LIFE AND CAREER SKILLS

SERIES

Volume 3

Health and Wellness

LIFE AND CAREER SKILLS

SERIES

Volume 3

Health and Wellness

Miranda Herbert Ferrara and Michele P. LaMeau,
Project Editors

GALE
CENGAGE Learning®

Farmington Hills, Mich • San Francisco • New York • Waterville, Maine
Meriden, Conn • Mason, Ohio • Chicago

**Life and Career Skills Series,
Volume 3: Health and Wellness**

Project Editors: Miranda Herbert
Ferrara and Michele P. LaMeau

Editorial Service : Thomas Riggs &
Company

Indexing Service: Laura Dorricott

Production Technology Support:
Mike Weaver

Rights Acquisition and Management:
Moriam M. Aigoro, Ashley
M. Maynard

Imaging: John Watkins

Product Design: Kristine Julien

Manufacturing: Wendy Blurton

Vice President and Publisher,
New Products and GVRL:
Patricia Coryell

For product information and technology assistance, contact us at
Gale Customer Support, 1-800-877-4253.
For permission to use material from this text or product,
submit all requests online at **www.cengage.com/permissions.**
Further permissions questions can be emailed to
permissionrequest@cengage.com

Cover images: ©PureSolution/Shutterstock.com (icon) and ©Aleksandr
Markin/Shutterstock.com (woman and man at the gym exercising).

While every effort has been made to ensure the reliability of the information
presented in this publication, Gale, a part of Cengage Learning, does not
guarantee the accuracy of the data contained herein. Gale accepts no payment
for listing; and inclusion in the publication of any organization, agency,
institution, publication, service, or individual does not imply endorsement of the
editors or publisher. Errors brought to the attention of the publisher and verified
to the satisfaction of the publisher will be corrected in future editions.

EDITORIAL DATA PRIVACY POLICY: Does this product contain information
about you as an individual? If so, for more information about our editorial data
privacy policies, please see our Privacy Statement at http://solutions.cengage
.com/Gale/Data-Privacy-Policy/.

LIBRARY OF CONGRESS CATALOGING-IN-PUBLICATION DATA

Health and wellness / Miranda Herbert Ferrara and Michele P. LaMeau, project
editors. — 001
     pages cm. — (Life and career skills series ; volume 3)
   Includes bibliographical references and index.
   ISBN 978-1-4103-1763-6 — ISBN 1-4103-1763-3
   1. Health—Popular works. 2. Hygiene—Popular works. 3. Medicine, Preventive—
Popular works. I. Ferrara, Miranda Herbert, 1950- editor. II. LaMeau,
Michele P., editor.

RA776.H43584 2015
613—dc23
                                                                2015001883

Gale
27500 Drake Rd.
Farmington Hills, MI, 48331-3535

ISBN-13: 978-1-4103-1763-6
ISBN-10: 1-4103-1763-3

This title is also available as an e-book.
ISBN-13: 978-1-4103-1771-1   ISBN-10: 1-4103-1771-4
Contact your Gale sales representative for ordering information.

Printed in China
1 2 3 4 5 6 7 19 18 17 16 15

Contents

Preface

The *Life and Career Skills Series (LCSS)* is designed to supply foundational information in an accessible format to provide direction for personal life decisions. This collection of thematically focused volumes centers on the life and career issues people face on a day-to-day basis, as well as key organizations and suggested resources for further reading. Written in an engaging, approachable, and informative question-and-answer style, the series provides users with the tactical information needed to accomplish their life goals—whether in the context of transitioning from school and/or college into the workplace or transitioning into the next stage of life.

Topic Selection

The first four volumes of the series contain topics that consist of the most relevant, current, and useful subjects surveyed in the market. Entry topics have been selected for the *Life and Career Skills Series* through a variety of methods to assure that the most timely and useful information would be provided. When needed or warranted, the list of topics was reviewed by subject matter experts to ensure that the materials being covered were presented accurately and appropriately.

LCSS Entry Features

Each volume of *LCSS* includes entries on topics appropriate to that volume's particular theme. Entries have been divided into four major sections, then the individual essays grouped under thematic subsections so that like topics fall together. Each of the major sections begins with a **table of contents** outlining the essay coverage immediately followed by an **overview essay** that sets out the themes for the section. The overview entry is followed by two or three **composite entries** bringing together information on that particular theme. Each composite entry is followed by a list of books, periodicals, and websites where the reader can find more information.

Each composite entry in an *LCSS* volume begins with an **In This Section listing** that clearly outlines the topics and key concepts covered.

Throughout the text of the entry the reader will find **icons** used as visual cues to indicate paragraphs or sections of text where key terms or particularly important or helpful information can be found. The icons are more fully explained in the User's Guide following this preface.

LCSS entries feature **in-text key terms** that the authors and editors feel will aid overall reader comprehension of the topic.

Many *LCSS* entries also contain **sidebars**. Sidebars highlight information such as historical data about the entry topic, biographical information about people involved with the topic, case studies, statistics, hints, and "fun facts."

The entries are **heavily illustrated** with color photos, charts, tables, and other graphics, allowing users to further contextualize the information they are being provided.

Authoritative Sources

Entries have been compiled by combining authoritative data from government sources, professional associations, original research, and publicly accessible sources both in print and on the Internet. These sources include periodicals, white papers, and books, as well as websites and blogs.

The *Life and Career Skills Series* overview and composite entries contain a selection of relevant print and electronic sources where the reader can find further information on the topic. In addition, there is a list of **Resources for More Information** at the end of each volume listing books, periodicals, and websites that can be used for further research.

Organizations

A **List of Key Organizations** follows the Resources for More Information. Although not an exhaustive list, these organizations are important in the field and provide another source of information for interested readers.

The list gives the address and home page url of each organization and has a short description of the organization when available.

Fully Indexed

Each *LCSS* volume has a comprehensive index of concepts, names, and terms enabling readers to locate topics throughout the volume. Because many subjects are not treated in separate entries but are discussed within the context of larger composite entries, the index guides readers to discussions of these subjects quickly.

About *Life and Career Skills Series, Volume 3: Health and Wellness*

Life and Career Skills Series, Volume 3: Health and Wellness helps readers take charge of their well-being. The essays guide readers in making healthy choices about hygiene, diet, exercise, and medical care. They present easy-to-understand information about health-care coverage options and offer overviews of the types of available medical care, from general practitioners to alternative medicine and mental health providers. They also offer practical guidance about private insurance, government programs, and community health resources.

Questions addressed in this volume include: "What Are Some Tips for Fitting Fitness into a Busy Schedule?," "How Much Sleep Should I Get Each Night?," "How Can I Avoid Stress?," and "What Services Does the Veterans Health Administration Provide?" The essays offer contemporary context for healthy living, offering up-to-date information about the Affordable Care Act, considering the effects of social media on wellness, and drawing on recent scientific and policy studies.

Suggestions Welcome

Comments on this *LCSS* volume and suggestions on topics for future volumes are cordially invited. Please write:

The Editors
Life and Career Skills Series
Gale, Cengage Learning
27500 Drake Rd.
Farmington Hills, Michigan 48331-3535

Gale, Cengage Learning, does not endorse any of the organizations, products, or methods mentioned in this title.

The websites appearing in the *Life and Career Skills* Series have been reviewed by Gale, Cengage Learning, to provide additional information. Gale is not responsible for the content or operations policies of these websites. Further, Gale is not responsible for the conduct of website providers who offer electronic texts that may infringe on the legal right of copyright holders.

PLEASE READ—IMPORTANT INFORMATION

Life and Career Skills Series, Volume 3: Health and Wellness is a health reference product designed to inform and educate readers about a wide variety of health and wellness issues; diagnostic tests and procedures; nutrition and dietary practices beneficial to health and wellness; and various treatments, including drugs. Cengage Learning believes the product to be comprehensive, but not necessarily definitive. It is intended to supplement, not replace, consultation with a physician or other healthcare practitioners. While Cengage Learning has made substantial efforts to provide information that is accurate, comprehensive, and up-to-date, Cengage Learning makes no representations or warranties of any kind, including without limitation, warranties of merchantability or fitness for a particular purpose, nor does it guarantee the accuracy, comprehensiveness, or timeliness of the information contained in this product. Readers should be aware that the universe of health and medical knowledge is constantly growing and changing, and that differences of opinion exist among authorities. Readers are also advised to seek professional diagnosis and treatment for any medical condition or health concern, and to discuss information obtained from this book with their healthcare provider.

User's Guide

Throughout the text of each entry in the *Life and Career Skills Series*, there are three icons used as visual cues to indicate paragraphs or sections of text where key terms or particularly important or helpful information can be found.

Icons

Know This — Indicates a paragraph where a key concept or larger theme that must be known to understand the main idea of the entry is located.

Helpful Hint — Indicates a paragraph where a helpful tip or idea, a suggestion for consideration, or a best practice is located. These suggestions may be helpful when putting concepts presented in the entry into practice.

Key Term — Indicates the paragraph and provides the definition of an essential term in an entry necessary to understand the overall topic and core concepts presented.

Nutrition, Exercise, and Personal Care and Hygiene

Overview: Nutrition, Exercise, and Personal Care and Hygiene

I Want to Improve My Overall Health. Where Should I Start?

No matter how old you are, taking steps to improve your health can make a positive difference in your life. You can't eliminate all your health risks—everyone has a genetic background that helps determine their likelihood for getting certain diseases and conditions. However, you can control aspects of your environment, including what you eat, how active you are, how much sleep you get, and how much stress affects your daily life.

Changing these personal factors is key to improving your health. For example, according to the American Cancer Society, people who quit smoking cut their risk for heart disease by half after one year, and after five years their risk for mouth and throat cancer also drops by half. In two to five years people who quit smoking have the same risk for stroke as a nonsmoker does.

Avoiding tobacco is just one of many important steps toward better health. As you commit to leading a healthier lifestyle, you will likely begin to feel better and look better. The first step is to take a good look at how your current lifestyle may be affecting your health.

© MYPOKCIK/ SHUTTERSTOCK.COM.

What Key Aspects of My Lifestyle Can Affect My Health?

Throughout your day there are many opportunities to improve your health. The number of possible healthy changes might seem overwhelming at first. The good news is these steps work just as well if you take them one at a time. In fact, starting small may make it easier to stick with new habits.

Begin by looking at what you eat. It is no surprise that your diet plays an important role in your health. Eating the right foods can give you vitamins and other nutrients that help prevent a number of diseases, and avoiding unhealthy foods can work to lower your health risks, including high cholesterol and high blood pressure. For people with food allergies or intolerances, choosing foods carefully is essential to preventing uncomfortable or dangerous reactions.

Exercise is another important avenue to health. It goes hand-in-hand with your diet to help control your weight. People who exercise regularly also have a lower risk for heart disease and stroke, type 2 diabetes, and certain cancers, including colon and breast cancer. In addition, exercise can help strengthen your bones and muscles, lessen the symptoms of arthritis, and improve your mood. It can even help you live longer. The United States Centers for Disease Control and Prevention (CDC) reports that people who are physically active for about seven hours each week have a 40 percent lower risk of dying early than those who get fewer than 30 minutes of activity a week.

Immune system:
The body's system of natural defenses that helps the body resist harmful substances or microorganisms— bacteria, viruses, parasites, and fungi.

Next, consider your sleeping habits. It's easy to think about sleep as just a few hours of down time. But adequate sleep is necessary for your body to function. It is the time when body cells and tissues are repaired and hormones that boost the *immune system* are released. Sleep is also essential for learning, memory, and emotional function. Over time lack of sleep can raise your risks for many diseases and conditions, including obesity, diabetes, heart disease, and infection. It can also make it difficult for you to function at work, at home, and in relationships. Sleep needs vary by age and from person to person, but according to the National Sleep Foundation, most adults do best with between seven and nine hours of sleep each day.

Diet, exercise, and sleep all affect your weight, which is another key factor in your health. Being overweight or obese raises your risks for cardiovascular conditions such as heart disease and stroke, which are linked to high levels of cholesterol in the blood. High blood cholesterol usually results from diets high in saturated fats, which are found in foods such as whole milk and fatty meats. People who carry most of their weight around their waist are at even higher risk for cardiovascular problems.

Carrying too many pounds also makes you more likely to develop type 2 diabetes and gynecological problems such as infertility. According to the National Cancer Institute, some types of cancer, including cancer of the breast, colon, esophagus, kidney, gallbladder, are linked to being obese. And added pressure on joints from excess weight can lead to osteoarthritis.

What Are Some Less Obvious Factors That Can Affect My Health?

Some everyday activities that may seem automatic can also affect your health. For example, grooming habits such as basic cleanliness are essential to defend against a variety of bacteria, viruses, and fungi that can cause disease. Cleanliness and other aspects of grooming are also important for successful work and social relationships. Personal hygiene habits, such as hand washing and avoiding germs on surfaces, can help you stay well while at home and in other settings, such as at work, at the gym, and while traveling. In addition, proper care of bedding, clothing, and personal items can help minimize health problems such as exposure to allergens, infestation with parasites, and the spread of *infectious diseases*.

Infectious disease:
A disorder caused by bacteria, virus, fungi, etc. that can be passed from person to person.

Another aspect of health that is often neglected is stress. Bodies respond to stress and anxiety with physical symptoms such as pain, high blood pressure, insomnia, upset stomach, and weight gain or loss. This is known as the mind-body connection, and it can also work to enhance your health. People who find ways to minimize stress and focus on positive facets of their lives may be able to avoid some diseases and health problems.

I've Been Eating Unhealthy Foods for Many Years. How Can I Change My Diet?

Eating habits are among the hardest to change. Unhealthy food choices may be part of your family's lifestyle, which can challenge your willpower. If you are used to sweet, fatty, or processed foods, healthier choices may taste strange and unfamiliar. People who are used to eating take-out and restaurant meals may have to learn cooking skills.

Changing your eating habits can be easier if you develop a plan to reach your goals. According to the National Institutes of Health (NIH), one way to do that is to work with a series of steps that starts with committing to forming new habits. Take time to consider the advantages of a healthy diet, such as weight loss and lower health risks. Eating more fruits and vegetables and fewer fatty meats can lower your risks for cardiovascular disease and some cancers. These plant-based foods contain vitamins and other nutrients that are essential to health. Whole grains provide more nutrients as well as fiber, which helps with digestion. Keeping these benefits in mind can help you take action.

Once you are confident that you want to make your diet more healthy, formulate several specific goals, such as replacing meat with a vegetable dish one night a week. Goals should also be reasonable. So, "Eat fresh fruit five days a week" is better than "Lose 20 pounds," which may take months to achieve. It will be easier to stay on track if you plan ahead for overcoming obstacles such as snacking while watching TV. Have some cut-up vegetables ready instead of chips and dip.

New eating habits can be hard to maintain in a restaurant setting, where meals often arrive in large portions. According to the CDC, restaurant meals and drinks have increased in size since the 1970s until most now exceed federal standards for serving sizes. When you eat out, share a meal with a friend or take some home for another meal. Avoid large portions at home by using smaller plates when you dish up your food.

Tracking your progress is a good way to reinforce good eating habits. Try keeping a journal of how well you have met your goals. When you have a success, such as learning to cook a new healthy meal, reward yourself with a nonfood item such as a movie or an afternoon off. And know that setbacks happen to everyone, so if you slip up on your new eating habits, don't give up. Instead, look over your goals to make sure they can work, and start again.

I'm Not Used to Exercising. How Can I Get Started?

Inactive people need to start slowly when they begin a program of regular exercise. Though rare, there is an elevated risk for heart attack in people who jump suddenly into vigorous aerobic exercise. In addition, people who have chronic health problems such as arthritis, diabetes, or heart disease should talk to their doctor before they start exercising. Some forms of exercise could be dangerous for these people.

Even for people with health problems, the benefits of exercise usually outweigh the risks. But getting started can be difficult. Just as with changing what you eat, establishing the habit of regular physical activity can be easier if you create a plan with specific goals, track your progress, and reward yourself for successes. For example, plan a goal of taking the stairs instead of the elevator or walking around the block at lunch time. As these goals become habits, move on to more ambitious activities such as riding a bike or swimming. Record how far you walk or ride, and give yourself a reward when you reach a benchmark.

© ALEXMILLOS/
SHUTTERSTOCK.COM.

A few tips can help you turn regular exercise into a habit. One is to choose activities that you enjoy. People who like to shop may do well at walking the entire length of a mall or grocery store. If you walk the dog every evening, add a few more blocks to the walk. Hiking, fishing, gardening, and yard work can also be good exercise.

Another tip is to find a friend who is also interested in becoming more active. Exercising together can keep you both motivated to continue. And exercise doesn't have to be done all at once. Even 10-minute sessions of activities such as climbing your stairs at home or lifting weights while you watch TV can add up. Eventually, exercise should become a regular part of your day.

I Don't Want to Take Medicines to Help Me Sleep. What Else Can I Do?

Prescription sleep medicines are often used for short-term treatment of sleeplessness. Less often, these drugs are prescribed for longer-term use by people with severe, chronic insomnia. Sleep medicines should always be used with caution because they can be habit forming or cause rebound insomnia (the inability to sleep after you stop taking them), making things worse. They also can interact with other medicines or mask an underlying medical problem. Over-the-counter sleep aids should only be used occasionally. If you try one, be sure to tell your doctor what you are taking.

To treat insomnia without medicines, start by establishing a regular bedtime and wake time to help regulate your body's natural clock.

Try to get some exercise, but not right before bedtime. It is also best not to nap during the day, since that can make it harder to fall asleep later.

People who have trouble sleeping should avoid food and drinks with caffeine close to bedtime. Caffeine is a stimulant, and according to the National Sleep Foundation, it can stay in your body for six hours or more. Heavy meals and alcohol can also disturb sleep, so avoid them within two to three hours of bedtime. It's also best to stay away from tobacco. Besides being a major health risk, smoking can disrupt sleep.

Your bedroom can also affect your sleep. Keep it dark, cool, and quiet. Ear plugs and eye shades can help, and some people use a fan, a humidifier, or another device to create "white noise." Keep distractions such as TVs, computers, and work materials out of your bedroom. If your bed is uncomfortable, consider getting a better mattress.

If none of these sleep strategies helps, talk to your doctor. He or she may recommend that you have a sleep study to help diagnose any problems you may have. For example, sleep apnea can cause people to wake up multiple times during the night.

What Simple Hygiene and Grooming Habits Can I Use to Protect My Health?

Personal grooming and cleanliness are essential for getting along in social and work situations. Good habits in grooming and hygiene also help you avoid bacteria, viruses, fungi, and other organisms that can cause disease. These organisms, often referred to as germs, are a major cause of illness and death worldwide.

To avoid infectious diseases, your first line of defense is to wash your hands frequently. The CDC recommends washing under warm or cold running water. Lather with soap, and scrub the backs of your hands, between your fingers and under your nails. Do this for at least 15 seconds, then rinse under clean running water and air dry your hands or use a clean towel. Wash your hands before and after you prepare food and before you eat. It is also important to wash before and after caring for a sick person and after using the toilet, changing diapers, coughing, or sneezing. Handling contaminated materials, such as garbage or animal waste, also should trigger hand washing.

When you can't wash your hands, an alcohol sanitizing gel or wipe can help. Use one after you touch surfaces that many people touch, such as door knobs, shopping-cart handles, and elevator and ATM buttons.

Keeping your hands and body clean will be easier if you follow good grooming habits. For example, maintain trimmed and filed fingernails and wash your hair often enough to keep it from looking greasy. Men with facial hair should keep it neatly trimmed and washed frequently. Everyone should brush their teeth at least twice a day, including after eating and before bed.

It is also important to keep up with hygiene when you are away from home. At work, sanitize items such as your keyboard, phone, and mouse. People who operate machinery can avoid germs by sanitizing surfaces such as door handles, steering wheels, and other controls. Try not to touch seats and armrests in public places, such as lobbies or on public transportation, since they are likely places for germs. If possible, push doors open with your shoulder or elbow. At the gym, use a sanitizer to clean seats and grips on exercise machines before and after you use them.

I Can Tell That Stress Is Affecting My Health. What Can I Do to Relieve It?

Stress is a normal part of life, and no one can escape it completely. In most cases you can find ways to cope with stress and minimize its effects. However, sometimes stressful events seem overwhelming and lead to sadness, anxiety, and depression. Too much stress can even cause physical symptoms such as back pain, headache, insomnia, nausea, and high blood pressure.

People who have a lot of stress in their lives may have weakened immune systems, making them more likely to get illnesses such as colds and other infections. And according to the NIH, psychological factors can play a major role in heart disease and other illnesses.

Emotional difficulties can cause physical symptoms, which illustrates what is known as the mind-body connection. This connection is also at work when people improve their health by reducing the effects of stress in their lives. So, while you often can't control stressful events, you may be able to minimize how they affect your health.

One way to improve your response to stress is to make time for yourself. Set aside an hour or longer to do something you enjoy, such

Meditation: *A practice that helps one to center and focus the mind; sometimes used to help recovering addicts.*

as listening to music or reading. Some people use relaxation techniques such as *meditation* and deep breathing. Talking to a good friend can also help, especially if you can express some of your feelings. Exercise is an excellent stress reducer, so try to stay active as much as possible. In addition, use healthy sleep habits to get enough sleep.

If these self-help techniques do not help, consider seeing a counselor or therapist. These professionals can help you examine the causes of stress in your life, how you respond to stress, and how you can learn to manage it.

For More Information

BOOKS

Hartwig, Melissa, and Dallas Hartwig. *It Starts with Food*. Las Vegas: Victory Belt Publishing, 2014.

Rath, Tom. *Eat Move Sleep: How Small Choices Lead to Big Changes*. Arlington, VA: Missionday, 2013.

Rosenberg, Robert. *Sleep Soundly Every Night, Feel Fantastic Every Day: A Doctor's Guide to Solving Your Sleep Problems*. New York: Demos Health, 2014.

Willett, Walter C., with P. J. Skerrett. *Eat, Drink, and Be Healthy: The Harvard Medical School Guide to Healthy Eating*. New York: Free Press, 2005.

PERIODICALS

Farley, Thomas A. "The Public Health Crisis Hiding in Our Food." *New York Times*, April 21, 2014: A21. This article can also be found online at http://www.nytimes.com/2014/04/21/opinion/the-public-health-crisis-hiding-in-our-food.html.

Ornish, Dean. "Eating for Health, Not Weight." *New York Times*, September 23, 2012: SR4. This article can also be found online at http://www.nytimes.com/2012/09/23/opinion/sunday/the-optimal-diet.html?_r=0.

Taubes, Gary. "Why Nutrition Is So Confusing." *New York Times*, February 9, 2014: SR5. This article can also be found online at http://www.nytimes.com/2014/02/09/opinion/sunday/why-nutrition-is-so-confusing.html.

WEBSITES

Bekiempis, Victoria. "Junk Food Isn't Only Addictive, It Makes You Avoid Trying New Foods." *Newsweek*. http://www.newsweek.com/junk-food-addictive-avoid-trying-new-foods-266803 (accessed October 30, 2014).

ChooseMyPlate.gov. http://www.choosemyplate.gov/ (accessed October 30, 2014).

"Fitness & Nutrition." *New York Times*. http://www.nytimes.com/pages/health/nutrition/ (accessed October 30, 2014).

"Food Pyramids and Plates: What Should You Really Eat?" *Harvard School of Public Health.* http://www.hsph.harvard.edu/nutritionsource/pyramid-full-story/ (accessed October 30, 2014).

"Sleep." *New York Times.* http://topics.nytimes.com/top/news/health/diseases conditionsandhealthtopics/sleep/index.html (accessed October 30, 2014).

"Wellness." *Washington Post.* http://www.washingtonpost.com/lifestyle/wellness/ (accessed October 30, 2014).

Health and Diet Concerns

Why Is a Healthy Lifestyle Important?

Eating the proper foods and exercising are the very foundations for a healthy and functioning body. There are a variety of reasons for maintaining a healthy diet, such as preventing disease, controlling weight, and sustaining an overall longer and better quality of life.

Eating with family or friends can help keep your eating habits on track. © BLEND IMAGES/ SHUTTERSTOCK.COM.

A poor diet and lack of proper exercise have been linked to heart disease, several different forms of cancer, and diabetes. According to the American Cancer Society, for example, consuming processed and fried meats and alcoholic drinks increases the risk for colon and liver cancers. Unhealthy eating habits and an inactive lifestyle have also been linked to a variety of anxiety issues and depression. An eight-year study by the American Council on Exercise showed that even light exercise significantly reduced the participants' odds of premature death when compared to those in the study who exercised infrequently or not at all.

How Can I Make My Diet Healthier?

Many people who want to eat a healthy diet but fail to do so tend to have a fear of making a drastic change. However, the change to a healthier diet can be made more manageable by making simple, minor adjustments. Focus on finding foods that you like and that are easy to prepare in order to motivate yourself. Then simply make sure to include fruits and vegetables, lean protein, and grains in your daily diet, while limiting the consumption of fat, sugar, and alcohol.

Starting slowly as you shift your diet to healthier choices is a smart way to help you change how you think about food. Adding a small green salad with your dinner or switching to olive oil from butter when cooking may seem like small adjustments, but making a few such adjustments in how you eat each day will ease you into better eating habits. Reducing food portion sizes is another helpful step. Studies have shown that portion sizes have noticeably increased from the late twentieth century to the early twenty-first century. For example, surveys by the U.S. National Institutes of Health indicate that food portions commonly served in restaurants have in many cases more than doubled in size over the past 20 years.

A good way to gauge a healthful-sized portion of fish, chicken, or red meat is to compare it to the size of a deck of cards. Choosing smaller dishes and plates to eat from at home can help you control the amount you eat. Sharing an entrée with a friend when you eat out is also an excellent way to limit your food intake.

What Are the Current Recommendations for a Balanced Diet?

A healthy diet balances the amount of calories you consume with an adequate amount of nutrients. Caloric needs are determined by such factors as sex, age, and weight. According to the U.S. Department of Agriculture, each day most people should consume about 2,000 calories, and the food they eat should include about 2 cups of fruit and 2½ cups of vegetables. Another recommendation is that you eat at least 3 ounces of whole-grain products every day and consume 3 cups per day of fat-free or low-fat milk.

Overall, you should consume a variety of nutrient-dense foods and beverages. A nutrient-dense food is one that provides a large amount of

Keeping a Food Diary

Keeping a food diary that records everything you eat each day is one of the best ways to keep your healthy diet on track. However, tracking the calories you consume and burn can feel daunting. If you want to keep track of your calories on paper, choose a notebook that will be easy to carry with you. You may want to invest in a book that lists calorie counts for commonly eaten foods. If you have access to the Internet, you can find out the calorie content of most foods with a quick Internet search.

If you prefer to track your calories electronically, there are several tools that can make the process easy. LIVESTRONG's MyPlate (http://www.livestrong.com/myplate/) and MyFitnessPal (http://www.myfitnesspal.com/) offer programs that are available as apps or through a web interface. These programs guide you in setting your daily caloric goal, allow you to access calorie and nutritional information for many foods or enter your foods manually, and track the calories you consume and burn. If you use a smartphone to access these apps, you may be able to scan packaged food to obtain nutrition information. Having these trackers at your fingertips throughout the day can help you meet your goals.

nutrients relative to its volume. You should select healthy food choices from the five basic food groups (vegetables, fruit, grains, protein, and dairy) and limit your consumption of trans fats and *saturated fats*, cholesterol, sodium, sugars, and alcohol. You should also avoid foods that provide only "empty calories" (foods that provide few or no nutrients).

Saturated fat: *Fat that is solid at room temperature.*

How Much Exercise Should I Be Getting?

The U.S. Department of Health and Human Services recommends that every week you get either 150 minutes of moderate, aerobic exercise or 75 minutes of vigorous exercise. Moderate exercise includes brisk walking, slow swimming, and mowing the lawn. More vigorous aerobic exercise includes jogging, skipping rope, and aerobic dancing. Strength training, such as lifting weights, rock climbing, and heavy gardening, twice a week is also recommended.

A good general goal is to exercise for 30 minutes each day. If you do not have that much time available to you in a single period during the day, you can break up the exercise into increments, such as three 10-minute walks, and you will still receive the benefit of the exercise. If your goal is to lose weight, you can increase the minutes of exercise or increase its level of intensity.

How Can I Figure Out How Many Calories I Need to Consume Each Day?

You can calculate how many calories you need to take in each day by means of the Harris-Benedict formula. The formula allows you to calculate your basal metabolic rate (the number of calories you need simply to be awake), which varies for men and women, and then find the metabolic rate for different types of activity.

Women: $655 + (4.35 \times$ your weight in pounds) + (4.7 $\times$ your height in inches) $- (4.7 \times$ your age in years).

Men: $66 + (6.23 \times$ your weight in pounds) + (12.7 $\times$ your height in inches) $- (6.8 \times$ your age in years).

After determining your basal metabolic rate above, multiply it by the factor corresponding to your daily activity level as follows:

- Sedentary (little to no exercise): 1.2
- Lightly active (light exercise/work 1 to 3 days per week): 1.375
- Moderately active (moderate exercise/work 3 to 5 days per week): 1.55
- Very active (hard exercise/work 6 to 7 days a week): 1.725
- Extra active (very hard exercise/work 6 to 7 days a week): 1.9

The final number you have is the daily number of calories you need to maintain your current weight. Eating more and burning fewer calories will cause you to gain weight, and consuming fewer calories and increasing your exercise level will cause you to lose weight.

How Can I Motivate Myself to Stick with a Healthy Diet?

Setting healthy habits is the best way to keep your diet on track. Motivational techniques are also helpful, such as keeping a list of reasons why you want to lose weight and then referring to it when you feel weak. Keep yourself accountable with a friend, family member, or coworker who can check in with you via e-mail, text, or a phone call.

During meals or snacks, eat everything gradually while you are sitting down, and always focus on carefully tasting the food. This approach will make it easier to stick to your diet and to avoid binge eating. In addition, work to break bad eating habits and embrace good ones. Giving in and eating food not in your plan simply reinforces the habit of surrendering to this tendency. In contrast, each time you make healthier choices in your diet, you assert the habit of control, which helps strengthen a routine that makes dieting easier.

Does Healthy Eating Mean Giving Up All of My Favorite Foods?

Eating a healthy diet does not mean you need to give up all your favorite foods. Remember that there is not one perfect diet or a single, ideal combination of foods. Not completely limiting or cutting a favorite food from your diet will also help you avoid feeling as if you are punishing yourself. You should allow yourself once a day to eat one of your favorite foods in moderation or a substitute made by modifying your favorite food with lower-calorie or lower-fat ingredients. For example, if your favorite comfort food is macaroni and cheese, substitute the high-fat ingredients whole milk and regular cheese with skim milk and low-fat cheese.

Fruits, vegetables, and grains are part of healthy eating. ILLUSTRATION BY ELECTRONIC ILLUSTRATORS GROUP. © 2014 CENGAGE LEARNING.

You can also enjoy your favorite foods by eating them less often or by reducing the portion size. If you enjoy having a chocolate bar every day, purchase smaller-sized versions or eat only half a bar. Alternatively, you can eat a full chocolate bar but only once a week or once a month as a reward.

I Do Not Have a Lot of Time to Cook. Can I Still Eat a Healthy Diet?

It is possible to eat a healthy diet even without having a lot of time to cook. With modern technology, preparing healthy meals is as simple and quick as having a bag of your favorite frozen vegetables at hand. Pour them into a bowl and microwave for five minutes, and you have a healthy side dish for your meal. Microwaved baked potatoes are also a good standby that can be cooked in eight minutes or less. A butter substitute or low-fat yogurt will give them a quick and tasty touch-up.

Packets of oatmeal kept in a cabinet by your microwave make a quick and healthy breakfast. Keeping bags of frozen fruits and yogurt on hand will allow you to blend an easy breakfast smoothie. Use weekends to plan meals for your workweek. Make enough salad for lunches for two days, buy two weeks' worth of yogurt, and put together a large batch of low-fat stew or chili and then freeze it into meal-sized portions to eat for the rest of the week. With a little bit of thinking ahead, cooking for healthy eating when you have little time is as simple as preparing the meal itself.

What Are Some Tips for Healthy Eating away from Home?

Healthy eating is possible even while traveling, whether for business or pleasure. Heeding some simple tips will keep your diet in control and even offer you some pleasant, new food experiences.

Protein: *An organic substance made of amino acids that are necessary for human life.*

For breakfast find a local juice bar and order a soy milk fruit smoothie, perhaps adding protein powder or other immune-system boosters. If you find yourself eating at the hotel restaurant, consider ordering oatmeal and adding raisins, nuts, or even splash of skim milk for added flavor. For egg-based items, such as omelets, order the item with egg whites only. Also keep in mind that having eggs prepared poached will reduce the fat content. Lunch should be the largest meal of your day. With half of the day ahead of you, you can use the food energy better than you can near the end of the day. Find a salad bar and add chickpeas, beets, sunflower seeds, and other brightly colored vegetables to your salad. Choosing hearty soups will give you a boost of *protein* and fill you up more quickly. At dinner, search the menu for vegetarian options. Many Chinese and Indian restaurants offer a vegetarian menu. Japanese and Thai restaurants use a variety of vegetables and typically offer tofu for a low-fat protein option.

If your hotel has a fitness room or workout area, take full advantage of the amenities after dinner by walking on a treadmill or spinning on a stationary bike for a short time. This will help you digest your meal before bedtime.

What Is the Best Way for Me to Lose Weight?

In order to lose weight, you need to consume fewer calories each day than the number needed to maintain your weight. There are 3,500 calories in a pound of body fat. To lose one pound in a week, you will need to net 500 fewer calories each day. You can reach this goal by eating fewer calories or burning more calories through exercise. Tools such as heart-rate monitors and online calculators can help you figure out how many calories you are burning when you exercise.

Studies have shown that lowering your intake of carbohydrates rather than fats can lower your weight, even without increasing how much you exercise. Limit your carbohydrate intake, but do not eliminate what are considered "good" carbs, such as fruits, vegetables, and whole grains, which are essential to your body's healthy functioning. You should also favor foods with polyunsaturated or monounsaturated fats over foods with saturated fats. Fish that are high in polyunsaturated fat include tuna, trout, mackerel, sardines, and herring. Good plant sources of polyunsaturated and monounsaturated fats include flaxseed, soybean and olive oils, and nuts and other seeds such as walnuts and sunflower seeds.

The best way to lose weight is to form healthy eating habits and get regular exercise. Making these choices and taking these actions will help you lose weight and help you maintain that weight and live an overall healthier life.

Food, Weight, and Body Shape

What Are Some Basic Guidelines for Healthy Eating?

Healthy eating is an important component of a healthy lifestyle and can help you maintain an appropriate body weight and reduce your risk of chronic disease. A healthy diet starts with basic knowledge of your nutritional and energy needs. In addition, you should know which types of foods should make up the majority of your caloric intake and which foods you should consume in moderation or cut out entirely.

 The caloric needs of adults are determined by such factors as age, gender, and activity level. In general, men need more calories per day than women. Also, people who are inactive need fewer calories than those who exercise regularly or those who perform manual labor. The U.S. Department of Agriculture (USDA) issues general guidelines for the daily caloric needs of children and adults. These recommendations are laid out by age range and gender and can be accessed on the USDA website (http://www.cnpp.usda.gov/dietaryguidelines).

Paying attention to caloric intake alone will not guarantee that you are maintaining a healthy diet. It is also important to pay attention to the quality of the calories you consume and to make sure that you are eating a good variety of nutritious foods. In general, research suggests that the majority of Americans eat too many calories overall and get too few of these calories from vegetables, fruits, whole grains, low-fat dairy, and seafood. Salt, sugar, refined grains, and saturated fats, by contrast, are overconsumed.

How Many Fruits and Vegetables Should I Eat per Day?

Fruits and vegetables are an excellent source of vitamins, and most are also a good source of fiber. The USDA recommends that at each meal you try to fill about half of your plate with fruits and vegetables. Aim to eat a variety of each.

Fruits often have more sugar and, therefore, more calories than vegetables, so it is a good idea to familiarize yourself with the caloric content of various fruits to make sure you are not eating more calories than you had planned. Fruit juices and smoothies can be particularly high in calories, so paying attention to nutritional labels is important.

What about Grains?

Grains are a staple in most American diets and can be classified as either whole grains or refined grains. The USDA recommends that no more than half of the grains you eat be refined, and it is a good idea to stick with whole grains whenever possible. Whole grains contain the grain kernel in its entirety, including the bran, germ, and endosperm. Examples of whole-grain products include whole-wheat bread, oatmeal, brown rice, bulgur, and faro. It's important to read labels carefully when you choose grains because products can have labels such as "multigrain," suggesting that they are not refined grain products when, in fact, they are.

Refined grains have been processed to remove the bran and germ portions of the grain kernel, stripping them of vitamins but making them more palatable and, in the case of white rice, much faster to prepare. Many refined grains have been enriched with B vitamins and iron, but they still lack the fiber contained in whole grains. Most bread not specifically labeled "whole wheat" contains mostly refined grains, as does white rice and snack foods such as crackers.

What Are Some Good Protein Choices?

Protein comes from a variety of animal and plant sources, including beef, poultry, pork, eggs, seafood, soy, beans, and nuts. The USDA recommends that you consume a variety of proteins, either from meat- and plant-based sources or, for vegetarians, from plants alone. When selecting meats, you should choose mainly lean cuts, which are relatively low in fat. Nuts may also be high in fat and calories, so consume them in moderation.

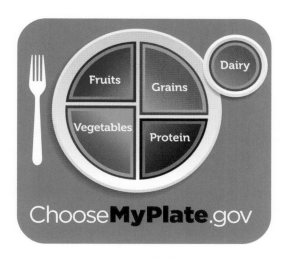

The U.S. government has designed this graphic to help people remember proper portion sizes for the different types of foods: fruits, vegetables, grains, protein (both plant and animal), and dairy.

Protein is important for building bones, muscles, and cartilage and is also essential for manufacturing blood cells, among other functions. Meat, poultry, and nuts also contain essential vitamins and minerals. Iron is particularly important for adolescent girls and women of child-bearing age, who lose a percentage of blood cells each month during menstruation. The omega-3 fatty acids found in seafood such as salmon are also important for healthy triglyceride levels in your blood, among other benefits. If you do not eat seafood you can get omega-3s from supplements.

What Should I Know about Dairy?

Cow's milk and some other foods made from milk, along with calcium-fortified soy milk, are considered part of the dairy group. Foods made from milk that do not contain calcium, such as butter, are not considered part of this group. When choosing dairy products, you should be mindful of the USDA recommendation that the majority of your dairy choices be low in fat or fat free.

Sufficient dairy intake is especially essential for children because it helps the body build healthy bones and teeth. Calcium is also important during adulthood, especially for women, because it helps reduce the risk of osteoporosis. Dairy products are also a good source of potassium, which helps the body regulate blood pressure, and vitamin D, which is important for bone development.

What Are Some Healthy Fats?

While not officially a food group, healthy oils are an essential part of your diet because they contain fatty acids necessary to the function of the human body. Oils are derived from a variety of plant sources, such as nuts and seeds, as well as from fish. Oils that are high in monosaturated or polysaturated fat and low in saturated fat are the healthiest options, although they should still be consumed in moderation because they are high in calories. Olive oil is one of the healthier options for cooking, as well as for use in salad dressing. You can also get healthy oils from eating foods such as nuts and avocados.

Solid fats, such as butter, margarine, and shortening, derive from animal sources through a process called hydrogenation. These fats are much less healthy than most oils and should be used sparingly or avoided. Plant oils that are solid at room temperature, such as palm oil and coconut oil, also belong in this category.

How Much Should I Weigh?

As part of most physical exams, your doctor will compare your weight to a range of weights typical for your gender and height. You can also find this information online. While such comparisons may give you a general idea of whether your weight is in the healthy range, they do not take into account factors such as body composition. Very muscular athletes, for example, can be heavier than average but still be a healthy weight.

Body Mass Index (BMI), which estimates your percentage of body fat, is now considered a more accurate indication than your weight alone in measuring whether you are overweight. BMI can be roughly calculated from your height and weight but is also measured with calipers or via hydrostatic underwater weighing, which is sometimes available at larger medical centers. Those with a body fat percentage under 18.5 percent are typically considered underweight; those with a BMI between 18.5 and 24.9 percent are in the normal range; those between 25 and 29.9 percent are considered overweight; and those in the 30 percent and above category are considered obese. A BMI measure does not differentiate between fat and muscle, so it is best to consult with your doctor if you are unsure whether you fall within the healthy range.

Are Some Body Shapes Less Healthy than Others?

In addition to checking your weight and BMI, your doctor may take the circumference of your waist to assess your health and determine whether you are at increased risk of certain diseases. Whether male or female, the more fat you have at your waist versus around your hips, the greater your risk for developing conditions such as heart disease and type 2 diabetes. In general, for men, the risk goes up with a waist circumference of 40 inches or greater, while women with a waist measuring more than 35 inches are at an increased risk of developing these conditions.

Some advertisements for diet aids or fitness devices present claims that you can melt off fat from problem areas if you buy and use their product. However, it is typically impossible to reduce body fat in one specific spot, so if your waist measurement is high, you will need to lose weight to address the situation. Weight loss is best achieved through a healthy diet in addition to regular physical activity.

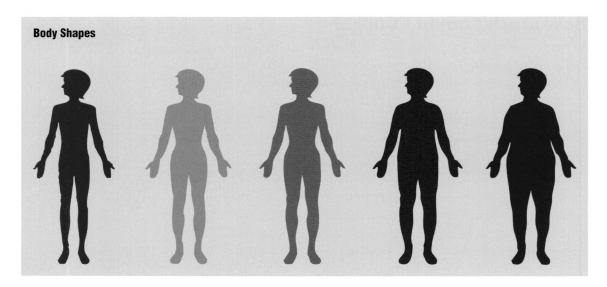

Body Shapes

Whether you are male or female, the more fat you have at your waist versus around your hips, the greater your risk for developing certain health conditions. ILLUSTRATION BY FRANK FORNEY. © 2015 CENGAGE LEARNING.

How Can I Reach and Maintain a Healthy Body Weight?

The National Institutes of Health (NIH) has published some guidelines that you may find helpful when you are trying to lose weight and maintain weight loss. First, it is important to think in terms of making sustainable changes to your diet and activity level rather than just focusing on immediate weight loss. People who successfully control their weight typically set specific, attainable goals that are flexible enough to accommodate a variable schedule. When setting goals, you should consider your present habits so that you do not choose targets that are unachievable. For instance, if you have been inactive for a number of years, it is unrealistic to plan to run several miles a day, five days a week. While this may be a goal that you would like to work toward eventually, you should start with something more in keeping with your present level of fitness, such as 20 minutes of walking five days a week. You can always recalibrate your goals as you progress.

You may find that keeping a record of your food intake and exercise will help you achieve goals by tracking your behavior. For instance, you may be shocked by how easy it is to consume your daily caloric allowance in one or two large meals or by excessive snacking. Self-monitoring will give you a more realistic idea of what your habits are now, so that you can make adjustments in both your behavior and your goals. You can also share these records with your doctor or other medical provider to make sure that you are eating and exercising in a safe manner.

A regular weigh-in can also be a good check on your progress. Most experts suggest that you weigh yourself no more frequently than once a week. You should plan to weigh yourself at the same time of day, typically in the morning, before you have consumed any food or liquids. In this way, you will avoid being discouraged by normal fluctuations brought on by such factors as water retention. It is generally not suggested that you lose more than one pound per week unless you are under close medical supervision. If you do not lose a pound each week, however, try to avoid becoming discouraged. Instead, look for a downward trend over the weeks and months that you are monitoring. If you cannot lose weight or are stalled at the same weight for a number of weeks, you should see your doctor to rule out medical causes such as a thyroid problem.

Food Allergies and Intolerances

What Are Food Allergies and Intolerances?

Food allergies and food intolerances are sometimes confused with each other, but they are separate conditions. Both allergies and intolerances can make you feel sick after eating a particular food. However, food allergies are much more serious. While a food intolerance may upset your stomach or make you feel a little sick, an allergic reaction to a food can kill you.

Immune system: *The body's system of natural defenses that helps the body resist harmful substances or microorganisms—bacteria, viruses, parasites, and fungi.*

The underlying causes of these two conditions are also different. Food allergies are the result of your body's *immune system* mistakenly reacting to a specific protein in a food as if it were a threat. As a result, your body releases chemicals to attack the protein. These chemicals can disrupt your digestive system, nose, lungs, throat, or skin. You may break out in hives or a rash, vomit, or have trouble breathing. Allergies can be triggered by tiny amounts of food; even breathing peanut dust can cause a reaction in people allergic to peanuts.

A food intolerance, by contrast, does not involve the immune system. Instead, it is the result of your digestive system becoming irritated by a food substance or your inability to digest a food properly. For example, people with lactose intolerance do not produce the enzyme lactase, which is necessary to break down lactose, the sugar in milk. Food additives, such as monosodium glutamate (MSG), and substances called sulfites can irritate the stomach or intestines in people who are sensitive to them. MSG is a food additive commonly found in Japanese and Chinese food, and sulfites are a preservative commonly found in wine and dried fruits and vegetables. People may also be sensitive to naturally occurring substances in foods, such as gluten, which is found most commonly in wheat and wheat-derived products.

How Common Are Food Allergies and Intolerances?

According to the American Academy of Family Physicians, about 6 percent of children and 2 percent of U.S. adults have a true food allergy.

Accounting for Increased Food Allergies

A 2013 study published by the United States Centers for Disease Control and Prevention (CDC) reported that childhood food allergies increased 50 percent between 1997 and 2011. The causes of this increase are not known with certainty, however, there are several theories, including what is known as the "hygiene hypothesis." This hypothesis holds that the hygiene practices of the developed world have reduced childhood exposure to germs and subsequently limited the development of our immune systems. Proponents of the hygiene hypothesis point to the fact that children who grow up in environments where they are more likely to be exposed to germs (such as those who grow up with pets, come from large families, or live in rural settings) have lower rates of allergies of all kinds when compared to other children.

Other researchers believe that the rise in food allergies is tied to a recent trend of delaying the introduction of food, particularly foods associated with allergies, to young children. Researchers have noted that cultures that introduce foods such as peanuts earlier have lower rates of food allergies than those cultures that delay their introduction. It is also likely that more food allergy cases are being diagnosed because of greater awareness of the issue.

"FOOD ALLERGY FACTS AND STATISTICS IN THE U.S." *FOOD ALLERGY RESEARCH AND EDUCATION.* HTTP://WWW.FOODALLERGY.ORG/DOCUMENT.DOC?ID=194 (ACCESSED OCTOBER 17, 2014).

As the digestive system matures, children typically outgrow allergies to milk, soy, wheat, and eggs. Children are less likely to outgrow allergies to nuts and shellfish. Allergies sometimes return later in life. You are at a higher risk for food allergies if you have asthma or other allergic reactions, such as hay fever or eczema. Having a close relative with any of these conditions or with a food allergy also increases your risk.

Food intolerance is much more common than food allergies. However, the risk factors for food intolerance are less clear than they are for allergies. Lactose intolerance, the most common food intolerance, occurs in about 10 percent of Americans, according to the Cleveland Clinic. It also sometimes runs in families. Lactose intolerance is more common in adults than in children, although it can occur even in premature babies. As these infants mature and their systems begin to make lactase, the condition usually goes away.

What Are the Symptoms of a Food Allergy?

The American Academy of Family Physicians reports that 90 percent of food allergies result from just eight foods: tree nuts, peanuts (technically

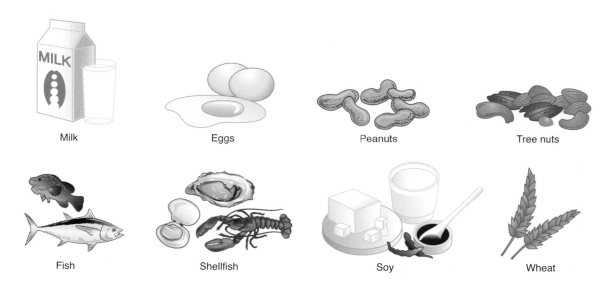

The American Academy of Family Physicians reports that 90 percent of food allergies result from these eight foods. ILLUSTRATION BY ELECTRONIC ILLUSTRATORS GROUP © 2013 CENGAGE LEARNING.

a legume, not a nut), cow's milk, eggs, soy, wheat, fish, and shellfish. Your first exposure to the food primes your immune system. Symptoms will not occur until the next time you eat the food, when white blood cells are sent to attack the protein and cause the allergic reaction. An allergic reaction may start right away or a few hours after ingesting the substance. You may have red itchy skin, swelling, or hives. Sneezing, an itchy or stuffy nose, and teary eyes can also occur, as can vomiting and diarrhea.

 Some people with food allergies have wheezing, throat tightness, and trouble breathing. In some cases this becomes so severe that the person's airways become blocked. This is called anaphylaxis, and it is a life-threatening event. If you or someone you are with has these symptoms, call 911 right away. A medicine called epinephrine, administered with an auto-injector into the upper thigh, can relieve these symptoms and save the person's life if given in time.

What Are the Symptoms of a Food Intolerance?

If a particular food repeatedly causes gas, cramping, or bloating in the stomach, you might have an intolerance. An intolerance can also cause heartburn, headache, nausea, vomiting, diarrhea, or stomach pain. Although some symptoms of a food allergy and food intolerance are similar, those caused by a food intolerance are less severe and tend to come on more slowly. People with a food intolerance can often eat small amounts of a particular food without a problem, but for those with an allergy, even a small amount can cause big problems.

Hives is one reaction to food allergies. © ALAMY.

Typical foods that cause intolerance include citrus fruits, apples, strawberries, tomatoes, and bananas. Milk and milk products, coffee, and chocolate may also cause problems. Foods that are fermented, such as wine and beer, may cause intolerance. Many people have an intolerance to gluten, which is a protein in wheat, barley, and rye grains. This type of intolerance is not the same as celiac disease, which is an autoimmune disease that causes inflammation and other serious problems in the intestines when foods containing gluten are eaten.

If you have nausea, diarrhea, or vomiting one to eight hours after a meal, you may have food poisoning. This is different from either a food allergy or food intolerance. Food poisoning is caused by toxins produced by *bacteria* or other organisms on spoiled or contaminated food, such as meats that are undercooked. With food poisoning, other people who ate the same food will likely have similar symptoms.

Bacteria: *Single-celled microorganisms, some of which are beneficial to the body while others can cause disease.*

How Can I Find Out If I Have a Food Allergy or Intolerance?

The first thing you should do if you suspect a food allergy is to avoid that food altogether. Then make an appointment with your doctor or an allergist to diagnose your condition through tests. You may be allergic to more than one food, and cross reactions can occur between foods and other allergens, such as pollen from grasses and trees. For example, people who are allergic to ragweed pollen may also react to bananas or melons. Tests will be able to tell you more.

Your doctor will ask about your symptoms and what foods caused them, how long it took for your symptoms to appear, and how severe they were. He or she may also ask if anyone in your family has allergies and if you had any allergies as a child. These factors raise your risk for a food allergy. Your doctor will also check for other conditions that could be causing your symptoms, such as inflammatory bowel disease.

To determine which foods are causing problems, your doctor may ask you to keep a food diary. A food diary lists everything you eat on a daily basis, what symptoms you have, what medications you use, and if they help. Allergists also use a skin-prick or skin-scratch test to find out how your body reacts to specific foods. This entails introducing a small amount of the possible allergen under the top layer of skin in order to provoke a controlled allergic reaction. If redness or bumps result, you test positive for that substance. Doctors frequently perform several skin-prick tests at the same time, usually on the back or the arm, to compare the reactions of different substances.

Once certain foods are identified as possible allergens, your doctor may ask you to avoid them completely for a week or two. Adding one at a time back into your diet can help link specific foods to your symptoms. This is known as an elimination diet, and it can be used to test for food intolerances as well as food allergies.

Food allergies can also be identified with a blood test that checks how your blood reacts to various foods. An oral food challenge looks for bodily reactions directly by having you eat small amounts of a suspect food in your doctor's office. If you have a dangerous allergic reaction, your doctor can treat it immediately.

If tests do not reveal a food allergy and your symptoms are not severe, you may have a food intolerance instead. Some food intolerances can be diagnosed with specific tests. For example, lactose intolerance can be determined by tests that analyze your breath or stool. Using an elimination diet can help identify problem foods, so keeping a food diary to track what you eat and when you have symptoms is always a good idea.

How Are Food Allergies Treated?

There is no cure for food allergies, although children sometimes outgrow them. Mild allergic reactions to food can often be treated with antihistamines, which relieve swelling, itching, and hives. Some can be bought without a prescription, which are called-over-the-counter drugs, and others require a prescription from your doctor. However, do not rely on antihistamines if you have severe symptoms. In these cases, your best defense is to avoid the food altogether. This is crucial if your allergy is severe or life threatening.

To make sure you avoid all food allergens, read the ingredients on all food packaging. Frozen, canned, or boxed meals may contain ingredients that are not always obvious. At restaurants ask your server what is in the dish you want to order; most restaurants are familiar with allergy issues and will accommodate you. If you have a child with food allergies, make sure his or her teachers, caregivers, and friends know what the problem foods are.

People who have had a severe food reaction should carry an epinephrine auto-injector, a device that releases a hormone that prevents or reverses anaphylactic shock. Brand names of these devices include EpiPen, Twinject, and Auvi-Q. Some experts recommend carrying two of these devices in case one does not work or it takes first responders more than 20 minutes to reach you. Injecting yourself as soon as you realize you are having an allergic reaction can save your life. You should also wear a medical alert bracelet or necklace that tells others you have a food allergy in case you become incapacitated before you can administer epinephrine.

How Are Food Intolerances Treated?

As with food allergies, the best way to avoid problems with a food intolerance is to stay away from problem foods. Read food labels to uncover hidden ingredients, and ask servers about the dishes you order in restaurants. Prepared foods and condiments often contain substances such as MSG that can trigger intolerance symptoms.

However, people with a food intolerance can often eat small amounts of a food or eat it on occasion without a problem. Sometimes you can take steps to aid digestion of the food. For example, people with lactose intolerance can take pills containing the lactase enzyme before they drink milk or eat dairy products. Lactose-free milk is also available. Other digestive enzyme products are available for people who have trouble with beans, broccoli, and other foods that cause gas.

How Will a Food Allergy or Intolerance Affect My Daily Life?

People with mild food allergies or intolerance usually experience little disruption in their daily lives. The habit of avoiding certain foods can become routine, and treatments such as antihistamines or enzyme products can be effective. Also, some food allergies go away over time. This is especially true for children, who often outgrow allergies to milk.

Those with a severe food allergy, however, need to be very careful. Reactions can get worse with each exposure to the problem food. Or you may have no reaction with one or two exposures, have a mild reaction on the third or fourth exposure, and go into anaphylactic shock on the fifth or sixth exposure. You should also talk to your doctor about cross-reactions with other allergens, such as ragweed pollen, so you can avoid them as well. People with severe allergies to peanuts must be especially careful because peanut dust or oil is in many products, including prepared foods, candies, and even skin care lotions. In some cases, just standing near someone who is eating peanuts can cause a life-threatening allergic reaction.

For More Information

BOOKS

U.S. Department of Agriculture and U.S. Department of Health and Human Services. *Dietary Guidelines for Americans 2010*. Washington, DC: Government Printing Office, 2010.

PERIODICALS

Bowman, Alisa. "Food Intolerance and Allergies." *Women's Health*, February 3, 2009. This article can also be found online at http://www.womens healthmag.com/nutrition/healthy-lunch-tips.

Park, Alice. "Why We're Going Nuts Over Nut Allergies." *Time*, February 26, 2009. This article can also be found online at http://content.time.com/time/magazine/article/0,9171,1881985,00.html.

WEBSITES

"Aim for a Healthy Weight." *National Heart, Lung, and Blood Institute*. http://www.nhlbi.nih.gov/health/educational/lose_wt/index.htm (accessed November 7, 2014).

American Academy of Allergy Asthma and Immunology. "Food Allergy Overview." http://www.aaaai.org/conditions-and-treatments/allergies/food-allergies.aspx (accessed October 7, 2014).

Cleveland Clinic. "Problem Foods: Is It an Allergy or Intolerance?" http://my.clevelandclinic.org/health/diseases_conditions/hic_Allergy_Overview/hic_Food_Allergies/hic_Problem_Foods_Is_it_an_Allergy_or_Intolerance (accessed October 7, 2014).

"Diet and Nutrition." *WebMD*. http://www.emedicinehealth.com/nutrition_and_diet/page3_em.htm (accessed October 22, 2014).

"Dietary Guidelines for Americas, 2010." *Health.gov*. http://www.health.gov/dietaryguidelines/2010.asp (accessed November 7, 2014).

"Eat Healthy, without Spending Time Cooking." *AskMen*. http://www.askmen.com/sports/foodcourt/40_eating_well.html (accessed October 22, 2014).

"5 Benefits of Healthy Habits." *Healthline*. http://www.healthline.com/health/5-benefits-healthy-habits#1 (accessed October 22, 2014).

"Food Intake Patterns." *Centers for Disease Control and Prevention*. http://www.cdc.gov/healthyweight/healthy_eating/ (accessed October 22, 2014).

"Food Portion Sizes Double over 20 Years as People Grow Fatter." *Nation of Change*. http://www.nationofchange.org/food-portion-sizes-double-over-20-years-people-grow-fatter-1383734122 (accessed October 22, 2014).

"How Much Should the Average Adult Exercise Every Day?" *Mayo Clinic*. http://www.mayoclinic.org/healthy-living/fitness/expert-answers/exercise/faq-20057916 (accessed October 22, 2014).

Li, James T. C. "What's the Difference between a Food Intolerance and a Food Allergy?" *Mayo Clinic*. http://www.mayoclinic.org/diseases-conditions/food-allergy/expert-answers/food-allergy/faq-20058538?_ga=1.223874011.1544103679.1410220920 (accessed October 7, 2014).

National Institute of Allergy and Infectious Disease. "Is It Food Allergy or Intolerance?" http://www.niaid.nih.gov/topics/foodAllergy/understanding/Pages/foodIntolerance.aspx (accessed October 7, 2014).

"Nutrition and Health Eating." *Mayo Clinic*. http://www.mayoclinic.org/healthy-living/nutrition-and-healthy-eating/in-depth/fat/art-20045550 (accessed October 22, 2014).

"Reasons Why It Is Important to Eat Healthy Foods to Stay Healthy." *Livestrong*. http://www.livestrong.com/article/82340-reasons-important-eat-foods-stay/ (accessed October 22, 2014).

"Serving Sizes and Portions." *National Institutes of Health*. http://www.nhlbi.nih.gov/health/educational/wecan/eat-right/distortion.htm (accessed October 22, 2014).

"Thinking Thin." *Psychology Today*. http://www.psychologytoday.com/blog/thinking-thin/201001/10-tips-stick-your-diet-0 (accessed October 22, 2014).

"Tips for Eating Healthy away from Home." *BetterHealthUSA*. http://www.betterhealthusa.com/public/267.cfm (accessed October 22, 2014).

Healthy Routines

What Is a Mind-Body Connection?

There is a connection between your physical well-being and your mental well-being. Regular exercise can help you manage physical conditions, such as high blood pressure or diabetes, but it can also have a positive effect on issues connected with your mind or emotional health, including stress, depression, anxiety, self-confidence, self-esteem, and your ability to learn and remember.

Different theories exist about which kinds of activities create a mind-body connection. Some believe that in order for physical activity to have a positive impact on your mental well-being, it should include self-reflection, awareness of your body, and attention to your breathing, which are elements of practices such as yoga and Pilates.

The link between physical and mental well-being can be traced back thousands of years. © DE VISU/SHUTTERSTOCK.COM.

Others believe that aerobic exercise is the best way to address issues such as anxiety. However, any kind of physical exercise you do can have a positive effect on your mind.

What Is the History of the Mind-Body Connection?

The link between physical fitness and mental health goes back to ancient times. The practice of yoga originated in India over 5,000 years ago as part of the Hindu philosophy of the connection between mind, body, and spirit, and it is considered to be beneficial for the health of the body's organs. This relationship has also been explored in more recent centuries. The idea was promoted in Great Britain by Archibald MacLaren (1820–84). In his book *A System of Physical Education* (1867), MacLaren discusses the importance of having both physical and mental activities and how each benefits the other. He also describes how physical fitness helps manage stress and fatigue.

In the United States, President Dwight D. Eisenhower formed the President's Council on Youth Fitness in 1956. President John F. Kennedy later changed the name to the President's Council on Physical Fitness. Both presidents believed that fitness was essential not only for physical health but also for mental abilities and emotional health. In a 1962 article in *Sports Illustrated*, President Kennedy stated that "physical fitness is the basis for all other forms of excellence."

How Does the Mind-Body Connection Work?

Scientists have conducted many studies to find out how and why physical activities are connected to the mind. One basic concept is that exercise, and aerobic exercise in particular, gets more blood and oxygen flowing throughout the body, including the brain. When brain tissue receives more blood and oxygen, it becomes healthier and better nourished.

Scientists have also found that exercise helps create, protect, and repair neurons, which are cells that transmit information. The creation of new neurons is called neurogenesis. New neurons created by exercise are mostly found in the hippocampus, the part of the brain where learning and memory happen. Exercise helps the brain improve cognitive flexibility, which is the ability to think about different ideas at once or easily switch from one idea to another.

Tai Chi

Tai Chi has gained popularity for the unique combination of physical and mental health benefits that it offers. The practice originated as a martial art in China roughly 2,500 years ago. Its dual purposes were to prepare practitioners for battle and to help them develop inner peace. Over subsequent centuries different styles of Tai Chi emerged. The major styles, each named for the family that originated it, are Chen, Sun, Wu, and Yang, the latter of which has attained the greatest popularity inside and outside of China.

Tai Chi involves slow motion exercises combined with deep, meditative breathing. Because it is a low-impact activity, it is appropriate for people of all ages. The health benefits of Tai Chi are thought to include increased flexibility and balance and lowered blood pressure. It is also believed to aid in combatting the effects of arthritis and other chronic conditions. Because of the increased flexibility that Tai Chi cultivates, it is often promoted to help senior citizens avoid falls and other injuries.

Endorphins, chemical hormones produced in the pituitary gland at the base of the brain, are released when you exercise or when your body experiences pain, stress, or excitement. Usually, the brain begins producing endorphins about 30 minutes after you start exercising. Endorphins act as the body's natural antidepressant because they can create a feeling of euphoria, which among runners is called a "runner's high."

How Can Physical Activity Benefit My Mental Abilities and Well-Being?

Physical activity can help you alleviate stress, and it can help reverse damage to your brain from past stress by creating new brain cells. Exercise can also improve your ability to sleep, which in turn can help you manage stress. Physical activities have been shown to increase concentration, alertness, and memory, and they can improve general cognitive skills as well as emotional health, mood, and self-esteem.

Studies have shown that exercise can lessen some of the negative impacts of aging and may have the potential to help combat the effects of dementia and *Alzheimer's disease.* A study published in the *New England Journal of Medicine* in 2003 reported that people who went ballroom dancing at least twice a week were less likely to develop dementia. A study at Cambridge University published in 2014, which looked at a decade of studies on dementia, concluded that even one hour of exercise per week can reduce the risk of Alzheimer's by almost half.

Alzheimer's disease:
A serious condition usually found in older adults that affects the parts of the brain that control thought, memory, and language.

Exercise can also help prevent memory loss. The hippocampus naturally shrinks with age, but exercise helps offset this process by promoting the creation of new brain cells. A 2012 *New York Times* article cited a study in which older men and women participated in a walking program, and after a year their hippocampi had grown.

Exercise can increase nerve cell production, and these nerve cells create neurotransmitters, or chemical substances, that pass on information about emotions, appetite, and other behaviors and bodily functions. The increased production of neurotransmitters is thought to help relieve depression. Exercise also helps combat stress, which is known to suppress the production of nerve cells. Some believe that exercise works as effectively as antidepressant medication.

Physical activity is connected to improving your learning skills, and this can be particularly true for children and young adults whose brains are still forming. Numerous studies have shown that students who are involved in regular physical activities do better academically and have improved concentration and attention spans. However, exercise can help improve your mental abilities at any age.

Which Types of Exercises Are Best for the Mind-Body Connection?

Yoga, tai chi, and Pilates have gained popularity in the late twentieth and early twenty-first centuries as exercises that particularly focus on the mind-body connection. The practice of yoga includes specific body postures, breathing exercises, and meditation. Tai chi, an ancient Chinese discipline, involves sequences of slow movements. Pilates is an activity that includes stretching and doing low-impact exercises on specific equipment. All of these forms of exercise are thought to be particularly beneficial in helping people relax and deal with stress more effectively.

Aerobic activities are often cited as important to improving mental health and cognitive functioning. These exercises include strenuous and sustained exercises such as jogging, swimming, or bicycling. Aerobic means "with oxygen," and the increased oxygen and blood flow created by aerobic activity nourishes the brain. Aerobics are particularly known to help alleviate anxiety and depression, increase energy, and improve brain performance.

Aerobic exercise can also help people who are recovering drug and alcohol addicts. When the body experiences any type of pleasure,

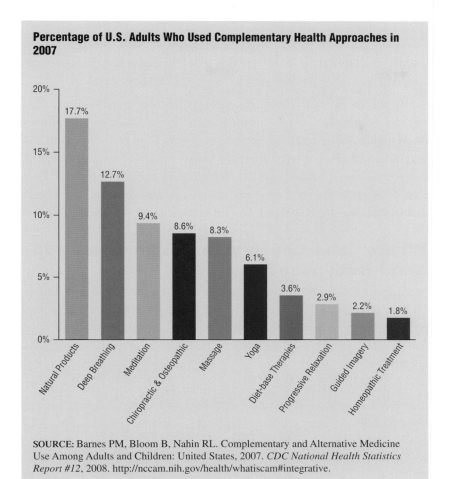

Percentage of U.S. Adults Who Used Complementary Health Approaches in 2007

SOURCE: Barnes PM, Bloom B, Nahin RL. Complementary and Alternative Medicine Use Among Adults and Children: United States, 2007. *CDC National Health Statistics Report #12*, 2008. http://nccam.nih.gov/health/whatiscam#integrative.

Complementary health approaches include mind-body techniques such as deep breathing, massage, and yoga.
ILLUSTRATION BY LUMINA DATAMATICS LTD. © 2015 CENGAGE LEARNING.

it releases a chemical called dopamine. Dopamine can be produced by drugs or alcohol, but it can also be generated by aerobic exercise. When people are trying to recover from addictions, aerobic exercise can help satisfy their body's craving for dopamine.

Which Type of Exercise Is Best for Me?

Exercise plans vary according to individual preference. Some people may prefer one form of exercise over another, but any regular physical activity or movement can be helpful to your overall wellness. The ideal way to plan an exercise routine is to choose an activity that you enjoy that also works with your lifestyle. Perhaps going to the gym or jogging before work might help you start your day off right or tai chi might help you relax in the evening. Incorporating more than one type of exercise into your workout regularly may be even better for you than focusing on just one activity.

It will be easier to meet your goals if you are realistic about what you can accomplish. If you try to relieve stress by undergoing a strenuous daily workout, you may not only set yourself up for failure, but you may also add to your level of stress. It may be better to start out with something you know you can handle and work up to bigger goals. Even a small amount of regular physical activity can help increase your energy and mental sharpness and give you some relief from anxiety.

Where Can I Get Help in Designing a Good Mind-Body Plan?

Starting your own mind-body program can be as simple as deciding to take an after-dinner walk every night. However, there are many people who can offer guidance on what type of plan might work for you, teach you various types of exercises or practices, or give you support and encouragement.

A personal trainer can work with you to develop a plan that will not only improve your physical health but also help you lessen anxiety, improve self-confidence, and manage other mind-body issues. He or she can help you discover which types of exercise are right for you and can advise you as to how frequently and how long you should work out. There are also trainers who focus on exercise programs such as yoga and stretching. Many gyms offer personal trainers who can meet with you either for a single session or on a regular basis to help motivate you and keep you on track with your goals.

 If you are looking for more general or less expensive options, a local gym or community center may provide access to exercise equipment along with a variety of classes in activities such as aerobics or tai chi. Sometimes a local house of worship or a college or university offers classes and may even be able to help you plan a balanced mind-body program for yourself. If you are looking for support but are not interested in a formal class, you can check out neighborhood bulletin boards or look online for local websites to see if there are groups you can join. If you don't see any opportunities that work with your needs, you might try putting up flyers or announcing on your Facebook page that you would like to start an exercise group.

However, if your schedule is erratic or you would prefer to work out at home, there are many videos, computer programs, smart phone apps, and television programs that can provide specific workouts oriented toward the mind-body connection. Your family doctor can also help you figure out a plan that might work for you or recommend some good places to start. He or she can be a particularly important guide if you want to target specific issues such as depression, anxiety, or memory loss. If you have certain medical challenges or medical history, it is always a good idea to check in with a health-care provider or other professional before you start any activity plan.

Choosing a Physical Activity

How Can I Choose a Physical Activity That Is Right for Me?

Choosing a physical activity that suits you depends on many factors, including your goals, your age, your present health, where you live, and even your budget. In addition, your temperament can be a major factor in choosing an activity. Are you the type of person who gets bored easily or prefers to stick to a regular routine? Do you like team sports or do you prefer to compete against yourself? Do you live in an area with numerous professional gyms equipped with top-notch equipment and trainers? Or do you live in an area where the only gyms are built with high school athletes in mind?

Consider your general physical condition and what stage of life you are in. Raising children can limit your choices by restricting the time you have available for exercise. At a later stage of life, arthritic joints might limit the activities you can endure. Failing to consider these factors could sabotage your goals and new healthy routines before they become established.

If coming back to exercise after a lengthy period of inactivity, you may want to consider a sport or an activity that you have enjoyed in the past, such as playing softball, basketball, or rollerblading. However, if your health is good, you may want to kick it up a notch with a cross-training program, rock climbing, downhill skiing, or step aerobics. As long as you respect your body's limits, almost any activity is good for you.

Why Is Physical Activity Important?

The human body is designed to move. The framework for movement is composed of over 200 bones, which are held together by hundreds of muscles and ligaments that are designed to be flexible yet strong enough to perform numerous movements. Nerves carry messages from the brain

PHYSICAL ACTIVITY PYRAMID

Different types of physical activity should be done for various lengths of time for the best fitness results.
© ELENABSL/
SHUTTERSTOCK.COM.

throughout the body to signal and coordinate movement. If your muscles and ligaments are not used, they will become weak and atrophy or waste away. Therefore, it is extremely important to use the body as it was designed, and this means exercising regularly.

The benefits of physical activity go beyond maintaining the health and conditioning of muscles, ligaments, and bones. Physical activity also develops a strong cardiovascular system and can improve mental health. It often results in weight loss and better sleep. It can provide a defense against diabetes, certain cancers, osteoporosis, stroke, depression, high blood pressure, and other chronic health conditions. Ultimately, the benefits of regular physical activity are usually a longer, healthier life and lower health-care costs.

Take time to plan activities that are effective and that you will enjoy. When possible, combine exercise with other activities, such as walking

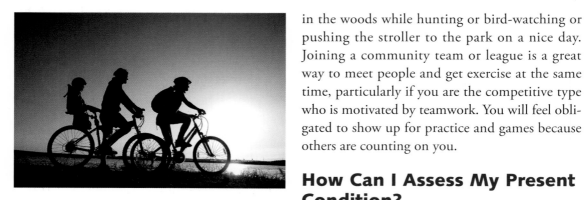

Involving family and friends can help you (and them) choose an activity everyone will like.
© YANLEV/SHUTTERSTOCK .COM.

Calorie: *A unit of energy contained in the food and liquids that people consume.*

in the woods while hunting or bird-watching or pushing the stroller to the park on a nice day. Joining a community team or league is a great way to meet people and get exercise at the same time, particularly if you are the competitive type who is motivated by teamwork. You will feel obligated to show up for practice and games because others are counting on you.

How Can I Assess My Present Condition?

Before starting any exercise program, assess your present health and general physical condition. If you have a known disease or condition or if you have not had a physical in the last 12 months, make an appointment with your doctor. Be sure to tell the doctor your plans during this screening appointment. Gather test results and measurements, which will include your weight, blood pressure, body mass index, cholesterol, and blood sugar. Make sure you learn what they mean and record them as your beginning benchmarks. Discuss with your doctor what these numbers should be and the best methods to attain them.

In addition to your present health situation, factor in your family history. Genetics can be a prime predictor of your future health. In addition to genetics, your true family history will include diet and environmental factors. If your family traditions include large home-cooked meals with generous portions of meat, potatoes, or pasta, for example, without a corresponding level of physical activity, chances are you eat too many *calories* for the energy you expend. Family traditions that include smoking and drinking can also influence health. One of the most effective exercises is putting down the fork and pushing yourself away from the table.

Your self-assessment should be objective, honest, and optimistic. It is a starting point, not the end. Your body is designed to heal itself and respond to positive changes. You are the one in charge of what goes in your body, how your body moves, and much of your physical and mental health.

How Do I Set Goals?

Most people begin a fitness program for specific reasons, such as losing weight, counteracting a health condition, or developing abdominal muscles to show off at the beach. Whatever your goal, you can find a variety

44

of activities and intensity levels to achieve them. If you want to change your body measurements, your personal health chart will be invaluable. As your numbers begin to change, you will likely become motivated to change them even more. Most fitness experts recommend a combination of aerobic and anaerobic activities, which generally means both cardiovascular exercises and strength training, for the best results. The President's Council on Fitness, Sports & Nutrition recommends that adults exercise at least 30 minutes a day for five days a week.

If you do not see improvements or positive changes in your weight or other measurements, reassess your goals. Perhaps you have just begun to condition your body and all you need to do is step up the intensity or duration of your activity. For example, if you are walking 15 minutes at a leisurely pace of 20 minutes per mile, pick up the pace and walk 2 miles in 30 minutes. Walk, do not ride in the cart, at the golf course. If you are using 5-pound weights for strength training, switch to 8- or 10-pound weights. Instead of 50 crunches, do 100. Also, be honest with yourself. Have you been rewarding yourself with more food because you are getting more exercise? That is a sure-fire way to sabotage your plan.

Consider hiring a personal trainer for a few sessions. A reputable, certified trainer will check that you are performing activities properly, will determine which activities reduce your risk of injury, and make sure that you are performing the right types of activities to meet your goals. To save money, consider getting two or three friends together for a group rate.

How Can Budget Impact Activity Choice?

Your budget will impact your chosen physical activity. Gym memberships can be expensive, and they are not always necessary. However, many people find them motivational; these people believe they are more likely to attend the gym regularly if they have paid good money to join. Also, the social aspects of going to the gym, not to mention access to modern exercise equipment, may also prove to be motivational. A gym may provide many different types of classes to stave off boredom and promote total fitness. Some gyms offer child care or other services that make them a good option for busy parents.

If your budget it limited, you can start a great exercise program with nothing more than a good pair of running shoes. Walk or run around your neighborhood, a nearby park, track, or shopping mall and then perform push-ups, sit-ups, and other anaerobic activities at home. You may find that having an exercise partner will provide motivation on those days when you would rather not venture into the heat or cold.

Making exercise a family affair is also inexpensive and enjoyable; you can play tennis at a nearby school, kick a soccer ball, or take a family bike ride. If vigorous aerobics are not your style, you can learn a few yoga poses and practice them on your own rather than signing up for classes. Finally, consider yard work and gardening. Being active while raking leaves, shoveling snow, or pulling weeds accomplishes two things at once. Choosing a physical activity that is convenient and inexpensive is important for developing a long-term, consistent activity.

If you do not have access to a gym, you can create your own. Equipment does not have to cost a small fortune. Garage sales and websites such as Craigslist are loaded with used equipment that can be purchased at a fraction of the cost of new equipment. Whether you have a separate room to use as a fitness sanctuary or use a corner of your family room, do not forget to track your results. Pin your personal health chart to a bulletin board or keep it near your workout area.

How Do I Maintain a Balanced and Flexible Approach?

The best way to maintain a balanced approach to physical activity is by recognizing that first and foremost, you are doing it to maintain your health. Running a marathon is an admirable goal, but if it is unrealistic given your weight and exercise history, you are likely setting yourself up for failure. Walking a 5k is a good first goal. When you achieve it, you may set another goal of running a 5k. In time, you may work your way up to a 10k or even a half marathon. By setting and achieving realistic goals, you are more likely to experience success and continue your exercise program.

Remaining balanced means not comparing yourself to others, especially to individuals who have been exercising for years or who have a completely different body type. A flexible approach means that you can create workarounds for obstacles. For example, if your knee hurts from aerobic activity, perhaps you switch to swimming for a while, even if it is not your favorite activity. Your knee will heal, and you will still get an awesome workout. If the roads are too icy to run in winter, get a temporary gym membership to use the treadmill. Flexibility means you maintain your commitment to physical activity even if some of the specifics change.

Balanced and flexible also means not overworking your body. Allow days off for rest, but not so many that you lose the strength and stamina you have acquired. Vary your routine to engage different muscle groups and to continue to challenge yourself. For example, if running 3 miles becomes easy, try embarking on a long bike ride of 20 miles or more. You may find that your body responds in an entirely different fashion. Plus, a new experience can reinvigorate your exercise program.

Should I Focus on Cardiovascular Activity or Muscle Strength?

Cardiovascular (cardio) workouts are those that primarily involve your heart and lungs. These are aerobic activities that you perform for 20 minutes or more in order to raise your heart rate. They will make you breath heavily and sweat. The goal of cardio activity is to make your heart, which is a muscle, stronger. Strength training, or anaerobic activity, focuses on small bursts of activity that may not result in a sustained, elevated heart rate. However, strength training, such as lifting weights, helps you reduce fat and gain muscle. Building muscle reduces fat, and cardio exercises burn calories; both are crucial for long-term health. Additionally, stronger muscles will improve your aerobic performance.

Gaining muscle strength can be achieved by numerous activities and does not require expensive equipment. You can perform numerous exercises for all muscle groups using a chair for stability, a wall to lean against, or simple barbell weights. Find programs online or through books and DVDs at your local library. Like aerobic activity, strength training requires warming up and cooling down by stretching your muscles. This flexibility will help you avoid injuries. If you are new to strength training, you may want to try yoga. It is low impact and allows you to work at your own pace, gaining strength and stability in a non-competitive and soothing environment. If your goal is to gain muscle mass, you will probably need to increase your *protein* intake. The more you exercise, the more you will realize how integral your diet is to your success.

Protein: *An organic substance made of amino acids that are necessary for human life.*

Physical activity is a lifelong pursuit. You may have one set of goals given your current assessment, but these will likely change over the years. Always be willing to try something new if you get in a rut or as your financial, health, or family circumstances change.

Establishing and Maintaining a Fitness Routine

What Is a Fitness Routine?

A fitness routine consists of regular exercise to help develop a fit, strong, and healthy body. To establish a routine, you do not have to do the same exercises every day. In fact, fitness experts recommend that you vary your exercises so that you work different parts of your body. If you overwork some muscles, they may become used to the exercise and it may lose its effectiveness. Overworking muscles can also lead to injury, so it is a good idea to choose various exercises that use different parts of your body.

Chronic illness: *A long-lasting condition that can be controlled but not cured. Also called Chronic disease.*

Establishing and maintaining a fitness routine is an important part of developing a healthy lifestyle. Exercising is one of the best things you can do for your health. Exercise improves your body's physical fitness. Physical fitness refers to your overall state of well-being and your ability to perform physical tasks. If you have a healthy body, you will be less likely to suffer an injury or develop a *chronic illness*. A healthy body is stronger and more likely to recover from illness or stress than an unhealthy body. Exercise can also help you lose weight or maintain a healthy weight, as well as reduce your chances of developing certain medical problems, such as type 2 diabetes, hypertension (high blood pressure), and heart disease. It can also improve your mood and help you combat depression.

How Can I Motivate Myself to Make Fitness Part of My Routine?

First consider why you are participating in a fitness routine. Perhaps you have certain goals in mind, such as becoming fit to have more energy to spend time with your friends and family or staying fit to help prevent future health problems. Setting goals is a good way to motivate yourself to exercise. These goals, though, should be long term and ongoing. A goal of becoming fit to look good at a class reunion, for example, will only last until the class reunion. Long-term goals will motivate you to continue to exercise.

If you are overtired by or bored with your exercise routine, you will probably feel less motivated to exercise. By performing different exercises and exercises that target different body parts, you incorporate variety into your workouts. Changing up your routine regularly can reduce stress on your body and may ease boredom.

Another way to motivate yourself is to choose exercises that you enjoy. If you enjoy social activities, you can schedule regular walks, runs, or bike rides with a friend. If you like playing team sports, you can join a sports league that has regular games or competitions. Finding activities that are naturally attractive to you will make exercise seem less like work and more like a fun activity.

How Often Should I Exercise?

Exercising regularly is important. How much and how often you exercise depends on the type of exercise you perform, how intensely you exercise, and other factors. The American College of Sports Medicine (ACSM) recommends that healthy adults should perform at least 150 minutes of medium-intensity cardiovascular exercise every week. The ACSM suggests that you exercise five days a week at a moderate level of intensity or and three days a week at a higher level of intensity.

The ACSM offers recommendations for other types of exercise as well. For example, healthy adults should perform exercises that use weights or other types of resistance two or three days a week, with at least one day of rest in between those types of exercise routines to allow the body time to rest and recover. The ACSM guidelines state that healthy adults should perform flexibility exercises two or three days a week and should also spend two or three days a week performing neuromotor exercises such as yoga. Neuromotor exercises are those that help people with their balance, coordination, and *agility*.

Agility: *The ability to quickly react to unexpected shifts in supply and demand.*

The ACSM recommendations are general guidelines, not strict rules. Specific factors such as your fitness level and age might affect your exercise routine. If you are an older adult or are just beginning to exercise, the ACSM suggests that you exercise less intensely and perform fewer repetitions of each exercise when you begin your fitness routine. When you are more accustomed to exercising, you can gradually increase your

THREE TYPES OF EXERCISE

Stretching, for flexibility

Weight-bearing, for strengthening muscles and bone mass

Aerobic, for the heart

Different types of exercise target different parts of the body: stretch for flexibility, lift weights for strength and bone mass, and do aerobics for your heart. ILLUSTRATION BY ELECTRONIC ILLUSTRATORS GROUP. © 2013 CENGAGE LEARNING.

intensity and repetitions. The ACSM says that, even if you cannot meet its guidelines, you should still try to exercise, since some exercise is better than none at all.

When Should I Exercise?

Because people perform different kinds of exercises for different reasons, it is not surprising that they exercise at different times. You might prefer to exercise when you wake up in the morning. Maybe you prefer morning exercise because it gives you an energy boost or because mornings are the only time you have to exercise. Some people prefer to exercise in the morning because their gym or health club is near or even at their workplace.

Fitness instructor and personal trainer Jessica Smith warns that morning workouts can have a major drawback, however: they could deprive you of sleep. In a 2013 article for *Shape* magazine, Smith said that you should engage in morning exercise only if you are not robbing yourself of sleep. She noted that sleep deprivation (not having enough sleep) has been linked to fatigue, weight problems, and susceptibility to certain diseases. Smith suggested breaking up your exercise routine into different segments throughout the course of the day instead of one long workout that cuts into your sleep time.

The ACSM also recommends incorporating multiple shorter workouts throughout your day instead of one long workout. This can make it easier to fit exercise into your busy schedule. It ensures that you are getting your regular exercise and working toward the 150 minutes of weekly exercise that the ACSM recommends.

What Are Some Tips for Fitting Fitness into a Busy Schedule?

Don't let a busy schedule be an excuse for not exercising. There are many ways to incorporate workouts into even the busiest schedules. Even 5 or 10 minutes of exercise can contribute to physical fitness and overall health. In the morning, perform 5 to 10 minutes of weight or flexibility exercises, or take a quick walk or run with a pet. During your workday, try to fit in some exercises, such as stretches, that you can perform while sitting or standing at your desk. Take a walk or run or climb stairs during your lunch or other work breaks. Some workplaces even offer on-site fitness classes or gym memberships to help their employees stay fit.

At home, you can add exercise to your daily activities. Perform stretches to improve your flexibility while folding laundry or putting away dishes. Do weight and resistance exercises while watching television, or do cardiovascular exercises (such as walking on a treadmill or using a stationary bike) while reading a newspaper or magazine. Of course, you can also engage in more traditional workouts at gyms or by following routines featured in books, magazines, DVDs, and other sources. Many of these workouts allow you to customize the intensity level and length of your fitness routine.

My Fitness Routine Is Not Producing the Results I Had Hoped. What Should I Do?

Sometimes you find that maintaining a regular fitness routine is not creating the results you want. Your routine might not be working at all, or it may have worked well when you started exercising but is becoming less effective over time. While these developments are frustrating, they are common and can be fixed.

Finding a fitness routing you like will help you stick to it.
© BLEND IMAGES/ALAMY.

If your fitness routine never worked in the first place, you could be exercising improperly. To learn how to do exercises properly, you can join a gym or hire a fitness instructor such as a personal trainer. You can look online for reputable websites that relate to fitness and physical education. Exercise and fitness organizations, government agencies, and many universities offer these kinds of Internet resources. You can also consult books, magazines, and DVDs to learn more about exercise.

This research could tell you if you are using your body improperly during certain exercises and it can help you correct your form. Or you might find that you are doing your exercises properly but are not exercising intensely enough. You might need to lift heavier weights or run faster during certain exercises. Remember that changes in the type and intensity of your exercise are also good because your body becomes accustomed to certain exercises over time, which can slow or stop your fitness progress. Changing your routine forces your muscles to work in new ways.

I Am Having Trouble Maintaining My Fitness Routine. What Should I Do?

When you began your fitness routine, you were likely motivated by one or more factors. You may have begun exercising to lose weight, reshape your body, build endurance, or improve your overall health. Even if you are meeting your fitness goals, it can be difficult to stay motivated over time. You may become bored with your routine. You may have noticed that your weight loss has plateaued or that your progress toward your health goals has slowed. Alternately, if you exercise outdoors, you may find your motivation dwindling in colder weather. These factors, however, can all be overcome.

Changing your routine can prevent you from getting bored and abandoning your regimen. If bad weather prevents you from exercising outdoors, see if you can find a gym or indoor track where you can work out. Another way to keep your momentum going is to reward yourself for sticking to your routine. You can set milestones along your fitness journey and reward yourself for meeting those goals. For example, treat yourself to a movie after exercising five days a week for two consecutive weeks or buy yourself a new outfit after you lose 10 pounds.

Social support can also help you stick to your exercise routine. Exercising with a friend can help you look forward to exercising and enjoy the actual exercise itself. An exercise partner can encourage you on days when you do not feel like exercising, teach you new ways to exercise, and help you increase the intensity of your workouts. Experts have found that the encouragement of friends and family members increases the likelihood that a person, particularly a woman, will stick with a fitness routine.

What Are the Benefits of Fitness Routines for Different Types of People?

The health benefits of establishing and maintaining a fitness routine can vary from person to person, depending on age, gender, regimen, and other factors. Physically active women are less likely to develop osteoporosis, a condition that weakens the bones and is found most often in women. Regular physical exercise can help reduce depression, a condition twice as likely to afflict women as men. Men are more likely to develop heart disease, but people of both sexes can suffer its effects. Experts recommend engaging in cardiovascular (also known as aerobic) exercise, which is exercise that engages the heart and increases the body's consumption of oxygen.

Regardless of your gender or your fitness level, you should consider some things before exercising. If you are pregnant, are over the age of 50, or have heart disease, high blood pressure, or another medical condition, you might want to consult a doctor before starting a new fitness routine. You can further maximize the effectiveness of your workouts by following a healthy diet that is low in fat and sodium and that meets other nutritional guidelines. Finally, if you have an inactive lifestyle, you should consider adding more physical activity to your life in addition to your workouts. These steps can help you live a healthier life.

Sleep

Why Is Sleep an Important Part of Establishing a Healthy Routine?

Osteoporosis: *A degenerative bone disease that causes a decrease in bone mass, making bones more brittle and fragile and likely to break.*

Getting a good night's sleep not only makes you feel good, but medical studies have shown that it is also good for your health. During sleep, scientists say, the human brain and body work to repair themselves in complicated, essential ways. You may notice that you are more alert and can concentrate better after eight hours of sleep. The right amount of sleep may have other health benefits, including regulating your weight; protecting you from type 2 diabetes; and lowering your risk of Alzheimer's disease, depression, *osteoporosis*, and cancer.

During sleep, fluids in and around the brain get rid of toxins, and your body checks on the internal balance of various systems. While you are awake, your brain creates toxins, called free radicals, that cause aging and trigger disease. While you are asleep, however, your brain creates other chemicals, called antioxidants, that clear away these toxins. If you don't get enough sleep, your brain doesn't have a chance to manufacture enough antioxidants, and this can lead to the death of some brain cells.

The brain changes in other ways while you are sleeping. Your brain cells shrink in size, allowing the fluids that are washing away toxins to have more room to do their job. Studies point to evidence that less sleep can result in fewer antioxidants and less time for the fluid to wash the brain, which may create conditions for aging and even the onset of disease.

How Much Sleep Should I Get Each Night?

Getting the right amount of sleep is important, yet most Americans do not get enough. Recommendations for the ideal amount of sleep vary and are different for various age groups. For adults over 18, 7.5 to 9 hours of sleep is considered optimal. For teenagers the range is 8.5 to 10 hours per night. The right amount of sleep for you may be somewhat different from

The Role of Sleep in Maintaining a Healthy Weight

Most people understand that getting enough sleep is important for health, but many overlook the connection between sleep and maintaining a healthy weight. Sleep and weight are connected in several important ways. Individuals who get enough sleep at night are more likely to have energy for exercise during the day, but those who are sluggish from lack of sleep will, on average, burn fewer calories during the day than their more rested counterparts.

Sleep is also important in regulating hormones that affect weight. Studies have shown that individuals who get fewer than five hours of sleep a night have higher levels of hormones tied to hunger, while they also have lower levels of hormones that suppress it. Not getting enough sleep can also have a negative effect on your brain's impulse control, which can make you more likely to indulge in unhealthy food choices. Although you still need to exercise and eat a healthy diet even if you get plenty of sleep, establishing healthy sleeping patterns is an important part of keeping your energy levels high and taking control of your weight.

that for another person your age, but the range for each age group is well defined. The quality of your sleep is also important and may be determined by factors such as how easily you fall asleep and whether you wake often.

According to the National Institute of Neurological Disorders and Stroke (NINDS), if you feel drowsy during the day, fall asleep at night in less than five minutes, or sleep for very brief times during the day, then you probably aren't getting enough sleep on a regular basis. Occasional long periods of sleep, such as on a weekend or vacation, may help you catch up but will not completely reverse the negative effects of too little sleep.

Some people believe that they need less sleep as they get older, but sleep researchers say that people still need the same amount of sleep later in life. About half of people over 65 have problems such as sleeping lightly or for short periods of time.

What Are Some Tips for Making Sure I Get Enough Sleep?

Recognizing the importance of sleep to your overall health is the very first step in getting enough sleep. To find your optimal amount of sleep, begin keeping track of when you go to sleep, when you wake up, and how you feel during the day. Even a half hour more or less on a regular basis can make a difference in how you feel when you wake up, how alert

A good night's sleep is an integral part of a healthy lifestyle.
© BIKERIDERLONDON/
SHUTTERSTOCK.COM.

you feel throughout the day, whether you get drowsy in the afternoon, and whether your body has the time to rejuvenate itself.

You should plan ahead to allow yourself the amount of sleep you need. If you do best with 7.5 hours of sleep, you can count backward from the time you need to wake up to find the ideal time to go to sleep. For example, if you need to be up by 6:30 a.m., you should plan to go to bed by 11 p.m. Your sleep times should be regular, and if you go to sleep at the right time you should be able to wake up without an alarm. If you need an alarm or use your snooze button, these may be signs that you aren't getting enough sleep.

If you have a short night of sleep or even a week of shortened sleep, it may be helpful for you to add up the total hours you have missed from your optimal amount of sleep. You can make those hours up by adding an hour or two each night until the deficit is cleared.

I'm Getting the Recommended Amount of Sleep, So Why Do I Feel Tired?

If you are getting between seven and eight hours of sleep per night but still feel tired, you may need more sleep. Most adults do not need nine or more hours of sleep, but some do. It may help for you to try increasing your sleep time by just 15 or 30 minutes for a two-week period to see whether you notice a difference. Even if you are getting enough sleep, you may need to improve the quality of your sleep. There are several stages to the normal sleep cycle, and your body needs to go through all of them to get full benefits from sleep.

The first stage of sleep lasts just 5 to 10 minutes and is a transition from wakefulness to sleep. Your brain begins to slow down, but if you wake during this period you will not feel rested. The second stage of sleep lasts for about 20 minutes and is referred to as light sleep. During this period your body temperature cools down, your heart rate slows, your eye movement stops, and your brain produces rhythmic bursts of brain activity called sleep spindles. The third stage of sleep is deep sleep. This stage is characterized by slow brain waves called delta waves and may last from 30 minutes to an hour. People in deep sleep are difficult to wake. The fourth stage of sleep is called REM, which stands for Rapid Eye Movement. During this stage, your brain becomes more active, your muscles become less active, and you dream. You may cycle through stages two, three, and four about four or five times during a night of sleep. The first instance of REM sleep occurs, on average, about 90 minutes after you fall asleep and usually lasts longer with each cycle.

If your sleep is interrupted before you complete the sleep cycles, you may not feel rested afterward. Many things can interfere with sleep, and sometimes you may not be aware that your sleep is being interrupted. If you drink alcohol or take a sedative before bed, you may wake when the effects wear off. You may also awaken if your room is too warm or if your work schedule has changed. Pain, muscles cramps, or a condition called apnea may also interrupt your sleep and cause you to feel tired in the morning.

How Much Sleep is Enough?

The amount of sleep you need each day changes over the course of your lifetime. Although sleep needs vary from person to person, this chart gives general recommendations for different age groups.

Age	Recommended Amount of Sleep
Newborns	16–18 hours a day
Preschool-aged children	11–12 hours a day
School-aged children	At least 10 hours a day
Teens	9–10 hours a day
Adults (including the elderly)	7–8 hours a day

SOURCE: National Heart, Lung, and Blood Institute. "How Much Sleep Is Enough?" http://www.nhlbi.nih.gov/health/health-topics/topics/sdd/howmuch.

ILLUSTRATION BY LUMINA DATAMATICS LTD. © 2015 CENGAGE LEARNING.

I'm Having Trouble Falling Asleep at Night. What Should I Do?

Falling asleep at night should take between 5 and 10 minutes. If it takes longer, there are several things you can do to regulate your internal circadian, or biological, clock. Your circadian clock is made up of a group of cells in the back of your brain that respond to light, telling your body when to be awake and when to feel drowsy. This part of your brain, located in the *hypothalamus*, sends signals that control the release of melatonin, the hormone most associated with sleep regulation. When there is less light, your body secretes melatonin and makes you drowsier. To help your body's natural sleep/wake cycle, it is best to get plenty of natural light during the day and to stay away from bright light while you are winding down to go to sleep. The bright lights of electronic devices can inhibit your body's production of melatonin and make it harder for you to fall asleep.

While it is tempting to nap during the day to catch up on sleep deficits, sleep experts warn that napping may disturb the pattern you've established for nighttime sleep and can make it harder for you to fall

Hypothalamus: *The section of the brain responsible for hormone production.*

Factors That Can Cause Sleep Problems

- Physical (such as ulcers)
- Medical (such as asthma)
- Psychiatric (such as depression and anxiety disorders)
- Environmental (such as alcohol)
- Stresses (such as job loss or change, death of a loved one, or moving)
- Illness
- Environmental factors (such as light, noise, or extreme temperatures)
- Narcolepsy (a neurological disorder of sleep regulation, which has shown to be genetic)
- Work hours that may not coincide with sleep patterns
- Some medications
- Aging (as many as half of all adults over the age of 65 have some sort of sleep disorder)

SOURCE: The Cleveland Clinic. www.clevelandclinic.org

TABLE BY PREMEDIAGLOBAL.
© 2013 CENGAGE LEARNING.

asleep at night. Other tips from sleep experts include getting exercise during the day; having a relaxing routine before bed such as bathing, reading, meditation or light yoga; and making your bedroom and bed comfortable spaces where you can reduce light and sound.

When Should I Consult a Doctor about Sleep Problems?

Insomnia is one of the most common sleep problems. More than a third of adults report sometimes having symptoms of insomnia, which include difficulty falling asleep, staying asleep, or feeling tired after sleeping. If you have these symptoms consistently, you should consult your doctor.

Circadian rhythm disorders refer to conditions in which a person sleeps a normal amount of time but has difficulty falling asleep or waking up during socially acceptable times. This type of disorder is often associated with shift workers and people who travel frequently across different time zones.

Other conditions that doctors can help with include obstructive sleep apnea, excessive sleepiness disorder, parasomnias, and restless leg syndrome (RLS). Obstructive sleep apnea is caused by blocked or constricted airways and may be indicated by loud snoring accompanied by pauses in breathing. Persistent daytime sleepiness or fatigue may be symptoms of narcolepsy (disabling sleepiness), cataplexy (sudden loss of muscle tone), or other medical conditions. Parasomnias are abnormal behaviors that occur while you are sleeping, including nightmares, sleepwalking, or sleep-related paralysis. If you suffer from an overwhelming urge to move your legs while you are trying to fall asleep, you may have restless leg syndrome. There are many medical approaches to helping with these problems.

Many people have trouble sleeping at times or have periods of time when they don't get enough sleep. If you have problems that seem serious, however, or if they consistently disturb your sleep or the sleep of those around you, try to document the trouble you are having and make an appointment to talk to your doctor. You may have a medical condition that is interfering with your sleep, and lack of enough sleep may also contribute to other illnesses.

For More Information

BOOKS

Avritt, Julie Jordan. "Women's Fitness." In *The Gale Encyclopedia of Fitness*, edited by Jacqueline L. Longe, 923–26. Detroit: Gale, 2012.

Centers for Disease Control and Prevention. *The Association between School-Based Physical Activity, Including Physical Education, and Academic Performance.* Atlanta: U.S. Department of Health and Human Services, 2010. This paper can also be found online at http://www.cdc.gov/healthy youth/health_and_academics/pdf/pa-pe_paper.pdf.

MacLaren, Archibald. *A System of Physical Education: Theoretical and Practical.* Chestnut Hill, MA: Adamant Media Corp., 2001.

"Physical Activity (Exercise) for Depression." In *Encyclopedia of Emotion*, edited by Gretchen M. Reevy, 440–41. Santa Barbara, CA: Greenwood Press, 2010.

Wells, Ken R. "Men's Fitness." In *The Gale Encyclopedia of Fitness*, edited by Jacqueline L. Longe, 547–49. Detroit: Gale, 2012.

PERIODICALS

Donnelly, Laura. "One Hour of Exercise a Week 'Can Halve Dementia Risk.'" *Telegraph*, July 13, 2014. This article can also be found online at http://www .telegraph.co.uk/health/healthnews/10964854/One-hour-of-exercise-a-week-can-halve-dementia-risk.html.

Kennedy, John F. "The Vigor We Need." *Sports Illustrated*, July 16, 1962, 12–15.

Park, Alice. "The Power of Sleep." *Time*, September 11, 2014. This article can also be found online at http://time.com/3326565/the-power-of-sleep/.

Reynolds, Gretchen. "How Exercise Could Lead to a Better Brain." *New York Times*, April 18, 2012. This article can also be found online at http://www .nytimes.com/2012/04/22/magazine/how-exercise-could-lead-to-a-better-brain.html?pagewanted=all&_r=0.

Roy, Sree. "Safeguarding America's Sleep." *Sleep Review*, July-August, 2014, 8+.

"Sleep and the Brain." *Focus on Healthy Aging*, April 1, 2014, 6.

Smith, Jessica. "8 Well-Meaning Workout Strategies That Backfire." *Shape*, March 28, 2012. This article can also be found online at http://www.shape .com/fitness/workouts/8-well-meaning-workout-strategies-backfire.

Verghese, Joe, Richard B. Lipton, Mindy J. Katz, Charles B. Hall, Carol A. Derby, Gail Kuslansky, Anne F. Ambrose, Martin Sliwinski, and Herman Buschke. "Leisure Activities and the Risk of Dementia in the Elderly." *New England Journal of Medicine* 348 (2003): 2508–16.

WEBSITES

"ACSM Issues New Recommendations on Quantity and Quality of Exercise." *American College of Sports Medicine.* http://acsm.org/about-acsm/media-room/news-releases/2011/08/01/acsm-issues-new-recommendations-on-quantity-and-quality-of-exercise (accessed September 30, 2014).

"The Benefits of Physical Activity." *Harvard School of Public Health.* 2014. http://www.hsph.harvard.edu/nutritionsource/staying-active-full-story/#the-cost-of-inactivity (accessed October 21, 2014).

"Brain Basics: Understanding Sleep.*" National Institute of Neurological Disorders and Stroke.* 2014. http://www.ninds.nih.gov/disorders/brain_basics/understanding_sleep.htm (accessed October 2, 2014).

Bryant, Cedric X. "Why Is It Important to Vary My Workout Routines?" *ACE.* http://www.acefitness.org/acefit/healthy-living-article/60/1210/why-is-it-important-to-vary-my-workout/ (accessed September 30, 2014).

"Cardiovascular Exercise." *ACE.* http://www.acefitness.org/acefit/fitness-fact/1/cardiovascular-exercise/ (accessed September 30, 2014).

"Fitness Training: Elements of a Well-Rounded Routine." *Mayo Clinic.* http://www.mayoclinic.org/healthy-living/fitness/in-depth/fitness-training/art-20044792 (accessed September 30, 2014).

Hauri, Peter. "The Sleep Disorders." *National Sleep Foundation.* 2014. http://sleepdisorders.sleepfoundation.org/ (accessed October 6, 2014).

"Overcoming Barriers to Physical Activity." *Centers for Disease Control and Prevention.* http://www.cdc.gov/physicalactivity/everyone/getactive/barriers.html (accessed September 30, 2014).

Smith, Melinda, Lawrence Robinson, and Robert Segal. "How Much Sleep Do You Need?" *HelpGuide.org.* http://www.helpguide.org/articles/sleep/how-much-sleep-do-you-need.htm (accessed October 2, 2014).

Walcutt, Diana L. "Stages of Sleep." *Psych Central.* http://psychcentral.com/lib/stages-of-sleep/0002073 (accessed October 2, 2014).

"Ways to Be Active." *President's Council on Fitness, Sports & Nutrition.* http://www.fitness.gov/be-active/ways-to-be-active/ (accessed October 21, 2014).

Personal Care and Hygiene

In This Section

- Basic Hygiene Habits
- Basic Grooming Habits
- Clothing, Bedding, Towels, and Personal Items
- Healthy Habits When Away from Home
- For More Information

Why Is Good Hygiene Important?

The human body is vulnerable to a variety of bacteria, germs, and fungi that are readily found in our environment and easily transmitted from person to person via bodily contact and touching things that others have touched. Establishing and sustaining good hygiene habits are vital to protecting yourself from illness and to maintaining health. In addition, good hygiene can help you avoid spreading germs to others.

Maintaining personal cleanliness is socially and emotionally beneficial because it allows you to fit in with others and feel good about yourself. People who do not keep themselves clean in line with the standards of the culture in which they live may have a difficult time socializing with others and finding and keeping a job.

What Are Some Good Basic Hygiene Habits?

Good hygiene starts with keeping your hands clean. Every day your hands come into contact with germ-covered surfaces, such as door

The Debate over Hand Sanitizers

Since the late 1990s hand sanitizers have gained popularity as a quick and easy way to kill germs, including those that cause stomach bugs. Marketed in convenient pump and travel-sized containers for on the go, these alcohol-based preparations have been embraced by consumers as an option for cleaning hands when soap and water are not available. They have quickly become a staple in homes, schools, and medical facilities.

Not everyone is a proponent of hand sanitizers, however. One of the greatest causes for concern is that most hand sanitizers have a higher alcohol content than hard liquor. Although alcohol poisoning from these products is rare, as little as one ounce of hand sanitizer could be fatal to a small child if ingested. A 2006 *New York Times* article warns consumers to be aware of the alcohol content in hand sanitizers—not because it could be dangerous but because it could be ineffective. The article explains that not all of the sanitizers on the market contain enough alcohol to be effective in killing germs. When purchasing a hand sanitizer, make sure you read the label. To be effective, it must be at least 60 percent alcohol.

Those who are wary of hand sanitizers also point out that extensive use of antibacterial products, including hand sanitizers, is contributing to the development of bacteria that are resistant to antibiotics. Similarly, hand sanitizers do not differentiate between good bacteria and bad bacteria. Killing too much good bacteria can ultimately leave you vulnerable to illness.

handles, in public spaces. Daily activities such as using the bathroom, touching pets, and handling meat and other foods can also contaminate hands with illness-causing agents, which you can in turn leave on surfaces and spread to others. Frequent hand washing, especially before and after touching food and after using the bathroom, can greatly cut the risks of getting sick. Hand washing is especially essential during cold and flu season, when people spend a lot of time indoors and germs are very prevalent. When washing your hands, you should thoroughly lather and rub them together for at least 20 seconds before rinsing. You should also dry your hands completely on a clean towel.

Cleaning and trimming your fingernails is also an important part of hand hygiene. It's important to scrub the underside of your nails with a scrub brush and soap routinely. Long fingernails provide a place for dirt and bacteria to hide, so it is better to keep nails trimmed. Always keep clippers and nail files clean to avoid the spread of bacteria. If you routinely receive professional manicures or pedicures, you should be sure the equipment being used is sterilized thoroughly between clients, since poor hygiene practices in nail salons have been known to spread serious infection.

Regular bathing is also an essential part of any hygiene routine. A bath or shower daily is ideal during hot weather and for those who participate in intense exercise or hard physical labor. Bathing washes away germs, and it helps eliminate unpleasant body odors. When you bathe, it is important to clean all body parts thoroughly from head to toe. Many people tend to neglect their feet, assuming that standing in a hot shower is enough to clean them. Feet can be especially prone to developing fungal infections, so always be sure to wash them, including between your toes, with soap and water. Belly buttons, too, are often neglected and should be cleaned thoroughly each time you bathe.

Shaving, washing your hands, and brushing your teeth not only keep you clean, but they also help prevent you from getting sick.
© AUREMAR/
SHUTTERSTOCK.COM.

Daily hair washing is somewhat controversial. Unless your hair is very oily or gets dirty because of your job or other lifestyle factors, daily shampooing may be more than is necessary and can cause your hair to overproduce oil. While it is important to keep hair clean to avoid lice, as well as an unkempt appearance, washing hair every other day or a few times a week may be sufficient.

Ideally, the washcloths and towels you use during and after bathing should be laundered between uses. While loofas and bath puffs have grown in popularity over recent years, they can be hard to clean and should therefore be used with caution as they may harbor bacteria, especially when stored on wet surfaces or in a humid bathroom. It is also important to keep your tub or shower clean, including regularly laundering your cloth shower curtain and replacing your rubber curtain at the first sign of mildew.

What Can I Do to Prevent or Treat Acne?

Acne is a skin disorder that occurs when the skin's oil glands become overactive, leading to plugged pores and outbreaks of pimples, usually on the face, neck, chest, and back. While acne is not caused by bacteria, as is sometimes mistakenly believed, and is not dangerous, it can lead its sufferers to experience low self-esteem. Further, severe acne can permanently scar your skin. Acne is typically caused by hormonal fluctuations, especially around *puberty*. Although it may not be preventable, there are things you can do to reduce its severity.

Puberty: *The onset of sexual maturation, during which adolescents develop characteristics of their sex and become capable of reproduction.*

> **Hand Washing—a Good Hygiene Habit**
>
> **When to Wash Your Hands**
> - Before, during, and after preparing food
> - Before eating food
> - Before and after caring for someone who is sick
> - Before and after treating a cut or wound
> - After using the toilet, changing diapers, or cleaning up a person who has used the toilet
> - After blowing your nose, coughing, or sneezing
> - After touching an animal, animal feed, or animal waste
> - After handling a pet, pet food, or pet treats
> - After touching garbage
>
> **How to Wash Your Hands**
> - Wet your hands with clean, running water (warm or cold), turn off the tap, and apply soap.
> - Lather your hands by rubbing them together with the soap. Be sure to lather the backs of your hands, between your fingers, and under your nails.
> - Scrub your hands for at least 20 seconds—the time it takes to hum the "A-B-C" song once.
> - Rinse your hands well under clean, running water.
> - Dry your hands using a clean towel or air dry them.
>
> **SOURCE:** Centers for Disease Control and Prevention. "Handwashing: Clean Hands Save Lives." http://www.cdc.gov/handwashing/when-how-handwashing.html.

ILLUSTRATION BY LUMINA DATAMATICS LTD. © 2015 CENGAGE LEARNING.

When you have acne, you should wash your face with a gentle cleanser every morning and evening and after any heavy exertion such as exercise or hard labor. You may be able to get a special cleanser from a doctor or dermatologist, as well as acne creams to apply topically after cleansing. Stay away from astringents and harsh soaps since these can actually make acne worse. You should also avoid picking at or "popping" pimples because this practice can introduce bacteria and lead to infection.

How Can I Maintain Healthy Teeth?

Brushing your teeth regularly is also an important hygiene habit, since the warm, humid climate of the human mouth can be a breeding ground for bacteria. Moreover, reports by the U.S. National Institutes of Health have suggested that problems such as heart disease may worsen due to poor tooth health. Most dentists recommend that you brush your teeth at least twice daily with fluoride toothpaste and a soft-bristled toothbrush. Brushing should occur once after eating breakfast and once before bed at night. Regular flossing at least once daily is a good idea to remove debris from between teeth. When you brush your teeth, you should be sure to brush your gums and your tongue as well. Bacteria on your tongue in particular are a known culprit of bad breath. You should replace your toothbrush every three to four months or when it shows signs of wear. In the meantime, running your toothbrush through the dishwasher can be a good way to sanitize it.

Besides daily brushing, you should plan to visit your dentist every six months to get a thorough cleaning of your teeth and gums. Your dentist will be able to assess the condition of your mouth and address any problems, such as cavities, that may arise.

How Can I Care for My Ears without Causing Damage?

Ears are delicate, so it's important to clean them very carefully. The external portion of the ears can be washed with a cloth and gentle soap. However, you should never insert anything, including washcloths or cotton swabs, into your ear canal because this can cause permanent damage to inner ear structures and damage your hearing. In addition, small wounds caused by cleaning can lead to painful infections. If you wear headphones, particularly ear buds, it is important to clean them frequently and make sure that all portions of the ear bud have been removed from your ear when you are done using it.

Sometimes a buildup of earwax will affect your hearing and may produce an unpleasant smell. You may be able to clear a blockage at home by dropping a small amount of baby oil, mineral oil, or commercial drops in the ear. Hydrogen peroxide drops may also be effective. Alternatively, you can use an ear irrigation kit, which can be purchased in drugstores and other retail establishments. These kits generally use a solution of water or saline, which is warmed to body temperature and placed in the ear canal for 15–30 minutes. If you are not comfortable performing this procedure yourself, you should visit your family doctor. Ear candles, which are placed in the ear canal and lit, have been found to be dangerous by the U.S. Food and Drug Administration (FDA) and should never be used.

How Should I Care for My Eyes If I Wear Contact Lenses?

Like ears, eyes are very delicate organs. Many people choose to wear contact lenses to help correct vision problems, and doing so is safe, provided you practice good habits and take good care of your supplies. First, you should always wash your hands before handling your lenses to lessen the chances of getting infection-causing bacteria in your eyes. Contacts should be removed and cleaned daily, unless you have a special prescription that allows for overnight wear.

Choosing the correct supplies and taking good care of them will also help you maintain good eye hygiene. Your contacts should be cleaned daily using the solution recommended by your eye doctor. Before storing your contacts in their case, you should empty the case of any old saline solution and rinse it out thoroughly. Generally speaking, it's best to replace your case every three months.

What Are Some Tips for Maintaining Good Hygiene during My Period?

Menstruation: *Monthly shedding of the lining of the uterus in females, which results in the discharge of blood and tissue.*

Women have a variety of sanitary products to choose from during *menstruation*. Tampons are worn internally and allow you to catch the bulk of your menstrual flow before it leaves the body. While tampons are generally safe to use, you should follow the instructions on the box regarding how often to change them. Toxic Shock Syndrome (TSS), a bacterial infection, is a rare but dangerous side effect of failing to remove and change tampons in a timely manner.

A menstrual cup, also worn internally, is a flexible cup, typically made from medical-grade silicone, which collects menstrual fluid. A menstrual cup can usually be worn from 8 to 12 hours, about twice as long as a tampon. Reusable cups should be removed and washed when full. Disposable cups, which are discarded after a single cycle should be cared for in the same manner, then disposed of at the end of your cycle. Single-use cups are also available. Whichever kind of cup you choose to use, you should follow the manufacturer's instructions for cleaning and replacement.

Sanitary pads, worn externally, are another option to use during your period. While the use of pads carries little risk of infection, you should change your pad before it gets completely saturated in order to avoid leakage onto your clothing.

How Can I Teach My Kids Good Personal Hygiene?

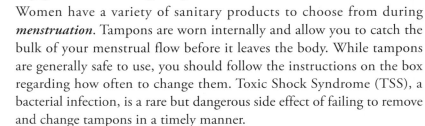

Teaching your children good personal care habits is important for keeping them healthy and promoting self-esteem and social acceptance. You should start by modeling healthy habits. This means staying consistent with your hygiene routines, even when you are pressed for time in the morning or exhausted in the evening after a long day.

Teach your kids about the importance of hand washing and the basics of how germs are spread between people. Teachers and day care providers are typically helpful in this area because they, too, are invested in cutting down on germs in the environment. Objects such as bath toys and toothbrushes that light up and sing to indicate the proper length of time to brush can make routine hygiene activities fun for younger children.

Basic Grooming Habits

Why Is Good Grooming Important?

Good grooming is an essential part of self-care. Being neat, clean, and well put together will benefit you in social and employment situations, which in turn is good for your self-esteem. On the flip side, people who do not maintain cultural standards of cleanliness and tidiness may have a difficult time finding and keeping a job, making friends, and forming romantic relationships.

Human beings are vulnerable to a variety of bacteria, germs, and fungi, which, along with natural bodily processes, can produce unpleasant odors and an unsightly appearance. Establishing and sustaining good grooming practices with regard to your body and clothing can help you overcome these challenges and present a positive image to others. Taking care of yourself communicates a desire to participate in your community, and it indicates respect for those with whom you come into contact daily.

What Are Some Good Basic Grooming Habits?

Good grooming starts with basic cleanliness. A daily bath or shower is the best way to keep yourself clean and smelling fresh. It is especially essential to bathe daily if you engage in activity that causes sweating and body odor such as frequent exercise, recreational sports, or hard physical labor. You should bathe with mild soap and water, paying particular attention to areas such as armpits and feet that can produce an unpleasant odor. Most adults should use a deodorant, which is best applied to clean skin. It is also a good idea to moisturize skin after bathing, especially during the winter months. Doing so can prevent uncomfortable and unsightly patches of dry skin.

Regular hand washing and fingernail care is also a fundamental part of being well groomed. Hands can spread germs, and noticeably dirty hands and nails are distasteful to others, especially when you shake hands or pass items between you. When washing your hands you should thoroughly lather them with soap and then rub for at least 20 seconds before rinsing. You should also scrub the underside of your nails with a small brush to eliminate dirt. Nail cleaning is especially essential if you have long fingernails. Maintaining a neat manicure, with trimmed, filed nails, is a good idea for both men and women. You can manicure your own nails at home or pay to have them done professionally. Women may also choose to wear colored nail polish, although this practice is typically less acceptable for men. Women who hold jobs in conservative fields or work in service positions may also be limited in this respect.

Good grooming starts with basic cleanliness which includes keeping your hair clean. © ROBERT HOETINK/ SHUTTERSTOCK.COM.

How Should I Care for My Hair?

Clean, well-cut, and styled hair is something other people often notice when forming a first impression. To ensure that your hair looks attractive, you should plan on washing it regularly. Exactly how often you should wash your hair depends on factors such as your hair type and lifestyle. In general, you do not need to wash your hair daily, and doing so may cause your scalp to overproduce oil. Instead, you should wash your hair often enough to keep it from looking greasy and to reduce your chances of contracting head lice (tiny insects that feed on blood from the human scalp). You may also want to use a conditioner, which can help hair look smooth and shiny. Conditioner may leave fine hair looking greasy, however, so it is best to use it sparingly if your hair falls into this category. If you are not able to wash your hair, dry shampoo can work in a pinch to cut grease and make hair look clean and shiny.

Regular haircuts can also help keep you looking your best. Stylists recommend that you get a cut every four to eight weeks, depending on the length and condition of your hair. As a general rule, short hair will need to be cut more frequently to maintain the style. Also, hair that is chemically processed should be cut every four to six weeks to keep the ends from looking frizzy or "fried." If your hair is longer than shoulder length, a trim ever eight weeks is probably sufficient.

If you have a beard or moustache, you should keep it neatly trimmed to avoid looking scraggly. © AJP/ SHUTTERSTOCK.COM.

What about Facial and Body Hair?

Many men choose to shave their facial hair partially or completely. Either option can be attractive, provided it is neatly maintained. If you shave, particularly if you are employed, you should do so frequently enough to avoid heavy stubble. The amount of time you can go between shaves will vary. However, if you decide to grow a beard or moustache, you should keep it neatly trimmed and combed to avoid a scraggly appearance. You should also wash facial hair regularly when you wash your face. Washing will keep the skin underneath your facial hair clean, and it will eliminate food particles from accumulating in it. If desired, you can follow the wash with an application of beard oil, which will make your beard softer.

Women do not generally have enough facial hair to shave. If you do have unwanted facial hair, you can pluck or lighten it using a bleaching kit made for facial use. Eyebrow plucking or waxing can be an easy and inexpensive way to present a well-groomed look. However, plucking can be a delicate operation since it is easy to over pluck or to end up with uneven results. Many women opt for professional facial hair treatments that can then be maintained at home.

The amount of body hair considered desirable for both sexes varies from culture to culture. In the United States, most women remove hair from their legs and armpits, either by shaving, waxing, or using a chemical depilatory cream. Hair removal from the bikini line is also common. You can remove body hair at home, or you can have it removed professionally. Professional hair removal can have the advantage of long term results via permanent removal methods such as electrolysis (destruction of the hair root by an electric current) or laser hair removal. Chest and back hair removal for men is also becoming more common.

How Can I Keep My Mouth Clean and Prevent Bad Breath?

To keep your mouth clean and your breath fresh, you should brush your teeth at least twice daily with fluoride toothpaste and a soft-bristled toothbrush. Ideally, you should brush after eating breakfast and again before going to bed at night. It is also important to brush your gums and tongue. Your tongue, in particular, can harbor bacteria that are a known culprit of bad breath. Regular flossing at least once daily is a good idea to remove odor-causing food particles from between teeth. Finally, finishing your oral hygiene regimen with mouthwash can help keep your breath fresh. Be sure to drink plenty of water between brushings and use breath freshening spray, mints, or gum if you are worried about bad breath.

Regular visits to your dentist for a thorough cleaning of your teeth and gums are important. Dentists can also remove stains from your teeth to keep your smile looking bright. There are a number of whitening procedures available, using both chemical solutions and lasers to whiten stained teeth. Whitening kits are also available for home use, although the results might not be as dramatic.

What Can I Do to Prevent or Treat Acne?

Outbreaks of pimples on the face, neck, chest and back are caused by acne, a skin condition occurring when the skin's oil glands become overactive. Acne is generally considered unattractive and can cause its sufferers to experience low self-esteem. In addition, severe acne can permanently scar skin. While acne is not entirely preventable, there are things you can do to reduce its severity.

First, you should wash your face twice daily with a gentle cleanser, and more frequently if you exercise or work hard enough to get sweaty. Special cleansers and other topical treatments for acne may be available from your doctor or dermatologist. You should stay away from harsh soaps and astringents as these may actually worsen acne. You should also avoid "popping" pimples; this practice can introduce bacteria into your skin and lead to a painful and unsightly infection.

What Are Some Guidelines for Wearing Makeup and Fragrance?

Whether to wear makeup is a personal choice that depends on your taste and lifestyle. Many women feel attractive in makeup, while others do not like the effect. Whatever your preference, there are some general guidelines for wearing makeup, especially in a professional situation. For example, most beauty experts caution that "less is more." When applying makeup, you should use a light hand and a good editorial eye. If you are unsure which products are available and what looks good on you, you can often get a free or low-cost consultation at a department store makeup counter.

Fragrances are also a matter of personal choice, but your choices on this front will also affect those around you and should, therefore, be made with that in mind. When wearing perfume or cologne, apply it once in the morning, ideally after bathing. Rather than spraying it directly on your skin, you can mist it into the air and walk into the stream. This helps keep the scent from being too heavy. Also, you should avoid reapplying scent during the day, especially if you work in a crowded environment. While you may not be able to smell your fragrance after a period of time, others probably will, and an overpowering scent can detract from the impression you want to create of being well mannered and well groomed. Some workplaces have a no-fragrance policy, so you should check to make sure it is okay before wearing perfume or cologne to work.

How Can I Look Well Dressed and Put Together?

Choosing clothing that flatters your body type and taking good care of it will go a long way toward making you look good. Investing in good-quality staples such as a high-quality sweater or a good suit is ideal if you can afford to do so. If the fit of a piece is not perfect or if it changes over time as you gain or lose weight, you should consider having it altered by a tailor.

Before you leave the house in the morning, you should check your clothing for loose buttons, hanging threads, and lint. These details, while small, can spoil an otherwise polished look. They can be easily remedied with a sewing kit and a lint roller, which you may choose to carry along with you. Clothing that needs to be ironed should always be well pressed, and clothes that require professional dry cleaning should be taken in regularly to keep them clean and flattering.

Caring for your accessories can also go a long way toward making you appear well groomed. Polishing leather bags and shoes will prolong their life and will keep them looking sharp. Keeping jewelry clean and watches in good working order is also essential in presenting a put-together image.

Clothing, Bedding, Towels, and Personal Items

Why Is Washing Clothes, Sheets, and Towels an Important Part of Personal Hygiene?

Keeping your clothes, household linens, and other personal items clean and dry is an important part of personal hygiene. Your clothes collect *microbes*, including bacteria, fungi, and viruses as you wear them. Similarly, your sheets, towels, and other personal items will collect microbes during normal use. It is common for the microbes in your clothes and household linens to come from your own body, other people, pets you come in contact with, contaminated surfaces, or food preparation. These microbes can cause odor and result in the spread of illness if they are allowed to grow. Furthermore, bedbugs, lice, and mites can live in your clothes and linens. These tiny insects can cause skin irritation and rashes, which can potentially lead to more serious infections. If not properly eliminated, these pests can proliferate and spread.

Microbe: *An extremely small living organism that can only be seen with a microscope.*

The first step in preventing the growth and spread of microbes and pests is to use good laundering practices. These include washing clothes and linens regularly, using laundry products that have been proven to kill microbes and pests, and ensuring that laundry is completely dry before it is put away. As you clean your clothes and household items, take a look at the care instructions offered by the manufacturers. Most items have a laundry care label attached to them that lists the type of fabric in the item and the best washing and drying methods to use. Following these instructions can help preserve the quality of the item for a longer period of time.

What Products Are Needed for Cleaning Laundry?

Make sure you have all the laundry products you need for washing and drying your clothes and household items before you start your wash loads. This will enable you to finish the process without stopping, which is important

A lint brush can help you keep your clothes looking neat between cleanings. © AUSTINADAMS/ SHUTTERSTOCK.COM.

because leaving wet clothes in the washer can cause microbes to begin growing again. To completely get rid of the microbes in all of your clothes and bedding, you will need detergent, regular chlorine-based bleach, non-chlorine bleach, and a pine-oil-based disinfectant. Optional products include an enzyme presoak, fabric softener, and antistatic dryer sheets.

When choosing a detergent there are several things to take into consideration. Liquid detergents work best on oily food soils and can be used as a stain remover prior to washing. Powdered detergents work best on ground-in dirt. However, for most laundry, either one will work fine. If you are allergic to fragrance, you will want to use a fragrance-free detergent.

Most detergents are formulated to work in hard water, which has high amounts of calcium and magnesium. However, some of the detergent's cleaning power is used to soften the water, meaning that laundry may look dingy as a result. If you have hard water, you may want to try using a little bit more detergent than the recommended amount. There are also products available specifically for softening water in the washing machine. Baking soda or borax can also be used.

Chlorine-based bleach is a disinfectant and stain remover but can only be used on white fabric. Non-chlorine, oxygen-based bleach can be used as a stain remover and color brightener but not as a disinfectant. To disinfect colored fabric, you can use a pine oil or phenolic disinfectant.

Before you buy and use laundry products, make sure you read the labels printed on the box or bottle. These labels will provide you with information about the product's intended uses, how much of the product to use, and when to add the product to the washing cycle.

What Are Some Tips for Preparing Laundry for Washing?

The first thing to keep in mind, even before laundry day, is keeping soiled things separate based on how contaminated the items may be.

INTERNATIONAL WASHING CARE

Knowing the international laundry symbols can help when deciding how to launder or dry clean your clothing and other items. © SYQUALLO/ SHUTTERSTOCK.COM.

Put potentially highly contaminated laundry into a separate basket from other items. The most highly contaminated household items are uniforms of health-care workers, clothing worn by family members who are sick or have been in the hospital, clothing of people who have wounds or skin diseases, sports jerseys or exercise clothes, pet blankets, and diapers. Towels and dishrags used during food preparation should also be separated from other items.

When you are ready to do the laundry, you should further separate the items into groups that you will wash together. You need to wash things separately not only based on the kind and level of contamination but also based on the color and kind of fabric. Dark-colored dyes, including red, purple, black, and dark blue, can stain lighter-colored fabrics. In order to prevent discoloration, you should wash white and light-colored items separately from dark-colored items.

Items made of similar fabrics that can tolerate the same water temperature should also be washed together. In general, white cotton, polyester, and cotton-polyester blends can tolerate hot water. Light-colored cotton and polyester need warm water. Dark-colored cotton and polyester as well as all colors of linen, spandex, and Lycra need cool water. Rayon, silk, and wool need to be hand washed in cool water. However, if your washing machine has a very gentle or "hand wash" cycle, you can use that with cool water.

Just as they should be kept in separate laundry baskets when dirty, dishrags, kitchen towels, cloth napkins, and other items used in food preparation should be washed in a load by themselves. Similarly, the linens of a sick person or those that have been soiled with bodily fluids and the uniforms of health-care workers should be washed separately.

How Does Laundering Sanitize Clothing and Household Items?

There are three essential ways that laundering kills microbes: physically washing them away, killing them with heat, and killing them with chemicals. During your washer's main cycle, detergent loosens dirt and microbes to be washed away. The dirt and microbes are detached from the fabric and suspended into the wash water. This mechanism is often referred to as dilution. The rinse and spin cycles then get rid of the suspended dirt. It is important to note that detergent and water alone do not kill most microbes. Instead, heat, bleach, and other disinfectants are needed to kill microbes. Sun drying and the heat of a tumble dryer also kill microbes.

The water in your washing machine needs to be at least 140 degrees Fahrenheit (60 degrees Celsius) in order to kill most microbes and properly disinfect clothes and other items. However, you may not know how hot your washing machine water gets, and not all fabrics can be washed in hot water. Thus, to achieve complete sanitation of your laundry, you will need to use a disinfectant in addition to hot water.

You can use chlorine-based bleach (sodium hypochlorite) in any temperature of water. It is important that you do not soak material in bleach but rather add the detergent and bleach to the washing machine water before putting in the items to be washed. When you use bleach, always use two rinse cycles to make sure all the bleach is rinsed out.

Chlorine-based bleach, though an excellent disinfectant, will also remove the color from clothes and is too harsh for many fabrics. For clothing that cannot take chlorine bleach because of color or fabric, you can use a pine-oil-based disinfectant such as Pine Sol. Add the pine-oil-based disinfectant to the wash water at the same time as the detergent.

How Can Stains Be Removed from Clothing and Household Items?

For stain removal on colored fabrics, you can use a non-chlorine bleach in the washer with detergent. Many brands of detergent have a non-chlorine bleach in them. Non-chlorine bleach uses an oxygen release formula often referred to as "oxy." These "oxy" products are not intended as disinfectants and do not kill microbes. Only use household chlorine-based bleach as a stain remover on white fabric.

Enzyme presoak products are best for protein-based stains such as blood and other bodily fluids, egg, grass, baby formula, and dairy products. Other stain removers, which come in a spray, bar, stick, or gel, should be applied as quickly as possible and prior to washing on oil-based stains such as those due to animal fats, body soils, cooking oils, cosmetics, and motor oils.

What Are Good Laundering Practices for Eliminating Bedbugs, Head Lice, Scabies, and Other Mites?

It is possible that your home will experience an infestation of bedbugs, lice, or mites at some point. These tiny insects can cause bites, sores, and rashes, so it is important to see a health professional to heal any skin issues they have caused. Then, to ensure that you do not continue to experience these itchy and sometimes painful symptoms, it is important to eliminate the pests from your home. Depending on the type and severity of the infestation, you might want to enlist the help of professional exterminators, but no matter what, you will need to launder all of your clothes, sheets, blankets, and other fabric items.

Research has shown that all stages of bedbugs, lice, and mites in clothes or other fabric can be killed in several ways, including by freezing the infested item below 0 degrees Fahrenheit (-17.8 degrees Celsius) for at least 10 hours; washing it in water heated to at least 140 degrees

Caring for Personal Items

In order to keep your hygiene routine on the right track, it is important to care for your personal items. For example, you probably know that good oral hygiene requires regular tooth brushing. However, over time, toothbrushes collect germs from your mouth, as well as from the environment in which they are stored. Be sure to rinse your toothbrush thoroughly after each use, and store it in a place where it can air-dry. To avoid spreading germs, never share a toothbrush, and don't allow toothbrushes stored in the same holder to touch. It is also important to replace your toothbrush regularly. The American Dental Association (ADA) recommends that you replace your toothbrush every three to four months. You should replace your brush sooner if you have been ill or if the bristles become frayed, as worn out brushes won't clean as well. Although you can purchase devices designed to sanitize toothbrushes, they are unnecessary. If you'd like to clean a toothbrush, just run it through the dishwasher.

Grooming tools such as brushes, combs, and razors also need routine cleanings. Each time they are used they collect hair and skin particles. You can remove hair from a brush using a fine-tooth comb. At least once a month, you should wash your combs and brushes with shampoo and warm water. Keep your razor clean while you shave by rinsing it under water after every two or three strokes. Rinse it thoroughly after you finish shaving to remove hair and shaving cream. To sanitize your razor, dip it into a cup of rubbing alcohol and allow it to air-dry.

Fahrenheit for a 30-minute cycle; or putting it in a hot tumble dryer (104 to 122 degrees Fahrenheit; 40 to 50 degrees Celsius) for at least 30 minutes. Dry cleaning will also kill the pests, but you will need to check with your dry cleaner before bringing them any infested items.

What Are Some Tips for Drying Clothes and Household Items?

After washing, it is important to make sure that your clothes are completely dry. The microbes and pests on dirty laundry spread from item to item and grow faster when fabric is damp. You should never put wet things into the laundry basket.

 Use the high-spin option on your washer to get out as much water as possible before drying. Whenever possible, dry your clothes in the sun, because sunlight is a disinfectant and will kill microbes. After items have dried in the sun, throw them in the dryer for a short time to make sure all dampness is gone and to soften them.

If it is not possible to dry your items outside, you can use your dryer to disinfect them, as long as the temperature in your dryer reaches at least 104 degrees Fahrenheit. Keep in mind, however, lower temperatures are easier on most fabrics. To save energy, use the moisture-sensor option on your dryer and clean your lint filter after each load to improve the airflow in the dryer.

Why Is It Necessary to Clean Washing Machines and Dryers?

In order to ensure that your clothes are getting as clean as possible, it is important to keep your washing machine clean. Over time, the inside of your washing machine may become discolored and develop an unpleasant, mildew-like odor that will transfer to your clothes. This odor is a sign of the presence of mold or bacteria. Once a week, you should do a hot-water, empty-load wash with bleach or other disinfectant. If you continue to notice a discoloration or odor, you can clean the inside of the machine with a weak bleach solution made of 1 cup of bleach to 2 pints of water.

It is also important to ensure that your dryer is clean and operating efficiently. If you use dryer sheets to get rid of static electricity and to soften your clothes, a film can form on the dryer's lint filter. You should clean it once a month by rubbing it with a toothbrush. This will help improve airflow, enabling your clothes to dry faster.

Healthy Habits When Away from Home

Why Are Healthy Habits Important?

Paying attention to personal care and hygiene does more than help you look and feel your best. It also helps you stay healthy. For example, according to the United States Centers for Disease Control and Prevention (CDC), simply washing your hands is one of the most important ways to keep from getting sick with illnesses such as influenza, salmonella, pneumonia, and many others.

Personal hygiene can be especially important when you are away from home. When you travel, or even during a day at work, there are more opportunities to come into contact with germs and other agents that can make you sick. Keeping up good personal hygiene habits can make an important difference in your health.

What Are the Basic Rules for Healthy Personal Hygiene Habits Away from Home?

 The hallmark of good personal hygiene is hand washing. According to the CDC, frequent hand washing can reduce the number of people who get sick with diarrhea by 31 percent and those who get respiratory illnesses, such as colds, by 21 percent. Scrub your hands for at least 20 seconds and rinse under clean running water. Air dry your hands or use a clean towel. Sanitizing gels help get rid of germs, but they do not work as well as soap and water, especially if your hands are visibly dirty.

It is also important to avoid touching your face with your hands. Even if you have just washed your hands, you could pick up new germs from touching a contaminated surface. For example, the CDC reports that the influenza virus can survive on hard surfaces for two to eight hours. Touching your face can allow germs to enter your body through your eyes, nose, or mouth and cause infection.

When you use a public bathroom, remember that people usually touch the stall door handle, sink faucets, and soap dispensers before they have washed their hands. After you wash your hands, leave the restroom without touching any surfaces. Open the door with your shoulder or with a fresh paper towel.

How Can I Practice Healthy Habits While at Work?

When commuting time is included, many people spend more waking hours at work than at home. Work may also bring you into contact with more people, who in turn are likely to carry germs, raising your risk for getting an infectious illness. These factors make it important to incorporate strategies for staying healthy into your workday.

Healthy habits can start even before you get to work. If you use public transportation, try not to touch surfaces that can harbor germs, such as seats and arm rests. Carry a small bottle of alcohol hand sanitizer or a package of alcohol wipes to clean your hands when you can't wash with soap and water. If possible, use your shoulder or elbows to push open doors.

You should also sanitize your work area regularly. If you work in an office, clean your keyboard, computer mouse, and telephone with an alcohol wipe. Researchers have found that the average desktop has about 100 times more bacteria than a kitchen table, and some of those germs could cause disease. Avoid eating at your desk, since that can transfer germs to your mouth. If you operate machinery, use an alcohol wipe on surfaces you touch such as door handles and controls. Tools that are shared can also be sanitized with alcohol wipes. This is easier to remember if you do it every day.

If employees at your workplace share a refrigerator, try to agree on a schedule for keeping it clean. Check the temperature to make sure it is 40 degrees Fahrenheit or lower. Bacteria that cause food-borne illnesses can grow quickly on food at warmer temperatures. The CDC reports that each year one in six Americans gets a food-borne illness, also known as food poisoning. You should also check expiration dates on packaged food. Throw out anything past its "use by" date, along with any food that looks or smells suspicious.

In any work environment, it is important to limit contact with fellow workers who seem ill. Part of good personal hygiene is helping to keep other people from getting sick as well. Avoid spreading germs by

Sneezing into your elbow is one way to prevent germs from getting into the air and infecting others. © TYLER MCKAY/ SHUTTERSTOCK.COM.

Infection: *A disease caused by an invasion of bacteria, viruses, or fungi.*

covering your mouth with a tissue or with your elbow when you cough or sneeze. Washing your hands also helps keep those around you safe from germs. If you are sick, it's best to stay home.

How Can I Avoid Illness at the Gym?

Exercising at a gym is a great way to stay healthy, but gyms and health clubs also have the potential for causing illnesses. Certain areas, such as wet places around pools, showers, and hot tubs, encourage the growth of bacteria, viruses, and fungi. Germs can also thrive on wet towels and on equipment where sweat is left to dry.

You can minimize your risk for *infection* at the gym by practicing a few healthy habits. Start with washing your hands frequently, and if your gym has an automatic sanitizer dispenser, use it often. Wipe down seats and grips on equipment before and after you use it. Sanitizing the grips with alcohol gel or wipes gives you more protection.

In the shower, locker room, or around a pool, wear shower shoes or flip-flops. Bare feet can pick up viruses and bacteria as well as fungi that can cause problems such as toenail fungus or athlete's foot. If you use a sauna, sit on a towel instead of a bench.

Pools, hot tubs, and other recreational water areas can be contaminated by several types of bacteria that cause diarrhea. It takes time for chlorine to kill these bacteria, even in a properly maintained pool, so try not to swallow any water. You can help keep your gym pool safe by showering before you swim.

How Do I Avoid Germs at Other Public Places, Such as Restaurants and Theaters?

In any public place, the fewer surfaces you touch, the lower your risk for infection. That's especially true for surfaces such as doors and doorknobs, shopping-cart handles, and elevator and ATM buttons. You can't avoid touching all these surfaces, so remember to wash your hands or use a hand sanitizer frequently.

In restaurants, wash your hands before you eat. Check salad bars and buffets to be sure they are clean and that the food seems fresh. If food that should be hot seems only warm, don't eat it. At the table, consider using an alcohol wipe to sanitize containers of ketchup and other condiments. They are likely to be touched by many people and may not be cleaned regularly. If you have concerns about a particular restaurant, you can get information from your local health department about how the establishment rated in recent on-site inspections.

Theater seats and armrests may not be cleaned or sanitized regularly, and studies have found that these surfaces often contain disease-causing bacteria. If you eat or drink while watching a movie, try not to touch the armrest because you could transfer germs to your mouth. If you put your purse or backpack on the theater floor or on a seat, clean it before you place it on a surface in your home.

Students and others who share desks should avoid touching their faces while sitting in class. Germs from other students can linger on the desk surface. During cold and flu season, consider cleaning the desk surface with an alcohol wipe.

What Should I Do to Stay Healthy While I'm Traveling?

Many of the personal hygiene principles for other situations apply to travel as well. For example, hand washing is essential to lower your risk of infection. If you can't wash with soap and water, use an alcohol sanitizer. Avoid touching surfaces when possible and try not to touch your face.

If your trip includes an airline flight, you will be in close quarters with many people who could carry germs. Try to avoid physical contact with others while standing in line or with the person sitting next to you. Consider wiping down the seat tray and armrests with an alcohol sanitizer. If you use the bathroom, do not touch any surfaces after you wash your hands. Use a paper towel to open the door, and try not to touch seat backs as you return to your seat.

Hotel rooms can also harbor bacteria and other germs from previous visitors. Check your room for obviously unclean areas and ask for a room change if you find any. You should also check for bedbugs,

Bedbugs, like this one, can infest even the most expensive hotels. © JAREYNOLDS/ SHUTTERSTOCK.COM.

which can infest even expensive hotels. To do this, look closely at the mattress and headboard for tiny flecks that look like small flax seeds. If you see any, leave the room immediately, ask for a refund, and stay in a different hotel.

You can also minimize your risk by putting your bag on the luggage rack instead of on the bed and placing your toiletries on a towel or tissue. Sanitize the TV remote, phone, and light switches. If you use a glass, wash it first. If you order room service and eat in your room, remember to wash your hands first.

Travel to foreign countries can expose you to diseases not present in the United States. If you plan international travel, see your doctor at least six weeks before you leave. He or she can advise you about vaccines to protect you from illnesses known to exist at your destination. Some vaccinations take that long to become fully effective.

In some countries, there is a high risk for getting a food-borne illness. You can find out about this and other travel risks for your destination by visiting the CDC's Travelers' Health page at http://www.cdc.gov/travel. If you will be at increased risk for food-borne illness, it is especially important to avoid food from street vendors, unpasteurized dairy products, and raw or uncooked seafood. Your best bet is to stick with well-cooked food served hot. If you eat fruit, wash it in bottled water and peel it yourself. Use only bottled water for drinking and brushing your teeth and avoid ice.

It is also a good idea to use an insect repellent in foreign countries, since insects often carry disease. That's true for local travel as well, especially if you will be hiking or camping. Bites from mosquitoes, ticks, and other pests can cause illnesses such as Lyme disease, Rocky Mountain spotted fever, and West Nile virus.

Campers should also be careful to keep perishable foods cold and to wash their hands before eating or preparing food. Drink plenty of water, especially if the weather is hot.

Whether you are traveling to a distant location or camping close to home, you should carry a first aid kit. Include hand wipes and sanitizers, antibiotic ointment, adhesive bandages, and sunscreen. Consider adding pain relievers such as ibuprofen or acetaminophen and a medication for diarrhea. Tweezers, nail clippers, and a thermometer can also come in handy. You should always carry your prescription medications in their original containers.

For More Information

BOOKS AND PAPERS

Bloomfield, S. F., et al. "The Infection Risks Associated with Clothing and Household Linens in Home and Everyday Life Settings, and the Role of Laundry." Somerset, UK: International Scientific Forum on Home Hygiene, 2011. This paper can also be found online at http://www.ifh-homehygiene.org/best-practice-review/infection-risks-associated-clothing-and-household-linens-home-and-everyday-life.

"Clothing, Household Linen, Laundry & Home Hygiene." Somerset, UK: International Scientific Forum on Home Hygiene, 2013. This leaflet can also be found online at http://www.ifh-homehygiene.org/factsheet/clothing-household-linens-laundry-home-hygiene.

PERIODICALS

Chen, Joanne. "16 Tips For Staying Healthy While Traveling." *Condé Nast Traveler*, October 28, 2014. This article can also be found online at http://www.cntraveler.com/stories/2014-10-28/travel-tips-how-to-stay-healthy-while-traveling.

Tobak, Steve. "An Entrepreneur's Guide to Personal Grooming." *Entrepreneur*, January 28, 2014. This article can also be found online at http://www.entrepreneur.com/article/231052.

WEBSITES

"Before You Go." *American Academy of Family Physicians*. http://familydoctor.org/familydoctor/en/prevention-wellness/staying-healthy/travel/international-travel-tips-for-staying-healthy.html (accessed October 16, 2014).

"Best Practices: Clothes Washer Tips." *Energy Star*. https://www.energystar.gov/index.cfm?c=clotheswash.clothes_washers_performance_tips (accessed October 23, 2014).

"Body Hygiene." *Centers for Disease Control and Prevention*. http://www.cdc.gov/healthywater/hygiene/body/index.html (accessed October 16, 2014).

"Flyers' Survival Guide for Airports, Planes." *WebMD*. http://www.webmd.com/a-to-z-guides/features/airport-germs-healthy-travel?print=true (accessed October 16, 2014).

"Food Poisoning Prevention." *National Institutes of Health*. http://www.nlm.nih.gov/medlineplus/ency/article/001981.htm (accessed October 16, 2014).

"Good Grooming: Taking Care of Your Personal Image." *Emily Post*. http://www.emilypost.com/everyday-manners/your-personal-image/866-good-grooming (accessed October 16, 2014).

"How Can We Prevent Recreational Water Illnesses (RWIs)?" *Centers for Disease Control and Prevention.* http://www.cdc.gov/healthywater/swimming/rwi/rwi-prevent.html (accessed October 16, 2014).

"Hygiene Fast Facts: Information on Water-Related Hygiene." *Centers for Disease Control and Prevention.* http://www.cdc.gov/healthywater/hygiene/fast_facts.html (accessed October 16, 2014).

"Is Your Desk Making You Sick? New Survey Finds Desktop Dining Poses Food Poisoning Risk." *Academy of Nutrition and Dietetics.* http://www.eatright.org/Media/content.aspx?id=6442464916#.VD6iORaTdEI (accessed October 16, 2014).

"Laundry." *Hygiene for Health.* http://www.hygieneforhealth.org.au/around_home_laundry.php (accessed October 23, 2014).

"Laundry Basics—Sorting It Out." *American Cleaning Institute.* http://www.cleaninginstitute.org/clean_living/sorting_it_out.aspx (accessed October 23, 2014).

Merchant, Mike. "Insects in the City." *Texas A&M Agrilife Extension.* http://insectsinthecity.blogspot.com/2010/03/guidelines-for-killing-bed-bugs-in.html (accessed October 23, 2014).

"Preventing Seasonal Flu Illness." *Centers for Disease Control and Prevention.* http://www.cdc.gov/flu/about/qa/preventing.htm (accessed October 16, 2014).

"Protect Your Eyes." *Centers for Disease Control and Prevention.* http://www.cdc.gov/contactlenses/protect-your-eyes.html (accessed October 16, 2014).

"Show Me the Science—Why Wash Your Hands?" *Centers for Disease Control and Prevention.* http://www.cdc.gov/handwashing/why-handwashing.html (accessed October 16, 2014).

"6 Gym Health Hazards." *WebMD.* http://www.webmd.com/fitness-exercise/features/6-health-risks-to-avoid-at-the-gym?page=2&p (accessed October 16, 2014).

"10 Healthy Hotel Hygiene Habits." *Fodors.* http://www.fodors.com/news/10-healthy-hotel-hygiene-habits-6538.html (accessed October 16, 2014).

"When and How to Wash Your Hands." *Centers for Disease Control and Prevention.* http://www.cdc.gov/handwashing/when-how-handwashing.html (accessed October 16, 2014).

"Work and Hygiene." *Hygiene Council.* http://www.hygienecouncil.org/explore/advice-and-tips.aspx (accessed October 16, 2014).

Preventive Health Care, Medications, and Alternative Medicine

Overview: Preventive Health Care, Medications, and Alternative Medicine

What Is the Role of Preventive Medical Care in a Healthy Lifestyle?

Many people view doctors and other health-care professionals as resources of last resort. That is, they only seek medical care when they are dangerously ill or injured or when over-the-counter medication and home remedies have failed to help. However, a number of medical researchers believe that preventive medical care, combined with modern advances in medical knowledge and techniques, may contribute to a longer, healthier life. This is due partly to new methods of curing disease but also to a growing awareness of the importance of preventing illness through patient education.

A healthy lifestyle is largely defined by your everyday choices. More than just the absence of disease or injury, living a healthy lifestyle means paying attention to each area of your life and attempting to ensure that, as often as possible, you make the choice that contributes to your overall wellness. This means eating fresh, healthful foods, exercising regularly, and avoiding harmful substances such as tobacco. It also means developing habits that increase your physical and mental well-being, such as maintaining regular sleep patterns, drinking plenty of water, and exploring ways to reduce stress. A supportive relationship with your medical provider can help you understand the fundamental ingredients of a healthy lifestyle and to recognize symptoms of distress before they turn into serious illness.

Regular medical care includes several elements. One of the most important is the health examination, or check-up. An annual check-up can provide baseline information about your health that can help your doctor recognize when harmful changes occur. Your medical team can also keep you informed about which tests and inoculations are appropriate for your

© KENTOH/SHUTTERSTOCK. COM.

age group and make sure that you keep up to date on necessary procedures. Vaccinations and medical tests, when administered on a regular basis, can help prevent serious diseases such as polio, tetanus, and flu and can give early warning of the onset of cancer or heart disease. If you do become ill, seeing a doctor during the early stages of a disease can prevent the development of more serious problems. Medications prescribed by a doctor can help you manage serious chronic conditions, and they can greatly increase your quality of life.

The idea of holistic health care took root within the medical system in the late twentieth and early twenty-first centuries. Using many ancient medical traditions as a foundation, the holistic approach views the patient as a complete system, composed of mind, body, and lifestyle choices. While science-based medicine has been very successful in treating the symptoms of disease and in perfecting drugs and surgeries to resolve them, a number of alternative systems have developed based on a holistic view of the human body as a self-healing organism. Many people have been drawn to alternative health-care practices, finding them less invasive than mainstream medicine. Modern medical doctors have increasingly embraced the idea of holistic health care, recognizing the importance of a strong doctor-patient relationship in building the health awareness that helps maintain a healthy lifestyle.

What Is the Difference between Preventive and Curative Medicine?

Curative medical care generally identifies the symptoms of a disease or injury and works to relieve those symptoms and restore health. Western mainstream medicine focuses on curing disease or repairing injuries, and many medical procedures and medications have been developed with these goals in mind. In the curative method, doctors and other health-care workers approach their patients' symptoms as puzzles to be solved through scientific reasoning. Appointments are often brief and focused on a limited number of clear symptoms. Medications or procedures may be prescribed to resolve these symptoms. If prescription medications cause unwanted side effects, other medications may be prescribed to relieve those effects.

Curative medicine has proved effective in combating certain diseases and in healing injuries. For example, many bacterial infections that were once life threatening, such as flu and pneumonia, are now regularly cured through the use of antibiotics. Setting a broken bone or replacing damaged knee or hip joints are also examples of curative procedures.

Rather than concentrating on relieving the symptoms of disease, preventive medicine focuses on the ways in which illness and injury can be prevented. Practitioners of preventive medicine approach this goal from several directions. One of these is developing guidelines for safety and cleanliness for individuals, institutions, and health-care professionals. Wearing automobile safety belts, frequent hand washing, and wearing protective gloves and masks are examples of the preventive approach. Another aspect of preventive care is health screening. Regular use of medical screening tests can reveal a decline in health before it becomes a serious disease. Some tests, such as those for bone density, can help prevent injury by showing weakened areas in the body's structure. A third focus of preventive medicine is lifestyle management. Through education and support, such as offering nutritional advice and smoking-cessation classes, health-care practitioners can help patients increase overall wellness and prevent a number of dangerous conditions.

Palliative care is another approach to medical treatment. In contrast to preventive medicine, palliative care is designed for those who are already seriously ill. Unlike curative medicine, the palliative approach does not seek to cure disease but to increase the comfort and quality of life of those affected by serious chronic (ongoing) or terminal (fatal) illnesses. Palliative care is generally administered by a team of health-care workers; these may include social workers, massage therapists, and mental health counselors, in addition to doctors and nurses. The tools of palliative care are generally medications to reduce pain and anxiety and medical equipment to enhance comfort. Palliative medicine is frequently part of end-of-life care for the terminally ill, but it may also be an important part of caring for those with debilitating chronic conditions such as Alzheimer's and heart disease.

What Are Complementary and Alternative Medicine, and How Are They Different from Standard Medicine?

The term *complementary and alternative medicine* (CAM) is used to describe a number of nonmainstream health-care practices. These include medical philosophies that stem from ancient cultural traditions

© DORA ZETT/
SHUTTERSTOCK.COM.

from around the world, as well as more recently developed care systems. Almost all CAM health care is based on a holistic approach and the belief that your body contains the elements necessary to heal and repair itself. Many CAM methods are founded on a philosophy that the body is regulated by the same laws that govern the natural world and on the belief that the best route to healing is through natural remedies. These include herbs, vitamins, and minerals, as well as lifestyle changes such as improved diet and exercise systems that reduce stress. Some CAM practitioners consider common mainstream treatments, such as surgery and drugs, to be invasive and destructive to the body's self-healing process.

Although alternative medical approaches may be practiced on their own, as a substitute for standard medical care, they are more commonly used as a complementary form of treatment. That is, you may choose to explore a nonmainstream form of medicine while continuing to consult your medical doctor. This has the advantage of ensuring that you receive the benefits of scientific research and modern treatment options while learning about natural and self-motivated systems of building lasting health through lifestyle management. For example, while an alternative treatment for cancer may consist only of following a special diet and taking certain herbal remedies, a complementary approach might suggest that you combine following the diet and using herbs with conventional chemotherapy (chemicals used to treat or control a disease) treatments prescribed by your medical doctor. With the approval of your doctor, an alternative practitioner may be able to recommend natural treatments, such as acupuncture, that may help reduce the uncomfortable effects of chemotherapy.

As some alternative procedures have become more widely accepted, a philosophy of integrative medicine has evolved, in which some conventional medical providers have adopted a more holistic approach. Integrative medical centers have begun to offer alternative treatments such as herbal medicine, massage, yoga, and acupuncture alongside standard, science-based treatments.

What Kinds of Medical Providers Are There, and What Kinds of Care Does Each Provide?

In caring for your health, you have a choice of a variety of both conventional and nonconventional medical providers. For standard, science-based medical care, you may consult a medical doctor, a physician assistant, or a nurse practitioner. All can provide basic medical diagnosis, suggest treatment, and prescribe medications. Many doctors choose a specialty, or a field of medicine in which they receive extra training. For regular health maintenance, you may choose to see a doctor who specializes in internal medicine (health care for adults). Specialists in family medicine can offer comprehensive medical care to people of all ages. Women should have regular checkups with a gynecologist, who specializes in the care and treatment of the female reproductive system. Pediatricians focus on the health and diseases of children, and geriatricians specialize in treatment of the elderly.

If you are diagnosed with a serious disease or are concerned that you might be in danger of contracting one, you will probably be referred to

Referral: *A request from the primary care physician for a patient to see another doctor.*

a specialist. Cardiologists deal with diseases of the heart and circulatory system. Neurologists specialize in treatment of disorders of the nervous system, including the brain and spinal cord. Oncologists treat patients with cancer. Orthopedists work to correct problems of the bones and joints. Dermatologists treat skin ailments, pulmonologists focus on lung disease, and podiatrists specialize in problems of the feet. If you have a problem with a particular condition, you may want to ask your health-care provider for a *referral* to a doctor who specializes in that area.

Under the umbrella of alternative health care, there are a number of different kinds of providers. The most widely accepted by the mainstream medical establishment are osteopaths, chiropractors, and naturopaths, all of whom are required to complete several years of medical training and to pass rigorous examinations in order to practice. Osteopaths and chiropractors specialize in treatment of the spine, using manipulation of the bones and muscles as a primary healing tool. Naturopaths are holistic practitioners who use a variety of herbal remedies as well as vitamin and mineral supplements in their treatments. Massage therapists, who treat injury and stress by manipulating muscles and other tissues, are also alternative health-care workers who have been accepted into the mainstream.

Other holistic medical providers you may want to consider are practitioners of ancient health-care traditions, such as traditional Chinese medicine and Ayurveda, the traditional medicine of India. These healers use their own herbal preparations in combination with diet, exercise, and other lifestyle therapies. Traditional Chinese medicine practitioners may also employ the treatment technique of acupuncture, in which thin needles are inserted at various mapped points in the body. Practitioners of homeopathy, called homeopathists, base their treatment on the idea that a disease can be cured by administering remedies made from trace amounts of substances that cause symptoms similar to that disease. Most alternative practitioners will examine and treat your overall health rather than focusing on a particular symptom or set of symptoms.

Do I Need to Choose a Primary Doctor?

A primary doctor, also called a primary care provider (PCP), is a health-care worker who sees patients on a regular basis and provides for most of their nonurgent medical needs. Your PCP may be a doctor, but physician assistants and nurse practitioners may also serve as PCPs. If you prefer an alternative holistic approach to health care, you may choose an osteopath, a naturopath, or a chiropractor to serve as your PCP. However, many insurance plans do not provide coverage for alternative practitioners. PCPs often specialize in such general medical fields as family medicine, internal medicine, gynecology, or pediatrics. You may visit your PCP for regular checkups and tests, as well as when you experience a minor illness or injury.

Many insurance plans, especially health maintenance organizations (HMOs), require members to choose a primary care provider. Within the HMO structure, PCPs are often described as "gatekeepers," because they not only provide most kinds of basic medical care but also decide which tests or treatment you may need and can refer you to another doctor for more specialized treatment if they consider it necessary.

Even if your insurance provider does not require you to select a PCP, you may want to choose a doctor from a general field of care, such as internal medicine, family medicine, or gynecology, to be your primary doctor. Forming a relationship with a primary doctor can help you maintain important wellness habits, such as regular checkups and screening tests, which can increase your awareness of any developing illness. If you do become ill, it can be both comforting and medically useful to have a health-care professional with knowledge of your personal history to help you negotiate the medical system, obtain necessary medications, and make decisions about treatment.

How Can I Choose the Right Health-Care Provider for Me?

Selecting a health-care provider is a very personal decision. It is important to consider your individual personality and health issues when choosing what type of provider to consult. You may wish to see a medical doctor to ensure that established medical tests and treatments are available to you. You may consider exploring alternative medical systems if you are interested in a more holistic approach to improving your overall health, wish to avoid the use of drugs or surgery, or have a chronic condition that has not responded to conventional treatment. Your choice of medical providers may also be limited by financial considerations, since many insurance providers will not pay for alternative forms of medicine. Affordable alternative care, such as community acupuncture clinics, is available in some communities.

One good approach to finding a medical provider is to ask your friends for a recommendation. Insurance companies also frequently provide lists of approved doctors. Professional associations may be another resource. If you have a disease or chronic condition, organizations or websites devoted to that condition may provide lists of providers with special qualifications in its treatment.

If you have an interest in alternative medicine, websites such as the University of Rochester's *Health Encyclopedia* (http://www.urmc .rochester.edu/encyclopedia/content.aspx?ContentTypeID=85&Conten tID=P00189) can help you learn about the different types of treatment available. You may also ask your medical doctor to recommend qualified alternative practitioners. Always be sure to check with your doctor before seeking any alternative treatment.

Once you have names of possible practitioners in hand, it is a good idea to interview a provider before forming an ongoing relationship. Note your first impression of the receptionist and office staff. Are they professional, respectful, and courteous? Is the process of making an appointment convenient and easy? Many offices offer e-mail communication to allow you to reach your doctor easily. When you meet your doctor, you should ask some questions to determine if you communicate well and if his or her philosophy of treatment agrees with yours. For example, if you do not like to take medications unless absolutely necessary, you may work better with a doctor who is conservative about prescribing drugs. The ability to talk to your doctor openly and receive a sympathetic and understandable response is one of the most important elements of any health-care relationship.

For More Information

BOOKS

American Medical Association. *American Medical Association Guide to Talking to Your Doctor*. New York: John Wiley and Sons, 2001.

Knight, Joseph A. *A Crisis Call for New Preventive Medicine: Emerging Effects of Lifestyle on Morbidity and Mortality*. River Edge, NJ: World Scientific, 2004.

McKeown, Thomas. *The Role of Medicine: Dream, Mirage, or Nemesis?* Princeton, NJ: Princeton University Press, 1979.

Niles, Nancy J. *Basics of the U.S. Health Care System*. Burlington, MA: Jones and Bartlett Learning, 2010.

PERIODICALS

Bowden, Jonny. "An Ounce of Prevention." *Better Nutrition* 76, no. 4 (2014): 61.

"A Doctor's Office That's All about You: More than 25,000 Doctors Commit to Patient-Centered Care." *Consumer Reports*, July 2013. This article can also be found online at http://consumerreports.org/cro/magazine/2013/07/a-doctor-s-office-that-s-all-about-you/index.htm.

Rabin, Roni Caryn. "You Can Find Dr. Right, with Some Effort." *New York Times*, September 29, 2008. This article can also be found online at http://www.nytimes.com/2008/09/30/health/30find.html?_r=0.

Redwood, Daniel. "A Culture of Collaboration at an Integrative Health Center: Interview with David Fogel, MD." *Topics in Integrative Health Care* 5, no. 3 (2014). This article can also be found online at http://www.tihcij.com/Articles/A-Culture-of-Collaboration-at-an-Integrative-Health-Center--Interview-with-David-Fogel-MD---Interviewed-by-Daniel-Redwood-DC.aspx?id=0000433.

Thompson, Tommy. "Quality Is in Our Hands." *Modern Healthcare* 37, no. 30 (2007): 26, 28.

WEBSITES

"East Meets West: How Integrative Medicine Is Changing Health Care." *Exploring IM: Integrative Medicine.* http://exploreim.ucla.edu/health-care/east-meets-west-how-integrative-medicine-is-changing-health-care/ (accessed October 31, 2014).

"Hospice and Palliative FAQ's." *Taking Charge of Your Life.* http://takechargeofyourlife.org/hospice_faqs.php#terminallyill (accessed October 31, 2014).

"Preventive Health Care Helps Everyone." *World Research Foundation.* http://www.wrf.org/preventive-healthcare/preventive-healthcare.php (accessed October 31, 2014).

"Types of Health Care Providers." *Medline Plus.* http://www.nlm.nih.gov/medlineplus/ency/article/001933.htm (accessed October 31, 2014).

Preventive Health Care

What Does It Mean to Be Proactive about My Health?

The term *proactive* refers to a general philosophy of approaching problems by planning ahead rather than waiting for events to occur. Proactive behavior involves both imagination to help you envision future possibilities so you can prevent them and research to help you deal with them if they do occur. There are a number of life situations in which a proactive approach may help you avoid being unprepared when sudden events or changes take place. If you spend time examining possible situations at work or in your family life, you can ensure that you have a plan of action in place to cope with challenges. Having a proactive attitude does not mean obsessing over possible tragedy. Rather, it means developing a realistic idea of what problems you may face and constructive ways to approach them.

In terms of your family's health, a proactive approach may include making sure you have a health-care plan in place to help you in the event of a medical emergency. If you do not have access to health insurance through an employer, you may want to investigate options that became

Flu shots and other vaccinations help prevent the occurence of communicable diseases.
© ALEXANDER RATHS/ SHUTTERSTOCK.COM.

available with the passage of Affordable Care Act (https://www.healthcare.gov/) in 2010 or see if you qualify for government programs such as Medicaid. Proactive strategies also involve educating yourself about common health problems that members of your family may encounter and taking steps to prevent or manage them.

If someone in your family has an accident or illness that places them within the medical system, proactive behavior includes asking questions of every medical professional involved in order to learn and evaluate your options. It may also include voicing your concerns and desires about treatments. While you should listen carefully to the advice of your doctor and other professionals, being proactive and educating yourself about your options may lead you to seek a second opinion or choose a different medical provider.

What Is Preventive Medicine?

Preventive medicine involves steps to help you avoid an illness or injury rather than wait until a problem occurs. Washing hands and keeping a clean environment to avoid spreading germs have been important in the development of preventive medicine. Vaccinations, or inoculations, which are widely given to prevent the outbreak of certain diseases, are another important factor in preventive health care, as are screening tests to learn if you have or are developing an illness.

Since the late 1900s preventive medicine has been an established medical specialty in the United States, under the administration of the American Board of Preventive Medicine. The board governs preventive practices in certain specific fields. These include aerospace medicine, which treats conditions and threats to health in those who work in the airline and spaceflight industries; occupational medicine, which focuses on work-related illness and maintaining a healthy work environment; and public health and general preventive medicine, which is concerned with protecting the public from such threats as disease and toxic contamination of food and water.

Smoking Cessation

If you are one of the estimated 42.1 million smokers in the United States, one of the most proactive things you can do for your health is to commit to quitting smoking. The United States Centers for Disease Control and Prevention (CDC), which gathers statistics regarding the prevalence and impact of smoking, reports that smoking is the leading preventable cause of death in the country, leading to roughly 480,000 deaths each year. Smoking is tied to a wide range of ailments, from lung and other cancers to chronic obstructive pulmonary disease (COPD), coronary heart disease, and stroke.

The benefits of quitting smoking are immediate. According to the CDC, within 1 year of quitting, your chances of having a heart attack fall dramatically. Within 2 to 5 years of quitting,

your risk of stroke will be no greater than that of a nonsmoker. Within 10 years, your risk of developing lung cancer will be cut in half.

Many resources are available to help you stop smoking. Some of them are available free of charge. Because of the high health-care costs associated with the use of cigarettes and other tobacco products, many employers sponsor tobacco-cessation programs to help their employees kick the habit. If no such program is available to you, search for programs in your local community. The Internet is also a valuable resource to support your efforts. The CDC offers resources and tips online at http://www.cdc.gov/tobacco/quit_smoking/how_to_quit/. The government provides additional support for smoking cessation at http://smokefree.gov/.

Another aspect of the preventive approach to health does not involve direct patient care but instead works to promote health by changing public policy. This may include lobbying lawmakers to pass protective legislation that sets standards for clean air and water and the disposal of toxic waste. It may also involve educating the public about health issues and attempting to change social behavior, such as promoting the use of condoms to prevent the spread of sexually transmitted diseases.

How Long Has Preventive Medicine Been Around?

The idea of preventing an illness rather than simply treating it may date to 1000 CE, when children in China were given matter from smallpox sores in an effort to protect them from the disease. This idea that giving someone a very mild case of smallpox might provide immunity from a severe case of the disease became accepted in China by the mid-1600s and in Europe by the early 1720s, where it was introduced in England by the feminist intellectual and author Mary Wortley Montagu (1689–1762).

Typical Health Screenings

Health screenings are available to help identify a variety of conditions and diseases. Talk to your healthcare professional for more information.

- Abdominal Aortic Aneurysm
- Blood Cholesterol Level
- Breast Cancer (mammogram)
- Cervical Cancer (Pap smear)
- Colon Cancer (Stool test, colonoscopy)
- Depression
- Diabetes
- Hepatitis C Virus

- High Blood Pressure
- HIV
- Lung Cancer
- Osteoporosis (Bone Thinning)
- Overweight and Obesity
- Prostate Cancer (Prostate-specific antigen or PSA)
- Sexually Transmitted Infections

SOURCE: Compiled from U.S. Department of Health and Human Services, Agency for Healthcare Research and Quality. "Women: Stay Healthy at Any Age, 2014 Update." (AHRQ Pub. No. 14-IP007-A); and "Men: Stay Healthy at Any Age, 2014 Update." (AHRQ Pub. No. 14-IP006-A). http://www.ahrq.gov/patients-consumers/patient-involvement/healthy-men/index.html.

ILLUSTRATION BY LUMINA DATAMATICS LTD. © 2015 CENGAGE LEARNING.

Though the ancient Babylonians (c. 1000 BCE) and Greeks (c. 500 BCE) had some knowledge of the health benefits of sanitation and clean water, this awareness had been largely lost in European society by 1000 CE. A number of epidemics spread through medieval Europe, aided by open sewers, ignorance about personal hygiene, and the crowded, unsanitary conditions of most cities. By the mid-1880s the work of a number of doctors, engineers, and other socially concerned citizens led to a Sanitation Movement, which introduced the idea that disease was caused by the dangerous fumes from the sewage and garbage that filled many city streets. Although the citizens involved with the Sanitation Movement did not understand the role of bacteria and other organisms in the spread of disease, they were responsible for the construction of contained sewage systems. The movement also introduced many healthful practices of cleanliness that are still in use in the early twenty-first century.

The ideas of inoculating against disease and the importance of sanitation and clean water to health formed the basis of preventive medicine. One of the earliest preventive programs of the American Medical Association (AMA), founded in 1847, was a 1912 report on the prevention of tuberculosis. By the early 1920s the AMA had established a Section of Preventive and Industrial Medicine and Public Health. In 1948 the American Board of Preventive Medicine and Public Health was formed to advance the study of preventive health care. It changed its name to the American Board of Preventive Medicine in 1952, and preventive medicine became a medical specialty. The American College of Preventive Medicine was established in 1954. A number of other organizations support preventive health care, including the U.S. Preventive Services Task Force, founded in 1984 to recommend effective preventive procedures.

What Are Strategies for Preventing Illness?

In terms of active protection against disease, immunization may be your most important tool. Check regularly with your health-care provider to ensure that your vaccines are up to date and to learn what screening tests you should undergo. Develop sanitary practices such as regular hand-washing and sneezing or coughing into disposable tissues (if you do not have a tissue, use the crook of your elbow rather than your hands). When possible, avoid sharing personal items such as toothbrushes and towels.

Activities that strengthen your overall health will fortify you against a variety of illnesses. Eating healthy fresh foods can contribute to overall body strength as well as help prevent heart, liver, and kidney problems; diabetes; and high blood pressure. If you must buy prepared foods, read labels carefully to avoid those that contain high amounts of sugar, fat, sodium, and chemical additives.

Building regular exercise into your schedule can help reduce your risk of heart disease, diabetes, stroke, and depression, as well as strengthen bones and muscles. To be successful in preventing illness, try to find exercise that is enjoyable so that maintaining it will be a pleasure rather than an unpleasant chore. Walking, running, swimming, gardening, dancing, and playing active games are all forms of healthy exercise. You may want to combine several in your weekly exercise routine.

A number of diseases or conditions, including certain cardiovascular diseases, digestive problems, and mental illnesses, may be prevented through healthy relaxation methods. Check out the offerings at your local community center for classes stress-reducing activities. For example, meditation and yoga, a form of exercise that includes stretching and breathing techniques, are often successful in increasing physical and emotional relaxation. Getting enough restful sleep is also important in building overall health.

A preventive approach to illness may also mean not engaging in certain behaviors. Most medical professionals agree that smoking cigarettes contributes to a number of illnesses, including heart disease, circulatory problems, and several lung ailments. While some experts recommend drinking a small amount of red wine for heart health, most agree that excessive alcohol consumption leads to a number of health problems, including liver and kidney damage. You may reduce the risk of sexually transmitted disease by using condoms and by not engaging in sexual activity without knowing your partner's sexual history.

What Are Strategies for Preventing Injuries?

Injuries typically fall into two categories: unintentional and intentional. Unintentional injuries are those caused by accidents or errors, such as car accidents, falls, burns, or eating or drinking a poisonous substance. Intentional injuries include personal attacks, such as assault or rape, and damage resulting from attempted suicide.

One of the most effective approaches to preventing injuries has been through changes in public policy. Consumer groups have been responsible for the introduction of a wide variety of protective legislation to help prevent unintentional injuries. These include laws that require automobile seat belts for adults, safety car seats for children, and motorcycle helmets, as well as labeling laws for toxic substances and bans on flammable fabrics. Civic intervention can also help prevent intentional injuries, including increased street lighting for crime prevention and suicide-prevention barriers on bridges.

Health maintenance organization: *In the United States, an organization of physicians and other health-care professionals that provides health services to subscribers and their dependents on a prepaid basis. Also called HMO.*

Your personal proactive approach to preventing injury should include obeying these protective laws, even when they are inconvenient. For example, resist the temptation to leave your seat belt unbuckled for a short trip to the store, bicycle without a bike helmet, or drive yourself home from a party when you have been drinking. In addition, follow common-sense safety rules and pay careful attention when you are involved in any household task, from using a knife in the kitchen to stepping into a bathtub. Many accidents result from distraction or from hurry, such as using an unstable chair rather than a stepladder to change a light bulb.

Does My Insurance Pay for Preventive Care?

Most insurance companies provide some coverage of basic preventive measures such as inoculations and screenings. You will need to check with your insurance provider to learn exactly which procedures are covered and what percentage of costs will be paid. ***Health maintenance organization*** (HMO) insurance providers tend to focus on preventive care and frequently offer lower-cost preventive services than preferred provider organizations (PPOs) do. The Patient Protection and Affordable Care Act, passed by the U.S. Congress in 2010, requires that all policies in its Healthcare Marketplace offer complete coverage of a wide range of inoculations, screening tests, and other measures, with no additional charge to the insured person.

The preventive procedures and tests covered by health insurance vary depending on your age, gender, and other personal characteristics that may increase your vulnerability to various diseases. For example, on many plans, women over the age of 40 are eligible to receive a mammogram to screen for breast cancer every 1 to 2 years. All adults over the age of 50 may be tested for colorectal cancer either every 1 to 2 years or every 5 to 10 years, depending on the type of test. Immunization shots are likewise offered free to qualified patients by many insurance plans. These include influenza (flu) shots, which are recommended yearly for all people over the age of six months, and the measles, mumps, and rubella vaccine, usually given to children in two doses at around one year and four years of age.

How Can I Promote Accident and Illness Prevention at My Workplace?

Workplace health issues are considered so important that they are one of the three major areas of concern for the American Board of Preventive Medicine. Because health and safety problems can increase absenteeism and reduce production, your employer may be receptive to suggestions for a proactive approach to preventing illness and workplace accidents.

On-the-job accidents can cause injury at any type of workplace. Some of the common causes of workplace injury are vehicle accidents, falls, exposure to toxic substances, and equipment accidents. The damage caused may range from a slight injury requiring little beyond first aid to serious injury requiring extensive time off work to disability or death. An important first step in accident prevention is employee education about existing safety procedures. You might want to suggest that your employer set up a committee to examine the records of workplace injuries in order to brainstorm ways to prevent them.

A growing concern in the modern computerized workplace, as well as in the factory, is repetitive motion injury, in which a relatively minor movement can cause serious damage when carried out repeatedly over a long period of time. The science of ergonomics is devoted to designing equipment that places less strain on the workers who use it. The U.S. Department of Labor's Occupational Safety & Health Administration (https://www.osha.gov/dsg/topics/safetyhealth/index.html) offers Injury and Illness Prevention Programs to help businesses identify and reduce the causes of workplace injuries, including repetitive motion injuries.

Education about the importance of healthy lifestyle habits is also a key part of illness prevention programs. Employers may wish to reinforce this message by providing healthy snacks and offering lunchtime exercise programs. Basic sanitation, such as covering coughs and sneezes and frequent hand-washing, should also be emphasized, as should regular preventive medical care, such as vaccinations and screenings. Businesses can also promote employee health by offering special programs such as on-site mobile medical services.

Regular Checkups and Doctor's Visits

Why Are Checkups and Regular Doctor's Visits Important?

Making regular visits to the doctor is an important part of maintaining good health and preventing illness and injury. Checkups provide you with an opportunity to discuss any health concerns you may have with your medical provider, get vaccines such as an annual flu shot, and participate in decisions about your health. Regular visits help your doctor monitor your overall state of health, evaluate your risk factors for certain diseases, and request any necessary screenings.

When you arrive for your checkup, you will probably be taken to an examination room by a nurse who works with your doctor. He or she will check and record basic physical information, such as height, weight, temperature, blood pressure, and heart rate. You will then be asked about your medical history, including any procedures or serious illnesses you have had, along with information about your family's history of disease. You may also be asked questions about your bodily functions, such as digestion, sleep, and bowel movements. These details will help your doctor form a picture of your general health.

Regular checkups allow you to participate in decisions about your health.
© MUCHAELJUNG/ SHUTTERSTOCK.COM.

When your doctor arrives, he or she will perform a physical exam. This may include a wide variety of procedures, such as listening to your heart and lungs, examining your eyes and ears, and looking down your throat. Your doctor may tap your abdomen to check for pain or unusual organ size. He or she may also perform or schedule a number of tests, depending on your age, gender, and medical history. These may include a Pap test, commonly given to women between the ages of 21 and 65 to screen for cervical

Regular Dental Checkups

It is important to make regular dental appointments a part of your health-care regimen. Dental checkups allow your dentist to clean your teeth thoroughly and make sure that you are brushing and flossing effectively. They also provide an opportunity for dental staff to offer you tips for making your dental routine more effective. During a checkup your dentist will evaluate you for early signs of gum disease, tooth decay, and oral cancer. Early detection can prevent these problems from becoming more serious and difficult to treat. Depending on your age and the condition of your teeth, your dentist may also recommend preventive treatments such as the application of fluoride or sealant to crevices in your teeth.

All adults should have at least one dental checkup each year. However, it is recommended that you have two checkups and cleanings per year, which most insurance plans will cover. If you fall into a high-risk group, you should see your dentist more frequently. High-risk groups include smokers and people with gum disease, diabetes, or weakened immune systems. Adults who have physical or mental disabilities that limit their ability to care for their teeth should also see a dentist more regularly.

cancer, or a colonoscopy, which is often advised for adults over 50 to detect signs of colorectal cancer. A blood test to determine blood sugar and cholesterol levels may be performed in order to detect or prevent diabetes and heart disease. Your doctor may also offer you health counseling based on your examination, medical history, and lifestyle, and you may ask him or her any questions you may have about your health or your exam results.

A medical checkup allows your doctor to establish baseline information on your health. This means that your doctor will learn how the different systems of your body are working when you feel well and help your doctor recognize and treat any problems in their early stages. Your provider will also attempt to identify any signs of illness and will advise you about how to proceed if problems are found. In addition, he or she may counsel you in preventive measures that can improve and maintain your health, such as changes in diet and exercise.

Health maintenance organization: *An organization of physicians and other health-care professionals that provides health services to subscribers and their dependents on a prepaid basis. Also called HMO.*

What Is a Primary Care Doctor?

The term "primary care physician," or PCP, is principally used by *health maintenance organizations* (HMOs). Within the HMO structure, your PCP is the first doctor you will see for your medical needs. PCPs are often described as "gatekeepers" of the HMO medical system, because they not only provide most kinds of basic medical care but also decide which tests or treatment you may need. They also can refer you to another doctor for more specialized treatment if they consider it necessary.

PCPs also have their own medical specialties, which they study during a three-year residency program after graduating from medical school. Most PCPs are specialists in one of the following: family medicine, internal medicine, obstetrics and gynecology (OB/GYN), or pediatrics. Family medicine practitioners learn a variety of skills to help them

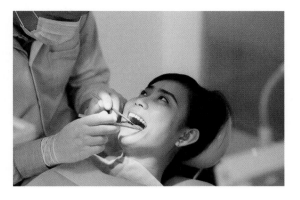

Routine dental examinations are one way of preventing dental problems. © DRAGON IMAGES/SHUTTERSTOCK. COM.

care for all members of a whole family, including children, men, women, and older adults. Internists focus on the medical needs of adults, while OB/GYN doctors help women with pregnancy, childbirth, and diseases of the female reproductive organs. Pediatricians specialize in the treatment of children and childhood diseases. As the population of senior citizens in the United States continues to increase, the rapidly growing specialty of geriatrics, or the care of the elderly, has become another primary-care field.

In addition to their field of specialty, primary care doctors learn skills to help them fulfill their role as the point of first contact for patients. They also practice preventive medicine, counseling patients on healthy habits and tracking which screening tests and *immunizations* may be appropriate. PCPs are responsible for diagnosing and treating a wide range of conditions.

If you are not insured through an HMO, your insurance plan may be a preferred provider organization (PPO). PPOs do not require a PCP for referrals. Instead, they offer patients a network of preferred providers, or medical professionals who are covered by your insurance plan. You may choose doctors or other care providers who are not on your plan, but you will be asked to pay a higher percentage of the cost of services. Even though you are not required to have a PCP manage your care, you may wish to choose a central doctor from one of the general primary care specialties to help you manage your health.

Immunization:
The introduction of disease-causing compounds into the body in very small amounts to allow the body to form antigens against the disease.

What Are Nurse Practitioners and Physician Assistants?

Many of the professionals providing primary care services are not actually medical doctors but are members of other health-care professions. Nurse practitioners (NPs) and physician assistants (PAs) are trained and licensed medical professionals who can provide a wide range of treatments and other services, such as prescribing medication and referring patients for tests or specialized treatment.

Nurse practitioners are professionals who have completed the requirements to become registered nurses along with additional education and clinical training. This generally means four years of schooling to obtain a bachelor's degree in nursing, plus two more to obtain a master's degree. Specific licensing requirements for NPs are determined by the state in which they practice. NPs were first licensed in 1965, and as of the early 2000s they have become an important part of the medical establishment in every state. NPs are qualified to perform most healthcare services, including health evaluations, diagnosis, patient education, and treatment. They may work independently within a clinic or may be part of a medical team that also includes physicians and nurses.

Though the licensing requirements for physician assistants also vary from state to state, the average length of study—after earning a bachelor's degree—is 27 months. As their title suggests, PAs are generally required to work under the supervision of a licensed medical doctor. One doctor may supervise several PAs in a clinic setting, and PAs often see patients independently, consulting with their supervising physician only when the need arises. The first class of PAs graduated from a training program at Duke University in 1967, and since then the profession has continued to grow. By the early twenty-first century there were PAs practicing in every state. Like NPs, PAs can provide most medical services, such as health maintenance, diagnosis, and prescriptions. PAs may also assist in surgical procedures and supervise their own assistants.

What Is a Medical Specialist?

A medical specialist, or physician specialist, is a doctor who has chosen to obtain advanced education and training in a particular field of medicine. Most doctors attend four years of college and four years of medical school, followed by a year of clinical practice called an internship or residency. During this first year of residency, most medical interns rotate through a variety of medical specialties in order to learn about each. These may include emergency medicine, surgery, internal medicine, pediatrics, or OB/GYN, among others. Interns who choose to specialize in a particular field of medicine must complete two to four additional years of residency, or clinical training, in that field.

Vaccine Recommendation Information

The Advisory Committee on Immunization Practices (ACIP) of the Centers for Disease Control and Prevention (CDC) is a group of medical and public health experts that develops recommendations on how to use vaccines to control diseases in the United States. The recommendations stand as public health advice that will lead to a reduction in the incidence of vaccine-preventable diseases and an increase in the safe use of vaccines and related biological products.

ACIP has links to their recommendations covering the following diseases on their website, http://www.cdc.gov/vaccines/hcp/acip-recs/index.html.

- Anthrax
- BCG
- DTaP
- Hepatitis A
- Hepatitis B
- Hib
- HPV
- Influenza
- Japanese Encephalitis
- Measles, Mumps, and Rubella
- MMRV
- Meningococcal
- Pneumococcal
- Polio
- Rabies
- Rotavirus
- Smallpox (Vaccinia)
- Tdap/Td
- Typhoid
- Varicella (Chickenpox)
- Yellow Fever
- Zoster (Shingles)

ILLUSTRATION BY LUMINA DATAMATICS LTD. © 2015 CENGAGE LEARNING.

Your primary care doctor may decide that you need to see a specialist if you have a problem that requires a more thorough knowledge of a specific medical field. For example, if you have a serious problem with your knee and your PCP is unable to determine the cause, she or he may refer you to an orthopedist, a physician who specializes in treating bone and muscle ailments. If a routine test indicates the possibility of cancer, you may be referred to an oncologist, who specializes in cancer treatment. Referral to a specialist need not be a cause for alarm. Your PCP will want to ensure that you receive the best possible care, and a doctor who devotes his or her entire career to one type of medicine is often in the best position to serve your needs.

How Do I Go about Finding a Primary Care Doctor?

The best time to look for a PCP to manage your health care is while you are healthy. Though it may seem unnecessary to seek out a doctor if you are not ill, it can be far more difficult to make good decisions when you are feeling unwell and vulnerable. If you have a medical team in place that you trust, illness can be far less stressful. Establishing a relationship with a doctor can also help you maintain your health, because a PCP can help you with preventive measures such as screenings and immunizations.

When looking for a doctor, your first step should be to contact your insurance provider. Some providers may assign you a PCP, while others will provide a list of medical professionals for you to choose from. Even if you are assigned a doctor, most plans will allow you to change to another doctor on their list of preferred providers at any time. If you are receiving medical coverage through the federal Medicaid program, you may have more difficulty finding physicians who are willing to serve Medicaid patients. Local medical societies may provide lists of doctors who take Medicaid, and you can visit the program's official website (http://www.medicaid.gov) to find information on resources specific to your state.

Alternative medicine: *Medical practices that fall outside the spectrum of conventional allopathic medicine.*

Once you have a list of possible doctors, you can evaluate them with your needs in mind. For example, if you know that you are more comfortable with a doctor of the same gender, you can narrow your list. If you have friends who attend the same clinic or have the same insurance, you can ask them for references. A visit to a doctor's website may give you an idea of his or her general medical philosophy, and you may also be able to call and arrange a brief telephone interview. If you do this, you should spend some time thinking about what is most important to you about your health care so that you can ask questions that will help you make your decision. For example, if you are interested in ***alternative medicine***, you may want to ensure that your doctor is open to these types of remedies and treatments.

No matter how much thought you put into choosing a PCP, you will not really know how well you will get along with that doctor until you meet in person, and perhaps not until you have had several appointments. If you decide that you and the PCP you have chosen are not a good match, you should not hesitate to change doctors. It is important to your health that you have a doctor with whom you feel comfortable and safe.

How Often Should I See a Doctor?

Many people never consider seeing a doctor unless they are unwell. Even adults who take their children in for regular medical checkups do not always maintain their own health as carefully. Those who do not have medical insurance are even less likely to have regular checkups, and they are sometimes forced for financial reasons to seek their medical care in hospital emergency rooms. However, there is much evidence that routine checkups can have positive health benefits.

If you are in good health, most doctors recommend an exam every one to five years to monitor important health indicators such as blood pressure and cholesterol levels. Young adults may go less often, but by the age of 50 most adults should plan to see their doctor once a year. Young children may need to see a doctor more often than adults. Infants often have at least six appointments in their first year, tapering off to once a year by the age of four. Many doctors recommend regular "well child" appointments to maintain health and prevent illness. Of course, if you are ill, you should make medical appointments as often as your doctor recommends.

For adults, routine screenings frequently reveal warning signs of serious disease. For example, mammograms and Pap tests can give your doctor early indications of breast and cervical cancer. Colon cancer screenings help prevent one of the most commonly diagnosed cancers by allowing early removal of precancerous growths. Diseases such as diabetes and hypertension (high blood pressure) can be controlled with medication once they are discovered but can have damaging or fatal results if left undetected.

Perhaps the most important benefit of regular medical checkups is that they represent a commitment to your health. Taking the time to make an appointment for a checkup and thinking of questions to ask your doctor are important steps in taking control of your health care. Your medical professionals are important resources for health-care information, and your regular checkup is an important source of information about the development of your personal health.

Chronic Conditions

What Does It Mean to Have a Chronic Condition?

The word *chronic* means lasting for a long time or recurring repeatedly. In terms of health, chronic conditions or diseases are those that persist over a long period of time or come back over and over. The National Center for Health Statistics defines a chronic illness as one that lasts longer than three months. Diseases that may be described as chronic include diabetes, heart disease, asthma, epilepsy, cancer, and Alzheimer's disease, as well as a variety of auto-immune disorders. Some chronic health issues are not diseases but ongoing physical conditions that may contribute to health problems. These include high blood pressure (hypertension) and excess body fat (obesity).

Having an ongoing medical challenge can compromise your health and lead to the development of additional chronic conditions. Chronic medical conditions have become widespread in modern society. The U.S. Department of Health and Human Services' Center for Disease Control (CDC) estimated that in 2012 almost half of all American adults experienced some sort of chronic condition and that one in four had two or more chronic problems. Most chronic illnesses and conditions cannot be "cured" or completely eliminated by medical treatment, but many can be effectively controlled with appropriate care. In addition, you can avoid a number of chronic problems entirely by developing healthy lifestyle habits and following preventive medicine guidelines, such as undergoing regular medical checkups and screenings.

How Does a Chronic Disease Affect My Health?

Chronic illnesses pose a major threat to your health. Government statistics show that chronic disease is the leading cause of death worldwide

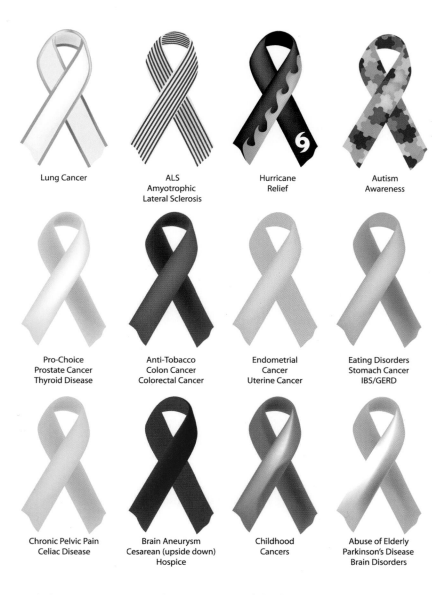

Lung Cancer

ALS
Amyotrophic
Lateral Sclerosis

Hurricane
Relief

Autism
Awareness

Pro-Choice
Prostate Cancer
Thyroid Disease

Anti-Tobacco
Colon Cancer
Colorectal Cancer

Endometrial
Cancer
Uterine Cancer

Eating Disorders
Stomach Cancer
IBS/GERD

Chronic Pelvic Pain
Celiac Disease

Brain Aneurysm
Cesarean (upside down)
Hospice

Childhood
Cancers

Abuse of Elderly
Parkinson's Disease
Brain Disorders

Chronic conditions include various illnesses, auto-immune disorders, or physical conditions.
© INKSPOTTS/
SHUTTERSTOCK.COM.

and that it is responsible for 70 percent of deaths each year in the United States. Chronic conditions are also a major cause of disability. Even when chronic ailments do not cause severe disability, they can affect your quality of life in significant ways. For instance, allergies are an example of a chronic condition that may begin as a relatively minor inconvenience. However, as allergies worsen, they may affect your ability to go to friends' homes or public places, limiting your choices and restricting

Chronic Diseases: The Leading Causes of Death and Disability in the United States

Chronic diseases and conditions—such as heart disease, stroke, cancer, diabetes, obesity, and arthritis—are among the most common, costly, and preventable of all health problems.

- As of 2012, about half of all adults—117 million people—have one or more chronic health conditions. One of four adults has two or more chronic health conditions.[1]
- Seven of the top 10 causes of death in 2010 were chronic diseases. Two of these chronic diseases— heart disease and cancer—together accounted for nearly 48% of all deaths.[2]
- Obesity is a serious health concern. During 2011–2012, more than one-third of adults, or about 78 million people, were obese (defined as body mass index [BMI] $\geq$30 kg/m^2). Nearly one of five youths aged 2–19 years was obese (BMI $\geq$95th percentile).[3]
- Arthritis is the most common cause of disability.[4] Of the 53 million adults with a doctor diagnosis of arthritis, more than 22 million say arthritis causes them to have trouble with their usual activities.[5]
- Diabetes is the leading cause of kidney failure, lower limb amputations other than those caused by injury, and new cases of blindness among adults.[6]

References

1. Ward BW, Schiller JS, Goodman RA. Multiple chronic conditions among US adults: a 2012 update. *Prev Chronic Dis.* 2014;11:130389. DOI: http://dx.doi.org/10.5888/pcd11.130389.
2. Centers for Disease Control and Prevention. Death and Mortality. NCHS FastStats Web site. http://www.cdc.gov/nchs/fastats/deaths.htm. Accessed January 8, 2015.
3. Centers for Disease Control and Prevention. NCHS Data on Obesity. NCHS Fact Sheet Web site. http://www.cdc.gov/nchs/data/factsheets/factsheet_obesity.htm. Accessed January 8, 2015.
4. Hootman JM, Brault MW, Helmick CG, Theis KA, Armour BS. Prevalence and most common causes of disability among adults—United States, 2005. *MMWR Morb Mortal Wkly Rep.*2009;58(16):421-426. http://www.cdc.gov/mmwr/preview/mmwrhtml/mm5816a2.htm?s_cid=mm5816a2_e. Accessed January 8, 2015.
5. Barbour KE, Helmick CG, Theis KA, et al. Prevalence of doctor-diagnosed arthritis and arthritis-attributable activity limitation—United States, 2010-2012. *MMWR Morb Mortal Wkly Rep.*2013;62(14): 869-873. http://www.cdc.gov/mmwr/preview/mmwrhtml/mm6244a1.htm. Accessed January 8, 2015.
6. Centers for Disease Control and Prevention. *National Diabetes Fact Sheet, 2011.* Atlanta, GA: Centers for Disease Control and Prevention, US Dept of Health and Human Services; 2011.http://www.cdc.gov/diabetes/pubs/pdf/ndfs_2011.pdf. Accessed January 8, 2015.

SOURCE: Centers for Disease Control and Prevention. "Chronic Diseases and Health Promotion." http://www.cdc.gov/chronicdisease/overview/index.htm.

ILLUSTRATION BY LUMINA DATAMATICS LTD. © 2015 CENGAGE LEARNING.

your life. Repeated allergy attacks can inflame your airways and lead to asthma, a more serious chronic condition. Similarly, people with chronic high blood pressure may have almost no symptoms. However, if left untreated, high blood pressure can result in life-threatening events, such as a brain aneurism or stroke.

Serious chronic diseases can have far-reaching consequences for your health. For example, chronic kidney disease may eventually require daily use of a dialysis machine to replace kidney function, and it may even result in a kidney so damaged that you must undergo a kidney transplant. Likewise, if not properly controlled with diet and medication, diabetes can cause damage to blood vessels, kidneys, eyes, and the nervous system. Some long-term diabetics develop blindness or sores on their feet so severe that they face amputation of their feet or legs.

Aside from their numerous physical effects, chronic conditions can have a devastating impact on your mental health as well. Dealing with symptoms of illness over time can lead to exhaustion, depression, and a deep sense of loss. Chronic illness can also be isolating, since many people with chronic diseases do not have the energy to socialize. Family and friends may become drained by the ongoing support required by those with long-term health problems. Medical bills and other support services may become a financial burden for families dealing with chronic illness.

What Are Auto-Immune Diseases?

The body's immune response works to protect you from disease and harmful substances. When that response malfunctions, the immune system can begin to attack your own body, causing inflammation throughout the system. When this inflammation persists over time, it can cause a number of chronic conditions that are classified as auto-immune diseases. Auto-immune disorders have become increasingly common. According to the National Institutes of Health, in 2013 at least 23.5 million Americans were affected by more than 80 such diseases. Common auto-immune diseases include lupus, multiple sclerosis, Crohn's disease, and rheumatoid arthritis.

Auto-immune diseases can affect your general health. They can also be unpredictable, with periods of reasonably good health interrupted by "flare-ups" of acute symptoms. Early signs of an auto-immune disorder include intense pain or weakness in joints or muscles, numbness in hands and feet, persistent fatigue, blurry vision, difficulty concentrating, and skin rashes. If you suspect that you may have an auto-immune disease, contact your doctor immediately for testing. You may need to be patient and persistent. Auto-immune diseases can be difficult to diagnose because many have similar symptoms.

How Can I Prevent Chronic Conditions?

The good news about chronic conditions is that many can be prevented by taking a proactive approach to safeguarding your health. The CDC identifies four major categories of high-risk behavior that should be avoided or improved in order to avoid contracting a chronic illness: cigarette smoking, high alcohol consumption, inadequate exercise, and unhealthy eating. You can substantially reduce your risk of chronic health problems by avoiding cigarettes completely and by limiting your alcohol intake to no more than one drink a day. In addition, your overall resistance to disease will be increased if you incorporate at least 30 minutes of exercise into your daily routine. Improving your nutrition may mean replacing processed foods and fast-food restaurant meals with healthy, fresh options such as fruits and vegetables. If you must buy prepared foods, read labels carefully to avoid those that contain high amounts of sugar, fat, sodium, and chemical additives.

Another important element of preventing and controlling chronic disease is regular medical supervision. If you are between the ages of 21 and 50, you should see a doctor for a general checkup every three to five years. After the age of 50, yearly checkups become more important. A medical checkup can identify problems before they become serious, when treatment may be most effective. Your doctor may suggest screenings appropriate to your age and sex that will monitor your health in a number of areas. For example, a bone density scan, recommended for women over the age of 65, can indicate the earliest stages of the chronic condition of osteoporosis, or loss of bone density. This can allow patients to take precautions to avoid fractures and to begin treatment with dietary supplements or medication even before symptoms appear.

What Kind of Care Do I Need for a Chronic Disease?

The approach best suited to caring for a chronic illness is described as "holistic." Holistic health care does not simply focus on the symptoms of a disease but addresses the variety of ways that an illness affects you physically and emotionally. Because chronic conditions go on for long periods of time and are not responsive to "cures," they can become damaging to your general health and sense of well-being. The treatment approaches that work best for chronic problems are those that take into account not only the particular disease being treated but also the effect of that disease on your overall health, mental attitude, and family relationships.

Primary care physician:
The doctor who is responsible for the total care of a patient and refers patients to other doctors or specialists.

This holistic approach is not traditionally a part of health care in the United States, although it has become more common in the early twenty-first century. In a traditional medical setting, you will probably see your ***primary care physician*** (PCP) for your basic care, and she or he will refer you to one or more medical specialists who have detailed knowledge of your particular condition. For example, if you are diagnosed with asthma, your PCP may suggest that you see a pulmonologist, or lung specialist, for more in-depth testing and treatment. If your pulmonologist thinks that your condition may be complicated by sleep apnea, a disorder in which breathing is repeatedly interrupted during sleep, you may be referred to a sleep clinic for further testing.

Dealing with a variety of doctors, appointments, tests, and treatments can leave those with chronic illness feeling overwhelmed and confused. If you are experiencing a chronic condition, you may gain a greater sense of control if you become your own holistic health-care manager. Because you have a unique understanding of your own experience, you are in the best position to decide which treatments work best for you.

Managing your chronic condition means listening to and recording your doctors' recommendations. It may also mean educating yourself about your disease and treatment alternatives. You may want to design a wellness plan that provides a schedule for lifestyle changes, such as finding a type of exercise that you are able to do and setting up a schedule to make it part of your daily routine. Your doctors may be able to direct you to peer support groups, where you can meet and learn from others experiencing the same chronic condition.

Can I Qualify for Disability Benefits If I Have a Chronic Disease?

Social Security Disability Insurance (SSDI) provides benefits for those who cannot work due to disability and their dependents. If your chronic condition is severe enough that it prevents you from working for at least one year, you may apply for benefits through SSDI. Social Security disability payments are available to you if you have worked for approximately 10 years at a job where Federal Insurance Contributions Act (FICA) deductions were withheld from your paycheck or if you were self-employed and paid Self-Employment Tax with your federal income tax.

However, there may be obstacles to receiving SSDI benefits for chronic conditions. The Social Security Administration publication "Disability Evaluation under Social Security" (available online at http://www.ssa.gov/disability/professionals/bluebook/AdultListings.htm) is a detailed listing of medical conditions that qualify for disability benefits, specifying the exact diagnosis and degree of impairment required. Your doctors may be able to help you by providing records of all your test results as well as letters confirming that you are unable to work because of your chronic illness.

Applications for SSDI are often rejected when they are first received because the government requires further evidence that the disabling condition prevents you from working. These initial denials may be reversed upon appeal, however. If you win the appeal, you will receive benefit payments dating back to the time of your original application. You may want to hire an attorney who specializes in SSDI appeals to help you through this process. SSDI lawyers generally work on a "contingency" basis, meaning that they are paid only if you win your case. Their fee will be a percentage (often one-quarter to one-third) of any payment you receive.

First Aid Basics

What Is First Aid?

First aid is immediate emergency care for people who are ill or injured. First aid is usually performed by individuals on the scene when a medical emergency arises and who take action to care for the victim until first responders (for example, firefighters and emergency medical technicians) arrive. Simple first aid, such as applying an adhesive bandage to a cut, may be carried out with little knowledge or training. More complex first aid procedures, such as cardiopulmonary resuscitation (CPR), are skills that require education and practice. Though certain procedures and principles are basic to all first aid, specific environments have led to the development of specialized emergency care, such as wilderness or mountaineering first aid, sports first aid, and workplace first aid procedures, including those for miners and for workers who deal with toxic substances.

First aid is an important skill that may be useful in many areas of your life. You may be called upon to respond quickly in case of an accident or sudden illness at home, work, or school; in public; or while traveling. Knowing the proper responses to common medical emergencies can calm victims and bystanders, prevent excessive bodily damage, and perhaps save a life. Learning first aid procedures can help you address crisis situations confidently and can even help you know what to do when you are injured yourself.

What Should I Do during a Medical Emergency?

If someone is hurt or sick, first determine whether or not there is an immediate threat of danger to you or others, then assess your own injuries and control your emotions. Remaining calm will help you make good decisions. Next, assess others' injuries. If they appear minor, use your first aid knowledge to help them. For example, you may apply a bandage to a superficial cut or apply cold water to a slight burn.

If you or someone else is seriously ill or injured, call or send for professional help immediately or ask someone else to do it. If possible call 911 and tell the operator your location and the nature of the emergency. Note that all cell phones are equipped for emergency calls even if they are not activated, and they can usually make emergency contact even if you are in a location where service is generally not available. When you are sure medical professionals are on the way, address the situation using some of the first aid techniques outlined below.

What Should I Do If Someone Is in Shock?

One of your first actions in administering first aid is to treat for shock. Shock is a life-threatening medical condition that can be caused by different kinds of trauma. It is generally produced by slowing circulation of the blood, which reduces the delivery of oxygen to the body's organs. Symptoms of shock can include pale and clammy skin, a weak pulse, rapid breathing, nausea, anxiety, and disorientation. Another sign of shock can be when injured people insist that they are fine and reject treatment. Everyone experiencing traumatic injury should be immediately treated for shock.

In assessing serious injuries, be careful not to move the injured person more than absolutely necessary to avoid causing or increasing damage to the spine. Look for excessive bleeding, then determine if the person is conscious and breathing by touching and talking to him or her.

Also listen for breath sounds. If the injured person is conscious, have the individual lie on his or her back with both feet elevated about 12 inches to aid circulation. Encourage the individual to remain still, and cover him or her with a blanket or coat for warmth. An individual who is choking or bleeding from the nose or mouth should be turned on his or her side to aid breathing. Do not give anything—even water—by mouth to a person in shock due to the danger of choking. If the injured person is unconscious, treat for shock in the same way, but check quickly for sounds of breathing. If breathing has stopped, clear blockages and perform CPR as described below.

Injuries can occur at any time or in any place. © WELLPHOTO/ SHUTTERSTOCK.COM.

Good Samaritan Laws

In an emergency, many people are afraid to help because they fear they could do something to further injure the victim. They also worry that they could be sued or even prosecuted for causing harm. Good Samaritan laws were created in order to protect you from exactly that possibility. All 50 U.S. states and the District of Columbia have some form of Good Samaritan laws, although the content of these laws varies from state to state. In some jurisdictions, these laws protect those who choose to act from being subject to legal proceedings after the fact. Such laws generally apply only to those who give assistance without any expectation of reward. In other jurisdictions, Good Samaritan laws require that bystanders provide a reasonable degree of aid at the scene of an emergency.

In 1998 the final two episodes of the long-running sitcom *Seinfeld* featured a plotline in which the central characters are arrested under a Good Samaritan law after they make jokes about the victim of a carjacking instead of helping him. Each is subsequently sentenced to one year in prison for failing to render aid.

What Should I Do If Someone Is Not Breathing?

Although breathing issues are life threatening and must be treated immediately, it is important to remain calm, both in order to reassure the victim and to enable you to act efficiently. If someone is conscious and having problems breathing, it may indicate an allergic response, especially if it follows obvious contact with an allergen such as a bee sting. Some allergies cause a reaction called anaphylaxis, in which the airways swell and close. If someone appears to be experiencing difficulty breathing, have him or her sit or lie down immediately and call for medical assistance. Some allergy sufferers carry an auto-injector pen that releases epinephrine, a synthetic form of *adrenaline*, into the system to stop the anaphylactic reaction. If one is available, administer it according to the directions on the label.

Choking on a foreign object, such as food, may also slow or stop breathing. Signs that a person is choking include the inability to breathe, cough, or talk. The skin and lips may begin to turn blue. If the victim appears to be choking, you can attempt to dislodge the blockage by striking his or her upper back between the shoulder blades sharply several times with your hand. You may also attempt the Heimlich maneuver. This involves placing your arms around the choking person

Adrenaline: *Also known as epinephrine, adrenaline is a hormone that is released during times of stress that causes the heart rate to increase and strengthens the force of the heart's contraction. Secretion of adrenaline is part of the human 'fight or flight' response to fear, panic, or perceived threat. Adrenaline also blocks the histamine response in an allergic reaction.*

What's in Your First Aid Kit?

The American Red Cross recommends that first aid kits for a family of four include the following:

- 2 absorbent compress dressings (5 x 9 inches)
- 25 adhesive bandages (assorted sizes)
- 1 adhesive cloth tape (10 yards x 1 inch)
- 5 antibiotic ointment packets (approximately 1 gram each)
- 5 antiseptic wipe packets
- 2 packets of aspirin (81 mg each)
- 1 blanket (space blanket)
- 1 breathing barrier (with one-way valve)
- 1 instant cold compress
- 2 pair of nonlatex gloves (size: large)
- 2 hydrocortisone ointment packets (approximately 1 gram each)
- Scissors
- 1 roller bandage (3 inches wide)
- 1 roller bandage (4 inches wide)
- 5 sterile gauze pads (3 x 3 inches)
- 5 sterile gauze pads (4 x 4 inches)
- Oral thermometer (non-mercury/nonglass)
- 2 triangular bandages
- Tweezers
- First aid instruction booklet

SOURCE: American Red Cross. "Anatomy of a First Aid Kit." http://www.redcross.org/prepare/location/home-family/get-kit/anatomy.

from behind, placing one fist just above the navel, grasping your fist with your other hand, and pulling up sharply several times. The Heimlich maneuver may be combined with blows to the back and may also be performed from the front on someone who is lying down.

If the person is unconscious and not breathing, you may attempt CPR, which employs a combination of chest compressions and rescue breathing (also known as mouth-to-mouth resuscitation) in an attempt to keep blood and oxygen flowing to the organs to prevent further damage. In order to perform CPR correctly, you should take one of the many courses available through such organizations as the American Red Cross. However, even without formal training, you can act to save a life in an emergency. Though traditional CPR alternates chest compressions with mouth-to-mouth rescue breaths, the American Heart Association suggests a CPR technique using chest compressions only for those who are untrained or reluctant to perform rescue breathing.

In order to perform compression-only CPR, first make sure the victim is on his or her back. Kneel over the person, then place your hands, one on top of the other, in the middle of his or her chest, just above where the ribs meet the bottom of the breastbone. Push down firmly, compressing the chest about two inches. Continue compressions at the rate of about 100 per minute until medical professionals arrive to take over.

While compression-only CPR has proved effective on adults, children respond better to a combination of compressions and rescue breaths.

If you wish to be prepared to help children in severe emergencies, you should take a training course to learn the proper method of delivering CPR to children and infants.

What Should I Do If Someone Is Bleeding Heavily?

Heavy bleeding can be one of the most frightening situations for the amateur first aid provider. Because a number of serious diseases can be transmitted by contact with bodily fluids, take precautions when handling a person who is bleeding. If possible, wear protective gloves made of latex, vinyl, or nitrile. If no medical gloves are available, you can substitute plastic bags or even work gloves, but these will not offer complete protection. Always wash your hands thoroughly after contact with a person who is bleeding.

The most effective method to stop bleeding is applying direct pressure to the bleeding wound. If possible, make a pad out of clean cloth and press it firmly against the wound. Elevate the injured area above the heart, and keep firm pressure until the bleeding stops or help arrives, adding more cloth if necessary. If bleeding to an appendage such as an arm or a leg is very severe and does not lessen, you may apply a tourniquet. A tourniquet is a bandage tied above the bleeding wound and tightened by inserting a stick (or a pencil, pen, wooden spoon handle, etc.) and twisting it to cut off blood flow. Tourniquets can cause significant damage to tissue and blood vessels and can result in the loss of a limb. Only consider using this method if the bleeding is so severe that the victim's life is in danger.

What Is the Proper First Aid for Burns?

Burns are a common household injury, and knowledge of how to treat them is an important first aid skill. Medical professionals classify burns into three categories depending on their severity. No matter how minor a burn is, if it occurs over a large portion of the body—or over especially vulnerable parts, such as the face, hands, feet, joints, or genitals—it should be treated as a serious injury, and medical help should be sought immediately. When dealing with serious burns, be sure to wash your hands and maintain a clean environment to avoid infection.

First-degree or minor burns are those that damage only the top layer of the skin. They are often caused by scalding water or steam, touching something hot, or overexposure to the sun. They are usually painful and cause swelling and redness of the skin. The most effective treatment for a minor burn is to cool the skin immediately by placing it under cool running water or using a cold compress for about 15 minutes. Do not use ice, which can damage sensitive tissue. Applying greasy creams or butter to first-degree burns is not advised, because they can seal in the heat and cause more damage. Pure aloe vera gel, available over the counter at most pharmacies, has proven to be effective in healing minor burns.

Second-degree burns are defined as those whose damage reaches the second layer of skin. The most noticeable symptoms of a second-degree burn are blistering and a shiny redness of the skin. Treat these burns with cool water as you would with first-degree burns, and bandage them loosely with sterile gauze for protection. If a large area is burned, treat for shock and call for help.

Third-degree burns are serious injuries that damage all layers of the skin and may affect underlying nerves, muscles, and bones. Third-degree burns appear blackened or white due to severe skin damage. Ensure that the burned person is not in contact with burning or smoldering materials. Check for breathing and administer CPR if necessary. Do not immerse a third-degree burn in water or remove clothing stuck to it. Cover burns lightly with sterile gauze or a clean sheet, gently separating burned fingers and toes. Treat for shock and call for help.

What Should My Home First Aid Kit Contain?

Every home should have a first aid kit containing the basic equipment needed for dealing with minor medical emergencies. You should have additional first aid kits in your car, as well as in any other places you spend time, such as a boat or vacation home. Make sure everyone in the family knows where the kit is, and check it regularly to ensure that supplies are refilled and up to date. You can buy first aid kits from the Red Cross or at various retail stores. Familiarize yourself with your kit's contents, and make sure it contains everything you might need.

Antibiotic: *A chemical substance that kills bacteria and stops their spread.*

The American Red Cross website (http://www.redcross.org/prepare/ location/home-family/get-kit/anatomy) contains a list of suggested supplies for a home first aid kit. These include several types of bandages, sterile gauze, antiseptic, and *antibiotic* ointment for cleaning and treating wounds. It also includes a lightweight emergency blanket to aid in treating for shock and several pairs of latex gloves to protect the first aid provider against infection. Common over-the-counter medications may be included, such as aspirin for pain and hydrocortisone cream to reduce inflammation and soothe allergic skin reactions. You may also want to include important prescription medications taken by members of your family, such as an epinephrine auto-injector to stop anaphylaxis in a person with severe allergies. One of the most important items in your home first aid kit should be a first aid manual that describes the proper response to various injuries and other medical emergencies.

For More Information

BOOKS

Edwards, Laurie. *Life Disrupted: Getting Real about Chronic Illness in Your Twenties and Thirties.* New York: Walker, 2008.

Roizen, Michael F., and Mehmet Oz. *You, the Smart Patient: An Insider's Handbook for Getting the Best Treatment.* New York: Free Press, 2006.

Rose, Geoffrey. *Rose's Strategy of Preventive Medicine.* New York: Oxford UP, 2008.

Subbarao, Italo, Jim Lyznicki, and James J. James, eds. *American Medical Association Handbook of First Aid and Emergency Care.* New York: Random House, 2009.

PERIODICALS

Haupt, Angela. "How to Find the Right Doctor." *U.S. News & World Report*, July 26, 2011. This article can also be found online at http://health.usnews.com/top-doctors/articles/2011/07/26/how-to-find-the-right-doctor.

Nighswonger, Todd. "Is First Aid First in Your Workplace?" *Occupational Hazards* 64, no. 4(2002): 45–7.

Overhage, J. Marc. "Proactive Medicine." *Modern Healthcare* 38, no. 5 (2008): 24.

Wiatrowski, William J. "Using Workplace Safety and Health Data for Injury Prevention." *Monthly Labor Review* 136, no. 10 (2013). This article can also be found online at http://www.bls.gov/opub/mlr/2013/article/using-workplace-safety-data-for-prevention.htm.

WEBSITES

"Chronic Disease Prevention and Health Promotion." *Centers for Disease Control and Prevention.* http://www.cdc.gov/chronicdisease/overview/index.htm (accessed October 2, 2014).

"First Aid: Information to Help You during a Medical Emergency." *Mayo Clinic.* http://www.mayoclinic.org/first-aid/ (accessed October 7, 2014).

Marcy, Jessica. "Chronic Disease Expert: U.S. Health Care System Needs to Treat 'Whole Person.'" *Kaiser Health News.* June 25, 2010. http://www.kaiserhealthnews.org/checking-in-with/lorig-chronic-disease.aspx (accessed October 7, 2014).

Shiel, William C., Jr. "Checkup." *eMedicine Health: Experts for Everyday Emergencies.* http://www.emedicinehealth.com/checkup/article_em.htm (accessed October 1, 2014).

"What Is Preventive Medicine?" *American Board of Preventive Medicine.* https://www.theabpm.org/aboutus.cfm (accessed September 30, 2014).

Medications and Supplements

What Are Prescription Medications?

Prescription medications are drugs that are only available to patients whose doctors specifically authorize them through written orders called prescriptions. These orders are given to the patient who takes them to a pharmacy, or drugstore, where prescription medications are formulated, measured, and sold. Prescriptions for some medications may also be transmitted by telephone or fax to the pharmacy of the patient's choice. Prescription drugs are prescribed for the particular *symptoms* of only one patient and are intended to be used by that patient alone. Taking medications that have been prescribed for someone else is illegal under both federal and state laws.

Symptom: *Something that indicates the presence of an illness or bodily disorder.*

Prescription medications must be approved by the U.S. Food and Drug Administration (FDA), which protects the public health by regulating which drugs are allowed on the market and how they are sold. All prescription medications undergo extensive screening through the FDA's New Drug Application (NDA) process, which requires a series of tests on both animals and humans to examine the effects of the proposed drug. The manufacturing process used to create the drug is also examined carefully. However, in spite of FDA safeguards, prescription drugs can have serious side effects and should always be taken strictly according to your doctor's instructions. Side effects are responses to a medication other than those for which the drug is prescribed. Side effects are not inherently negative, but the term is usually used to describe unpleasant or harmful effects caused by a drug.

What Does OTC Mean?

OTC means "over the counter" and is the term commonly used to refer to medications that the FDA has judged safe enough to be legally obtained without a doctor's prescription. OTC drugs can be purchased at a wide variety of locations, including pharmacies, grocery stores, and convenience stores, and are usually placed on shelves with other health-related products. Common OTC medications are headache and muscle pain relievers; cold and flu medicines; salves for relieving skin rashes and fungal infections; and digestive aids. Many people buy OTC medications to help with the symptoms of common ailments.

While you may ask your doctor or pharmacist to advise you about taking OTC medicines, you do not need their authorization to buy and use most OTC products. However, some OTC medications fall into a special restricted class, as defined by local laws. These are not displayed on shelves but are kept behind the pharmacy counter as prescription drugs are. Though you do not need a prescription to buy restricted OTC medications, you may need to show proof of your age or sign a register in order to ensure you do not buy a drug more often than allowed. Examples of restricted medications are pseudoephedrine, a decongestant that can be used to make the illegal drug methamphetamine, and emergency contraceptive pills, which are restricted to those over the age of 17. In some locations, cough syrups containing small amounts of the narcotic codeine are sold as restricted OTC medications, while in others they are sold only by prescription.

Medications come in all sizes, shapes, and colors.
© STEVE CUKROV/
SHUTTERSTOCK.COM.

Many OTC medications also go through the FDA's NDA process for new drug approval. Common OTC preparations that have been judged safe are recorded in FDA publications called monographs. If a proposed new OTC drug follows

Prescription versus Over the Counter (OTC) Drugs

Prescription Drugs	Over the Counter (OTC) Drugs
Prescribed by a doctor and intended to be used by the patient only	Do not require a doctor's prescription
Bought at a pharmacy	Bought off-the-shelf in stores
Regulated by the US Food and Drug Administration (FDA) through the New Drug Application (NDA) process	Regulated by the U.S. Food and Drug Administration (FDA) through OTC Drug monographs that cover acceptable ingredients, doses, formulations, and labeling

SOURCE: U.S. Food and Drug Administration. "Prescription Drugs and Over-the-Counter (OTC) Drugs: Questions and Answers." http://www.fda.gov/Drugs/ResourcesForYou/Consumers/QuestionsAnswers/ucm100101.htm.

ILLUSTRATION BY LUMINA DATAMATICS LTD. © 2015 CENGAGE LEARNING.

the "recipe" of an existing monograph, it may be approved for release to the public without further testing. Though OTC drugs are considered safe for unsupervised use, they also may have significant side effects and should be used with caution. OTC medications are not intended to replace medical care. If you are taking an OTC medication, you should follow all instructions on the medication carefully and see your doctor if symptoms persist.

Are Prescription Medications Better than OTC Medications?

Both prescription and OTC medications may be effective in combating disease. OTC drugs are generally recommended for mild cases of common ailments, such as headaches and colds, or for occasional flare-ups of manageable recurring conditions, such as allergies and athlete's foot. Prescription drugs are often stronger than their OTC counterparts and are recommended for severe symptoms. For example, if your allergies or headaches do not respond to OTC treatment, your health-care provider may suggest switching to a prescription medication.

Some medications come in both OTC and prescription strengths, with the prescription strength containing a larger amount of the drug's active ingredient. For example, the anti-inflammatory pain reliever ibuprofen is considered safe for over-the-counter sale in 200 milligram tablets, but doctors may prescribe tablets that contain 400, 600, or even 800 milligrams of ibuprofen for patients dealing with severe pain or inflammation. This is because ibuprofen may have significant harmful side effects, leading regulators to require medical supervision for larger doses. However, in some cases, the FDA will approve the prescription strength version of a medication for sale over the counter. The resulting product may be advertised as, "now available in prescription strength."

How Long Have OTC and Prescription Medications Been Viewed Differently?

The safety of medicinal substances has long been of concern, both to the public and to government agencies entrusted to protect public health. The Drug Importation Act of 1848, which required inspection of imported medicines, was one of the first legislative acts to attempt to safeguard the public from unsafe medications. The eighteenth and nineteenth centuries saw the appearance of a number of popular but unreliable remedies that were advertised as cures for a wide range of diseases and conditions. Although these were dubbed "patent medicines," they were usually not licensed by the government in any way, and many consisted of little more than alcohol and herbal extracts. Some, however, contained dangerous and addicting substances such as cocaine, heroin, and opium.

The 1906 Pure Food and Drugs Act worked to regulate the drug industry and stop sales of harmful substances. The act required labeling of medications containing certain dangerous ingredients and established national standards for the composition and dosage of medicines. However, government control remained lax, and untested medications continued to cause illness and death. In 1938 the U.S. Congress passed the Food, Drug, and Cosmetic Act, which tightened controls on the pharmaceutical industry, requiring manufacturers to prove a drug's safety before it could be marketed.

However, it soon became apparent that some drugs, even though they had met federal standards, were so strong that they required a doctor's supervision to be used safely. A number of these drugs were labeled with instructions that they were only to be used on the advice of a doctor and made available for purchase only with a prescription from a doctor or dentist. However, pharmacies were slow to enforce the new law, and illegal sales of restricted drugs continued.

In 1951 Congress passed the Durham-Humphrey Amendment to the Food, Drug, and Cosmetic Act, which set out clear standards for which drugs could be sold over the counter and which were only to be sold by prescription. Habit-forming drugs and other strong medications judged by the FDA to be safe only under a doctor's supervision were to be labeled "Caution: Federal law prohibits dispensing without prescription." Drugs proved by reliable tests to be safe and easy to use were allowed to be sold over the counter.

What Does a Pharmacist Do?

Pharmacists are medical professionals who prepare and dispense medications and advise patients on the proper use of both prescription and OTC drugs. Pharmacists are required to attend at least two years of college before completing a four-year pharmacy program. Many respected colleges and universities, such as Purdue University and Virginia Commonwealth University, have pharmacy schools. Upon completion, students receive a Doctor of Pharmacy degree. Most pharmacists work in retail drugstores or hospital and clinic pharmacies, but many work in other institutions, such as schools and prisons, and some work for companies that make and sell pharmaceutical drugs.

Your local pharmacist has the responsibility to make sure that the prescription and OTC medications in your pharmacy are well stocked and up to date. When you order a prescription drug, the pharmacist ensures that the prescribed dosage is measured out correctly and labeled with appropriate instructions and warnings. If you are receiving a medication for the first time, the pharmacist may speak with you to make sure you understand the correct way to use it and are aware of any specific side effects that the medication may cause. For example, some medications should be taken with meals, and some cause drowsiness and should not be taken before driving a car. Pharmacists are useful resources for advice about medication. While they cannot diagnose an illness or prescribe drugs, pharmacists are drug experts who can answer a wide range of questions and advise you about a variety of health issues.

Can Prescription and OTC Medications Be Abused?

Drug abuse (sometimes called substance abuse) is the use of a medication for nonmedical reasons such as recreation or altering one's mood. Drug abuse can lead to addiction—that is, physical, psychological, and emotional dependence on the substance being used. Common recreational drugs are alcohol, nicotine, marijuana, and cocaine. Both prescription and OTC drugs can be abused, both by those seeking a "high" and by those simply using them for a purpose for which they were not intended. Some drug abusers gain access to medications by stealing them, while others will pretend to have symptoms in order to obtain prescriptions from their doctors. Drug theft is a particular problem for parents of teenagers, who should ensure that all prescription medications are carefully secured and monitored.

Many prescription medications have mood-altering effects that can encourage abuse. For example, stimulants such as amphetamines and methylphenidate are often prescribed for those with attention deficit disorder (ADD) but are frequently abused by those seeking increased energy, alertness, and euphoria. Other medications, such as codeine and morphine, are prescribed for severe pain but are abused for their relaxing and intoxicating effects.

OTC drugs are often abused by young people who have less access to other legal and illegal recreational drugs. OTC products such as diet aids and laxatives may be abused by those wishing to lose weight quickly, a problem most often found among young women and girls. Dextromethorphan, a common ingredient in many cold medicines, is frequently used in high doses to cause euphoria and hallucinations. Energy drinks and other medications containing caffeine may provide a rush of energy when used in large amounts. The use of any medication, even for therapeutic purposes, involves some risk. The use of large amounts to provide recreational effects is extremely dangerous and should be discouraged with education and close supervision of all home medical supplies.

How to Read Labels and Drug and Medication Information Sheets

Why Do I Need to Read the Labels on My Medications?

When you visit the doctor due to an illness or other medical condition, he or she may give you a prescription for medication to be filled at a pharmacy. When you receive your medication, there will be a specially printed label on the bottle or box in which it is packaged. This label contains important information that you should know how to read in order to protect your health.

The most important reason why you should become skilled at reading medication labels is safety. Label information will confirm that you have the exact medication and dosage prescribed by your doctor and will inform you of the correct way to take or use the medication. Labels also contain any necessary safety warnings, convenient contact information for your pharmacy, and information you will need in order to obtain refills. Medication labels can also help you become an informed consumer by disclosing both the brand name and the generic name of the medicine so that you can more easily research information about the drugs you are taking.

What Should I Ask My Doctor about My Medications?

Even before you have a prescription filled, you can begin learning about your medications by asking your doctor about them. Never hesitate to ask detailed questions about any aspect of your medical care, especially about drugs that may have a serious impact on your health. No question should be considered unimportant or silly when you are trying to understand your treatment. If your health-care professional does not answer

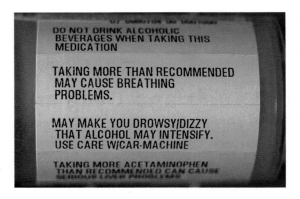

DO NOT DRINK ALCOHOLIC BEVERAGES WHEN TAKING THIS MEDICATION

TAKING MORE THAN RECOMMENDED MAY CAUSE BREATHING PROBLEMS.

MAY MAKE YOU DROWSY/DIZZY THAT ALCOHOL MAY INTENSIFY. USE CARE W/CAR-MACHINE

TAKING MORE ACETAMINOPHEN THAN RECOMMENDED CAN CAUSE SERIOUS LIVER PROBLEMS

Prescription medications often come with warnings that you should read and follow.
© DBA IMAGES/ALAMY.

Narcotic: *Originally, any drug that induces sleep; in modern usage, any drug derived from opium whose use is prohibited by law or has a high potential for abuse and dependence.*

your questions willingly and openly, you might consider changing to a different doctor with whom you can communicate more easily.

When your doctor suggests prescribing a medication for you, you should ask how the drug will help your condition and what other effects (commonly called side effects) it may have. You may also ask your doctor if there are foods or other substances, such as alcohol or caffeine drinks, that you should avoid when taking your medication. It is also a good idea to inquire about whether the drug has any known reactions to any other medication you may be taking.

You may want to find out details on how the medicine is used. For example, you might ask: How many times a day should I take this medication? What time of day should I take it? Should it be taken with meals? If it is not taken with meals, how long should I wait after eating before taking the medication? It is also a good idea to ask if you can engage in all parts of your normal daily routine, such as exercise or driving a car, while taking the medication or if there are any activities you should avoid.

Furthermore, you should request that your doctor clarify how long you should take the medication and explain the procedure you should follow if you miss a dose. If you will be taking the drug for a longer period of time, ask how many refills your prescription allows and discuss the procedure for getting refills. Some prescriptions may include a specific number of refills, while others, such as those for *narcotics* or other potentially habit-forming drugs, require a doctor's authorization for any additional medication. Your doctor may also require an office visit to determine how the medication is working before issuing a refill prescription.

What Kind of Information Is on the Label of My Prescription Medications?

Prescription drug labels contain a variety of important information. This information is generally printed in a standard format, though the exact placement of specific drug facts on labels may differ from pharmacy to pharmacy. Regardless, on each container of medication you should find the name, address, and telephone number of the pharmacy where the medication was purchased and the prescription number. This number is specific to your particular prescription and is an important reference when you have questions for your doctor or pharmacist or when you request a refill by phone or online. Also printed on the label are the name of the person for whom the drug is prescribed, the prescribing doctor's name, and the date the prescription was filled.

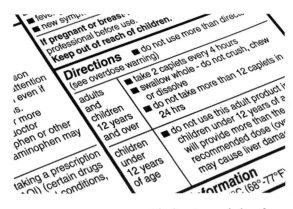

The directions on the box of an over-the-counter (OTC) cough syrup. © STEPHEN VANHORN/ SHUTTERSTOCK.COM.

Directions for the drug's use, such as "Take twice a day, with meals," are usually printed in all capital letters. The brand name of the medication and the generic name of the formula typically appear just below use instructions. For example, the brand name Advil will be accompanied by its generic name, ibuprofen. The size and number of tablets, or the liquid measurement of fluids, are also printed on the label. The number of allowable refills will be noted, along with the expiration date of the medication, which may be written as "Expires 00/00/00" or "Use before 00/00/00."

In addition, a number of safety warnings may appear, either printed on the label or on attached stickers. One common warning on all medications is "Federal law prohibits transfer of this drug to any person other than the patient for whom it is prescribed." Other common safety cautions include "Do not use this medicine if you are pregnant or plan to become pregnant," "Do not drink alcoholic beverages when taking this medication," "May cause drowsiness or dizziness," and "Do not take other medicines without checking with your doctor or pharmacist."

Because each pharmacy may print labels slightly differently, you should read the label on all prescription medication carefully and ask the pharmacist to explain anything you do not understand completely. For example, some labels may tell you to take a medication twice a day, without indicating how many hours should elapse between each dose. Your pharmacist will be able to clarify whether that means taking a dose every 12 hours or if you should take one tablet in the morning and one in the evening, at least eight hours apart. Be especially careful to read all warnings and ask for clarification where necessary.

The FDA Online Label Repository

The U.S. Food and Drug Administration (FDA) maintains an online database of prescription drug labels called the FDA Online Label Repository. Although a fact sheet is included with most prescriptions, the site can be helpful if you misplace this information. The database (http://labels.fda.gov/) is continually updated to include the most recent information available as it has been submitted to the FDA by drug companies. The FDA reformats the information to make it easier to read and understand.

There are several ways to search the repository. The most accessible options for consumers seeking information are Proprietary Name Search, which allows you to search for a brand-name prescription drug such as Zithromax, and Company Search, which lets you to search by a specific manufacturer such as Pfizer. You can click on the search results to access detailed drug information, including indications and usage, dosage and administration, and warning and precautions.

The FDA Online Label Repository also provides links to other useful prescription resources, including veterinary drugs, unapproved drugs, and nonprescription products. These resources can help you stay informed about your medications.

What Information Is on the Labels of Over-the-Counter Medications?

Over-the-counter (OTC) medications are those that the U.S. Food and Drug Administration (FDA) has judged safe enough to be sold directly to consumers at pharmacies and other retail stores without the need for a doctor's prescription. OTC medications also feature informational labels on their packaging. Thorough reading of these labels may be even more important than those of prescription drugs, because patients frequently buy OTC medications without the supervision of a doctor. However, you should feel free to ask your doctor any questions you may have about OTC drugs. Your pharmacist is also a valuable resource for information and advice about the use of OTC medications.

Federal and state laws require that OTC medication packages carry labels detailing a number of facts that consumers should know about any drug they consider taking. Under the general heading "Drug Facts," you will find a list of the active ingredients, which are the elements of the medication that give it a healing effect, and the inactive ingredients, which are other materials, such as coloring agents and starches, that may hold the active ingredients together and help shape them into a tablet, a capsule, or another form.

What's on the Label?

Usage and warning information: All Over-the-Counter (OTC) medicine labels have detailed usage and warning information so consumers can properly choose and use the products.

Active Ingredient(s): Therapeutic substance(s) in the product; amount of active ingredient per unit.

Uses: Symptoms or diseases the product will treat or prevent.

Warnings: When not to use the product; conditions that may require advice from a doctor before taking the product; possible interactions or side effects; when to stop taking the product and when to contact a doctor; if you are pregnant or breastfeeding, seek guidance from a health care professional; keep product out of children's reach.

Inactive Ingredients: Substances such as colors or flavors.

Purpose: Product action or category such as antihistamine, antacid, or cough suppressant.

Directions: Specific age categories, how much to take, how to take, and how often and how long to take.

Other Information: How to store the product properly and required information about certain ingredients such as the amount of calcium, potassium, or sodium the product contains.

The expiration date: When applicable (date after which you should not use the product).

Lot or batch code: Manufacturer information to help identify the product.

Name and address of manufacturer, packer, or distributor.

Net quantity of contents: How much of the product is in each package.

What to do if an overdose occurs.

These labeling requirements do not apply to dietary supplements, which are regulated as food products, and are labeled with a Supplement Facts panel.

SOURCE: U.S. Food and Drug Administration. "The Current Over-the-Counter Medicine Label: Take a Look." http://www.fda.gov/drugs/emergencypreparedness/bioterrorismanddrugpreparedness/ucm133411.htm.

ILLUSTRATION BY LUMINA DATAMATICS LTD. © 2015 CENGAGE LEARNING.

Under the heading "Uses," OTC drug labels list the symptoms for which the medication is intended. This is followed by a list of "Warnings" that you should note before taking the drug. OTC label warnings frequently suggest that you ask a doctor or pharmacist before using the medication if you have certain medical conditions. They typically also include general warnings such as a notification that the drug may cause drowsiness.

The warnings are followed by "Directions," which are detailed instructions for how the drug should be taken. These instructions are often divided by age group such as "adults and children 12 years and over," "children 6 years to 12 years," and "children under 6 years." A final section titled "Other Information" may contain important information on how your medication should be safely stored. For example, the label may instruct you to "Store at 20–25°C (68–77°F) and protect from moisture."

Before purchasing any OTC medication, you should read its label carefully to ensure that it is intended for the symptoms you have and to determine if you have any conditions that may make the drug dangerous for you. If you have any questions, do not hesitate to ask your pharmacist for clarification. Because OTC medication packages may be small, the print on their labels may also be small and difficult to read. This can pose a serious problem for consumers with poor eyesight. If you cannot clearly read everything on an OTC label, ask your pharmacist.

What Is a Medication Information Sheet?

When you purchase a prescription drug, you may be given one or more pages, called medication information sheets or patient information sheets, that contain much more detailed information about the drug than what appears on the label. Medication information sheets may also be found folded inside the boxes containing some prescription and OTC drugs. In an effort to ensure that you are provided with the most complete information possible, the FDA requires the manufacturers of many drugs to provide government-approved medication guides with their products. Many pharmacies also hand out their own fact sheets with the medications they sell.

However, the comprehensive nature of medication information sheets can make them difficult to use. Often printed in very small type, drug fact sheets frequently contain so much information that they can be overwhelming to the average consumer. In addition, many information sheets use complicated language and unfamiliar terms that reduce their usefulness to the nonmedical reader.

Adverse effect: *The formal term for a harmful side effect of a drug or dietary supplement.*

Pharmacy information sheets may include such information as the name of the medication, the symptoms for which it is recommended, and directions for its use. They may also include a thorough listing of all known *adverse effects* associated with the drug, as well as any necessary safety precautions. Many provide a list of drugs with which your medication is known to have a harmful interaction as well as instructions about how to handle a missed dose or an overdose. Recommendations for proper storage of the drug are also frequently included.

FDA medication guides provide similar information, but it is usually presented in a more easy-to-read question-and-answer format. Although pharmacies are required by law to include FDA-approved guides with a number of medications, sometimes they neglect to do so. If you do not receive a medication guide with your prescription drug purchase, you should request one. The information these guides provide about drug interactions and side effects is especially important as it may be much more extensive than what appears on medication labels. In taking any medication, it is wise to be prepared for any unpleasant secondary effects you may experience, and careful reading of patient information can alert you to possible problems before they occur.

What Are Generic Drugs?

When a pharmaceutical company develops a drug, it generally receives a patent, or license, granting that company permission to be the only manufacturer of the drug for a set period of time. After the drug is proved to be safe in a series of FDA-required tests, it is marketed under a brand name. For the duration of the patent, the brand-name product is the only form of the drug available to the public. Once the patent expires (often approximately 20 years after it was issued), other companies may develop drugs using the formula of the brand-name drug. These are termed "generic" drugs, because they are known only by the name of the medication's active ingredient. For example, Advil, the original brand-name medication, is only manufactured by the Pfizer drug company, while a number of manufacturers produce ibuprofen, the generic form of the drug. Generic drugs may vary in their inactive ingredients but will all have the same active, or therapeutic, ingredient as the brand-name drug of the same type.

The Institute for Safe Medicine Practices suggests that both the brand name and the generic name of a medication should appear on package labels of the drug. Even if you purchase a generic brand, your label or medication information sheet should list common brand names to help you avoid accidentally taking both the brand name and generic drug without realizing they are the same. If your medication's label or patient information papers do not indicate both the brand name and generic name of the drug you are taking, ask your pharmacist for that information.

Generic drugs are frequently much less expensive than brand-name medications. In many cases you can request that your doctor prescribe a generic substitute for a brand-name drug. However, generic drugs are not identical to their brand-name counterparts, and there have been cases in which the generic drug did not perform as well for certain individuals. In all cases, if you feel you are not responding well to any medication, consult your doctor immediately.

Vitamins, Dietary Supplements, and Herbal Remedies

What Are Dietary Supplements?

Dietary supplements are edible substances that you can add to your regular diet in order to improve your general health and nutrition. They include vitamins, minerals, and herbal (plant-based) products. Substances that form part of the chemical structure of foods, such as amino acids, may also be used as dietary supplements. Supplements are generally processed and packaged in a form that makes them convenient to use, such as tablets, capsules, powders, or liquids.

 Dietary supplements can help you improve your overall health. You might also take them to help combat the symptoms of an illness or chronic condition or to reduce the risk of one. Some dietary supplements, such as nutritional drinks, are designed to aid in gaining or losing weight. Others improve overall nutrition for those, such as the elderly, who may not maintain a daily diet with an adequate supply of necessary nutrients. However, manufacturers of dietary supplements are not legally allowed to claim that their products are effective in curing specific diseases.

How Do I Know Whether I Need a Dietary Supplement?

You might benefit from using dietary supplements if you do not get adequate nutrition from your normal diet. For example, appetite may decrease with age, causing many older people to eat an insufficient amount for their nutritional needs. Those on special diets, such as vegetarians, who do not eat meat, or vegans, who avoid all animal products, may need supplements to provide missing nutrients, as may those who limit their diet due to food allergies. Supplements may also be helpful if you have had a sudden weight loss or gain, consume alcohol regularly,

Essential Vitamins

Vitamin	Benefits
Vitamin A (beta carotene)	Promotes growth and repair of body tissues; reduces susceptibility to infections; aids in bone and teeth formation; maintains smooth skin
Vitamin B$_1$ (thiamin)	Promotes growth and muscle tone; aids in the proper functioning of the muscles, heart, and nervous system; assists in digestion of carbohydrates
Vitamin B$_2$ (riboflavin)	Maintains good vision and healthy skin, hair, and nails; assists in formation of antibodies and red blood cells; aids in carbohydrate, fat, and protein metabolism
Vitamin B$_3$ (niacin)	Reduces cholesterol levels in the blood; maintains healthy skin, tongue, and digestive system; improves blood circulation; increases energy
Vitamin B$_5$ (pantothenic acid)	Fortifies white blood cells; supports the body's resistance to stress; builds cells
Vitamin B$_6$ (pyridoxine)	Aids in the synthesis and breakdown of amino acids and the metabolism of fats and carbohydrates; supports the central nervous system; maintains healthy skin
Vitamin B$_7$ (biotin)	Aids in the metabolism of proteins and fats; promotes healthy skin
Vitamin B$_{12}$ (cobalamin)	Promotes growth in children; prevents anemia by regenerating red blood cells; aids in the metabolism of carbohydrates, fats, and proteins; maintains healthy nervous system
Folic acid (folate; considered a B-complex vitamin)	Promotes the growth and reproduction of body cells; aids in the formation of red blood cells and bone marrow
Vitamin C (ascorbic acid)	One of the major antioxidants; essential for healthy teeth, gums, and bones; helps to heal wounds, fractures, and scar tissue; builds resistance to infections; assists in the prevention and treatment of the common cold; prevents scurvy
Vitamin D	Improves the absorption of calcium and phosphorous (essential in the formation of healthy bones and teeth); maintains nervous system
Vitamin E	A major antioxidant; supplies oxygen to blood; provides nourishment to cells; prevents blood clots; slows cellular aging
Vitamin K	Prevents internal bleeding; reduces heavy menstrual flow

TABLE BY PREMEDIAGLOBAL.
© 2013 CENGAGE LEARNING.

or take several medications every day. However, you should make every effort to eat fresh, healthy foods, and you should never use dietary supplements in place of a nutritious diet.

Because there are so many dietary supplements on the market, it may be difficult to determine whether you need supplements and, if so, which ones you should take. Though most supplements that have been approved for sale by the Food and Drug Administration (FDA) are generally considered safe, many can have significant effects on the body and should be approached with care. A good first step in making any decision about your health is to consult your health-care professional. Your doctor can advise you about your need for supplements and suggest which vitamins, minerals, or other products may be appropriate

Symptoms of Iron Poisoning

Iron supplements are a staple in many medicine cabinets. They are commonly recommended for both infants and women of childbearing age, as well as individuals suffering from low iron levels, or anemia. Taking too much iron, however, can result in poisoning. If you are taking iron supplements or administering them to a child, you should read the label carefully and not exceed the recommended dose.

It is also important that anyone taking or administering iron supplements be aware of the signs of iron poisoning. Symptoms of an iron overdose include nausea, diarrhea, dehydration, low blood pressure, a fast and weak pulse, dizziness, flushed skin, and chills. Although these are also symptoms of many other conditions, if you have them while taking iron supplements, review your dosage and call your doctor. Early identification of these symptoms can help you avoid more dangerous side effects such as a buildup of fluid in the lungs, convulsions, shock, or coma, all of which require immediate medical attention.

Naturopathy: *A kind of alternative medicine that focuses on the body's inherent healing powers and works with those powers to restore and maintain overall health.*

for you. It is also a good idea to ask your doctor whether supplements you are considering might have a negative interaction with any medications you take.

Most medical doctors work primarily with medicinal drugs rather than dietary supplements. If you are interested in exploring nonmedicinal dietary supplements, you may want to seek out a doctor who is knowledgeable about them. You can also see an alternative health-care professional, such as a **naturopath**, who may be more familiar with a variety of supplements. For general questions, the purchaser who orders supplements at a local store may be able to offer some advice about the use of their products, and the pharmacist at your drugstore can be a valuable source of information about vitamins and other supplements.

What Are Vitamins?

Vitamins are specific compounds that enable the body to perform the functions of life. There are 13 vitamins that are necessary to help maintain the human metabolism, or the chemical processes required to keep your body working. These substances are generally found in the food you eat, except for vitamin D, which can also be obtained from sunlight. When food is processed by the digestive system, the vitamins it contains are used by the body in a wide range of vital processes that maintain health. For example, vitamin A is responsible for producing the chemical retinal, which is necessary for sight, and vitamin C is necessary for the creation of collagen, an important element of the connective tissue that holds the organs, bones, and muscles together.

There are two basic categories of vitamins: those that dissolve in fat and those that dissolve in water. The fat-soluble vitamins, A, D, K, and E, are stored in the body's fat reserves. When you eat foods containing these vitamins, your body can store excess amounts for use in times when they are not available in your diet. However, if you consume too much of these vitamins, harmful effects may result. For example, vitamin A is often prescribed for those with acne and other skin conditions, but taking too much vitamin A can sometimes cause problems such as severe redness or peeling of the skin.

The water-soluble vitamins are vitamin C and the family of B vitamins, which includes the nutrients folate, thiamine, riboflavin, niacin, pantothenic acid, and biotin along with vitamins B6 and B12. These vitamins do not dissolve in fat and are not stored in body tissue. Instead, when they are consumed, your body uses what it needs and then eliminates the rest in your urine. Because the body cannot create reserves of water-soluble vitamins, you need to receive a continuing supply of them, either in your diet or through supplements. Water-soluble vitamins are also more fragile than fat-soluble vitamins and can easily be destroyed by overcooking.

What Are Minerals?

Minerals are substances found in nature that are important to the healthy functioning of your body. The seven major minerals that your body needs are sodium, chloride, potassium, calcium, phosphorus, magnesium, and sulfur. A number of other minerals are equally vital, but smaller amounts are necessary to maintain health. These are called trace minerals and include iron, zinc, iodine, selenium, and others.

Minerals are important in building the elements of the body's structure, including bones, teeth, skin, and hair. They also help build blood and muscle, and they support the chemical processes that operate such systems as the nerves and digestion. Scientists continue to explore the complex ways that both major and trace minerals work within the body, but all agree that a large number of minerals are vital to good health. Minerals can influence each other, so it is important to keep them in proper balance. For example, in order for calcium to perform correctly in the body, a certain amount of magnesium must also be present.

You can get all of the minerals necessary for the proper functioning of your body from a well-rounded and healthy diet that includes plenty of fresh water. Processed foods may contain chemical compounds that negatively affect your body's balance of minerals. As with vitamins, some minerals, such as calcium and iron, are stored in the body, while excess amounts of others, such as magnesium and zinc, are eliminated in the urine and feces. Taking too much of a mineral that is stored in the body can cause serious health problems, while not getting enough of a mineral that is eliminated can cause an imbalance in the system. Because of the delicacy of the balance of minerals in the body, you should always consult your health-care provider before taking mineral supplements.

What Are Some Signs of Vitamin and Mineral Deficiency?

In many impoverished countries, vitamin and mineral deficiencies are common and life threatening. However, in most developed countries, the general availability of fresh fruits and vegetables year-round has reduced the problem, though the widespread use of highly processed foods continues to lead to nutritional deficiencies. In the United States, vitamin and mineral deficiencies can be a result of poverty, which may prevent people from buying enough healthy food products. It can also be caused by overconsumption of alcohol or the effects of some prescription drugs. Special or fad diets that eliminate certain food groups can lead to deficiencies in some nutrients. Women who breast-feed their babies can experience vitamin and mineral deficiencies, especially if they do not take supplements to replace the nutrients they lose.

Because each vitamin fulfills a number of important functions in your body, you may experience unpleasant symptoms if your diet does not contain enough of any one vitamin. A lack of vitamin A (found in liver, eggs, leafy vegetables, and orange fruits and vegetables such as carrots and peaches) may cause poor night vision, skin problems, and vulnerability to respiratory disease. Low intake of vitamin C (found in citrus fruits, tomatoes, and broccoli) can result in fatigue, slow healing of wounds, and gum disease. A lack of dietary thiamin (vitamin B1, found in egg yolks, red meat, and whole-grain wheat) can cause depression, confusion, and numbness in the fingers and toes.

Similarly, a lack of any one of the many minerals needed by the body can have serious results. Insufficient amounts of iron (found in meat, beans, and leafy greens) can lead to fatigue, weakness, and yeast infections. Painful leg cramps may result from deficiencies in calcium, magnesium, or potassium. Low levels of potassium can also result in irregular heartbeat and constipation. Some behaviors may place you at risk of nutrient deficiency. For example, excess consumption of carbonated or caffeinated drinks may reduce your body's ability to process magnesium.

The U.S. Department of Agriculture's National Agricultural Library (http://www.nal.usda.gov/wicworks/Topics/FG/AppendixC_NutrientChart.pdf) features a downloadable chart of all major nutrients, including their functions in the body, their most common food sources, and the symptoms you can expect if you consume too little or too much. You can print this chart as a handy reference for planning a well-rounded diet that meets your nutritional needs.

Some herbal remedies are used in their natural state as teas; however, many are processed into tablets, capsules, and tinctures for convenience and to aid in the measurement of standard dosages. © ELENA ELISSEEVA/ SHUTTERSTOCK.COM.

What Are Herbal Remedies?

Herbal remedies, also called botanicals, are medications made from the roots, leaves, and flowers of plants. Herbal medicine is an alternative approach to healing that has a long history of use by ancient doctors and traditional healers and is still in use around the world. Many pharmaceutical medications are based on herbal remedies. These include aspirin, the decongestant pseudoephedrine, and digitalis, a drug that is often prescribed for heart problems. Popular herbal remedies include echinacea, which is often used to treat colds, and garlic, which has antibiotic and antifungal properties. Goldenseal, used for colds and digestive problems, is also a common herbal remedy, and ginseng root has been used for thousands of years as a health tonic. The gel found in the leaves of the aloe plant is known to help heal minor burns, and the leaves of the gingko tree have become an increasingly popular remedy for memory problems and symptoms of premenstrual syndrome (PMS).

Though some herbal remedies are used in their natural state as teas, many are processed into tablets, capsules, and tinctures for convenience and to aid in the measurement of standard dosages. Herbal remedies are often described as more natural and gentle than prescription or over-the-counter medications. However, many herbal preparations have powerful active ingredients. Like any drug, herbal remedies can have serious side effects and interactions with other medications. For example, St. John's wort, commonly used to combat depression, also works as a blood thinner and should not be used by patients taking anticoagulant, or blood-thinning, medications. It may be generally safe to use herbal remedies that are widely known to be gentle and effective. For example, peppermint tea is sometimes used to calm an upset stomach. However, it is best to consult a health-care professional before prolonged use of herbal medicines.

 Some medical doctors may be knowledgeable about herbal medications, but alternative practitioners make use of these medications more frequently. Naturopaths and practitioners of Chinese medicine are two types of health professionals who use herbal remedies as their primary form of medication. Some naturopathic herbal formulations are powerful enough that they are available only with a prescription from a naturopathic doctor. If you decide to see a naturopath or other alternative practitioner, you should ask detailed questions about any herbal remedy that he or she may suggest, including how it may interact with your other medications. In addition, you should be sure to tell your medical doctor about any herbs that you consider taking.

Safe and Effective Use of Medications and Supplements

What Are the Most Important Safety Considerations When Taking Medications or Supplements?

It is important to think carefully about anything you consume, whether it is food, drink, or one of the many substances defined as medications or dietary supplements. Your body is a delicate and complex machine that can be easily thrown out of balance by careless use of medicinal substances. Even helpful supplements, such as vitamins and minerals, can have harmful effects if taken in excess.

Your first step when taking any medication should be to examine its source. Any drug or supplement that you take should be produced by a reputable manufacturer that provides detailed information about the substance's contents, uses, and effects. Tablets, capsules, and liquids should come in sealed packages and should be returned if the seal is broken. Using the remainder of a package of medication bought by someone else is risky. You should never use any prescription drug that has not been ordered by your doctor specifically for you and purchased from a reputable pharmacy.

Side effects and drug interactions are also major safety concerns when taking any medication or supplement. Side effects, or secondary effects, are responses that a drug may cause that are not among the intended effects for which it was prescribed. A drug interaction is a negative response that may occur if you take more than one medication or supplement at the same time.

There are a variety of resources available that can help you ensure that your health products are as safe and effective as possible, but you should always be cautious and alert. You should not assume that you will be told everything you need to know about medications. Take the time to read labels and to research the ingredients and effects of the medications

It is important to ask your doctor or pharmacist any questions you have about any medication you take regardless of whether it is prescription, herbal, or over the counter. © CHAMPION STUDIO/SHUTTERSTOCK .COM.

Chronic condition: *A condition that lasts a long time or occurs over and over again. Chronic conditions can be treated but not cured.*

you use, and make lists of questions to ask your doctor or pharmacist. Though you can and should consult your health-care professionals for information, help, and advice, you hold the ultimate responsibility for protecting your health and using medications safely.

What Is the Difference between Medications and Supplements?

A medication, or drug, is a chemical substance that has been tested and proven to be useful in combating the symptoms of a disease or *chronic health condition*. Some medications are only available with written orders from a medical professional who is authorized to prescribe drugs. Other medications are approved for over-the-counter (OTC) sale directly to consumers. In the United States all prescription and OTC medications must undergo testing and be approved for public use by the Food and Drug Administration (FDA).

Dietary supplements are edible substances that are added to your diet to improve general health and nutrition. Vitamins, minerals, and herbal medicines are all dietary supplements. Vitamins and minerals are necessary elements of human nutrition, while herbal, or botanical, medicines are remedies made from plants and used for a variety of healing purposes. You might use supplements to strengthen your overall health, prevent disease, or reduce the symptoms of an illness. Supplements can also assist in efforts to gain or lose weight, and they can boost nutrition for those who may not receive enough from the food they eat, such as young children, older people, or those on special diets.

One of the major differences between medications and supplements is that medications are considered to have therapeutic, or healing, value, while the benefits of supplements are not officially established. This means that the manufacturers of your prescription or OTC cough medication may legally advertise that their product will cure your cough, while manufacturers of dietary supplements are not allowed by law to claim that their products are effective in curing specific diseases or symptoms. Similarly, while your doctor may prescribe vitamin C to treat a disease such as scurvy, which is caused by vitamin C deficiency, sellers of the vitamin may not promise that it will cure or prevent a cold.

Who Regulates the Safety of Medications and Supplements?

Prescription and OTC medications are regulated by the FDA, which requires an extensive series of tests on both animals and humans before drugs are approved for sale to the public. OTC medications may be approved without testing if they follow existing formulas that have already been accepted by the FDA. The FDA issues regular drug safety communications that alert consumers to possible dangers from medications. These are published on the FDA website's Drug Safety and Availability page (http://www.fda.gov/drugs/DrugSafety/default.htm), which also includes information about recalls of drugs that have been found to be defective or harmful.

Dietary supplements are also under the supervision of the FDA but are regulated by different standards than those for either food or drugs. In 1994 the U.S. Congress passed the Dietary Supplement Health and Education Act, which makes the manufacturers of supplements responsible for ensuring that their products are safe before they are sold to the public. This means that supplements are not tested by the FDA and that the companies that produce them do not need to provide the FDA with evidence of their safety. However, the FDA does respond to safety complaints about supplements, and it monitors all labeling and information sheets about a product to ensure that no false or misleading claims are made. Advertising is monitored by the U.S. Federal Trade Commission (FTC), which responds to consumer complaints about false claims.

What Questions Should I Ask My Doctor or Pharmacist about My Prescription Medications?

Your medical team is an important resource for information about your health and medical care. This includes your primary-care doctor and any specialists you might see, as well as their staff of nurses and assistants. You should not hesitate to ask any member of your team questions you may have regarding your medications. Open communication with your medical professionals is an important part of your overall health care. If your health-care professionals do not answer your questions willingly and openly, you might consider changing to a different doctor with whom you can communicate more easily. Your local pharmacist is also a prescription drug expert who can often be a convenient source of information and advice.

Avoid Drug Interactions

Drug interactions may make a drug less effective, cause unexpected side effects, or increase the action of one or more of the medications. Some drug interactions can even be harmful to you. Read the label every time you use any drug and take the time to learn about drug interactions that may be critical to your health.

Questions to Ask Before Taking Any Medication

- Can I take this with other drugs?
- What foods, beverages, or other products should I avoid?
- What are possible signs of drug interaction that I should know about?
- How will the drug work in my body?
- Where can I find more information about the drug and my condition?

SOURCE: Council on Family Health in cooperation with the National Consumers League and the U.S. Food and Drug Administration. "Drug Interactions: What You Should Know." http:// www.fda.gov/drugs/resourcesforyou/ucm163354.htm.

Gaining as much information about your medications as possible will help you to use them more safely and effectively. Before taking a medication, you may want to ask your doctor or pharmacist about the medication's effects, when and how often it should be taken, how soon it should be effective, and whether there are other, nondrug treatments that you can try. You should also ask about side effects, known interactions with foods or other drugs, and what might happen if you miss a dose or take too much. You may wish to write down your questions before meeting with your doctor or pharmacist. If you are worried that you might forget some of the details, it may be helpful for you to record their answers.

What Questions Should I Ask about OTC Medications and Supplements?

Even though you do not need a prescription for OTC drugs, you can still seek advice from your doctor or pharmacist about how to use them safely. As with prescription drugs, your most important considerations should be whether or not you need the medication and how it will help you. You should also ask about all side effects and drug interactions and clarify how long you may safely take the medication. To ensure your safety, you should be sure to inform your doctor about any OTC medications you are taking.

You can also ask your doctor or pharmacist for advice about dietary supplements. If you buy supplements at a health-food or herbal store rather than a pharmacy, the person who purchases the products for the store may be a helpful resource. You should ask questions to determine whether you need the supplement, and you should also find out about the proper dosage and possible drug interactions and side effects. If you would like to make herbal or vitamin and mineral supplements a major part of your health program, you might consult an alternative health-care provider, such as a naturopathic doctor, who may be more familiar with and sympathetic to the use of supplements than your medical doctor. As always, you should inform your health-care provider of any vitamins, minerals, or herbal supplements that you take.

Where Else Can I Find Information about Medications and Supplements?

One of the most empowering things you can do to ensure the safe and effective use of your medications is to become an informed label reader. Manufacturers of prescription and OTC drugs and dietary supplements are required by law to include certain information on the labels of their products. Prescription drug labels include safe dosage instructions and any safety warnings about the use of the drug, as well as contact information for the prescribing doctor and pharmacy.

OTC medication labels include a facts section that outlines the drug's ingredients, instructions for safe usage by children and adults, the symptoms for which it is intended, and safety warnings. Dietary supplement labels are also required to include a panel of facts that lists the ingredients and nutritional content of the product as well as the percentage of the daily value (DV), or the amount of a nutrient that you need each day, that it provides.

You can also find detailed information on the fact sheets distributed by pharmacies and the manufacturers of medications and some supplements. These sheets may be obtained from your pharmacist and are sometimes found folded inside a product's packaging. They provide more complete lists of side effects and drug interactions as well as more detailed instructions for use. If an information sheet is not provided with your product, you can ask your pharmacist for one or contact the manufacturer. The National Institutes of Health website (http://ods.od.nih .gov/factsheets/list-all/) provides detailed information sheets on a wide variety of dietary supplements.

How Should I Safely Dispose of Expired Medications?

All medications and supplements are stamped with an expiration date. For some products this may mean that freshness and effectiveness are no longer guaranteed after this date, while for others it may mean that the medication is no longer safe. In any case, you should never use an expired medication or supplement but instead should dispose of it safely.

 You should not flush unused medications down the toilet or sink, as this may contaminate local waterways. Many medication labels offer instructions for safe disposal of their products, or you may ask your doctor for suggestions. The U.S. Drug Enforcement Agency (DEA) sponsors drug "take-back" events during which you can take unused prescription medications to special drop-off points. You can also check with your local garbage collection agency for similar programs in your area. If no authorized drug disposal program is available, the FDA suggests mixing unused medications with an inedible substance such as cat litter and placing the mixture in a sealed container in the trash.

For More Information

BOOKS

Grossberg, George T., and Barry Fox. *The Essential Herb-Drug-Vitamin Interaction Guide: The Safe Way to Use Medications and Supplements Together.* New York: Broadway Books, 2008.

Leahy, William. "Medications." In *Caregiving at Home.* Albuquerque, NM: Hartman, 2005.

Leonard, Basia, and Jeremy Roberts. *The Truth about Prescription Drugs.* New York: Rosen, 2012.

Talbott, Shawn M. *A Guide to Understanding Dietary Supplements.* Binghamton, NY: Haworth Press, 2003.

PERIODICALS

"Can You Read This Drug Label?" *Consumer Reports*, June 2011. This article can also be found online at http://www.consumerreports.org/cro/2011/06/can-you-read-this-drug-label/index.htm

Haupt, Angela. "Behind the Window: What Pharmacists Do." *U.S. News & World Report*, June 18, 2014. This article can also be found online at http://health.usnews.com/health-news/health-wellness/slideshows/behind-the-window-what-pharmacists-do.

"Health Tip: Use Medications Safely." *U.S. News & World Report*, December 2011. This article can also be found online at http://health.usnews

.com/health-news/family-health/childrens-health/articles/2011/12/23/
health-tip-use-medications-safely.

Gilbère, Gloria. "Minerals: The Body's Electrical System." *Total Health
Magazine*, August 29, 2010. This article can also be found online at http://
www.totalhealthmagazine.com/articles/vitamins-and-supplements/minerals-
the-bodys-electrical-system.html.

Miller, Anna Medaris. "Popular but Dangerous: Three Vitamins That Can
Hurt You." *U.S. News & World Report*, February 24, 2012. This article can
also be found online at http://health.usnews.com/health-news/diet-fitness/
articles/2012/02/24/popular-but-dangerous-3-vitamins-that-can-hurt-you.

WEBSITES

"Dietary Supplement Fact Sheets." *National Institutes of Health Office of Dietary
Supplements.* http://ods.od.nih.gov/factsheets/list-all/ (accessed October 13,
2014).

"The FDA's Drug Review Process: Ensuring Drugs Are Safe and Effective." *U.S.
Food and Drug Administration.* http://www.fda.gov/Drugs/ResourcesForYou/
Consumers/ucm143534.htm (accessed October 7, 2014).

"Finding Out about the Side Effects of Your Prescription Drugs." *Harvard
Health Publications.* http://www.health.harvard.edu/newsweek/Finding_
out_about_the_side_effects_of_your_prescription_drugs.htm (accessed
October 9, 2014).

"How to Read Drug Labels." *Office on Women's Health.* http://womenshealth
.gov/aging/drugs-alternative-medicine/how-to-read-drug-labels.html
(accessed October 10, 2014).

"OTC Treatments." *OTC Safety.* http://otcsafety.org/en/treatments/ (accessed
October 7, 2014).

"Q&A on Dietary Supplements." *U.S. Food and Drug Administration.*
http://www.fda.gov/Food/DietarySupplements/QADietarySupplements/
ucm191930.htm#FDA_role (accessed October 14, 2014).

Complementary and Alternative Medicine

In This Section

- Homeopathy and Naturopathy
- Traditional Chinese and Indian Medicines
- Meditation, Biofeedback, and Other Mind-Body Techniques
- Diet, Herbal Medicines, and Other Similar Therapies
- Chiropractic, Massage, and Other Manipulative and Body-Based Therapies
- Magnetic, Reiki, and Other Energy Therapies
- For More Information

What Is Homeopathy?

Homeopathy is an alternative form of medical treatment based on the idea that people can be cured of a disease by consuming a highly diluted form of a substance that causes symptoms similar to that disease. Homeopathic medical philosophy is founded on two main principles. The first is "like cures like," also known as the Law of Similars, which states that a substance that causes symptoms of a disease has the ability to cure those symptoms. For example, a homeopathic preparation of caffeine, which normally stimulates the nervous system, may be given to a patient who is anxious and has trouble sleeping. The active healing substances used in homeopathy are derived from plants, animals, and minerals.

The second principle of homeopathy is the Law of Minimum Dose, or the Law of Infinitesimals, which is the idea that a healing substance becomes stronger the more it is diluted in water or alcohol. Therefore, a properly diluted homeopathic remedy contains only a minute amount of

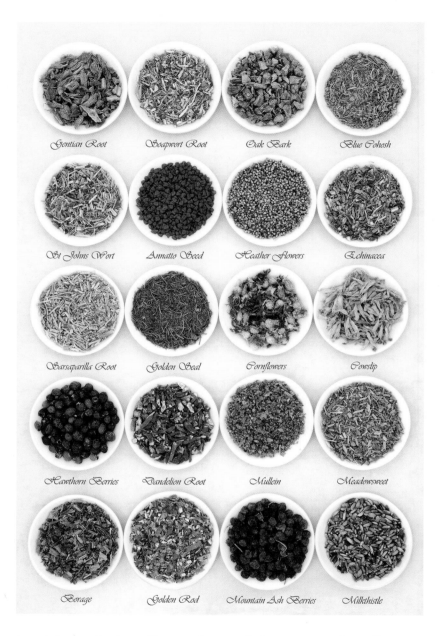

A variety of medicinal herbs.
© MARILYN BARBONE/
SHUTTERSTOCK.COM.

its original active ingredient, perhaps as little as one part ingredient to a trillion parts water. Homeopathic practitioners believe that this dilution greatly increases the curing power of homeopathic medicines. Another important aspect of the formulation of homeopathic remedies is succussion, or shaking. During the dilution process, homeopathic medicines

Dr. Samuel Hahnemann (1755–1843) was the founder of homeopathy. This monument, showing him in the center, is in northwest Washington D.C. THE GEORGE F. LANDEGGER COLLECTION OF DISTRICT OF COLUMBIA PHOTOGRAPHS IN CAROL M. HIGHSMITH'S AMERICA, LIBRARY OF CONGRESS, PRINTS AND PHOTOGRAPHS DIVISION. LC-DIG-HIGHSM-09945.

are repeatedly shaken and tapped vigorously in a process believed to increase the potency of the formula.

Many medical professionals have criticized homeopathic ideas and treatments as unscientific and outlandish. They argue that homeopathic remedies are so diluted that they contain virtually nothing but water and that any curative powers they possess are psychological. That is, people want and expect to be helped by homeopathic treatments, so they believe they have been helped. Nevertheless, homeopathy has a long history in both Europe and the United States, and many practitioners and patients believe that it is an effective treatment method. They claim that the dilution of homeopathic remedies makes them safer to use than many medications prescribed by medical doctors (MDs). Some point out that there are parallels to the homeopathic approach in traditional Western medicine. For example, some *stimulants* have proved effective in calming children with attention deficit hyperactivity disorder (ADHD), even though doctors do not completely understand why this is true.

Stimulant: *A type of drug given to increase alertness or wakefulness, or to improve concentration.*

How Long Has Homeopathy Been Around?

Although medical practitioners such as the ancient Greek philosopher Hippocrates explored the principle of "like cures like" as early as the fourth century BCE, modern homeopathy was invented during the late 1700s by a German physician named Samuel Hahnemann. The accepted practices of eighteenth-century medicine included many harsh and dangerous procedures that often harmed patients more than they helped. These included bleeding patients by cutting a vein or attaching

Samuel Hahnemann

German physician Samuel Hahnemann is considered the father of homeopathy. Hahnemann was born in Meissen, in what is now Germany, on April 10, 1755. He came from a family of modest means, and he used his natural facility for languages to support himself as a language teacher while completing his education.

After completing his medical studies in 1779, he began work as a doctor, practicing in several European cities before settling in Leipzig in 1789. An opponent of the common process of bloodletting (in which patients were bled in an attempt to cure disease and inflammation), Hahnemann sought alternative forms of treating patients. His breakthrough came when he noticed that quinine, a common treatment for malaria, mimicked the symptoms of the disease. Based on this observation, Hahnemann hypothesized that diseases are best treated by medicines that produce symptoms that are similar to those caused by the disease in healthy patients. He outlined this theory in *Organon der rationellen Heilkunst* (1810; *Organon of Rational Medicine*), which remains his best-known work.

Although it faced a backlash from some practitioners of conventional medicine, homeopathy gained popularity in Europe in the 1820s. In 1832 a hospital based on homeopathic principles opened in Leipzig. Hahnemann relocated to Paris in 1835. He established a thriving practice, which he maintained until his death on July 2, 1843.

a leech to the skin and administering doses of strong medicines, many of which contained poisonous substances such as mercury and arsenic. Dissatisfied with this approach to healing, Hahnemann stumbled across a new idea in 1789 while translating a medical text written by a prominent Scottish physician named William Cullen.

Cullen's book referred to a traditional South American herbal cure for malaria that, in strong doses, produced the high fever characteristic of the disease. The idea interested Hahnemann, who began experimenting on himself with a variety of substances and recording his findings. By the early 1800s he published his results in medical journals and homeopathic publications, proving, as he argued, the Law of Similars and the Law of Minimum Dose. The medical establishment generally rejected Hahnemann's ideas despite the fact that they had similarities with the era's new research into immunization, which involved infecting patients with a mild form of a disease-causing substance to protect them from a more serious infection.

Hahnemann's highly diluted, nontoxic medications provided an attractive alternative to the extreme cures offered by other physicians, and homeopathy grew in popularity across Europe and in the United States during the first half of the nineteenth century. In 1844 the American Institute of Homeopathy was established, opposed by the American Medical Association, which was founded in 1846 by allopathic, or traditional, medical doctors. Both the medical profession and the rising pharmaceutical industry objected to homeopathists, who challenged accepted methods of treatment and generally produced their own medications.

In spite of this opposition, homeopathy remained a respected form of medical treatment until the early 1900s, when it was widely discredited as quackery, or fraudulent medicine. By 1940 all homeopathic medical schools in the United States were closed, and by the 1970s only a handful of homeopathy practitioners remained. A revival of homeopathy began during the 1980s, resulting in the founding of a number of new colleges to train homeopathic physicians. Although it is still considered unscientific and ineffective by many, homeopathy has numerous followers. It is especially popular in many parts of Europe, such as Britain, where it is in some cases available through the country's National Health Service.

What Kind of Training Do Homeopathists Receive?

There are a number of colleges and training programs in various states offering diplomas and certificates in the study of homeopathy. A normal course of study is four years, but since homeopathic practitioners are not officially licensed, there is no legal requirement to complete training before practicing. Though homeopathists are sometimes referred to as doctors or homeopathic doctors, many have not attended medical school and so do not technically have the right to the title of doctor.

However, a number of health-care professionals, such as medical doctors, chiropractors, and naturopaths also study homeopathy, incorporating its principles into their regular practice. The states of Arizona, Connecticut, and Nevada allow medical doctors to become licensed as homeopathic physicians. Consulting homeopathic practitioners should include interviewing them carefully about their education and experience, as well as about any other medical licenses they hold. You may wish to broaden your treatment options by finding a medical or naturopathic doctor who also practices homeopathy.

What Is Naturopathy?

Naturopathy is an alternative form of health care based on preventing and treating disease using natural methods, such as nutrition, lifestyle management, and herbal remedies, rather than the chemical drugs and surgery that form the basis of traditional medical (allopathic) treatment. Naturopathy is rooted in a holistic approach to healing that does not simply focus on the symptoms of a particular disease but treats the patient as a whole, examining everything in the patient's life that contributes to disease. Naturopathic philosophy begins with the idea that your body has the power to maintain and restore health, and naturopathic practice works to remove the obstacles, such as stress, poor diet, and environmental toxins, that prevent your body from healing itself. Naturopathic doctors view themselves as teachers who help instruct patients about how to maintain their health.

Naturopathy may include a number of other alternative therapies, and naturopathic doctors may be proficient in such treatments as homeopathy and acupuncture, a traditional Chinese healing practice that involves inserting needles into the body at specific, mapped points. Herbal medicine is a central part of naturopathic practice. Homeopathic doctors often recommend herbal and nutritional supplements to accompany their treatments, and naturopathic pharmacies develop special preparations, some of which are available only by prescription. Some naturopathic formulas may be available at your local pharmacy or health-food store.

How Long Has Naturopathy Been Around?

Using the natural healing power of the body to combat disease was a principle of many early philosophies of medicine. As with homeopathy, the ancient Greek physician Hippocrates was one of the first advocates of curing through natural substances. The term *naturopathy* was coined by European practitioners in the 1800s to describe their methods of treating illness through the use of herbs, healthy diets, fasting (going without food for a certain length of time), water therapy, and other noninvasive techniques to aid the body's own healing process.

Naturopathy was introduced in the United States by Benedict Lust, a German immigrant who had been treated for tuberculosis in his homeland using a natural method. Lust helped establish naturopathy in the United States by founding the first school for naturopathic doctors in

1902, the American School of Naturopathy in New York. Naturopathy achieved great popularity during the 1900s for many of the same reasons that homeopathy became widespread—its methods were gentle and unlikely to injure the patient as the harsh treatments of allopathic doctors often did. By the early 1900s there were more than 20 naturopathic medical colleges in the United States, and thousands of naturopathic doctors were licensed in most states across the country.

During the second half of the twentieth century, Americans began to place increasing value on scientific and technological advancement, and nature-based treatments such as homeopathy and naturopathy were largely discredited. In the 1970s changing cultural values led an increasing number of people to reject the impersonal treatment and high costs that characterize much traditional medical care. This led to a revival of many alternative approaches to health care, including naturopathy.

As of 2014 the American Association of Naturopathic Physicians had more than 4,000 members, and naturopathic physicians were licensed to practice in 17 states, the District of Columbia, Puerto Rico, and the Virgin Islands. Although naturopathy is still discredited as unproven and unscientific by some members of the medical establishment, many medical doctors have begun to incorporate elements of holistic healing into their practices, using nutritional therapies and dietary supplements in addition to chemical medications. A few practitioners have earned licenses as both medical doctors and naturopathic doctors and integrate the two philosophies in their practices.

What Kind of Training Do Naturopathy Doctors Receive?

The education requirements for naturopathic practitioners are similar to those for medical doctors. Licensed naturopathic doctors (NDs) must complete four years of college before entering a four-year program of study at a naturopathic medical school. They receive two years of intensive study in the medical sciences, with a focus on holistic healing and the principles of naturopathy, followed by two years of clinical training. After graduation, naturopaths who want to specialize in a particular field may pursue postgraduate courses of study similar to those followed by medical specialists. Naturopathic doctors may specialize in such areas as cardiology (heart problems), obstetrics (pregnancy and childbirth), and homeopathy.

In states where they are licensed, naturopaths may prescribe medications and order blood tests and X-rays, just as medical doctors do. Naturopaths who work in states where they cannot become licensed doctors are more limited in their practice. If you are considering seeing a naturopath, especially if you live in a state where they are not licensed, ask about his or her education to ensure he or she has completed a program of study at an accredited college of naturopathic medicine. The Association of Accredited Naturopathic Medical Colleges website (http://aanmc.org/schools/) offers a list of the approved institutions for naturopathic training in the United States and Canada.

What Should I Expect When I Visit a Homeopathist or a Naturopath?

Homeopathy and naturopathy are holistic approaches to healing that focus on the entire patient rather than on a specific medical complaint. Therefore, your first visit to a homeopathic or naturopathic practitioner may take longer than you would expect from your experience with traditional medical doctors, perhaps one to two hours. Homeopathists and naturopaths are likely to ask you for detailed information about your general health, such as your sleeping habits, bowel movements, state of mind, and diet that may seem unrelated to your current symptoms. You may be given questionnaires about your health and habits to complete before your initial appointment.

After assessing your general health and lifestyle, as well as any illness you may be experiencing, both homeopathists and naturopaths will design a course of treatment and discuss it with you. Homeopathic treatments usually consist of a specific remedy, or combination of remedies, prepared by dilution and succussion. Remedies are most often in the form of small sugar tablets infused with the active ingredient and designed to be dissolved under your tongue. Tinctures, in which the active ingredient is steeped in water or alcohol, are another common form of homeopathic medication.

A naturopathic physician may order laboratory tests, such as blood or urine analysis, to help in deciding your treatment. He or she may prescribe dietary supplements, such as specially formulated vitamins, minerals, or herbal preparations, to build your overall health and boost your immune system, which works to protect your body from disease. These medications may be available for purchase at your doctor's office or through a naturopathic pharmacy associated with it. Your naturopath may also suggest lifestyle changes, such as a special diet that may improve your condition.

Will My Insurance Cover Naturopathic or Homeopathic Treatment?

Only a few states, including New Hampshire and Washington, have legal provisions requiring insurance companies to offer coverage for naturopathic and other alternative treatments, and even in these states there are exceptions to the requirement. The Patient Protection and Affordable Care Act of 2010, which introduced a number of reforms to the medical insurance industry, includes some provisions for coverage of alternative medical care, but by 2014 it was not yet clear how these changes would affect health-care coverage throughout the country.

Your best course of action is to call your insurance company and ask whether the kind of treatment you want is covered and whether your naturopath or homeopathist is included in your network of health-care providers. If your insurance does not provide coverage or offers only minimal coverage, you may want to ask your naturopath if he or she offers a payment plan or a low-income discount. If you live in an area that has a naturopathic medical college, there may be a student clinic where you can receive care, supervised by licensed naturopathic physicians, at a discounted rate.

Traditional Chinese and Indian Medicines

What Is Traditional Chinese Medicine?

Traditional Chinese medicine (TCM) is a health-care practice based on the belief that the body's natural healing abilities can be activated by the use of herbal remedies, diet, and physical routines that balance both body and mind. These routines may include acupuncture, an ancient Chinese treatment that involves inserting needles into the body at specific, mapped points; massage; and qigong and tai chi, traditional exercise systems that focus on flexibility and balance. TCM herbal preparations employ traditional Chinese herbs such as ginseng and dong quai, which may be administered in tablet form or as a dried plant mixture to be brewed into tea.

Derived from a healing tradition dating back more than 3,000 years, TCM is rooted in a number of ancient Chinese spiritual beliefs, such as the human connection to nature and the existence of a vital force (known as chi or qi) that animates everything in the universe, including the human body. Much of TCM is devoted to improving the flow of chi through the body. TCM practitioners often describe illness as an imbalance within the body. This imbalance may occur in the five basic elements (fire, earth, wood, metal, and water) that govern the natural world or in the forces of yin and yang, opposing principles (such as light and dark and masculine and feminine) that must combine to create life.

The philosophy of TCM is holistic, meaning that practitioners consider the patient's physical and emotional health as a whole rather than focusing on the symptoms of a particular disease. TCM treatments tend to be preventive and instructive, aiming to steer the patient toward a healthy lifestyle, a positive mental state, and harmony with the natural world. One of the methods TCM practitioners use to diagnose patients is pulsology, in which the pulse is measured at various spots in the body in order to determine where the flow of energy may be blocked.

Many allopathic, or science-based, medical doctors distrust the practice of TCM, regarding it as superstition based, ineffective, and even dangerous. They point out that holistic practitioners may overlook important symptoms of disease and that Chinese herbs and acupuncture treatments are untested and may cause considerable harm. However, increasing scientific research into TCM techniques has shown that such treatments as acupuncture and qigong have proven medical value, leading to wider acceptance for many elements of TCM. A growing number of allopathic physicians include holistic methods in their practice, some even studying and practicing acupuncture.

Herbs like these play an important role in Traditional Chinese Medicine. © YU LAN/ SHUTTERSTOCK.COM.

How Long Has Chinese Medicine Been Used in the United States?

TCM was introduced in the United States by the wave of Chinese immigrants who entered the country during the late 1800s. One of the earliest known practitioners was Ing Hay, known to his patients as "Doc" Hay. He opened a Chinese herb shop and clinic in the town of John Day, Oregon, in 1888. Traditional Chinese medical practice in the United States was largely limited to Chinese immigrants and their descendants until the 1970s, when President Richard Nixon visited the People's Republic of China. James Reston, a journalist with the *New York Times* who accompanied the president on his groundbreaking trip, was forced to undergo emergency surgery in the Chinese capital of Beijing. His widely read article about his doctor's use of acupuncture to relieve postsurgical pain contributed to a growing interest among Americans in traditional Asian healing techniques.

The National Institutes of Health (NIH) estimated that there were more than 10,000 practitioners of TCM in the United States by the end of the twentieth century and that more than one million patients had sought their help. Many of the elements of traditional Chinese medicine have gained broad popularity. A 2007 National Health Interview Survey revealed that more than 3 million Americans had been treated with acupuncture and that millions more had participated in tai chi or qigong exercise classes.

Five Popular Chinese Herbs Used in the United States	
Herb	**Purpose**
Astragalus (huang qi)	Builds immune system; offsets side effects of chemotherapy and radiation treatments
Dong quai (dang gui)	Stimulates the production of red blood and bone marrow; increases cardiovascular endurance; regulates menstrual disorders
Ginseng (ren shen)	Increases physical stamina; general tonic
Reishi mushroom (ling zhi)	Eliminates toxins; increases physical stamina
Schisandra (wu wei zu)	Prevents fluid loss (e.g., excessive sweating, runny nose, incontinence)

TABLE BY PREMEDIAGLOBAL. REPRODUCED BY PERMISSION OF GALE, A PART OF CENGAGE LEARNING.

How Can I Find a Chinese Medicine Practitioner?

As with any part of your health-care team, you should take time to investigate the credentials and background of any TCM practitioner you consider seeing. The National Certification Commission for Acupuncture and Oriental Medicine certifies more than 13,000 TCM providers across the country, and its website (http://www.nccaom.org/find-a-nccaom-certified-practitioner) offers a directory of reputable practitioners. Many states have professional organizations of TCM practitioners that may be able to advise you about a clinic in your area.

TCM schools, such as the Oregon College of Oriental Medicine in Portland, may also have lists of practicing TCM providers or offer student clinics where you may be treated at a reduced rate. A number of community acupuncture clinics offer affordable treatments. The People's Organization of Community Acupuncture's website (https://www.pocacoop.com/clinics/) has a list of clinics throughout the country. In addition, alternative health businesses such as health-food stores or shops that sell herbal supplements may have referrals for TCM providers.

What Should I Expect When Seeing a Chinese Medicine Practitioner?

As holistic health-care practitioners, TMC providers often devote considerable time to their patients, and you should expect your appointments to last longer than those with medical doctors. During your first visit, your practitioner will generally begin by asking detailed questions about every aspect of your health and lifestyle in order to understand the context of any complaint you may have. Before you go to your appointment, you may wish to make your own list of questions to ask your TCM practitioner about your health and treatment.

A TCM physical examination will probably include a close examination of your tongue, eyes, and skin, followed by the monitoring of as many as six pulses. Your practitioner will take your temperature and may touch your skin and press your abdomen to assess your internal organs. After a thorough examination, he or she will determine your course of treatment and discuss it with you. Again, feel free to ask questions. The ability to communicate freely is extremely important to any health-care relationship, and if you do not feel you have good communication with your practitioner, you may want to change providers.

Your TCM treatment may include herbal tablets or tea, usually available from your provider. Be sure to ask your provider about what effects you may expect from herbal remedies and what interactions they may have with other medications you are taking. It is also important to tell your medical doctor that you are seeing a TCM practitioner and about any herbal remedies you take.

Your practitioner may also suggest acupuncture treatments. These consist of very thin, sterilized needles that are inserted into specific points throughout the body. Typically, these needles do not cause pain, although you might experience a slight burning sensation. You will usually be asked to sit or lie down during an acupuncture treatment, and you should wear loose clothing to allow access to points on your arms and legs. Some practitioners use related treatments such as moxibustion, in which heat is applied to acupuncture points, or massage techniques that apply pressure to the same points. Your TCM provider may also suggest dietary changes or exercise routines, such as qigong, that serve to balance your entire system.

What Is Traditional Indian Medicine?

Like traditional Chinese medicine, the traditional medical system of India has its roots in ancient history. Developed more than 3,000 years ago, traditional Indian medical practices reflect the cultural, linguistic, and religious diversity of South Asian culture. The three major schools of traditional Indian medicine are the Ayurveda, developed from Hindu religious beliefs; the Siddha, grounded in the culture and language of

Ayurvedic practitioners use a variety of herbs in their treatments. © MUKESH KUMAR/SHUTTERSTOCK.COM.

southern India; and the Unani, originally founded in ancient Greece but also heavily influenced by Islamic culture. Although there are subtle differences in philosophy among the three schools, they are all based on a holistic approach to health and on using natural substances and lifestyle management to attain harmony within the self.

Ayurvedic medicine is the most common traditional Indian healing method practiced in the United States. In the ancient Hindu spiritual language Sanskrit, the word *Ayurvedic* means "science of life." The basic beliefs of Ayurvedic philosophy are similar to those of other holistic approaches to health care; that is, that the body has a powerful ability to heal itself and that illness results when the system is out of balance internally, due to stress or injury, or when it is out of harmony with the natural world. This balance is determined by the five basic elements of the universe (space, air, fire, water, and earth), which combine in a unique way in each person. To prevent or heal disease, Ayurvedic practitioners work to restore the body's natural balance through the use of diet, herbal remedies, massage, meditation, and yoga, a form of exercise that combines stretching with controlled breathing to increase flexibility, strength, and relaxation.

How Long Has Ayurvedic Medicine Been Used in the United States?

Like traditional Chinese medicine, Ayurvedic medicine was introduced to the United States by communities of immigrants from India who brought their traditional healing practices and beliefs with them. During the 1960s and 1970s rebellious American youth began to challenge many of the cultural beliefs and practices that had been accepted by previous generations. Many of them were particularly drawn to Eastern religions that focused on inner peace and to medical practices that prioritized natural cures over scientific methods and chemical medications.

The prominent Indian spiritual leader Maharishi Mahesh Yogi, who developed Transcendental *Meditation* during the late 1960s, contributed to the rise of Ayurvedic medicine in the 1980s by inviting a number of traditional Indian doctors to introduce their practice in the United States. During the 1990s the celebrated Indian American physician Deepak Chopra educated many people about the Ayurvedic approach through his books and television appearances.

Meditation: *A practice that helps one to center and focus the mind; sometimes used to help recovering addicts.*

The desire for a spiritually integrated form of health care has continued to draw Americans to Ayurvedic medical practitioners. However, Ayurvedic medicine has remained on the fringes of U.S. society and has been largely rejected by the medical establishment. The National Ayurvedic Medical Association was established in 1998 to promote Ayurvedic practitioners and to educate the public about the benefits of their treatments. In 1999 the American Academy of Ayurvedic Medicine was formed to increase connections between the Ayurvedic communities in the United States and in India, where it is much more accepted as a legitimate medical practice.

Although there were at least 30 schools for Ayurvedic healers in the United States by 2014, there was still no standardized credentialing process. This lack of certification, along with Ayurveda's nonscientific approach, has led many allopathic doctors to condemn Ayurvedic medicine as quackery, or fraudulent medicine. A few medical doctors, however, have learned Ayurvedic methods and have incorporated them into their practices.

How Can I Find an Ayurvedic Practitioner?

Because there is no legal certification for Ayurveda, training and skill levels may vary widely among practitioners. The website of the National Ayurvedic Medical Association (http://www.ayurvedanama.org/search/custom.asp?id=945) can help you find an Ayurvedic professional near you. The website also offers a downloadable "Scope of Practice" document that details the skills qualified practitioners should possess and what procedures they are permitted to perform. The California College of Ayurveda website (http://www.ayurvedacollege.com/resources/practitioners) also provides listings for practitioners throughout the United States.

Before you arrange any medical appointment with an Ayurvedic healer, you should ask about his or her education and experience. It may help to know that Ayurvedic practitioners in India must complete up to five years of training. Make sure that any professional you consider has attended a reputable school and has completed a full course of training.

What Should I Expect When Seeing an Ayurvedic Practitioner?

As with TCM, your initial appointment with an Ayurvedic practitioner will not be rushed and may take over an hour. Your practitioner will ask you detailed questions about your diet, emotional health, lifestyle habits, and routines, as well as your medical history and any current symptoms you may be experiencing. She or he will examine you by pressing or tapping on various parts of your body; listening to your voice and internal organs; and inspecting your tongue, skin, and nails. Like traditional Chinese practitioners, your Ayurvedic healer will take several different pulses, believed to be influenced by the vital elements of space, air, fire, water, and earth.

After your examination, your Ayurvedic practitioner may suggest a variety of therapies, such as treatment with medicated oils or herbal remedies, special massage techniques, and changes in diet and in daily or seasonal routines. Ayurvedic herbal formulas should be approached with caution, since some have been shown to contain toxic ingredients. Never take a dietary supplement that is not properly labeled with ingredients and dosage.

Ayurvedic practitioners generally expect that you will use their services in addition to those of your regular allopathic doctor. Ayurvedic healers are not permitted to diagnose disease, prescribe medicine, perform surgery or acupuncture, or use the title "doctor." An Ayurvedic healer should never suggest that you stop taking prescription medication or that you not follow your allopathic doctor's orders.

Meditation, Biofeedback, and Other Mind-Body Techniques

What Is Mind-Body Therapy?

Mind-body therapy is the name given to a wide range of techniques that address the effect of your mental state upon your health. Doctors and medical researchers have long noted that depression and other negative thoughts and emotions can cause or worsen physical illness. On the other hand, positive emotions and thoughts, such as affection, laughter, and hope, can speed healing and improve general health. Mind-body treatments are based on the idea that people can use this connection to combat illness and build overall wellness by consciously working to improve mental and emotional health.

There are a wide variety of mind-body therapies to choose from. Some, such as cognitive behavioral therapy, biofeedback, and hypnotherapy may require the support of trained professionals. Others, such as the exercise systems yoga, tai chi, and qigong, and relaxation practices such as meditation, guided imagery, and breathing exercises may be learned in classes and practiced on your own. If you are very self-motivated and disciplined, a number of self-help books are available that explain the basics of various mind-body techniques to help you start on your own individual therapy program.

How Long Has Mind-Body Therapy Been Around?

Many ancient cultures were deeply aware of the connection between emotions and thoughts and physical health. A number of traditional schools of healing, including traditional Chinese medicine and the Ayurvedic medicine of India, have practiced mind-body therapies for thousands of years. Most of these traditional systems are based on the idea that our bodies have a natural ability to heal themselves, and many of their therapies focus on removing the obstacles, such as stress, *toxins*,

Toxin: *A poison made by a germ.*

Meditation is a relaxation technique that can be done anywhere—even in your office.
© WAVEBREAKMEDIA/ SHUTTERSTOCK.COM.

and bad habits, that block the body's healing energy.

Around the 1600s a new philosophy of healing began to emerge in Europe, based on an increasing cultural value on rational thought and scientific experimentation. This medical theory is sometimes called "science-based," "evidence-based," or "allopathic" medicine. Allopathic doctors studied the parts of the body to understand their functions and often focused on specific diseases rather than viewing disease as an imbalance in the whole mind-body system. Science-based doctors generally viewed the mind and the body as separate and devoted themselves to healing the body. They developed chemical medications and surgical procedures to combat disease and tended to discredit other schools of medical thought as superstition and fakery.

Allopathic doctors and researchers have been enormously successful in studying and healing many diseases and injuries. However, some patients have found the purely scientific approach to medicine unsatisfying, and they have explored other healing techniques, from prayer to exercise. Beginning in the 1960s and 1970s a number of medical doctors began to discover that relaxation techniques and other mind-body approaches had a positive effect on their patients, particularly on those with chronic conditions such as rheumatoid arthritis and hypertension (high blood pressure). Research studies—including one conducted in 1989 by a Stanford University doctor David Spiegel on women fighting breast cancer—proved that patients who used mind-body techniques had more positive results and often lived longer than those who did not.

While mind-body therapies have remained a major part of many alternative healing systems, by the early twenty-first century the mind-body connection has become increasingly accepted by practitioners of allopathic medicine as well. A number of respected medical schools have mind-body medicine programs to teach the principles and techniques of "holistic" care, which treats the patient's physical and emotional health as a whole rather than focusing on the symptoms of a particular disease.

Organizations such as the Center for Mind-Body Medicine, founded in 1991, work to educate doctors and the public about the importance of the holistic approach to healing.

Why Do I Need to Learn Mind-Body Techniques?

One of the simplest and most valuable results of mind-body work is that it allows you to learn about your whole self. It is easy to get so caught up in day-to-day activities that you lose touch with how you feel, physically and emotionally, paying little attention to your body until it fails you through illness or injury. Mind-body therapies suggest that you stop, breathe, and quietly notice your physical and emotional feelings and thoughts, and just this simple action can begin the process of healing.

Biofeedback machines like these measure heart rate, blood pressure, and body temperature among other metrics.
© MONIKA WISNIEWSKA/ SHUTTERSTOCK.COM.

The Center for Mind-Body Medicine estimates that as much as 80 percent of all disease is related to stress. Stress is a growing problem in our increasingly fast-paced modern society and is known to cause or worsen a number of physical conditions, such heart disease, asthma, and digestive problems, among others. Most mind-body therapies teach relaxation techniques to help in managing stress to reduce the likelihood of stress-related disease and improve your general quality of life.

Practicing techniques of mind-body therapy may help you improve a number of ongoing health conditions, including insomnia, anxiety, depression, headaches, and skin rashes. Even life-threatening diseases such as diabetes, heart disease, and cancer may respond to a holistic approach. Using mind-body techniques will not necessarily cure you of a serious illness, but it may help you draw on your inner resources to overcome fear and anxiety, promote healing, and strengthen your immune system, which works to protect your body from disease.

If you decide to try a mind-body approach to maintaining your health, you may find it helpful to take a class to teach you the technique and help with discipline, at least at first. Classes also offer the support of meeting others who may have many of the same concerns, and learning in a group can be fun and stimulating. In most cases you will learn lasting skills that you can continue to use on your own as part of your health maintenance plan.

What Is Meditation?

Meditation is a relaxation technique that involves quieting the thoughts, calming the mind and body, and becoming aware of the state of your mind and body in the present moment. Becoming aware in this case does not mean thinking about how you feel but rather attempting to let your thoughts go and simply experience a quiet calm. There are many types of meditation, some with religious foundations and others that offer specific instructions on ways to control your conscious mind, such as chanting a special word or phrase (called a mantra). One of the simplest forms is "mindful" meditation, which suggests that you slow your breathing and focus your thoughts on your breaths as they move in and out of your body.

ILLUSTRATION BY LUMINA DATAMATICS LTD. © 2015 CENGAGE LEARNING.

If you want to try meditating, wear loose clothing and sit in a comfortable position. Lying down may prompt you to fall asleep. Close your eyes and focus your thoughts on one simple thing. This could be a candle flame, the sound of your breathing, or the image of a leaf floating on your breath. Do not become frustrated if thoughts intrude; this is quite normal. Simply notice the thought, put it aside, and continue to focus on your breath. Some experts suggest trying to develop the habit of meditation by beginning with only a few minutes a day. Even in this short time, you may feel relaxed and refreshed.

Another technique closely related to meditation is "guided imagery," in which you sit in a relaxed position while a teacher, therapist, or recorded voice leads you through a series of imaginary actions intended to relax you and promote healing. For example, your therapist may suggest that you imagine yourself in a beautiful landscape of your choice, such as a quiet beach or forest. You may be led through a series of sensory images, such as smells, sounds, and textures. Guided imagery may include specific healing ideas, such as picturing your immune system as a pack of helpful dogs rooting out cancer cells or imagining your skin pink and healthy and free of an eczema rash.

Mind–Body Techniques

The National Center for Complementary and Integrative Health (NCCIH) (National Center for Complementary and Alternative Medicine [NCCAM] until 12/17/2014) lists techniques that are considered mind-body therapies or practices. These techniques are administered or taught to others by a trained practitioner or teacher.

- Acupuncture
- Biofeedback
- Cognitive-behavioral therapy
- Creative arts therapies (art, music, or dance)
- Guided imagery
- Hypnosis
- Massage therapy
- Meditation
- Patient support groups
- Prayer
- Qigong
- Relaxation
- Spinal manipulation
- Tai chi
- Yoga

SOURCE: National Center for Complementary and Integrative Health (NCCIH) (National Center for Complementary and Alternative Medicine [NCCAM] until 12/17/2014). "Mind and Body Practices." http://nccam.nih.gov/health/mindbody.

What Is Biofeedback?

Biofeedback is a form of body-mind therapy that uses electronic machines to give you information about your internal bodily functions. These machines, which measure such vital activities as heart rate, blood pressure, and body temperature, allow you to "see" how your body functions. This outside evidence can help you to change bodily activities over which you may feel you have little control. For example, while you may have no idea how to calm yourself by lowering your heart rate, if a biofeedback machine wired to your heart shows a light that blinks every time your heart beats, you may find that by thinking calming thoughts you can slow the rate of the blinking light. Some body-mind experts have described biofeedback as meditation for Western minds, which may place more trust in medical machinery than in their own inner healing abilities.

Biofeedback has proved useful in treating such conditions as migraine headaches, digestive disorders, irregular heartbeat, depression, *anxiety*, and epilepsy. Biofeedback is usually administered in a healthcare provider's office, lab, or clinic, although there are devices you can purchase for use at home. An average course of biofeedback treatment may consist of 10 to 20 weekly appointments. In a normal biofeedback session, your doctor or technician will attach electrodes to your body to supply the necessary information, or feedback, about your body. Your practitioner will then lead you through a number of visualization exercises to help you exert control over your body's activities. You may also be given exercises to continue at home.

Anxiety: *An abnormal and overwhelming sense of worry and fear that is often accompanied by physical reaction.*

If you want to try biofeedback, you may ask your doctor for a referral to a competent practitioner. The Association for Applied Psychology and Biofeedback website (http://www.aapb.org/i4a/pages/index.cfm?pageid=3281) offers a directory of qualified biofeedback technicians all over the country.

Are There Other Mind-Body Techniques I Can Try?

There are a number of mind-body therapies that have proved effective for relaxation, behavior change, preventive care, and easing the symptoms of disease. These include hypnotherapy, cognitive behavioral therapy, *yoga*, tai chi, and qigong.

Yoga: *A form of exercise and a system of health that incorporates a series of exercises utilizing regulated breathing, concentration, physical postures, and flexibility.*

Hypnotherapy is a therapeutic technique in which a therapist places the patient under hypnosis, a state of deep relaxation, in order to suggest positive ideas and lifestyle changes. Though the relaxed state of hypnosis may make you more receptive to positive suggestions, it does not, as many films and television programs suggest, take away your control or allow the therapist to force you to do something you do not wish to do. Hypnosis has proved effective in changing habits, such as cigarette smoking; controlling phobias, such as fear of flying; and reducing or managing pain. A number of self-help books teach self-hypnosis, which uses techniques similar to those of meditation to achieve the relaxed and open state that may allow you to absorb positive ideas and changes.

Cognitive behavioral therapy (CBT) is a type of short-term mental health counseling in which the therapist and patient work together to change negative thought patterns and foster more positive feelings and behaviors. CBT offers a practical approach to dealing with such chronic conditions as depression and anxiety, as well as helping patients relax and form positive health habits. The website of the Association for Behavioral and Cognitive Therapies (http://www.abct.org/Help/?m=mFindHelp) provides a listing of reputable therapists as well as suggestions for useful self-help books.

Yoga, tai chi, and qigong are forms of exercise that combine physical movement with many of the elements of meditation, such as focused breathing, relaxation, and elements of spirituality. Yoga was developed from Hindu religious practice in India, while tai chi and qigong are part of traditional Chinese medicine. All three promote strength, flexibility, and relaxation. Though each discipline can take a lifetime to master, all can be performed by people of all ages, sizes, and levels of ability. Gentle classes for people with disabilities are available in many areas. The American Tai Chi and Qigong Association website (http://www.americantaichi.net/TaiChiQigongClass.asp) features a locator tool for classes in your area. The Yoga Finder website (http://www.yogafinder.com) lists yoga classes, workshops, and retreats around the world.

Diet, Herbal Medicines, and Other Similar Therapies

What Is Nutritional Therapy?

Nutritional therapy is a general term for health-care practices that focus on treating disease and improving general wellness through healthy dietary choices. There are various types of practitioners who employ nutritional therapy concepts. Some work within the science-based, or allopathic, medical system, while others embrace alternative forms of medicine such as naturopathy, which is based on preventing and treating disease using natural methods. A number of nutritional counselors are focused almost entirely on weight reduction, while others argue that promoting healthy lifestyle choices is more important than encouraging weight-loss diets, which may be unsafe and destructive to your health.

Most allopathic and alternative health-care workers agree that healthy nutrition is an important factor in healing and preventing disease. As processed and high-sugar foods have become increasingly popular, diet-related illnesses are on the rise, including diabetes, heart disease, and dental disease. A growing number of Americans, overwhelmed by the conflicting advertising claims of processed foods and weight-loss diets, feel increasingly out of touch with their dietary needs. In addition, food allergies have been found to be the root of a number of chronic conditions, such as allergies, eczema, and celiac disease. Nutritional counseling can help you identify deficiencies in your current eating habits and offer suggestions on how to improve your nutrition and overall health.

How Can Dietary Changes Improve My Health?

Though much of the discussion about diet in the United States revolves around weight loss, there are a number of ways in which the food you eat may affect your health. Learning about the components of a healthy

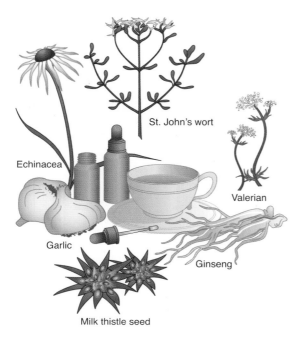

St. John's wort

Echinacea

Valerian

Garlic

Ginseng

Milk thistle seed

These are just a few of the many herbs used for healing. ILLUSTRATION BY ELECTRONIC ILLUSTRATORS GROUP. © 2014 CENGAGE LEARNING.

diet can help you prevent a number of diseases and chronic conditions, such as diabetes, high blood pressure, cardiovascular disease, and cancer. If you already have a chronic condition, there may be nutrients that can help you manage your condition or foods you want to avoid so as not to worsen your condition. Nutritional counseling can help you understand how what you eat has a direct effect on your health.

Food allergies are another nutritionally based problem. A food allergy occurs when the body's immune system has a damaging reaction to a type of food. The immune system normally helps the body combat disease or toxins, but it can become overly sensitive and trigger an extreme response to an otherwise harmless substance. Allergic reactions can range from uncomfortable (rashes, nausea, and diarrhea) to life-threatening (anaphylactic shock, in which the airways close and breathing is blocked). You can become allergic to food at any time, and existing allergies may worsen suddenly. In some cases, merely touching a food may set off a severe allergic reaction.

Food intolerance or sensitivities may also cause considerable discomfort and may be more common than food allergies. Those with intolerance to certain foods lack the necessary digestive chemicals to process that food. Lactose intolerance, which prevents the proper digestion of dairy products, and celiac disease, which causes severe reactions to certain proteins found in some grains, are examples of food intolerance. Discussing your responses to foods with a nutritionist can help you determine which foods are likely to provoke a reaction. You can then design a diet that avoids problem foods.

What Kinds of Nutritional Therapists Can I Consult?

There are a number of different types of nutritional therapists. The title "nutritionist" is an inclusive label that can include anyone from registered dieticians (RDs) to self-educated specialists who offer dietary counseling. Laws governing nutritional counseling vary from state

The American Herbalists Guild

Founded in 1989, the American Herbalists Guild is a nonprofit organization that promotes awareness of the medicinal use of plants and professionalism among practitioners of herbalism. It works to encourage the acceptance of herbal medicine, promote research into herbal medicines, and educate the public about the benefits of herbal treatment. It fosters cooperation between practitioners of herbal medicine and health-care providers from different backgrounds. The organization is a valuable resource for anyone interested in practicing herbal medicine. Because it develops and maintains standards for the profession, membership in the organization is a marker of professional competency.

The American Herbalist Guild holds an annual meeting that allows members to keep up-to-date on developments in the field and to attend sessions led by experts. The group publishes a periodical, the *Journal of the American Herbalists Guild*, which includes peer-reviewed articles as well as relevant book reviews and case histories. The organization's website (http://www.americanherbalistsguild.com) offers downloadable articles from the journal.

to state. Some, such as Florida, Ohio, and Wyoming, limit nutritional counseling to registered dieticians who are licensed by the state. Others, including Washington, Texas, and Virginia, have no licensing requirements and allow anyone to establish himself or herself as a nutritional therapist. Four states—Minnesota, Illinois, Maryland, and Delaware—require that nutritionists be licensed by the state, but they offer the possibility of licensing to those who are not RDs. If you wish to check the laws in your state, the website of the Center for Nutrition Advocacy (http://nutritionadvocacy.org/) offers an interactive map with detailed state-by-state information.

If you are referred for nutritional counseling by your allopathic doctor, you will probably consult a registered dietician. In the early twenty-first century the Academy of Nutrition and Dietetics allowed RDs to use the title "registered dietician nutritionist" (RDN). This reflects an increasing focus on nutrition rather than diet, which is largely associated with weight loss. RDs are required to complete a series of classes and an internship in *dietetics* and pass an exam. Some may complete postgraduate studies. RDs are often associated with hospitals or doctors' offices, but they may also set up their own private practices.

Dietetics: *The science of applying the principles of nutrition to the diet.*

If you are seeing an alternative health-care practitioner such as a naturopath, homeopath, or chiropractor, or if you have an interest in

Reference Values for Nutrition Labeling, Based on a 2,000 Calorie Intake, for Adults and Children 4 or More Years of Age

Nutrient	Unit of Measure	Daily Value
Total fat	grams (g)	65
Saturated fatty acids	grams (g)	20
Cholesterol	milligrams (mg)	300
Sodium	milligrams (mg)	2,400
Potassium	milligrams (mg)	3,500
Total carbohydrate	grams (g)	300
Fiber	grams (g)	25
Protein	grams (g)	50
Vitamin A	International Unit (IU)	5,000
Vitamin C	milligrams (mg)	60
Calcium	milligrams (mg)	1,000
Iron	milligrams (mg)	18
Vitamin D	International Unit (IU)	400
Vitamin E	International Unit (IU)	30
Vitamin K	micrograms (µg)	80
Thiamin	milligrams (mg)	1.5
Riboflavin	milligrams (mg)	1.7
Niacin	milligrams (mg)	20
Vitamin B_6	milligrams (mg)	2.0
Folate	micrograms (µg)	400
Vitamin B_{12}	micrograms (µg)	6.0
Biotin	micrograms (µg)	300
Pantothenic acid	milligrams (mg)	10
Phosphorus	milligrams (mg)	1,000
Iodine	micrograms (µg)	150
Magnesium	milligrams (mg)	400
Zinc	milligrams (mg)	15
Selenium	micrograms (µg)	70
Copper	milligrams (mg)	2.0
Manganese	milligrams (mg)	2.0

SOURCE: National Institutes of Health. Dietary Supplement Label Database. "Daily Value." http://www.dsld.nlm.nih.gov/dsld/dailyvalue.jsp.

an alternative approach to maintaining your health, you may want to see a holistic nutrition professional. Holistic health care is an approach embraced by many alternative medical practices, which is centered on the patient's whole health picture, including mental, physical, and lifestyle, rather than on symptoms of a particular disease. Because there are few official standards for alternative nutritional practitioners, you may wish to question any counselor you see about his or her education and experience in the field. The National Association of Nutrition Professionals website (http://nanp.org) provides a list of reputable schools, as well as help in finding a qualified holistic nutritionist and information about accepted standards of practice.

Another type of nutritional therapy is nutritional medicine, also called orthomolecular medicine, in which natural substances such as

Reference Values for Nutrition Labeling for Infants, Children Less Than 4 Years of Age, and Pregnant and Lactating Women

Nutrient	Infants	Less than 4 Years	Pregnant and Lactating Women	Units of Measure
Vitamin A	1,500	2,500	8,000	International Unit (IU)
Vitamin C	35	40	60	milligrams (mg)
Calcium	600	800	1,300	milligrams (mg)
Iron	15	10	18	milligrams (mg)
Vitamin D	400	400	400	International Unit (IU)
Vitamin E	5	10	30	International Unit (IU)
Thiamin	0.5	0.7	1.7	milligrams (mg)
Riboflavin	0.6	0.8	2.0	milligrams (mg)
Niacin	8	9	20	milligrams (mg)
Vitamin B_6	0.4	0.7	2.5	milligrams (mg)
Folate	100	200	800	micrograms (µg)
Vitamin B_{12}	2	3	8	micrograms (µg)
Biotin	50	150	300	micrograms (µg)
Pantothenic acid	3	5	10	milligrams (mg)
Phosphorus	500	800	1,300	milligrams (mg)
Iodine	45	70	150	micrograms (µg)
Magnesium	70	200	450	milligrams (mg)
Zinc	5	8	15	milligrams (mg)
Copper	0.6	1.0	2.0	milligrams (mg)

SOURCE: National Institutes of Health. Dietary Supplement Label Database. "Daily Value." http://www.dsld.nlm.nih.gov/dsld/dailyvalue.jsp.

ILLUSTRATION BY LUMINA DATAMATICS LTD. © 2015 CENGAGE LEARNING.

vitamins, minerals, amino acids, trace elements, and fatty acids are used to control disease and restore balance to the body. Orthomolecular medicine was introduced during the mid-twentieth century by American chemist Linus Pauling. Pauling argued that each individual has genetically engineered body chemistry, and illness can be cured or prevented by reducing or increasing the amount of body chemicals. Orthomolecular treatments often recommend high dosages of specific vitamins and other nutritional substances. The most well-known example is taking large amounts of vitamin C to ward off a cold. A number of groups still advocate Pauling's methods, including the International Society for Orthomolecular Medicine (http://www.orthomed.org/isom/isom .html) and Orthomolecular Development (http://orthomolecular.org/). However, many medical doctors warn that high doses of nutritional substances can be dangerous. You should inform your doctor about any nutritional supplements you consider taking.

What Is Herbal Medicine?

Herbal medicine, also called botanical medicine, is an alternative approach to healing that uses materials made from the leaves, roots, flowers, and bark of plants to strengthen the immune system and heal the symptoms of disease. Herbal medicine has a long history of use by ancient doctors and traditional healers and is still in use around the world. Many pharmaceutical medications are based on herbal remedies, such as the pain reliever aspirin, the decongestant pseudoephedrine, and digitalis, often prescribed for heart problems. A number of alternative medical systems rely heavily on herbal remedies, including naturopathy, traditional Chinese medicine, and the Ayurvedic medical tradition of India.

Medicinal herbs may be dried or powdered for use in teas. They may also be formulated into capsules, tablets, or tinctures (drinkable liquids) for more convenient use. Popular herbal remedies include peppermint, used for digestive problems; St. John's wort, often suggested for mood disorders, such as depression; and garlic, which has antibiotic properties and may be used to combat colds and flu. Though herbal remedies are generally perceived as more natural and gentle than the chemical medicines prescribed by allopathic doctors, herbs may have strong effects and should be approached with care. In addition, some herbs may have damaging interactions with other medications. Be sure to tell your doctor before beginning any course of herbal treatment.

Where Can I Get Advice about Herbal Medicines?

If you would like expert counseling in using herbal remedies, you may want to see a practitioner knowledgeable in herbal medicine. Naturopaths are doctors, recognized in many states, whose practice is based on preventing and treating disease using natural methods, such as nutrition, lifestyle management, and herbal remedies, rather than the chemical drugs and surgery that form the basis of traditional medical treatment. Naturopaths frequently prescribe herbal supplements. They often recommend herbal and nutritional supplements to accompany other treatments, and naturopathic pharmacies develop special preparations, some of which are only available by prescription. The American Association of Naturopathic Physicians website (http://www.naturopathic.org/AF_MemberDirectory.asp?version=1) includes a directory to help you find a qualified naturopath in your area.

Traditional Chinese medicine is another health-care discipline that relies on the use of herbs. Chinese medicine practitioners frequently suggest the use of preparations of traditional Chinese herbs, such as ginseng, dong quai, and many others, which may be administered in tablet form or as dried plant mixtures that are made into teas. The Indian healing tradition called Ayurveda also employs specially prepared herbal compounds. Ayurvedic medicine frequently combines herbal and nutritional remedies by suggesting the use of healing herbs as food or seasonings. Professional organizations such as the National Certification Commission for Acupuncture and Oriental Medicine (http://www .nccaom.org/find-a-nccaom-certified-practitioner) and the National Ayurvedic Medical Association (http://www.ayurvedanama.org/search/ custom.asp?id=945) can help you find practitioners in your area.

You may also consult a professional herbalist who specializes in the medicinal use of plants. The American Herbalist Guild, founded in 1989 to support herbal medicine practitioners across the country and promote high standards of professionalism, offers a list of members on its website (http://www.americanherbalistsguild.com/member-profiles) that may help you find a qualified herbalist near you. Because there are no legal standards for herbalists, you may wish to ask any herbalist you consult about his or her education and experience in herbal medicine. Herbalists are not allowed by law to diagnose illness or tell you that certain herbs will cure a disease. They may only suggest herbs that are known to provide specific effects.

If you wish to explore the use of herbal medicines on your own, there are numerous books available for study. In addition, you may ask at your local herb store if an herbalist there can advise you. Be cautious about using herbs with which you are unfamiliar, and always tell your doctor before taking any supplements. Like chemical drugs, herbs can have unpleasant side effects and dangerous interactions with other medications you take. For example, St. John's wort, often suggested to help with depression, is a blood thinner and should not be taken by those on prescription blood-thinning drugs.

Chiropractic, Massage, and Other Manipulative and Body-Based Therapies

What Is Body-Based Therapy?

Body-based therapy is a health-care practice that uses touch and movement of body parts to promote healing. Body-based practices usually involve treating your bones, joints, and muscles, as well as improving the circulation of the blood and lymph. Similar to how the circulatory system moves blood throughout your body, the lymphatic system is a network of organs and vessels that moves lymph, a clear fluid that contains white blood cells. White blood cells are important in fighting disease and infection, and the lymphatic system is a vital part of the immune system, which works to protect your body from illness and toxins. Improving the flow of lymph through your body is an important function of many body-based therapies.

Body-based therapies are sometimes called manipulative therapies because they involve moving, or manipulating, parts of your body to relieve pain or realign its structures. Two major forms of body-based therapy are spinal manipulations and massage. Spinal manipulations are generally performed by trained and certified doctors, such as chiropractors and osteopaths, who use their hands and other equipment to manually push parts of your spine into correct position. Therapeutic massage should be performed by licensed massage therapists and involves pressing or rubbing your skin, muscles, and other soft tissues to help in healing various injuries and ailments.

Body-based therapies can also have a psychological aspect. Some licensed massage therapists, for example, combine psychotherapy with massage, based on the idea that therapeutic touch can help uncover and heal hidden memories and feelings. Movement therapies such as dance therapy and the Eastern exercise systems of yoga and qigong can help to relax and refresh both your mind and your body while increasing flexibility and improving strength and balance.

Dr. Andrew Taylor Still (1826–1917) is considered the father of osteopathic medicine. LIBRARY OF CONGRESS. PRINTS AND PHOTOGRAPHS COLLECTION. LC-USZ62-111668.

Although you will generally need to consult a specialist to receive body-based therapy, there are some that you can try on your own. You can perform some types of massage, such as acupressure and *reflexology*, on yourself, after you have been instructed in proper methods. Many movement therapies, such as the Feldenkrais method, which helps your reeducate your body for pain-free movement, can be performed at home once you have learned the basics.

Reflexology: *A type of bodywork that involves applying pressure to certain points, referred to as reflex points, on the foot.*

Daniel David Palmer: Chiropractic Pioneer

Generally credited as the founder of chiropractic medicine, Canadian Daniel David Palmer was born near Toronto, Ontario, in 1845. He developed an interest in anatomy at an early age, although his education was cut short by the need to help provide for his family after the failure of his father's business. In 1865 Palmer and his brother traveled to the United States to make their fortune. They worked their way west, eventually settling in Davenport, Iowa. There, Palmer established himself as a magnetic healer. He developed a following for his treatment of rheumatism (a disease that causes stiffness, pain, and swelling in muscles and joints) and other common ailments.

During the course of his work, Palmer became convinced that manipulating the spine could provide relief from ailments and improve overall health. The new method gained notoriety when it was said to have cured the deafness of one of Palmer's patients. With his reputation growing, Palmer founded the Palmer School of Chiropractic in Davenport. His methods were not without controversy, however. In 1906 he was sued for practicing without a license and subsequently spent several weeks in jail. He died from complications of typhoid fever in Los Angeles, California, in 1913. The school that he founded remains one of the nation's top institutions of chiropractic study.

 Some forms of body-based therapy may be covered by your health insurance. Check with your carrier for specific information and for practitioners who are in your network.

How Do I Know If Body-Based Therapy Is Right for Me?

Body-based therapies have proved helpful in dealing with a number of physical and psychological issues. If you have chronic, or ongoing, pain in your back, joints, or muscles, you may benefit from body-based therapy to soothe inflamed tissues and correct any misalignments. Body-based therapies may also prove helpful if you are injured in an accident. Chiropractic treatment and some forms of physical therapy have been proven valuable in treating whiplash, a common neck injury in automobile accidents. Various massage therapies may be useful in treating muscle and ligament damage, such as sprains, which are common in sports-related injuries.

Body therapies may also help in treating ailments of the internal organs, including circulation problems, which often display such symptoms as cold hands and feet, shortness of breath, or swelling in the legs and feet. Massage and other therapies have been effective in treating constipation and asthma, as well as helping ease the pain of childbirth.

There are a number of massage techniques, including rubbing, kneading, and pressure, to relax and manipulate the muscles and other tissues in order to relieve pain and promote circulation of blood and lymph.
© DEAN BERTONCELJ/ SHUTTERSTOCK.COM.

Always consult your medical doctor first about any symptoms and get his or her approval before trying body-based therapy.

Stress is a major factor in a number of mental and physical ailments, including depression, anxiety, heart disease, high blood pressure, headaches, insomnia, and skin problems. If you regularly experience high levels of stress, you may find body-based therapy an effective way to address tension and maintain your health. Massage and movement therapies in particular may be helpful in teaching you relaxation techniques.

What Is Chiropractic Medicine?

Chiropractic medicine is an alternative health-care discipline that largely concentrates on the spine and the muscles and nerves connected to it. Chiropractic treatment is based on the theory that your body is an intricately interwoven network of systems and that balance among all these systems is necessary for good health. Since the nerves centered in your spine affect every organ and muscle in your body, chiropractors view proper alignment of your spine as central to the proper functioning of all your body's other structures. Chiropractors generally use touch to align the parts of the spine, believing that the bones, muscles, and nerves can be placed back into position without the need for invasive surgery.

Chiropractors take a holistic approach to healing, so they examine your mental and physical health as a whole rather than focusing on the symptoms of a particular disease or injury. Therefore, chiropractors are likely to perform a thorough diagnostic exam and recommend a prolonged series of treatments to correct persistent spinal misalignments. The education chiropractors receive is similar to that of medical doctors. In addition to a number of mandatory undergraduate courses, a doctor of chiropractic (DC) must complete four to five years of academic and clinical training at an accredited chiropractic college. After passing a strict written examination and a hands-on physical therapy examination, DCs may choose to do postgraduate work in a specialty field, such as sports medicine, pain management, or nutrition. The American Chiropractic Association website (http://www.acatoday.org/search/memsearch/) features a directory of accredited practitioners to help you find a chiropractor in your area.

Other practitioners who may employ spinal manipulation as part of their treatment are osteopaths and physical therapists. Doctors of osteopathy (DOs) are licensed in an alternative holistic school of medicine that is largely centered on the bones and muscles. Physical therapists are health professionals who use various techniques and exercises to help patients recover mobility and heal damage due to injury, surgery, or disease. The American Osteopathic Association website (http://www.osteopathic.org/osteopathic-health/Pages/find-a-do-search.aspx) and the American Physical Therapy Association website (http://www.apta.org/apta/findapt/index.aspx?navID=10737422525) both provide tools for finding practitioners near you.

What Should I Expect When I Visit a Chiropractor?

Before your first appointment with a chiropractor, you will probably be given a questionnaire to fill out regarding your medical history and the details of the injury or condition. This may include questions about your family's health history, as well as about any preexisting conditions you may have. In addition, you may be asked for a detailed description of any pain or discomfort you are experiencing, using questions such as "How much pain are you in on a scale of one to ten?" "Where is the pain located?" and "Is it a sharp or dull pain?"

Most chiropractors will want to begin your examination with a full set of X-rays to have the most complete picture possible of the state of your skeletal system. These can usually be taken in the doctor's office. If your injuries are extensive, your DC may request more thorough diagnostic tests, such as a magnetic resonance imaging (MRI) test, which produces an image of your body's soft tissue. These tests are complex and expensive and will probably require a visit to a special imaging center. If you have X-rays or other results from previous tests, bringing them with you may speed your treatment and reduce costs.

Because chiropractic is a holistic discipline, your DC is also likely to ask a number of questions about your overall lifestyle habits in order to gain a general picture of your health. Your chiropractor will also give you a physical exam, recording your vital signs such as pulse, blood pressure, respiration, and reflexes. In addition, he or she may analyze your posture, examine your walk and other movements, and administer tests to evaluate the flexibility of your spine.

Once the examination is complete, your practitioner will suggest a course of treatment. This will usually involve a series of physical manipulations, often called adjustments, to relieve pressure on nerves and muscles and to align the spine. You will probably remain dressed during adjustments, but you should wear loose clothing to allow ease of movement. Some chiropractors use handheld machines or have their patients lie on special tables to aid in the manipulation process. Adjustments may be administered during your first appointment, and your doctor will probably suggest a schedule of follow-up appointments to continue the process of adjusting your spine. He or she may also suggest exercises and dietary changes to support your healing process.

What Is Massage Therapy?

Therapeutic massage involves manual treatment of the muscles, ligaments, and other tissues that surround and support the bones and organs. Licensed massage therapists (LMTs) use a number of techniques, such as rubbing, kneading, and pressure, to relax and manipulate the muscles and other tissues in order to relieve pain and promote circulation of blood and lymph. Most massage is done with the hands, although elbows, forearms, specially designed implements, and even ice cubes may be used for certain effects.

There are many different types of massage. Some, such as Swedish massage, are chiefly geared toward relaxation, while others, such as Rolfing, aim to realign the entire body structure and can be quite deep and painful. Some massage systems have specific therapeutic goals, such as lymph drainage therapy, myofascial release (which works to relax connective tissue), and neuromuscular therapy (which focuses on the connections between muscles and nerves). Other systems employ elements of alternative medical traditions such as shiatsu and acupressure, which are based on Chinese and Japanese concepts of energy pathways in the body. Reflexology, developed in the early twentieth century, is rooted in the idea that massaging certain points on the hands, feet, and ears will have a positive effect on corresponding organs, joints, and tissues throughout the body. Medical massage is prescribed by doctors for those with certain conditions, while sports massage is specifically designed to help athletes prevent and manage injuries.

Most states require that LMTs receive specific training at an accredited massage school and pass strict written and practical tests in order to practice. The American Massage Therapy Association website (http://www.amtamassage.org/regulation/stateRegulations.html) provides a state-by-state list of regulations. Be sure to ask about the credentials and education of any massage therapist you consider seeing.

What Should I Expect When I Visit a Licensed Massage Therapist?

Though exact procedures may vary with the specific type of massage, you may generally make a massage appointment for 30 minutes, one hour, or an hour and a half. Most massage therapists begin with a brief interview in which they ask about your medical history and the specific complaint for which you are seeking relief. They may also explain their massage technique and invite you to tell them if you experience discomfort during the massage or if you would like a lighter or firmer touch at any time.

Massage usually takes place in a private room, which may have subdued lighting and calming music. Most therapists use a padded massage table with a cut-out area for your face. A thick sheet will be provided to cover your body. After talking with you, the LMT will leave the room to allow you to undress in private. Generally, people receiving massage are unclothed, but you may leave on some pieces of clothing if you are more comfortable doing so. The LMT will ensure that all parts of your body not being worked on are covered.

During the massage, make sure to follow your LMT's suggestion that you give feedback, and be especially careful to report any discomfort you may feel. Your therapist will usually have a variety of pillows and other articles to place under knees or ankles to reduce strain. Taking deep breaths can help you relax when tender areas are massaged. When your massage is over, you may want to take a few minutes to relax and then rise slowly. Most LMTs suggest drinking plenty of water following a massage to continue the bodily cleansing begun by the therapy.

Magnetic, Reiki, and Other Energy Therapies

What Is Energy Therapy?

Energy therapy is a broad term that includes a number of healing systems based on the idea that your health is influenced by energy fields both within the body and outside of it. Practitioners of energy therapies often describe a connection between the biofield, which consists of the electrical and magnetic forces in the body, and the physical energies that drive the natural world, such as the motion of the planets. Energy therapy frequently has a spiritual component, as the energy in the body is viewed as a vital spiritual force that connects the individual to the larger universe. In traditional Chinese medicine, this internal force is called chi or qi; in Japanese healing it is ki; and in Ayurveda, the traditional medical practice of India, it is called prana.

Even science-based medical doctors have long understood that electromagnetic forces in the body drive important functions such as nerve response and heartbeat. However, medical solutions to disruptions in bodily energy systems are generally quite different from those of energy-based practitioners, and they may involve medications or surgery.

Energy therapies fall into the category of complementary and alternative medicine (CAM). CAM includes a number of health-care practices that are not part of mainstream medical care, but that many people have found useful and effective. Most energy therapy practices work to balance the energy fields in the body and release blockages to allow the uninterrupted flow of energy. Some energy therapies, such as acupuncture, are ancient healing arts that have been practiced for thousands of years, while others, such as

These chakras—crowh, third eye, throat, heart, solar plexus, sacrum, root—are used in many Western systems of Reiki.
© UMNOLA/SHUTTERSTOCK .COM.

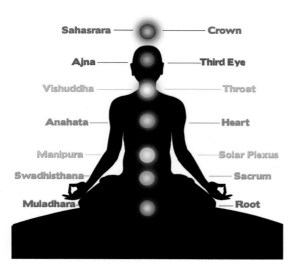

Sahasrara — Crown
Ajna — Third Eye
Vishuddha — Throat
Anahata — Heart
Manipura — Solar Plexus
Swadhisthana — Sacrum
Muladhara — Root

Physiological Reactions to Positive and Negative Magnetic Fields

Positive (stressful)	Negative (anti-stressful)
• Increased acid production	• Normalized pH
• Depleted oxygen production	• Inhibited growth of microorganisms
• Cellular edema (water retention)	• Negates free radicals
• Insomnia, restlessness, wakefulness	• Relaxation, rest, sleep
• Increased free radicals	• Increased oxygen production

ILLUSTRATION BY COREY LIGHT. © CENGAGE LEARNING, GALE.

transcutaneous electrical nerve stimulation, rely on modern technology. Although energy therapies have often been viewed as quackery or "magical thinking," many have remained popular, and some have gained acceptance as valid alternatives or accompaniments to traditional medical science.

What Is Acupuncture?

Acupuncture is a practice of traditional Chinese medicine in which very fine needles are inserted at various points in the body to relieve pain and combat illness. Developed in China between 2,000 and 4,000 years ago, acupuncture is based on the theory that energy, or chi, flows through the body in pathways called meridians and that illness results when these energy pathways are blocked. An acupuncturist works to relieve these blockages by placing needles at specified "acupuncture points" along the energy meridians.

Though once viewed in the West as outlandish and improbable, acupuncture has been tested by scientific methods and has proved to be effective in reducing pain and improving certain conditions such as insomnia and depression. According to Western medical researchers, acupuncture is effective because it stimulates nerves, muscles, and tissues, thereby increasing blood flow and sparking the release of pain-reducing brain chemicals. Increased acceptance in the West has resulted in acupuncture courses being offered by several prominent medical colleges. Additionally, acupuncture treatments are now being covered by some insurance companies.

Naturopathy: *A kind of alternative medicine that focuses on the body's inherent healing powers and works with those powers to restore and maintain overall health.*

A number of practitioners, including Chinese medicine practitioners, *naturopaths*, and some medical doctors, offer acupuncture treatments as part of their practice. Furthermore, there are a number of community clinics that offer acupuncture at reduced rates for low-income patients. For help in finding a qualified acupuncture professional, you may consult the website of the National Certification Commission for Acupuncture and Oriental Medicine (http://www .nccaom.org/find-a-nccaom-certified-practitioner).

What Can I Expect during an Acupuncture Appointment?

Acupuncture is a holistic approach to health care, which means that its practitioners tend to examine a patient's health and lifestyle habits as a whole rather than focusing solely on the symptoms of a particular disease. Therefore, your first acupuncture appointment may last an hour or more to give your practitioner time to ask you detailed questions about your habits, current health, medical history, and goals for treatment. After this interview, you will be given a physical exam, during which your practitioner may touch or press various parts of your body, examine your tongue, and take your pulse.

To prepare for an acupuncture treatment, dress in loose clothing to give your acupuncturist access to your arms and legs. You may also be asked to change into a gown at the appointment. When it is time for the actual treatment, you will be asked to lie down on a table, and the practitioner will insert very thin sterilized needles into your body. The acupuncturist may turn or move the needles or apply a slight electric current through them. Typically these needles do not cause pain, and you may not even feel them, though you might experience a slight burning sensation or an ache. It is not uncommon to experience a feeling of relaxation during the treatment. However, if you do feel any discomfort, be sure to tell your practitioner.

Your acupuncturist is likely to suggest several follow-up visits, which will be shorter, as they will usually involve only an examination and treatment. In addition, your practitioner may suggest changes to your diet, exercise, sleep patterns, and other health habits. Many acupuncturists tell clients to expect results after 3 to 12 treatments. If you do not feel results after 12 treatments, acupuncture may not be the best option for you.

What Is Transcutaneous Electrical Nerve Stimulation?

Transcutaneous electrical nerve stimulation (TENS) is an alternative treatment that uses pulses of very low voltage electricity to relieve muscle and joint pain. The treatment is administered by means of a small, battery-powered device that delivers electrical impulses through wires that are attached to the skin with adhesive patches. Many doctors and physical therapists use TENS to help their patients deal with chronic, or ongoing, pain without using pain-relieving medications. TENS has also proved valuable in treating pain following surgery, pain resulting from cancer, and pain related to labor and childbirth.

Despite the fact that it is unclear exactly why it works, TENS has been more widely accepted by the medical mainstream than other forms of energy therapy. Some researchers theorize that the electrical impulses create heat that allows deep muscles to relax, while others have suggested that TENS blocks the body's electrical nerve signals, thus reducing the feeling of pain. Still others believe that the electric current delivered by the TENS device stimulates the brain to release pain-reducing chemicals.

TENS is usually first administered in a doctor's or physical thera-pist's office. Once you have learned to operate the machine and place the electrodes properly on your body, you may be allowed to borrow or rent a device for home use. TENS devices are also available for purchase, although in some states a doctor's prescription is required. If you have long-term pain that has not responded to other treatments, you may want to ask your health-care practitioner about trying TENS. However, even if you live in a state where a doctor's prescription is not required, you should be sure to tell your doctor before beginning treatment. TENS may not be appropriate for some patients, such as those who have electronic pacemakers to help control their abnormal heart rhythms.

What Is Reiki?

Reiki is a Japanese healing practice that involves moving the vital force, or ki, through the body by the placement of hands on or near various body parts with the goal of relieving pain, reducing stress, and promot-ing healing. Introduced during the 1920s by Japanese religious scholar Mikao Usui, Reiki is now practiced around the world. One of the most mystical of the energy therapies, Reiki has deeply spiritual foundations. Its techniques are not taught in the usual sense but are transmitted to students by a Reiki master in an initiation ritual called an "attunement."

Though supporters of Reiki make strong claims about its effectiveness in treating a wide range of conditions, many mainstream health-care work-ers are skeptical of it, arguing that there is little proof that it works. How-ever, some reputable medical institutions, such as Johns Hopkins Medicine, consider Reiki to have sufficient value to place the practice among its suggested alternative treatments on its website (http://www.hopkinsmedicine.org/integrative_medicine_digestive_center/services/reiki.html).

Reiki treatments are generally noninvasive and harmless. During a treatment you remain clothed and sit or lie in a relaxed position while a Reiki master places his or her hands on or above your body in various positions. Reiki is not intended to replace regular medical care but to supplement it and aid in relaxation and healing. Because there are no legal licensing standards for Reiki practitioners, it may be difficult to find a qualified professional. However, the website of the International Center for Reiki Training (http://www.reikimembership.com/MembershipListing.aspx) offers a directory to help you find a trained Reiki master in your area.

There are a number of energy therapies similar to Reiki. These include Healing Touch (HT) and Therapeutic Touch (TT). HT is a holistic practice that combines several energy therapy techniques to promote circulation and reduce pain. HT practitioners are trained and certified through Healing Touch International (HTI), and HT is endorsed by a number of holistic health-care professionals and by the National Hospice and Palliative Care Organization. The HTI website (http://www.healingtouchinternational.org/) includes a tool for finding practitioners in your area.

TT is a healing system developed in the 1980s by a registered nurse and a psychic healer. With its roots in psychic healing, TT is less widely accepted by the mainstream medical establishment. TT practitioners may earn credentials through the Therapeutic Touch International Association. Its website (http://therapeutic-touch.org/about-us/qualified-practitioner/) provides a directory of qualified TT professionals.

What Is Magnetic Therapy?

Magnetic therapy is a form of energy healing in which magnets of various strengths are applied to or worn on the body to reduce pain and promote the healing of a variety of physical and mental ailments. Magnets were used for healing in ancient China and Japan and became popular in Europe during the Middle Ages. Their use was revived during the 1970s, and since that time the sale of therapeutic magnets has grown into a profitable industry.

Supporters of magnetic therapy have claimed that magnets promote health by stimulating the body's electromagnetic field and increasing the flow of vital substances such as blood, which is high in iron, a mineral attracted to magnets. Critics of the therapy argue that scientific research has failed to prove that magnets have healing effects. However, some medical institutions, such as New York University's Langone Medical Center, have found some value in the therapeutic use of magnets. In studies cited on the center's website (http://www.med.nyu.edu/content?ChunkIID=33778), magnets were found to be useful in reducing the pain of rheumatoid arthritis and post-polio syndrome, whose symptoms include muscle weakness, fatigue, and muscle and joint pain.

Many websites, such as Alternatives for Healing (http://www.alternativesforhealing.com/cgi_bin/practitioner-magnetic-therapy.php), can help you find a magnetic therapy practitioner in your area. However, you should be aware that the U.S. Food and Drug Administration prohibits manufacturers of magnets from making health claims about their products. In addition, magnets may interfere with internal medical equipment, such as pacemakers and implantable cardioverter defibrillators, with life-threatening effects. Be sure to tell your doctor about any alternative health care you may be considering.

For More Information

BOOKS

Beckett, Don. *Reiki: The True Story: An Exploration of Usui Reiki.* Berkeley: Frog Books, 2009.

Burke, Brad. *Living the Chiropractic Way: The Complete Lifetime Wellness Guidebook.* Indianapolis: Dog Ear, 2005.

Frank, Hoffmann Frank, and Martin J. Manning. *Herbal Medicine and Botanical Medical Fads.* New York: Routledge, 2002.

Huddleston, Peggy. *Prepare for Surgery, Heal Faster: A Guide of Mind-Body Techniques.* Thornton, CO: Angel River Press, 2013.

Pole, Sebastian. *Ayurvedic Medicine: The Principles of Traditional Practice.* Philadelphia: Singing Dragon, 2013.

Schmukler, Alan V. *Homeopathy: An A to Z Handbook.* Woodbury, MN: Llewellyn, 2006.

Van der Kolk, Bessel. *The Body Keeps the Score: Brain, Mind, and Body in the Healing of Trauma.* New York: Viking, 2014.

PERIODICALS

Berkowsky, Bruce. "Traditional Naturopathy: Living in Harmony with the Rhythms of the Natural Universe." *Total Health* 27, no. 2 (2005): 41–2.

Challem, Jack. "Natural Health Pioneers: These Visionaries Changed the Way We Think about Nutrition and Sparked a Wellness Revolution." *Better Nutrition.* 74, no. 7 (2012): 36.

Donaldson, Angela. "Good Vibrations: Three Therapies to Restore Balance and Trigger the Body's Natural Healing Mechanisms." *Good Health*, September 1, 2010.

Leeder, Jessica. "Alternative Health: When Conventional Medicine Isn't Cutting It, Some Parents Turn to Complementary Therapies Like Chiropractics, Craniosacral Massage, Acupuncture and Osteopathy. Are These Methods a Safe Solution for Your Family?" *Today's Parent*, November 2013: 41.

Morrison, Victoria. "Yoga Benefits the Body and Mind." *Occupational Health* 65, no. 6 (2013): 27–9.

O'Connor, Anahad. "Acupuncture Provides True Pain Relief in Study." *New York Times*, September 11, 2012. This article can also be found online at http://well.blogs.nytimes.com/2012/09/11/acupuncture-provides-true-pain-relief-in-study/?_php=true&_type=blogs&_r=0.

WEBSITES

"All About Massage Therapy." *Massage Today*. http://www.massagetoday.com/aboutmt (accessed October 27, 2014).

"The Feldenkrais Method of Somatic Education." *The Feldenkrais Guild of North America*. http://www.feldenkrais.com/method/the_feldenkrais_method_of_somatic_education/ (accessed October 27, 2014).

"Herbal Medicine." *University of Chicago Medicine*. http://www.uchospitals.edu/online-library/content=P00181 (accessed October 23, 2014).

"The History of Naturopathic Medicine." *Bastyr Center for Natural Health*. http://www.bastyrcenter.org/content/view/114/ (accessed October 17, 2014).

"Magnet Therapy." *NYU Langone Medical Center*. http://www.med.nyu.edu/content?ChunkIID=33778 (accessed October 28, 2014).

"Mind-Body Medicine." *University of Maryland Medical Center*. http://umm.edu/health/medical/altmed/treatment/mindbody-medicine (accessed October 21, 2014).

"Traditional Chinese Medicine: An Introduction." *National Institutes for Health: National Center for Alternative or Complementary Medicine*. http://nccam.nih.gov/health/whatiscam/chinesemed.htm (accessed October 20, 2014).

Wanjek, Christopher. "What Is Acupuncture?" *Live Science*, May 9, 2013. http://www.livescience.com/29494-acupuncture.html (accessed October 28, 2014).

Health-Care System

Overview: Health-Care System

What Is a Health-Care System?

A health-care system is a program by which physical or mental care is made available to a specific population. Services can be funded and regulated by private companies, the government, or a combination of both. Health-care systems generally provide services for individuals and families by physicians, hospitals, clinics, and other medical personnel or institutions. Health-care systems also oversee the safety and regulation of pharmaceuticals (medicinal drugs), the research and treatment of medical conditions, and the management and distribution of health information.

The United States has a multi-payer health-care system, meaning there are both private and public health insurers that either work independently or collaboratively. Private health insurance companies and federal, state, and local governments can help individuals and families pay for health care and also regulate, for example, cost control, quality of care, and access to care.

Despite major changes that increased governmental involvement in health care in the early twenty-first century, a majority of Americans still receive their medical coverage through the private sector. According to a 2013 World Health Organization (WHO) report, over one-sixth of the U.S. population did not have health insurance. The report predicted that the number of people without insurance would be cut in half when the key parts of 2010's Affordable Health Care Act, officially known as the Patient Protection and Affordable Care Act, were enacted.

How Did the U.S. Health-Care System Begin?

Medical practitioners competed to provide health care in the nineteenth century, but the quality of care was generally subpar. There was little if any oversight, poor training, and almost no regulation. Hospitals were

Disability insurance:
An insurance plan that replaces a portion of a person's income when he or she cannot work because of an accident or illness.

for people living in poverty who had no other options, whereas people with financial means received medical care at home. In the late nineteenth and early twentieth centuries, health care underwent a change, starting with improved training for physicians. In addition, hospitals became nonprofit organizations where resources were pooled so that physicians could have access to modern medical equipment and techniques.

As industrialization increased during this period, workers in highly dangerous jobs, such as miners and railroad workers, were given access to company doctors and clinics or infirmaries that were provided by unions. Businesses felt it was in their best financial interest to keep their workers healthy.

In 1910 American retailer Montgomery Ward offered one of the first employee group health insurance policies. The plan basically was *disability insurance* and did not cover medical care or hospitalization. The first union to offer medical services was the International Ladies Garment Workers Union (ILGWU) in 1914. In the first half of the twentieth century, there was some movement for the government to provide health care for all citizens. However, opposition from various stakeholders quashed this idea. Businesses were against it because of its potential costs, doctors were concerned there would be too much cost control, and some politicians thought it mimicked German socialism too closely. President Franklin D. Roosevelt was unsuccessful in his attempt to include required health care into the Social Security Act of 1935.

What Is Health Insurance?

Health insurance is a way for groups of people to share financial risk. Private health insurance is a system that allows you to receive medical coverage in exchange for regular payments, called premiums. The insurance company compensates you for part or all of the medical costs that might be incurred. Health insurance may also be acquired through a government-sponsored plan. Health insurance is important for general medical bills and is particularly vital if you are in an accident or have a serious illness that can lead to astronomical medical costs.

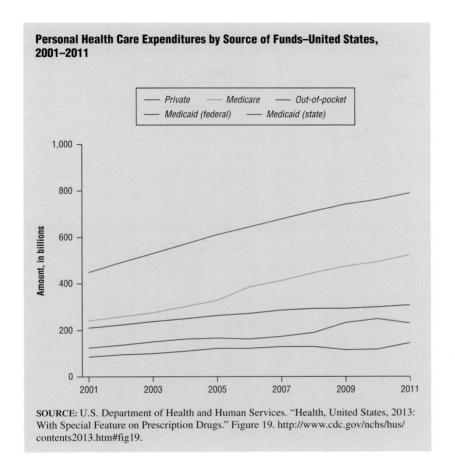

Personal Health Care Expenditures by Source of Funds–United States, 2001–2011

— Private — Medicare — Out-of-pocket
— Medicaid (federal) — Medicaid (state)

SOURCE: U.S. Department of Health and Human Services. "Health, United States, 2013: With Special Feature on Prescription Drugs." Figure 19. http://www.cdc.gov/nchs/hus/contents2013.htm#fig19.

ILLUSTRATION BY LUMINA DATAMATICS LTD. © 2015 CENGAGE LEARNING.

Premiums for private health insurance in the United States are often paid for in part or full as a benefit of employment or through membership in a union. The type and amount of health-care coverage you receive and the required financial contributions of you and your employer vary widely. If you have health insurance through your workplace or union, you, your employer, or your union pay toward a regular premium, which is then pooled and used to pay for individual or family medical expenses. Employers sometimes use top-notch health insurance programs to attract or retain employees. You can also purchase health insurance from a private company. The Affordable Care Act instituted a policy by which you can buy health insurance through state-regulated insurance exchanges (marketplaces).

Government health-care plans can include those funded by federal, state, or local governments and are generally aimed at particular groups of people. Programs can include large groups, such as Medicare (generally for people who are 65 and older) and Medicaid (for people with low incomes). There are also programs that target populations that have specific issues or are part of a particular demographic, such as the Veterans Health Administration/Military Health System (TRICARE), the Indian Health Service (IHS), the Program of All-Inclusive Care for the Elderly (PACE), and the Children's Health Insurance Program (CHIP). Some states have their own programs to help provide health insurance for people living with low incomes, such as the Oregon Health Plan and the Massachusetts Health Safety Net.

How Did Private Health Insurance Develop?

The first private health insurance company in the United States was Blue Cross, a *nonprofit* organization established in 1929. It began as insurance for hospital care and then extended to physician care. Those with the insurance were free to choose the hospital or physician they preferred.

Nonprofit: *An organization that has no shareholders, does not distribute profits, and is without federal and state tax liabilities. Also called Not for profit.*

During World War II (1939–45), the many Americans serving overseas created a shortage of workers at home. Additionally, the National War Labor Board froze wages because of the strained economy. Employers needed something other than high wages to attract workers, so they began offering health plans. Health coverage was doubly enticing because the government had ruled that health insurance was not considered taxable income. Unions not only supported these plans or offered their own plans, but they also began to negotiate for health insurance as part of employee contracts.

For-profit private health insurance took root after World War II. For-profit insurance companies used an "experience rating," whereby they charged different prices to groups of businesses based on their medical histories. For example, businesses with lower past medical costs were charged less money. Nonprofits such as Blue Cross, in contrast, used a "community rating," which meant insurance costs were the same for every group. Experience rating made for-profits more competitive in the marketplace, and eventually nonprofits also started to use this system to set insurance fees.

The number of people with private health insurance grew exponentially following World War II. In 1940 about 12 million people, or less than 10 percent of the U.S. population, had health insurance. By the next decade 75 million people, or half the population, were covered. In 2000 the percentage of people with health insurance peaked at 69.3 percent of the non-elderly population having employer-sponsored health plans, according to a 2012 survey by the Employee Benefit Research Institute. The percentage of people with health insurance started to decrease in the early twenty-first century, and by 2011 only 58.4 percent had employer-sponsored plans, primarily due to high unemployment and escalating insurance costs.

How Did Federally Sponsored Government Health Plans Develop in the Twentieth Century?

In the twentieth century government plans were created to assist, for example, those who were unemployed, had low incomes, had jobs without health benefits, or were retired. These programs became especially important as health insurance prices rose and purchasing plans without the benefit of employer-based pools became cost prohibitive.

In the 1950s and early 1960s, a number of charitable governmental health programs existed for people living in poverty. Federal and state governments would sometimes collaborate to help with medical costs for citizens on public assistance. With the 1960 Kerr-Mills Act, the federal government contributed to states to help seniors who were not on public assistance but were no longer covered by employer health insurance plans.

In 1962 President John F. Kennedy advocated for a program called Medical Care for the Aged, designed to help provide hospital insurance for senior citizens. He was unable to pass the legislation and was even accused of trying to socialize medicine. After Kennedy's assassination, President Lyndon B. Johnson continued to advocate for government-sponsored health plans. In 1965 the first major federal health insurance programs were enacted: Medicare and Medicaid. From the 1970s until the end of the millennium, many plans to provide different types of health insurance were introduced by the government, and most met with little success.

In 1971 Senator Edward Kennedy introduced a single-payer health plan by which the government would be the sole provider of health care for everyone. Many countries, such as the United Kingdom and Canada, use similar systems. President Richard Nixon, however, wanted a health-care plan that required private employers to provide coverage for workers and by which private insurance companies could not deny coverage for preexisting health conditions (such as a heart problem).

A successful compromise between the ideas of Kennedy and Nixon seemed possible, but other political issues intervened. Nixon was forced to resign as president in 1974, and his successor, Gerald Ford, did not work toward a national health plan. With an economic recession in the late 1970s, health care was again put on the back burner. In the early 1990s President Bill Clinton introduced an initiative that would require everyone to enroll in a health plan either through an employer or a state-based health insurance cooperatives, but it failed to pass through Congress.

How Did Public and Private Health Providers Respond to Health-Care Needs in the Late Twentieth Century?

Even though a nationalized system was not created before the end of the millennium, other governmental bills were enacted, and insurance companies created, changed, and expanded types of health-care plans. The HMO Act of 1973 was enacted as more employers offered health maintenance organization (HMO) options. In an HMO, the employee picks a physician from a limited list within a "network." The chosen physician provides all basic health care for the patient. Generally, the physician must refer the patient to a specialist in the network if additional care is required. Ideally, HMOs were supposed to provide better health care at lower costs. The HMO Act gave grants to help employers offer HMOs or expand existing HMOs and required employers with more than 25 employees to offer HMOs as an option. By the mid-1990s, approximately 50 million citizens were using HMOs.

Despite the advantages of HMOs, there were also problems. Many patients wanted more choices regarding health-care providers, yet insurance companies wanted to maintain restrictions in order to save money. In response, insurance companies began to offer preferred provider organizations (PPOs), managed health-care plans by which a patient could use a specified network of contracted health-care providers, clinics, and hospitals for free or at a reduced rate, provided the patient did not go outside the network. Some critics believed the lessening of restrictions on coverage was a primary reason for the escalating costs associated with health care.

Governmental agencies and various health organizations, such as the American Hospital Association, began to create a patient's bill of rights to help guarantee, for example, fair medical treatment and patient autonomy in making medical decisions. And in 1998 the President's Advisory Commission on Consumer Protection and Quality in the Health Care Industry adopted the Consumer Bill of Rights and Responsibilities. The majority of these bills were not legally binding.

In 1985 Congress passed the Consolidated Omnibus Budget Reconciliation Act (COBRA), which gave workers and their families the opportunity to retain their group health plans for specified amounts of time if they encountered circumstances such as job loss, reduction of work hours, divorce, or other major obstacles.

What Major Changes Occurred in Health Care in the Early Twenty-First Century?

According to a 2013 review by the WHO, the United States spent more per person on health care than all other countries—a staggering 53 percent more than the second-highest country, Norway. Furthermore, one in six Americans were uninsured and only 30 percent were covered by publicly financed health care, primarily Medicaid and Medicare. The rapidly rising costs of health care coupled with high unemployment and a recession in the early twenty-first century helped to bring about major changes in health-care policies.

In 2003 President George W. Bush signed into law the Medicare Prescription Drug, Improvement and Modernization Act. Its main benefit, which took effect in 2006 and was called Medicare Part D, provided prescription drug subsidies to Americans 65 and older. While some lauded the bill, others believed it had been too influenced by industry lobbyists and was only minimally helpful. A coverage gap, known as "the donut hole," was a central controversy. At a certain financial point, people had to pay the full cost of medication and continue paying premiums. In 2014, for example, if your drug costs were more than $2,850, you entered the donut hole and had to pay full price for prescriptions until your total costs were $4,550. The Affordable Care Act addressed this problem. Senior citizens would garner increased savings each year for prescription drugs, and the donut hole was scheduled to be completely eliminated in 2020.

The Affordable Care Act was enacted under President Barack Obama in 2010. It was the most comprehensive change to health care since the inception of Medicare and Medicaid. The act was more than 900 pages long with numerous provisions containing different rollout times. The bill went through a number of versions before gaining approval by Congress. Controversial measures included coverage of abortion procedures, new or increased taxes, and whether small businesses would be exempted from providing health care. The bill significantly shifted the health-care system toward greater governmental control.

The main goal of the Affordable Care Act was to expand access to health insurance, but it also had provisions to stress prevention and wellness; increase funding for primary care and public health; and improve quality of care, system performance, and consumer protections. There were dozens of congressional attempts to repeal the bill, and some of its provisions were brought before the U.S. Supreme Court. In 2012, for example, the Supreme Court ruled that the requirement for everyone to have health care or face a penalty was a tax and not a mandate and was, therefore, constitutional. However, the Supreme Court also ruled that states could opt out of the requirement to expand Medicaid.

For More Information

BOOKS

Askin, Elisabeth, and Nathan Moore. *The Health Care Handbook: A Clear and Concise Guide to the United States Health Care System*. St. Louis: Washington University Press, 2014.

Brill, Steven. *America's Bitter Pill: Money, Politics, Backroom Deals, and the Fight to Fix Our Broken Healthcare System*. New York: Random House, 2015.

Hoffman, Beatrix Rebecca. *Health Care for Some: Rights and Rationing in the United States since 1930*. Chicago: University of Chicago Press, 2013.

Sultz, Harry A. *Health Care, USA: Understanding Its Organization and Delivery*. Burlington, MA: Jones & Bartlett Learning, 2014.

WEBSITES

"Costs in the Coverage Gap." *Centers for Medicare & Medicaid Service*. http://www.medicare.gov/part-d/costs/coverage-gap/part-d-coverage-gap.html (accessed January 17, 2015).

"CPS Health Insurance Definitions." *United States Census Bureau.* https://www
.census.gov/hhes/www/hlthins/methodology/definitions/cps.html (accessed
January 17, 2015).

Dickerson, John. "Kennedycare: Fifty Years before Obamacare, JFK Had His
Own Health Care Debacle." *Slate.com.* http://www.slate.com/articles/news_
and_politics/history/2013/11/john_f_kennedy_s_health_care_failure_jfk_
and_barack_obama_s_tough_fights.2.html (accessed January 16, 2015).

"Focus on Health Reform: A Guide to the Supreme Court's Decision on the
ACA's Medicaid Expansion." *Henry J. Kaiser Foundation.* http://kaiserfami
lyfoundation.files.wordpress.com/2013/01/8347.pdf (accessed January 17,
2015).

"Health Plans & Benefits." *United States Department of Labor.* http://www.dol
.gov/dol/topic/health-plans/ (accessed January 17, 2015).

Mears, Bill, and Tom Cohen. "Emotions High after Supreme Court Upholds
Health Care Law." *CNN.com.* http://www.cnn.com/2012/06/28/politics/
supreme-court-health-ruling/index.html (accessed January 17, 2015).

Rice, Thomas; Pauline Rosenau; Lynn Y. Unruh; and Andrew J. Barnes.
"United States of America Health System Review." *World Health Orga-
nization.* http://www.euro.who.int/__data/assets/pdf_file/0019/215155/
HiT-United-States-of-America.pdf (accessed January 17, 2015).

U.S. Government Health Programs

What Is the Affordable Care Act?

The Patient Protection and Affordable Care Act (PPACA), commonly known as the Affordable Care Act (ACA) or "Obamacare," is a piece of legislation signed into law by President Barack Obama in 2010 that is meant to reform the American health-care system. The act is designed to curb the growth of health-care spending in the United States, while at the same time providing a greater number of Americans with reasonably priced medical care.

One of the central goals of the Affordable Care Act is to expand insurance coverage to allow all Americans to receive health care. The act aims to lessen the power of insurance companies and to provide consumers with more choices for health-care plans and medical providers. It is not a static set of laws. Rather, it is designed to provide health-care professionals with tools to make important changes in the way Americans are provided medical services.

Healthcare.gov is the portal to the government marketplace for the Affordable Care Act.
© TXKING/SHUTTERSTOCK. COM.

How Did the Affordable Care Act Come About?

The idea of a nationwide insurance system was not new when plans for the ACA were developed soon after Obama took office in 2009. For decades, lawmakers, largely Democrats, had sought some type of medical coverage for all Americans. When Obama was running for his first term as president, part of his campaign focused on overhauling the health-care system. Millions of Americans were either not covered by insurance at all or were receiving substandard medical services. Furthermore, medical costs in the United States were soaring.

In his first year in office, Obama, along with Democrats in the U.S. House of Representatives, introduced a plan to make major changes to a health-care-system that they viewed as broken. Drawing on the words of the late senator Ted Kennedy, Obama argued that reforming the health-care system was a moral issue. Leaving millions of Americans with no health insurance or care that was substandard, he argued, was a type of social injustice. Despite almost complete opposition from the Republican Party, the bill narrowly passed both the House and Senate. Obama signed the ACA into law in March 2010, and it went into effect on January 1, 2014.

What Are the Major Provisions of the Affordable Care Act?

Medicare: *In the United States, a national health-insurance program for citizens age 65 and older and disabled people.*

Key features of the Affordable Care Act are intended to provide Americans with better health care. The "Patient Bill of Rights" protects consumers from mistreatment by insurance companies. Insurance companies can no longer deny you coverage because of a preexisting condition (an ailment that was present before a person tried to enroll in an insurance plan). Furthermore, if you make a minor mistake on an insurance claim, insurance companies can no longer deny you coverage. The act also ensures your right to appeal a coverage decision by an insurance company if you feel the ruling is unjust. Among the most popular provisions of the ACA is that children can remain on their parents' policies until age 26.

Other provisions affect Americans receiving health-care coverage through *Medicare*. These include allowing people enrolled in Medicare

Case Study: Buying Insurance Online

Leah is in the market for health insurance under the Affordable Care Act (ACA). Since she knows how to use the Internet, she feels comfortable buying health insurance on the government's online health-care exchange, Healthcare.gov. After logging on to the website, however, Leah feels overwhelmed and anxious. Where should she begin? What if she picks the wrong plan? Unsure of what to do, she eventually sees an icon that says "Get Coverage." She clicks it. After entering her personal information, she is ready to shop on the marketplace.

Leah sees a list of different health insurance plans. Which one should she choose? First, she considers how much she is willing to pay each month for insurance (this amount is called a "premium"). This narrows her choices a bit.

From there, she analyzes each plan's out-of-pocket costs (the amount of money that must be spent on health care before her insurance will start contributing). Leah then researches each plan's provider networks (health-care facilities covered under a particular insurance plan). She lives in a rural area, so she wants to make sure that her insurance will cover health care in her region. After reviewing premiums, out-of-pocket costs, and provider networks, she chooses a plan that suits her budget, geographic area, and health-care needs.

Ultimately, Leah found the government's health-care website easy to use, and she is also happy that she is not penalized for preexisting conditions under the ACA. The only downside for her is the amount of time it took to sort through and consider all of the plans.

to receive important preventive health care at no cost and to purchase brand-name prescription drugs at greatly reduced prices. Various other programs are also being put into place under the ACA, such as accountable care organizations (ACOs). ACOs are groups of doctors, hospitals, and other types of health-care providers that have come together to share financial and medical responsibilities. Such programs, which are voluntary for Medicare participants, are designed to help doctors and other types of health providers work in tandem to provide better care.

How Has the Affordable Care Act Been Implemented?

The ACA features numerous reforms. The bulk of these were put in motion when the law took effect. However, states were not required to implement all of the reforms immediately. Instead, the reforms were to be rolled out over a number of years, with an estimated finish date of around 2022. The rollout plan is meant to provide additional time for

Affordable Care Act–Coverage Highlights as of November 14, 2014

General

- Health plans cannot limit or deny benefits to children under age 19 due to a pre-existing condition.
- Young adults under age 26 may be eligible to be covered under their parents' health plan.
- Insurers cannot cancel your coverage just because you made an honest mistake.
- You have the right to ask that your plan reconsider its denial of any payment.

Costs

- Lifetime limits on most benefits are banned for all new health insurance plans.
- Insurance companies must publicly justify any unreasonable rate hikes.
- Premium dollars must be spent primarily on healthcare not administrative costs.

Care

- Recommended preventive health services are covered with no copayment.
- Choose the primary care doctor you want from your plan's network.
- Allows you to seek emergency care at a hospital outside of your plan's network.

For More Information, read the full law, available online at http://www.hhs.gov/healthcare/rights/law/index.html.

SOURCE: HHS.gov/HealthCare. "About the Law." http://www.hhs.gov/healthcare/rights/.

ILLUSTRATION BY LUMINA DATAMATICS LTD. © 2015 CENGAGE LEARNING.

the federal government to give assistance to states that are not in a position to immediately comply with the reforms.

Not every state supports the ACA or has a plan for implementing the reforms the act requires. Generally speaking, there are three groups of states: 1) those that support all of the reforms called for in the legislation; 2) those that agree in part with the reforms; and 3) those that choose not to participate despite the federal mandate to do so. It will take time for the federal government to work with each state to ensure that all of the reforms are implemented.

How Has the Affordable Care Act Changed How Insurance Is Purchased?

In the relatively recent past, most people acquired their health insurance through their employer or directly from an insurance company. As a result of the ACA, many people now shop for insurance through "exchanges" (organizations set up to offer various insurance plans in each state). Exchanges are fundamentally changing the way that millions of Americans obtain their health insurance. In fact, many experts expect exchanges to be the way most Americans purchase their insurance in the coming years.

An exchange can be viewed as a store of sorts. When you go to a grocery store, you are usually provided with a number of options for similar types of foods. Some products are of a better quality than others, and prices and quantity vary across the range of choices. It is up to you to decide which product is best for you. Insurance exchanges are online stores that sell health-care plans. Consumers are offered different plans that provide different services at different prices. You can find all of this information in one location, allowing you to comparison shop and choose the best options for your situation.

Each state determines how its exchange operates. If a state does not wish to participate, the federal government will create an exchange and run it. Some states have chosen to partner with the federal government to create an exchange. Either way, the result is the same: All states have exchanges that can be used by citizens. Exchanges also can be used by small businesses.

Exchanges are important because they increase health-care options for consumers. These marketplaces are relatively easy to navigate, and people have a better chance of finding plans tailored to their needs. And since the exchanges cannot discriminate because of preexisting conditions or deny children coverage, they are becoming increasingly popular among many consumers.

What Is Healthcare.gov?

Healthcare.gov is a website operated by the federal government that was mandated by the Affordable Care Act. The site assists individuals who are looking for insurance or exploring alternatives to their current coverage. It is designed to help individuals and businesses to better understand how the reforms affect their particular circumstances and insurance needs. Healthcare.gov also helps people find information regarding preventive care, such as vaccinations or mammograms.

Most importantly, Healthcare.gov provides a central means of locating and purchasing insurance. It has often been described as a way to do "comparison shopping" for insurance, offering both private and public plans. In addition to looking at plans that suit your current health needs, you can compare prices for insurance in your state and see if you qualify for any types of health-care subsidies, such as *Medicaid*.

Medicaid: *A government-assistance program in the United States that provides health-care benefits to individuals and families with low income and limited resources. Also called Title XIX.*

How Can Healthcare.gov Be Used to Shop for Insurance?

When Healthcare.gov first went live in 2014, its many initial glitches were widely publicized. However, the problems were quickly fixed, and subsequently the site was viewed by many as being user friendly, even by those who are not computer savvy. You may also apply for an application by telephone, by mailing in a paper document, or with a person from the community who provides personal assistance.

The first step when applying online is to create an account. This is a simple process that requires little information from you. Much like starting an account for any other website, you need to create a user-name and password and answer some general security questions. Next is the application process, in which you provide information such as your annual income, how many people live in your household, and whether you currently have health-care coverage. Once that step is complete, you can find out if you qualify for any additional plans, such as Medicaid. This section is known as "eligibility results." Finally, you can choose a plan and enroll in it.

What Are the Key Arguments for and against the Affordable Care Act?

Co-payment: *A portion of each medical or dental expense for which an insured patient is responsible.*

Supporters of the Affordable Care Act routinely cite a number of its benefits. One of the greatest arguments in favor of the ACA involves senior citizens. The act seeks to make prescription drugs more afford-able, specifically regarding Medicare prescription drug coverage. The ACA also operates in a proactive manner, attempting to cover all preven-tive health services with no *co-payment*. Additionally, the ACA assists individuals and small business through tax credits. A crowning benefit of the act, according to supporters, is that it increases the number of low- and middle-class families that are insured.

Detractors of the ACA argue that it heightens political differences and that its ultimate costs are unknown. Certain individuals also do not like to have their actions dictated by the federal government. They argue that the act detracts from the ability of states to run their own health-care programs. Cost, however, remains perhaps the greatest concern. While opponents of the act may like the notion that someone cannot be denied coverage because of a preexisting condition, they contend that such a provision increases the price of everyone's insurance. Critics also worry that businesses will decrease their number of full-time employees to avoid the mandated coverage.

Medicare and State Health Insurance Assistance Program (SHIP)

What Is Medicare?

Medicare is a health insurance program sponsored by the federal government for U.S. citizens 65 or older. Some people with disabilities, some with end-stage renal disease (ESRD), and all people with amyotrophic lateral sclerosis (ALS, also called Lou Gehrig's Disease) who are under 65 also qualify for Medicare coverage.

There are four types of Medicare coverage. Part A, which is also called hospital insurance, covers hospital visits, nursing home stays, hospice care, and assorted home health services such as nursing care. Part B, or medical insurance, covers outpatient services that are medically necessary, such as a providing a blood sugar monitor for a person with diabetes, as well as services that are medically advisable, such as having a mammogram to screen for breast cancer. Part C, or Medicare Advantage, allows recipients to receive their Part A and B Medicare benefits from a private insurance company, including health maintenance organizations (HMOs) and preferred provider organizations (PPOs). Part D provides prescription drug coverage. (Some Medicare Advantage plans also provide prescription drug coverage.)

Passed into law in 1965 by President Lyndon Johnson, Medicare was designed to provide affordable access to health care for the elderly and disabled. According to the National Committee to Preserve Social Security & Medicare, before the passage of Medicare, approximately 50 percent of the elderly did not have health insurance and 35 percent were living in poverty. Medicare helps older and disabled people to remain financially solvent and as physically healthy as possible.

How Is Medicare Funded?

Funding for Medicare is provided by a variety of sources, including payroll taxes and Medicare insurance premiums. The Hospital Insurance

Many U.S. citizens become eligible for Medicare on their 65th birthday. © ZIMMYTWS/ SHUTTERSTOCK.COM.

Premium: *The fee for insurance coverage.*

Trust Fund and the Supplementary Insurance Trust Fund are government trust fund accounts administered by the U.S. Treasury that pay exclusively for Medicare. Medicare is administered federally by an agency called the Centers for Medicare and Medicaid Services (CMS), which is a part of the Department of Health and Human Services (HHS).

How Can I Tell If I Qualify for Medicare?

If you are a U.S. citizen or permanent resident aged 65 years or older, you qualify for Medicare if you or your spouse are eligible to receive Social Security benefits. To qualify for Social Security benefits, you must have worked 10 or more years for an employer who withheld payroll taxes. If you were self-employed for 10 or more years, you must have paid the federal self-employment tax. If you have worked for an employer that does not pay into the Social Security system, such as the federal government or the railroad, you qualify for Medicare as long as you have worked for that employer for a significant period of time.

If your spouse is at least 62 years old and you are 65 or older, you may qualify for Medicare based on your spouse's work history. If you are over 65 years old and are unable to qualify for Medicare based on your or your spouse's work history, you will pay *premiums* specific to the types of Medicare coverage you choose.

If you are a U.S. citizen or permanent resident under 65 years old, you may qualify for Medicare if you are disabled and have received Social Security benefits for at least 24 months, or if you receive a disability pension from the Railroad Retirement Board. If you have ESRD and you or your spouse have paid into the Social Security system for a specific period of time, you also qualify for Medicare. If you have ALS, you automatically qualify for Medicare. Qualified persons receive Medicare benefits only if they reside in the United States or affiliated territories.

How Do I Apply for Medicare?

Some people are automatically enrolled in Medicare, while others are not. You will be automatically enrolled in Medicare if you receive Social

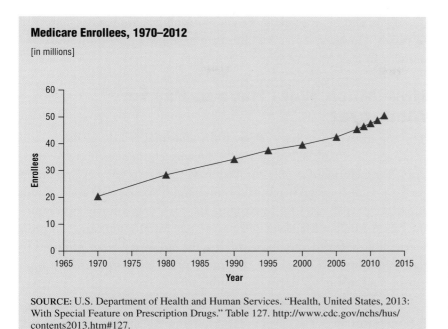

Medicare Enrollees, 1970–2012

[in millions]

SOURCE: U.S. Department of Health and Human Services. "Health, United States, 2013: With Special Feature on Prescription Drugs." Table 127. http://www.cdc.gov/nchs/hus/contents2013.htm#127.

As baby boomers have begun to retire, enrollment in Medicare has risen dramatically.
ILLUSTRATION BY LUMINA DATAMATICS LTD. © 2015 CENGAGE LEARNING.

Security or Railroad Retirement Board benefits and are over 65 years old; if you have received Social Security benefits due to a disability for two years or more and are under 65 years old; or if you have ALS. If you qualify for automatic enrollment, you will receive a Medicare card in the mail three months after your 65th birthday, after receiving disability benefits for two years, or immediately after receiving a diagnosis of ALS. Automatic enrollment occurs for plans Part A and Part B only.

You must personally enroll in Medicare if you do not receive Social Security benefits but qualify for Medicare. Reasons for not receiving Social Security benefits include remaining in the workforce after your regular retirement age. If you are nearing your 65th birthday and do not receive Social Security benefits, you are eligible to apply for Medicare in the six-month period starting three months before your birthday and ending at the end of the third month after your birthday. If you miss the enrollment period, you may apply between January 1 and March 31, during the open enrollment window. If you have ESRD, you must personally enroll in Medicare. To enroll, visit a Social Security office, call Social Security at 800-772-1213, or apply online at https://secure.ssa.gov/iClaim/rib.

If you choose to enroll in Part A, you will be automatically enrolled in Part B. However, if you enroll in Part B, you will not be automatically enrolled in Part A.

How Much Will I Have to Pay for Medicare?

The amount you will have to pay for Medicare depends on the type of plans you have enrolled in, as well as how much money you make each year. The majority of people enrolled in Medicare do not pay a premium for Part A, or hospital insurance. (However, if you or your spouse paid Medicare payroll taxes for fewer than 10 years, you will pay a premium for Part A.) Before Medicare will start to pay for hospital care, you must meet the specified deductible, which is the amount you are required to pay before insurance will pay. You must also pay a co-pay, which is an out-of-pocket sum for a specific health-care service.

Every person enrolled in Medicare will pay a premium for Part B, or medical insurance. The cost of your premium depends on your income. The more money you make each year, the higher your premium will be. If you do not enroll for Part B when you first become qualified to do so and you do not have other health insurance, you may have to pay a penalty fee.

If you receive Social Security, Railroad Retirement Board benefits, or civil service benefits, Part B insurance premiums will automatically be deducted from your monthly benefits payment. If you do not receive these benefits, you will receive a bill for your Part B premium. To pay your bill, you may send a check or money order to the Medicare Premium Collection Center or enroll in Medicare Easy Pay, a service that deducts your premiums from your bank account automatically.

The amount you pay for Part C, or Medicare Advantage, is decided by the private insurer that administers Parts A and B for you. Premiums, deductibles, co-pays, and other associated costs vary widely. In general, Medicare Advantage includes prescription drug coverage.

There is a low premium for Part D, which provides prescription drug coverage. Like Part B, the amount you pay for your premium depends on the amount of money you make. You will also pay a co-pay for prescriptions, and Medicare will not begin to pay for your prescriptions until you meet the deductible. If you have a very low monthly income, you may qualify for the Extra Help program, which will assist you in paying for the cost of prescription drugs.

How Can I Reduce My Medical Costs while on Medicare?

If you are enrolled in Parts A and B and these plans do not cover all of your health-care costs, you may apply for Medicare Supplement Insurance, known as Medigap, from a private insurer. Medicare does not cover the cost of Medigap, so you are responsible for the premium. Medigap is often used to help pay for costs associated with Part B that Medicare does not cover. It does not work in conjunction with Part C, Medicare Advantage. Neither Medicare nor Medigap cover certain health-care costs such as dentistry, eye care, and hearing aids.

If you cannot afford to pay your Medicare bill, there are a number of government programs in place that are designed to help you, known collectively as Medicare Savings Programs. These programs include the Qualified Medicare Beneficiary (QMB) Program, Specified Low-Income Medicare Beneficiary (SLMB) Program, Qualifying Individual (QI) Program, and Qualified Disabled and Working Individuals (QDWI) Program. For each program, you must not exceed the maximum monthly income limit in order to qualify. If you qualify for nursing home care, the Program of All-Inclusive Care for the Elderly (PACE) may be able to help coordinate and pay for your health care.

Where Can I Get Help with Navigating Medicare?

The State Health Insurance Assistance Program (SHIP), a federal program that began in 1990, gives monetary grants to state agencies to operate various programs that provide free assistance to people who need help navigating the Medicare system, whether they are already enrolled in Medicare or thinking about enrolling in Medicare.

The U.S. Department of Health and Human Services is a federal government agency that gives grants to state government agencies that offer various state SHIPs. These grants pay to train and support SHIP counselors, many of whom are volunteers. While the federal government pays for SHIP, state governments manage SHIP. State government agencies operate SHIP programs and services through various agencies. SHIP exists in all 50 states as well as in the District of Columbia, Puerto Rico, Guam, and the U.S. Virgin Islands.

How Can I Get Help through SHIP?

States administer SHIP programs through various state offices, generally offices on aging or insurance. For example, the Nebraska Department of Insurance administers its SHIP program, which it calls the Nebraska Senior Health Insurance Information Program (SHIIP). The California Department of Aging administers California's SHIP program, which is known in that state as the Health Insurance Counseling and Advocacy Program (HICAP). Some of the program names can be quite different from the term SHIP, such as GeorgiaCares, the state of Georgia's SHIP.

Despite all the name variations, finding your state's SHIP is relatively easy. Go to an online Internet search engine and enter terms such as "State Health Insurance Assistance Program" or "SHIP program" and the name of your state, and you should be able to find the SHIP for your state. You can also look for websites devoted to SHIPs, such as *SHIPtalk*. These websites have information about SHIPs and often allow you to search for the SHIP in your state.

To find a SHIP office, go online to find a website devoted to SHIPs, such as *SHIPtalk*. This site will help you find web pages for SHIP in your home state. If you live in the state of New York, for example, you will find a great deal of information about Medicare through the Internet pages of that state's SHIP, the Health Insurance Information, Counseling, and Assistance Program (HIICAP). If you do not have access to the Internet, call Social Security for assistance at 800-772-1213.

What Services Are Available through SHIP?

If you have questions or concerns about Medicare, taking advantage SHIP's resources may be helpful. Talking with a SHIP counselor could help you choose the right Medicare program for you. A SHIP counselor could tell you whether Medicare pays for certain types of medical expenses, inform you about other insurance plans that offer additional coverage, and explain insurance plans that could help you pay for your prescriptions. If you are already a Medicare recipient, a counselor could help you file a Medicare claim or help you with insurance problems. SHIP counselors could also help you find additional resources, since

SHIP offices are often affiliated with agencies that help older adults. Some SHIP offices sponsor events known as Medicare Mondays, where SHIP counselors discuss Medicare with members of the community at different locations.

You also can use the Internet to access some of SHIP's resources. HIICAP, the state of New York's SHIP, has webpages with a number of informative links. One page alone has links to overviews of various Medicare plans and New York's Medicare drug plan, as well as other drug plan information, an online handbook about Medicare, guidelines about reporting Medicare abuse and fraud, and an online notebook for HIICAP counselors. You can even access information on HIICAP's home page in more than 70 languages, although the information on the linked pages appears only in English.

Medicaid and Children's Health Insurance Program

What Are Medicaid and CHIP?

A government-sponsored program, Medicaid provides health insurance to low-income U.S. citizens and other qualifying residents. Medicaid offers health-care coverage supported by both state and federal funds for many people who cannot afford health insurance. Although federal law requires that certain groups of people are covered under the plan, including children, pregnant women, people with disabilities, and senior citizens, each state is allowed to create specific regulations regarding the economic eligibility and the inclusion of other populations under the plan.

Co-payment: *A portion of each medical or dental expense for which an insured patient is responsible.*

In 2014 Medicaid provided health services to almost 60 million Americans, making it one of the largest providers of health insurance in the United States. The program covers basic health-care needs as well as long-term care for the elderly and disabled. Medicaid also covers Medicare costs for low-income individuals who qualify. The Federal Coordinated Health Care Office, or Medicare-Medicaid Coordination Office, organizes and facilitates the delivery of benefits to Medicaid recipients. People who are enrolled in the Medicaid program do not have to pay monthly premiums. However, many are required to make small *co-payments* when they receive medical services.

A program closely related to Medicaid is the Children's Health Insurance Program (CHIP). Like Medicaid, CHIP provides health insurance coverage for children and pregnant women who cannot afford private insurance but whose incomes are too high to qualify for Medicaid. Funded by the federal and state governments, CHIP plans provide free or low-cost health insurance to eligible people. Each state is allowed to design its own CHIP income guidelines and policies, so eligibility requirements vary widely from state to state.

Depending on the state, CHIP plans provide a wide range of services. Most states pay for costs associated with routine types of medical care, such as children's checkups, doctors' visits, immunizations, hospital care, emergency care, prescriptions, X-rays and laboratory services, and dental care. CHIP plans provide pregnant women with a variety of options, paying for services such as prenatal care, labor, and post-delivery medical care for mother and baby. There are differences in each state's CHIP plan. Some states might pay your entire medical bill, while others may charge a co-pay for the medical services you receive.

CHIP provides free or low-cost health coverage for more than 7 million children up to age 19.
© MONKEY BUSINESS IMAGES/ SHUTTERSTOCK.COM.

How Long Have Medicaid and CHIP Been Around?

The Medicaid program was included in the 1965 Social Security Amendments signed into law by President Lyndon B. Johnson. Medicaid was designed to improve access to health care for the elderly, poor, and disabled. Modern subsidized health coverage is not a new concept, however. It traces its roots back to the late 1800s in Germany. By the mid-twentieth century, many European countries had adopted the idea of national health insurance with universal coverage. Due to a cultural emphasis on independence and self-reliance, U.S. citizens resisted the idea of government-assisted insurance until the early 1900s, when social activists pressed for affordable health care.

The Social Security Amendments of 1950 included a health-care program for low-income people receiving public assistance payments. The program was supported by state funds matched by the federal government. In 1960 the U.S. Congress implemented the Medical Assistance for the Aged program to provide medical coverage for elderly people who did not meet the low-income requirements established by the 1950 legislation but who still could not afford health insurance. Further extending the Social Security Amendments of 1965 allowed all individuals over the age of 65 to qualify for Medicare. This same act included the creation of the Medicaid program, which expanded low-income coverage and offered benefits not covered by Medicare, such as nursing home care.

The CHIP program came much later. During the 1990s several states recognized the lack of coverage available for children of low-income families who were not eligible for Medicaid. As a result, they implemented supplemental insurance programs specifically for these children.

Tips for Caregivers Applying for Medicaid

If you are a child of aging parents, you may find yourself becoming the primary caregiver when your parents experience a medical trauma or are incapacitated. This places the responsibility of finding in-home care or placing the parent in a nursing home on you. If you cannot afford such services, you will need to fill out a Medicaid application to request assistance. The Medicaid application is long and complex, and you may be required to provide financial and legal information going back as far as five years, including unpaid medical bills, pay stubs, health insurance premiums, tax returns, and bank statements. Once you have submitted the information and the eligibility form to your state's Department of Social Services office, you may receive a call from a social worker who will ask you to clarify information on the form, including any cash deposits that are not part of your parent's regular income.

This scenario is one that many adult children may face someday, so it is important for

you and your parents to prepare ahead of time. In the event that your parent suffers a stroke or an accident that impairs cognitive function, he or she will not be able to help you gather the necessary information, which will significantly slow down the application process. Talk to your parents and ask them to compile as much information as possible. It is a good idea to make a checklist of the information and documentation required on the Medicaid application so that you can put all the necessary paperwork in one folder, making it easy for you to locate if you need to apply for your parents. You should also talk to them about becoming their health-care proxy and about having them give you power of attorney. This allows you to make medical decisions on their behalf if they are incapacitated and to manage their finances in the event of an emergency. Being prepared will save you and your parents time and stress, since the process of applying for Medicaid is both detailed and challenging.

After the Bill Clinton presidential administration failed to implement a national health-care plan for all U.S. citizens, it searched for other ways to increase publicly funded health care and settled on expanding health-care coverage for children. Using the children's health insurance plan in Massachusetts as a model, Senator Ted Kennedy introduced a bill that would offer health-care coverage for children of low-income families. In 1997 CHIP was signed into law and became the largest expansion of children's health-care coverage since the implementation of Medicaid.

How Have Legislation and Government Involvement Affected Medicaid and CHIP?

Legislation has made government-funded health insurance complex. The Children's Health Insurance Program Reauthorization Act of 2009

What the Children's Health Insurance Program (CHIP) Covers

CHIP benefits differ by state, but all states provide comprehensive coverage, including:

- Routine check-ups
- Immunizations
- Doctor visits
- Prescriptions
- Dental and vision care
- Inpatient and outpatient hospital care
- Laboratory and X-ray services
- Emergency services

Individual states may provide additional CHIP benefits. Check with your state for information about covered services.

SOURCE: HealthCare.gov. "The Children's Health Insurance Program (CHIP)." https://www.healthcare.gov/medicaid-chip/childrens-health-insurance-program/.

ILLUSTRATION BY LUMINA DATAMATICS LTD. © 2015 CENGAGE LEARNING.

(CHIPRA) has allowed the federal government to provide more funding and guidance to state CHIP plans. This act also included provisions that allowed states to enroll people more easily in CHIP plans and Medicaid programs.

In 2010 government insurance programs underwent a major development when the Patient Protection and Affordable Care Act, commonly known as "Obamacare," was signed into law. Sponsored by President Barack Obama, the act created multiple changes to the health insurance system. Because many of the working poor did not meet the low-income guidelines but still could not afford health insurance, Medicaid was expanded to cover all individuals and families whose income is below 133 percent of the federal poverty level. A 2012 ruling by the U.S. Supreme Court allowed individual states to choose whether or not to expand their Medicaid guidelines, and, as of 2014, 20 states had decided against expanding Medicaid.

Who Is Eligible to Receive Medicaid or CHIP?

Although eligibility for Medicaid and CHIP usually depends on income level, each state has its own Medicaid regulations. Federal law requires that all states cover low-income children and their parents, pregnant women, the blind, the disabled, and people on specific government-assistance programs, such as Supplemental Security Income (SSI). In order to qualify in any state, the recipient must be a U.S. citizen or be classified as a "qualified non-citizen," a group that includes permanent residents, refugees, victims of domestic violence or sex trafficking, and immigrants from Cuba and Haiti. You must be a resident of the state in which you are applying and have a valid Social Security number.

States also decide the financial requirements necessary to qualify for Medicaid. Many states use the federal poverty level, issued each year by the Department of Health and Human Services, as a guideline. Although the Affordable Care Act expanded Medicaid guidelines to cover individuals with incomes up to 133 percent of the poverty line, some states opted not to implement this change. To determine Medicaid eligibility, many states look at other financial resources in addition to income and review applicants' financial histories to ensure that no assets that might make them ineligible for assistance have been hidden.

As with Medicaid, state governments administer CHIP plans with guidance from the federal Centers for Medicare and Medicaid Services. The operation of CHIP health plans varies by state. Some states manage CHIP plans separately from the Medicaid system. Other states oversee their state CHIP plans as part of the Medicaid system. Still other states offer a combination of the two and provide CHIP plans affiliated with Medicaid.

Regardless of how a state operates its CHIP plan, the federal government gives each state a certain amount of money to fund children's health insurance programs. States must match this amount to receive the funding. The federal government also gives states additional funding in the form of bonuses if they improve their enrollment procedures and increase their registration and retention of people in CHIP programs.

To qualify for CHIP, you must have an annual income that falls at or below a certain maximum, which varies from state to state. The Medicaid.gov website (http://www.medicaid.gov) provides links with information about CHIP plans in your state. There you can check your state's eligibility requirements so you can find out whether you or your children qualify for CHIP plans. You can also determine whether your state offers more than one health-care plan and compare multiple plans to find the right health-care solution for you.

How Do I Apply for Medicaid or CHIP?

Because the Affordable Care Act requires most Americans to find health insurance coverage, federal and state health insurance marketplaces were established to assist people who are not able to afford such coverage. State marketplaces are also known as state exchanges. You can learn about the federal health insurance marketplace by visiting the website HealthCare.gov (https://www.healthcare.gov). This site allows you compare different insurance plans, learn about eligibility requirements for programs such as Medicaid and CHIP, and ask questions about insurance coverage. During specific periods, known as open enrollment periods, you can complete a Marketplace application online to enroll in an insurance plan.

You also can learn about Medicaid and CHIP plans by visiting the Medicaid.gov site. The homepage features a number of links relating to CHIP plans, including one that allows you to search for CHIP plans in your state. The links also list the names of individual state CHIP plans, since some states have nicknamed their plans. Louisiana's LaCHIP incorporates the name of the state in the title, while Wisconsin's BadgerCare Plus is a nod to the state's nickname. Other states use more generic names, such as the Illinois All Kids program. Other links provide information about each state's eligibility requirements, including income limits and whether your state has implemented the Affordable Care Act changes to its Medicaid guidelines.

Medicaid and CHIP are distributed by individual states, so you usually apply through the Department of Social Services (DSS) in the state in which you reside. If you are already receiving SSI payments, you may automatically qualify for Medicaid without applying, but generally you must complete an application, which can be done in person at your local DSS office, online, or by mail. Many people choose to fill out an application for Medicaid or CHIP at home before meeting with a DSS agent because the enrollment process can take a long time.

For each person applying for benefits, you will need to make copies of certain documents, including proof of citizenship or immigration status, proof of identity, a Social Security card, proof of income for at least one month, recent statements from all bank accounts, and statements of any other payments you receive, such as a pension or veteran benefit. You will also need to provide a list of your assets and their value, including all motor vehicles and any homes or property you own. It is helpful to gather all of this information before applying since the application form is very detailed. You must provide honest and comprehensive answers to each question on the form so that you will not be disqualified.

Veterans Health Administration, Military Health System, and TRICARE

What Is the Veterans Health Administration?

The Veterans Health Administration (VHA) is a government-run health-care system that serves veterans of the U.S. armed forces. Operated by the U.S. Department of Veterans Affairs, the VHA is the largest integrated health-care system in the country, providing services to millions of veterans through its medical centers, clinics, and nursing homes. It is important to distinguish the VHA from the U.S. Department of Defense's Military Health System, which provides health services for those currently serving in the armed forces and to retired military personnel, as well as their dependents.

The Veterans Health Administration is directed by the undersecretary of the Veterans Affairs for Health. An experienced medical doctor often holds this position. The VHA's central offices are located in Washington, D.C., and its facilities are organized into regional service networks. These networks cover all 50 states as well as Guam, American Samoa, Puerto Rico, the U.S. Virgin Islands, and the Philippines.

According to the U.S. Department of Veterans Affairs' website, the mission of the Veterans Health Administration is to "Honor America's Veterans by providing exceptional health care that improves their health and well-being." As of 2014, out of the 22 million veterans in the United States, about 9.3 million were enrolled in the VHA health-care system.

How Did the Veterans Health Administration Come About?

Although the U.S. government had been providing pensions for its veterans since the Revolutionary War, the first time it sponsored veteran health care was in 1811. In that year the federal government established the Naval Home in Philadelphia, the first nursing home and medical facility specifically for veterans. In the 60 years that followed, a small number of similar facilities were added. After the American Civil War (1861–65), the need for health services for veterans greatly increased, and the federal government built many more veterans' nursing homes.

By the end of the 1920s many veterans were seeking and receiving medical care at these facilities for illnesses or injuries unrelated to their service. The veterans' homes therefore began to function similarly to hospitals, and the government responded by building veterans' hospitals. By 1930, when living U.S. veterans numbered 4.7 million, there were more than 60 veterans' hospitals in the United States. That year President Herbert Hoover persuaded the U.S. Congress to create the Veterans Administration (VA), which combined oversight of veterans' homes and health services with the administration of several other veterans' benefits, including pensions and life insurance.

Veterans Health Administration's doctors, nurses, and specialists provide a wide range of medical services to veterans of the U.S. armed forces. © MONKEY BUSINESS IMAGES/ SHUTTERSTOCK.COM.

When World War II ended in 1945, the number of veterans in the United States jumped to about 15 million, and the Veterans Administration was forced to increase in size. By 1950 there were 151 veterans' hospitals throughout the country staffed by more than 100,000 health-care workers.

In the late 1950s Congress began to provide funding to the VHA to research some of the mental and physical illnesses common to veterans. The Vietnam War (1955–75) resulted in a massive increase in numbers of wounded and disabled U.S. veterans, as well as veterans affected by psychological damage and unique medical issues such as exposure to Agent Orange (an herbicide sprayed over Vietnam by the U.S. military to make the leaves fall off plants). In 1979 Congress passed the Veterans Health Care Amendment Act, which included funding for Vet Centers. These provide access to counseling services for alcohol and drug addictions as well as *post-traumatic stress disorder (PTSD).*

Post-traumatic stress disorder (PTSD): *Reliving trauma and anxiety related to an event that occurred earlier.*

As services for veterans' health continued to grow, Congress altered the rules for access several times. In the 1980s new legislation mandated that higher-income veterans receiving treatment for medical conditions not related to their military service pay a portion of their fees. In

Total Military Health System (MHS) Population by Age and Gender, FY2011 (actual) and FY2017 (projected)

[in millions]

				Age Group					Total by	Total MHS
	≤4	5–14	15–17	18–24	25–34	35–44	45–64	≥65	Gender	Population
FY2011 Female MHS Beneficiaries	0.31	0.54	0.17	0.52	0.55	0.44	1.15	1.06	4.74	9.72
FY2011 Male MHS Beneficiaries	0.32	0.56	0.17	0.77	0.65	0.45	1.09	0.93	4.98	9.72
FY2017 Female MHS Beneficiaries, Projected	0.29	0.50	0.15	0.48	0.50	0.41	1.09	1.20	4.68	9.43
FY2017 Male MHS Beneficiaries, Projected	0.30	0.52	0.16	0.75	0.62	0.43	0.97	1.06	4.90	9.43

Source: FY 2011 from DEERS as of 12/30/2011, and FY 2017 estimates from Managed Care Forecasting and Analysis System (MCFAS) as of 12/28/2010.

SOURCE: Department of Defense. "Evolution of the TRICARE Program: Access, Cost, and Quality. Fiscal Year 2012 Report to Congress." 15. www.tricare.mil/hpae/_docs/TRICARE2012.pptx.

ILLUSTRATION BY LUMINA DATAMATICS LTD. © 2015 CENGAGE LEARNING.

1988 President Ronald Reagan approved legislation to raise the Veterans Administration to Cabinet-level status, and the following year it became the Department of Veterans Affairs.

The VHA has evolved to meet the needs of veterans of various conflicts and wars. It has also weathered much criticism about the quality and accessibility of its services. In the 1990s efforts were made to reform the VHA to address problems such as inefficient use of resources, high levels of surgical mortality, and lack of administrative accountability. Successful changes to the VHA in the 1990s and 2000s brought to veterans increased access to care as well as improvements to the quality and coordination of care.

How Is the Veterans Health Administration Funded?

The U.S. federal government funds the Veterans Health Administration. Congress must vote to approve budget appropriations to support four VA accounts, which include medical services, facility construction and maintenance, research, and medical administration. The level of funding changes year to year, as Congress evaluates and votes on each fiscal year's proposed VHA budget.

Co-payment: *A fixed amount of money that patients pay for each doctor's visit and for each prescription.*

The VHA is also funded in part through the Medical Care Collections Fund (MCCF). Enrollees pay into this fund either through *co-payments* for services or through third-party insurance payments.

The 2014 Veterans Health Administration Scandal

In 2014 the Veterans Health Administration (VHA) was rocked by a scandal after it was revealed in April that 40 or more veterans had died while awaiting care at severely backlogged VHA facilities in Phoenix, Arizona. Following the revelation, the Veterans Affairs (VA) Office of the Inspector General launched an investigation of delays in treatment throughout the VHA system. In May 2014 the scandal led to the early retirement of Robert Petzel, who as the VA undersecretary for health had served as the organization's head of health care, and the resignation of Eric Shinseki, secretary of Veterans Affairs.

In June 2014 an internal audit of the organization found that, across the country, more than 120,000 veterans either received no care or were forced to wait for care. Moreover, it was discovered that organization officials had manipulated data to make average wait times seem more acceptable. Based on these revelations, the Federal Bureau of Investigations (FBI) began a criminal investigation of the VA on June 11. In July 2014 Robert A. McDonald was sworn in as the new secretary of Veterans Affairs and tasked with reforming the VA. In August 2014 reform legislation known as the Veterans Access, Choice and Accountability Act was signed into law by President Barack Obama.

Other income that supports the VHA comes from pharmacy co-payments, fees collected from leasing facilities, and parking fees.

What Services Does the Veterans Health Administration Provide?

The Veterans Health Administration's doctors, nurses, and many specialists provide a wide range of services. These include preventive, primary, and critical care; surgery; mental health care; home health care; and geriatric care. Other, more specialized services include oncology (cancer treatment), dermatology (treatment of skin disorders), vision care, physical therapy, prosthetics, and, in some centers, organ transplants. Dental benefits are available to veterans who fit specific eligibility requirements and to those who purchase dental insurance through the VHA.

The VHA conducts research on special diseases and conditions and provides information to veterans about treatments and resources. On its website (http://www.publichealth.va.gov/exposures/) it offers extensive information about various military exposures, such as Agent Orange, radiation, and noise. The VHA also has several ways to connect veterans to treatment for such exposures, including through environmental health coordinators. These specialists work in dozens of locations to help evaluate veterans suffering from the effects of exposures and connect them to the appropriate care.

When combat veterans return home from deployment, they face a special set of difficulties, and the VHA's Vet Centers aim to assist veterans with this transition. These centers provide group and individual counseling for veterans and their families as well as assistance in finding other services. Helping with lifestyle readjustment, treating post-traumatic stress disorder, and preventing substance abuse and suicide are major focuses of these Vet Centers.

What Programs Does the Veterans Health Administration Sponsor?

The VHA uses the Internet to make hundreds of resources and tools available to veterans. The *My* Health*e*Vet website (https://www.myhealth.va.gov/) is an online resource that enables both veterans and active duty service members to access health resources, appointments, and their own medical records. It is also used by VHA health-care providers to access patients' records, including information about immunizations, appointments, and lab reports.

Infectious disease: *A disorder caused by bacteria, virus, fungi, etc. that can be passed from person to person.*

Extensive wellness programs provide veterans resources to improve their own health and well-being. These include crisis lines, nutrition guidance, weight-loss and smoking-cessation programs and information, immunizations, and access to chaplains. The VHA also offers multiple programs and initiatives for its own employees to safeguard and maintain their good health. These include initiatives for workplace safety, preventing the spread of *infectious disease*, and workers' compensation.

Understanding that caring for veterans often falls on others, the VHA provides many resources for caregivers, including a caregiver hotline, various home health resources, and caregiver support coordinators. These coordinators assist caregivers in finding appropriate health resources for the veteran for whom they care, and connects them to programs such as support groups. At many major VHA medical centers, the Fisher House Foundation (a nonprofit organization) provides comfort homes where family members or caregivers can stay for free when accompanying veterans who are receiving medical treatment.

How Does the Veterans Health Administration Serve the Needs of Female Veterans?

With a growing population of female veterans, the VHA has worked to include women's health care into its services and programs. Women veterans have access to all primary, preventive, and critical care services, as well as gender-specific care such as maternity care, cervical and breast cancer screenings, birth control, and menopausal support.

Female veterans are not as likely as male veterans to enroll in and use VHA health services, for a few reasons. Studies have shown that women veterans are often not familiar with what VHA benefits are available to them. Also, female veterans often perceive VHA care to be of lesser quality and less convenient than private-sector health care.

What Are the Advantages of Getting Care through the Veterans Health Administration?

The Veterans Health Administration offers veterans integrated, coordinated, comprehensive health care. While most health care for veterans' service-related conditions are free of charge, the VHA also evaluates individuals' finances to identify what, if any, co-payments enrollees must pay for other services. These co-payments are generally a small fraction of the overall cost of care.

Who Qualifies for Care from the Veterans Health Administration, and How Do I Apply?

Anyone who served in the active U.S. military and was released or discharged from that service, as long as the discharge was not dishonorable, is eligible for VHA services. Those who were called by federal order and completed active duty with the National Guard or Reserves are also eligible for VHA benefits.

To earn eligibility for services, a veteran must meet a minimum requirement for time served in the armed forces in active duty. For those enlisted after September 1980 or for those whose active duty began after October 1981, the VHA requires 24 continuous months of service or completion of the period of active duty to be eligible. There are exceptions to these rules, so all veterans who were not dishonorably discharged are encouraged to apply to find out if they are eligible.

Certain categories of veterans have enhanced eligibility when applying for VHA benefits. These can include former prisoners of war, those awarded a Medal of Honor or Purple Heart, and those who served in the Vietnam or Gulf Wars, to name a few.

Veterans may apply for VHA benefits by completing an application called the VA Form 10-10EZ. There are several ways to access and complete the application. On the Internet, it is located on the Veterans Health Administration website at http://www.va.gov/health. All local VHA health-care facilities have applications to fill out in person, and it is also possible to complete the application over the phone by calling 1-877-222-VETS (8387). Help with completing the application is available on the website, over the phone, and in person at local VHA facilities.

Veterans deemed eligible by the VHA receive a Veteran Identification Card that grants them access to services at all VHA medical facilities. Enrollees also receive a Veterans Handbook, which explains services, benefits, and how to locate facilities.

How Do I Find a Veterans Health Administration Provider?

As of 2014 the Veterans Health Administration maintained more than 1,700 facilities to support veterans' health. Once approved for VHA benefits, veterans can locate health services and providers in their area. All facilities are organized into Veterans Integrated Service Networks (VISN), which include more than 20 networks of care facilities grouped together geographically. For example, the Rocky Mountain Network covers most of Montana, Wyoming, Utah, and Colorado as well as part of Nevada.

Each VISN houses several types of facilities. These include the major hospitals, called VA Medical Centers, smaller Outpatient Clinics and Mobile Outpatient Clinics, and the often-rural Community-Based Outpatient Clinics. Community Living Centers, formerly called nursing homes, Vet Centers, and Mobile Vet Centers are also available nationwide. Locate the closest VHA facilities by clicking on the "Locations" page on the VHA's website. Veterans can also get assistance in locating facilities by calling the VHA's phone number, 1-877-222-VETS (8387). In addition, most private-sector health services can provide information on VHA facilities. Those already enrolled in the VHA can refer to their Veterans Handbook to locate facilities and providers.

Indian Health Service

What Is the Indian Health Service?

The Indian Health Service (IHS) is a federal agency that serves the health-care needs of roughly 2.2 million American Indians and Alaska Natives. These populations often face unique challenges when seeking health care due to the remoteness of their communities, lack of transportation to medical facilities, and higher-than-average rates of poverty. A division of the U.S. Department of Health and Human Services, the IHS works to identify and address health issues affecting native populations. It advocates for native peoples, promotes healthy lifestyles, and provides medical services.

The IHS serves members of federally recognized and sovereign tribes, all of which have a formal relationship with the U.S. government. The IHS ensures that its services are accessible to native populations and that they are sensitive to the cultural values and practices of native communities. In the early twenty-first century tribal governments have the option to receive care directly through the IHS or to partner with the IHS through self-governance contracts. In December 2013 the IHS had self-governance contracts with 60 percent of the 566 tribes recognized by the U.S. government.

How Did the Indian Health Service Come About?

The Indian Health Service was formally established by the Transfer Act of 1955 to assume the responsibility for providing health care to native populations, a role formerly performed by the Bureau of Indian Affairs (BIA). The roots of the IHS, however, can be traced to the late eighteenth century, when the U.S. government signed treaties with Native American tribes guaranteeing medical and other services in return for tribal lands ceded to the U.S. government. Federal involvement in

The Indian Health Service serves American Indians, Alaska Natives, and those who can provide reasonable proof of native descent. © ASHLEY COOPER/CORBIS.

Native American health care increased dramatically during the nineteenth century as smallpox spread rapidly through native populations. The federal government worked to contain the spread of the disease in native communities as a part of its larger overall strategy. At the same time government officials encouraged native peoples to embrace Western medicine as part of its broader effort to assimilate Native American tribes into American culture.

Attitudes toward assimilation evolved over the twentieth century and so, too, did federal policies regarding medical care for Native Americans. The Snyder Act of 1921 authorized funding specifically to provide health services to Native American tribes. Despite this funding, native communities experienced few gains in medical care and quality of life. Indian populations continued to experience high rates of infant mortality and death from infection. After the Transfer Act brought Native American health care under the IHS and the Department of Health and Human Services, efforts to improve health in native communities increased dramatically. As policy makers began to recognize the importance of encouraging tribal sovereignty, programs funded under the Snyder Act were transferred to tribal governments under the Indian Self-Determination and Education Assistance Act of 1975. Although the IHS has been plagued by funding shortages since 2000, it has continued to work toward improving health care across native populations.

How Is the Indian Health Service Funded?

The IHS is funded through congressional appropriations (money devoted to a special purpose). Like all other federal agencies, the IHS must submit a budget request by the first Monday in February. This budget request is written by the IHS Division of Budget Formulation. Input from the tribes served by the IHS is crucial to this process. After the budget request is submitted, it is reviewed by the House and Senate Committees on Appropriations. The IHS provides testimony in support of the budget, but Congress has the final say on how much money will be given to the agency each year.

The IHS budget is used to maintain facilities and pay for staff and medical services. Some services, however, are contracted to outside

Yvette Roubideaux

Yvette Roubideaux (1963–), MD, MPH, is the head of the Indian Health Service. A member of the Rosebud Sioux Tribe, Roubideaux was born in South Dakota in 1963. She was inspired to become a doctor after witnessing the problems plaguing the Indian Health Service and noticing that as a patient she never received care from an American Indian physician. She earned a medical degree from Harvard Medical School in 1989. After completing her residency, she practiced on reservations in Arizona for four years. During this period, she realized that she wanted to become involved in public health policy research. She returned to Harvard, earning a Master of Public Health from the Harvard School of Public Health in 1997.

After she completed her master's degree, Roubideaux made teaching and research the focus of her career. She joined the faculty at the University of Arizona College of Public Health and College of Medicine. She gained national prominence through her research into diabetes in American Indians. She joined national steering committees such as the National Diabetes Education Program Steering Committee and the Awakening the Spirit Team for the American Diabetes Association. She also served on the Department of Health and Human Services Secretary's Advisory Committee on Minority Health.

In May 2009 Roubideaux was confirmed as IHS director by the U.S. Senate, becoming the first woman to serve in that role. She was nominated for a second term by President Barack Obama in April 2013.

providers and reimbursed with IHS funds. Unlike programs such as Social Security, Medicare, and Medicaid, IHS services are not considered entitlements. This means that the agency is unable to guarantee payment, particularly for services provided by medical partners outside the IHS, even if patients meet all eligibility requirements. In 2014 the IHS estimated that the funds appropriated by Congress cover only 60 percent of the care that eligible American Indians and Native Alaskans need.

How Do I Qualify for Care from the Indian Health Service?

In order to be eligible for IHS services, you must meet one or more of the following criteria: be regarded as an American Indian or Alaska Native within your community, be a member of a Native American or Alaska Native group under federal supervision, live on tax-exempt land,

The Indian Health Care System (IHS) at a Glance

IHS services are administered through a system of 12 Area offices and 168 IHS and tribally managed service units.

Since 1992, the IHS has entered into agreements with tribes and tribal organizations to plan, conduct, and administer programs authorized under Section 102 of the Indian Self-Determination and Education Assistance Act. In 2014, over half of the IHS appropriation was administered by Tribes.

Urban Indian health care services and resource centers

There are 33 urban programs that provide services ranging from community health to comprehensive primary health care.

- **Population Served:**
  - Members of 566 federally recognized Tribes
  - 2.2 million American Indians and Alaska Natives
- **Annual Patient Services** *(Tribal and IHS facilities)*
  - Inpatient Admissions: 45,907
  - Outpatient visits: 13,180,745
- **Appropriations**
  - FY 2013 IHS budget appropriation: $4.1 billion
  - FY 2014 IHS budget appropriation: $4.4 billion
- **IHS Third-Party Collections**
  - FY 2012: $744 million
  - FY 2013: $810 million
- **Per Capita Personal Health Care Expenditures Comparison**
  - IHS expenditure on user population: $2,849
  - Total U.S. population expenditure: $7,713
- **Human Resources**
  - Total IHS employees: 15,630 (69% are American Indian/Alaska Native)
  - Includes 2,590 nurses, 790 physicians, 660 pharmacists, 670 engineers/sanitarians, 330 physician assistants/nurse practitioners, and 290 dentists
- **Facilities**
  - Hospitals: IHS: 28; Tribal: 17
  - Health Centers: IHS: 61; Tribal: 249
  - Alaska Village Clinics: Tribal 164
  - Health Stations: IHS: 34; Tribal: 70

SOURCE: Indian Health Service. "Year 2014 Profile: Based on 2000–2013 data—Numbers are approximate." http://www.ihs.gov/aboutihs/.

ILLUSTRATION BY LUMINA DATAMATICS LTD. © 2015 CENGAGE LEARNING.

actively participate in tribal affairs, or provide other reasonable proof of native descent.

In rare cases you may be eligible for care from the IHS even if you are not a member of a federally recognized tribe. For example, you will likely qualify for care if you are a woman who is pregnant with the child of an eligible tribe member, a member of an eligible American Indian's household, or a member of a Canadian or Mexican tribe residing in an area the IHS serves. In Alaska, nonnatives who live in remote areas with little access to other care providers can make use of IHS services for a fee.

What Services Does the Indian Health Service Provide?

The IHS offers comprehensive inpatient and outpatient health services, including *preventive care* and emergency medicine, dental care, counseling services, and pharmacies. Many of these services are provided through IHS facilities. This is known as direct care. Other services are contracted to providers outside of the IHS. This is known as purchased/referred care (formerly called "contract health services"). These services are paid out of the IHS budget, but each claim must be evaluated separately. Make sure you follow all procedures when using purchased/referred care to avoid having your claim rejected and being forced to pay for care yourself.

The IHS also provides behavioral health services. These services are offered to eligible patients who are experiencing challenges such as domestic violence, substance abuse, and mental health issues, as well as those who are at risk for suicide or violent behavior. The organization's Division of Behavioral Health provides mental health services that meet the unique needs of American Indians and Native Alaskans and coordinates with tribes to advocate for national policy development with respect to these issues.

Preventive care:
Medical care that helps to prevent disease such as immunization.

What Programs Does the Indian Health Service Sponsor?

In addition to providing basic health services, the IHS sponsors outreach programs aimed at promoting healthy living and disease prevention. Among the most prominent of these is the campaign to educate IHS clients about the prevention and treatment of type 2 diabetes, which is widespread in native communities. This program was launched in 1979 when Congress initiated the IHS National Diabetes Program; the Special Diabetes Program for Indians (SDPI) followed in 1998. IHS outreach programs also promote routine *immunization* and oral health care, combat substance abuse and obesity, and encourage good nutrition. The Native American and Alaskan Native communities have an accidental injury rate that is statistically higher than the national average. For this reason many IHS outreach programs focus on injury prevention, including the elimination of environmental hazards, which are often the cause of injuries.

The IHS strives to offer health education services that are appropriate to the cultures it serves. The goal is for IHS providers to be

Immunization:
The introduction of disease-causing compounds into the body in very small amounts in order to allow the body to form antigens against the disease.

knowledgeable about the language preferences, beliefs, values, and traditions of native communities and to use this knowledge to shape the ways in which health education information is conveyed. At times, however, budget and staffing shortages have prevented IHS providers in some locations from meeting this goal. IHS providers also work with traditional healers through the Traditional Medicine Initiative to integrate cultural beliefs about healing with Western medical technology.

What Are the Advantages of Getting Care through the Indian Health Service?

The primary advantages of obtaining medical services through the IHS are its low cost and accessibility. As long as funds are available, eligible patients can access approved services at no cost, regardless of their income. In most cases, the only costs that an IHS patient can expect to incur are the costs of transportation to and from an IHS facility.

Another advantage of the Indian Health Service is that its offices are generally located in close proximity to the populations they serve. The IHS is headquartered in Rockville, Maryland, and divides its services over 12 areas with offices in the following locations: Anchorage, Alaska; Albuquerque, New Mexico; Bemidji, Minnesota; Billings, Montana; Sacramento, California; Aberdeen, South Dakota; Nashville, Tennessee; Window Rock, Arizona; Oklahoma City, Oklahoma; Phoenix, Arizona; Portland, Oregon; and Tucson, Arizona. Many of the largest IHS facilities are located on the reservations of federally recognized tribes.

How Do I Receive Care from an Indian Health Service Provider?

Once you have verified that you qualify for the services of the IHS, you will need to locate an IHS facility and complete the registration process. You can find a facility online via the IHS website (http://www.ihs.gov/findhealthcare/). Select the city and state closest to you, and search for the kind of health-care provider you are seeking (hospitals, health centers, dental clinics, or behavioral health facilities).

After you have chosen a facility that meets your needs, you must complete the registration process in person. It cannot be done by mail, online, or over the phone. You must bring proof that you are an enrolled member of a federally recognized tribe to the facility where you wish to enroll. Each IHS facility has patient registration staff who can guide you through the process.

Does Indian Health Service Eligibility Mean I Don't Qualify for Other Government Health Programs?

Being eligible for services from the Indian Health Service does not preclude your eligibility for other government-assisted health-care programs such as Medicare and Medicaid. As a U.S. citizen, you are entitled to health benefits through these federal programs if you meet their eligibility requirements. In fact, one of the reasons that the IHS does not receive more funding is that it is assumed patients will be covered by these other programs. If you have questions about your eligibility for Medicare, Medicaid, or other government programs, contact the Department of Health and Human Services (http://www.hhs.gov/).

As an American Indian or Native Alaskan you are also eligible to enroll in the marketplace insurance plans under the Affordable Care Act of 2010. Additionally, depending on your income, you may not be required to pay any out-of-pocket costs normally associated with a marketplace plan. You are also exempt from the Affordable Care Act open enrollment period, meaning that you can enroll in a marketplace plan at any time of the year. If you choose not to purchase an insurance plan, you will be exempt from the penalty that is assessed on others who do not purchase insurance.

What Does the Future Look Like for the Indian Health Service?

Although the IHS has made considerable strides in improving the health of American Indians and Alaska Natives, it faces several serious financial and political challenges. In a 2010 report issued by the Health Rights Organizing Project, the chief operating officer of the IHS's Oklahoma City Indian Clinic noted a two- to three-month waiting time to get an appointment and, illuminating the need for a larger budget and more staff, described the frustrations of having "one optometrist, and one full-time dentist and a part-time dentist, for 16,000 patients."

In 2013 the agency suffered significant budget cuts as part of the federal budget sequestration, a series of automatic spending cuts set in motion by the Budget Control Act of 2011. As part of the sequestration, the IHS budget was reduced by approximately 5 percent. In March 2013 the *New York Times* reported that the cuts were estimated to result in "3,000 fewer inpatient admissions and 804,000 fewer outpatient visits each year." Given that the IHS struggled to provide services at its previous level of funding, it seems likely that the organization will continue to face challenges to care for all patients in a timely fashion in the future.

Despite these setbacks, however, the IHS remains committed to improving the lives and health of American Indians and Native Alaskans. In March 2014 the National Indian Health Board, which advocates for IHS funding, offered testimony to Congress in support of a budget increase. The 2015 budget proposed by President Barack Obama subsequently included a $200 million increase for the IHS. This budget increase, if passed, would include additional funds for purchased/referred care as well as funds to expand existing facilities and to cover medical inflation costs.

Program of All-Inclusive Care for the Elderly (PACE)

What Is the Program of All-Inclusive Care for the Elderly (PACE)?

The Program of All-Inclusive Care for the Elderly (PACE) is a federally funded program that provides community-based services to senior citizens with chronic health-care needs. As its title suggest, PACE offers a comprehensive approach to long-term care. Each participant and his or her family work with a team of professionals to develop a unique plan for care. PACE is a part of Medicare (a U.S. government program of health insurance to the elderly), but those who join have more benefits than are provided by Medicare alone. PACE services can also be offered as an option under Medicaid (a U.S. government program of health insurance for the poor). In addition to doctor care and prescription-drug benefits, PACE provides transportation, home health care, and nursing home care if it becomes necessary. PACE centers afford senior citizens opportunities for counseling and entertainment as well as medical treatment.

PACE is committed to helping senior citizens remain in their homes and communities despite their health challenges. Many of the elderly want to avoid the loss of autonomy and flexibility that comes with living in a nursing home. PACE participants must be in need of the level of care provided by nursing homes, but according to program statistics, only 7 percent of PACE participants actually live in nursing homes or other similar institutions. The support provided through PACE allows the vast majority of participants to remain in their own homes.

What Is the History of PACE?

PACE began in California in the early 1970s when concerned citizens recognized the need for long-term care for a generation of elderly

With the help of the PACE program, this senior can remain in her home despite her health challenges. © JIM WEST/ ALAMY.

residents who had immigrated to San Francisco's Chinatown-North Beach community. The efforts of a committee of community members led to the formation in 1971 of On Lok Senior Health Services, a nonprofit organization. *On Lok* means "peaceful, happy abode" in Cantonese. In 1973 the group opened an adult day-care center, one of the first of the kind in the United States. During the day the center provided hot meals, medical care, and social services for elderly members of the community, and in the evening they returned to their own homes.

The On Lok program grew over the next decade, developing in-home services for participants and expanding its medical services. Although it was initially funded through donations, the program began receiving federal Medicaid funds in 1974. In 1979 it received a four-year grant from the U.S. Department of Health and Human Services to create a model for long-term care of the elderly that could be implemented in other areas of the country.

In 1986 federal legislation provided funds for 10 programs similar to On Lok. These programs grew rapidly, and in 1990 they began receiving funding under the name Program of All-Inclusive Care for the Elderly (PACE). When the National PACE Association (NPA) was formed in 1994, there were 11 organizations in 9 states, and by 1996 there were 21 programs in 15 states. In 1997 the Balanced Budget Act of 1997 established the PACE model as a recognized provider for both Medicare and Medicaid, and PACE continued to grow. In 2014 there were 104 PACE programs operating in 31 states.

How Is PACE Funded?

The funding for PACE comes through the federal budget allocations for Medicare and Medicaid. The funding that PACE receives from these programs is capped. This means that PACE receives a predetermined amount per participant.

Many PACE programs rely on donations to augment the funds they receive from the government. Many also rely on community volunteers to lead recreational and social activities at their centers.

What Services Does PACE Provide?

PACE provides a variety of services for participants. Adult day care has been central to PACE's mission from the outset, and most PACE programs are centered in an adult day-care program. A PACE center provides preventive medicine and nursing care as well as recreational, physical, and occupational therapy services. PACE centers also provide an opportunity for participants to socialize with each other through activities such as watching movies and playing games. Recreational activities offered in PACE centers are designed to be therapeutic as well as fun. Volunteers may also offer specialty services, such as hairdressing, at PACE centers.

If you need care that is not available at a PACE center, you will receive a referral and will be eligible for transportation to your appointments. If you are unable to travel to a PACE center, you may qualify to receive services in your home. Once you become a PACE participant, you will receive all of your health care though the program. In addition to your regular checkups, which usually take place at the PACE center, PACE coordinates emergency and hospital care, laboratory and X-ray services, and even dentistry. There is a strong emphasis on preventive care to keep you healthy and active.

PACE also offers other forms of support, including nutritional and social work counseling and social services as necessary. Depending on your level of mobility, you may be eligible for meal services through PACE. PACE also provides training for your family and other caregivers. The training helps your caregivers take an active role in your care. PACE also offers support groups for family members.

Who Qualifies for PACE?

In order to be eligible for PACE, you need to be 55 years of age or older. You also need to live in an area served by PACE. You must meet your state's Medicaid requirements for nursing home care but be able to live safely in the community with support from the program.

Your primary care physician should be able to help you determine if your health needs meet program guidelines. Discussing your interest in PACE with your physician is also a good way to review your medical needs and to weigh the pros and cons of enrolling in the program.

How Much Will I Have to Pay for PACE Services?

Before enrolling in PACE, it is important to understand how it may impact you financially. Your costs for medical care through PACE depend on your income. If you qualify for Medicare, it will pay for any Medicare-eligible services that you receive through PACE. If your income makes you eligible for Medicaid, your share of these costs may range from nothing to a small monthly payment based on your income. If your income is too high to qualify for Medicaid, you will be responsible for a monthly payment and a premium for prescriptions drug coverage under Medicare Part D. If you do not qualify for either Medicare or Medicaid, you may be able to enroll in PACE and pay for your care privately, as long as you meet all other eligibility requirements.

Central to the PACE philosophy is the idea that participants should not miss out on services owing to a lack of financial resources. Regardless of your income level, if you are enrolled in Medicare as a PACE participant, you will not need to pay a prescription copay or pay a deductible for services approved by your medical team.

Are There Any Disadvantages to Participating in PACE?

Although there are many advantages to receiving all-inclusive health care through PACE, there are also potential disadvantages. PACE professionals are well qualified to meet your medical needs, but most programs require that you give up your primary care physician, because you will be receiving care through the program's doctors. This may feel like a major life change depending on your relationship and history with your existing physician. If you are worried about this provision, you should talk with your physician and PACE staff about possible ways to ease the transition.

Another potential disadvantage is that your PACE center may not be conveniently located. Rural PACE members, for example, may have to travel a large distance to reach a center. Even if transportation is provided, the trip itself may be daunting, particularly if you have a health condition that causes physical discomfort during travel. Although the PACE program is expanding, expansion into rural areas has been slow.

How Can I Enroll in PACE Services?

If you want to participate in PACE, first make sure that you live in an area that the program serves. You can access this information online by visiting the national PACE Association website (http://www.npaonline .org/). There you can access a list of PACE programs by state and a PACE map or search for programs by state or zip code. You can also obtain more information about PACE and local PACE programs by calling the Medicare hotline, 800-MEDICAR(E) (1-800-633-4227), or by visiting your local Medicaid office.

If you find that there is a PACE program in your area, make sure that you meet all eligibility requirements. You may want to speak with program staff to verify your eligibility and to make sure that the program is a good fit for your needs. Take a tour of your local PACE center and talk to participants about their experiences with the program. Once you are sure you want to participate, the final step is to sign an enrollment agreement with your PACE center.

What Happens after I Enroll in PACE?

PACE is tailored to the unique needs of each patient. When you become a PACE participant, you are assigned an interdisciplinary team of health-care professionals. The team may include medical professionals, such as doctors and nurses, as well as therapists, social workers, and nutritionists. They may also include home health aides if you will be receiving PACE services in your home. Your team members will all have experience in working with elderly patients and will help you meet any unique needs you may have. The program ensures that you will be able to access all services your team identifies as necessary regardless of your ability to pay.

Enrolling in PACE does not require a long-term commitment to participation in the program. You can choose to voluntarily terminate your enrollment agreement and leave the program at any time.

What Does the Future Look Like for PACE?

Several studies have attested to the value of PACE. A 1998 study headed by Pinka Chatterji found that PACE participants were less likely to be admitted to nursing homes for long-term care than were their nonparticipating counterparts. Studies also suggest that PACE participants are more likely to die at home, the preference expressed by the majority of the elderly. A 2014 study by the Florida Department of Elders Affairs and the Agency for Health Care Administration found that 24 percent of PACE participants died in hospitals, compared to 53 percent of Medicare beneficiaries in general. The preventive care that PACE provides is also cited as a reason for better levels of overall health in program participants compared to all senior citizens. These studies suggest the value of PACE and support its expansion into a larger number of states and communities.

In the communities that it already serves, PACE boasts high levels of satisfaction from both enrollees and their families and caregivers. Although costs vary by location, there is some evidence that the PACE model offers cost savings both to participants and the government. Although as of 2014 it was still relatively small, it continued to expand. This expansion was expected to continue in the foreseeable future.

State Pharmaceutical Assistance Programs (SPAPs)

What Are State Pharmaceutical Assistance Programs (SPAPs)?

State pharmaceutical assistance programs, or SPAPs, are state government programs that cover some or all of the costs of medical prescriptions for eligible individuals. Several states and the U.S. Virgin Islands offer SPAPs. Some of these programs require participants to pay a fee for each prescription, while others pay a certain amount of money toward prescriptions each month and require participants to pay the rest.

The benefits available through a SPAP differ by state. Some SPAPs help pay for prescriptions that treat specific types of chronic medical conditions, such as AIDS, diabetes, or kidney disease. Other SPAPs serve specific segments of the population, such as senior citizens, people with disabilities, or people with qualifying income levels.

SPAPs began in the 1970s, about a decade after the government programs Medicare and Medicaid began providing medical coverage for underserved segments of the U.S. population. By 2006 more than 20 states had started or authorized SPAPs, and other states had initiated similar programs to help residents pay for prescriptions. The number of SPAPs has fluctuated over time as state and federal governments have made changes to how they fund and operate their insurance programs.

Are SPAPs Related to Other Government Programs?

SPAPs have changed over time because of their complex relationship to Medicare. The federal government funds and operates Medicare, a program that provides medical coverage to Americans 65 and older, disabled Americans, and Americans with certain medical conditions. Medicare offers a number of plans, including the Medicare Prescription

SPAPs are one way to find resources to help you pay for your prescriptions. © FENG YU/ SHUTTERSTOCK.COM.

Drug Plan, commonly known as Medicare Part D. Medicare Part D provides prescription benefits through private insurers.

Prior to the roll out of Medicare Part D in 2006, many state governments were paying upward of 100 percent of drug subsidies for Medicare patients, some through SPAPs. In the early twenty-first century some states ended their SPAPs and replaced them with Medicare Part D's prescription drug coverage. Others restructured their programs so that Medicare Part D would provide eligible patients' primary coverage, while SPAPs would offer "wraparound coverage" to help qualifying participants pay their share of Medicaid Part D costs. In these cases, SPAP payments count toward a patient's out-of-pocket maximum. Once this maximum is reached, costs for subsequent services go down.

In some cases you can belong to a SPAP to help you pay for prescriptions even if you have another type of health-care coverage, such as private health insurance, veterans' benefits, or Medicare. In fact, SPAPs in a number of states require you to hold another type of insurance because the state plans pay for prescriptions or fees not covered by other types of insurance. Other states will not let you belong to a SPAP if you are eligible for government programs such as Medicaid.

How Can I Learn If My State Offers a SPAP?

Although SPAPs are not always well publicized, there are ways to find out what programs are available in your state. Searching the Internet is one of the easiest ways to determine if your state offers a SPAP. If you enter terms such as "SPAP" or "SPAP Medicare" into a search engine, you will find sites that provide general information about SPAPs and specific information about state SPAPs. A number of these sites, including Medicare.gov (http://www.medicare.gov/), allow you to search by state. If your state has a SPAP, you will be able to access detailed information about the kinds of assistance it provides, eligibility requirements, and how to apply.

During your Internet search, keep in mind that few states use the term "SPAP" in the name of their program. For example, Pennsylvania's

Pharmaceutical Assistance Programs

Even if your state does not have a state pharmaceutical assistance program (SPAP), you may be able to find other resources to help you pay for your prescriptions. Many pharmaceutical companies offer financial assistance programs for patients who cannot afford the full costs of prescription drugs. Some of these programs have higher income eligibility requirements than state programs, meaning that more people qualify for assistance. Although these programs differ by company, most require that patients provide proof of income, as well as proof that they lack insurance benefits to cover the costs. They may also require a doctor's signature. In order to have your application evaluated in a timely way, be sure to fill out all parts of an application carefully and accurately.

Some states or groups of states pool their resources to buy medications from pharmaceutical companies in bulk, lowering the costs of these medications for their residents. These state programs typically are available if you are enrolled in Medicaid. Still other state governments offer cards that give discounts on prescriptions for all of their residents, regardless of their ages or how much money they make. These bulk- buying programs and discount card programs are separate from SPAPs.

Many online resources are available to help you find and access to pharmaceutical assistance programs. The Medicare.gov website (http://www.medicare.gov/pharmaceutical-assistance-program/Index.aspx) allows you to search a database of drugs to find out if assistance is available for a specific prescription. You can click on a drug name to see the company that makes it, any drug programs available from that company, the eligibility criteria for programs, and contact information for the company. Other online resources to identify programs and access application materials include RxHope (https://www.rxhope.com/), NeedyMeds (http://www.needymeds.org), and RxAssist (http://rxassist.org/). As you search the Internet, however, be aware that there are some sites designed to take advantage of patients in need of help. Never pay a fee to access information about prescription assistance programs.

SPAP is known as Pharmaceutical Assistance Contract for the Elderly (PACE). Using a website that features links to all of the SPAPs can be a quick and easy way to find an individual SPAP and can help eliminate any name confusion.

If you do not have access to the Internet, call your local Medicare/Medicaid services office. To find the phone number or address, call the helpline at 800-MEDICAR(E). Another resource for information about the programs available in your state is the doctor who prescribes your medications or your pharmacist. Medical professionals are generally aware of prescription benefits available in your state, and they should be able to guide your search. They may be able to answer questions that you have about eligibility and the application process or refer you to someone who can assist you.

How Do I Learn about and Enroll in a SPAP?

The websites of different states' SPAPs provide useful information about the benefits they provide. They can help you determine if you qualify for SPAP benefits. Several sites list their state's eligibility requirements. You might need to be a certain age, have a certain income level, or have a specific medical condition to participate in a particular SPAP. If you do not meet these requirements, alternatives for receiving assistance with your prescriptions are often listed, such as enrolling in Medicare Part D or another type of state prescription program.

If you are eligible to join a SPAP, you may enroll online or call the phone number listed on the program's website for enrollment assistance. The Pennsylvania PACE website has a link that allows you to complete and submit an application to enroll in the state's SPAP. Once enrolled in PACE, you can go online to check the status of your benefits and learn more about PACE, such as updates regarding its coverage.

SPAPs offer different benefits in different states for different people and conditions. To belong to PACE, for example, you have to be a Pennsylvania resident who is 65 or older with a yearly income that is below a certain limit. You also cannot receive prescription benefits from Medicaid or other types of prescription-assistance programs. If you meet these requirements, you can enroll in PACE and receive its benefits.

Generic drug: *A drug that is approved by the Food and Drug Administration but is marketed under its chemical name, rather than its brand name, and is less expensive than a brand name drug.*

What Do SPAPs Offer?

Once enrolled in a SPAP, you pay a co-payment fee to receive brand-name and *generic* prescription drugs. A co-payment fee (also called a co-payment, co-pay fee, or co-pay) is the amount you are required to pay each time you use a medical service, such as receiving a prescribed medication or seeing a doctor.

Other SPAPs provide assistance with specific health needs. One such SPAP, the Texas Kidney Health Care Program (KHC), requires you to meet typical SPAP requirements, such as requiring you to live in a particular state (Texas), have an income under a certain level, and not be a recipient of full Medicaid benefits. Since it covers specific conditions, this type of SPAP requires you to have specific medical diagnoses and meet the definitions for certain conditions. This means that enrollees in the Texas KHC must be on dialysis or have received a kidney transplant and conform to Medicare's definition of end-stage renal disease. The Texas KHC also offers more comprehensive coverage than a typical SPAP. In addition to prescription coverage, it pays for medical care and medical-related travel expenses for qualified people who do not have insurance coverage or full Medicaid benefits.

The Texas HIV Medication Program (THMP) offers another Texas SPAP, the Texas HIV State Pharmacy Assistance Program. As with the state's kidney SPAP, Texas's HIV Medication Program and its SPAP require you to be a state resident with income below a certain level and insurance coverage needs. These programs also require specific medical diagnoses, which in this case is a diagnosis of HIV with certain cellular and viral characteristics. Once enrolled in Texas's HIV SPAP, you can receive antiretroviral drugs and drugs treating HIV-related infections. This SPAP also helps you pay for co-payment fees, insurance charges, deductibles (amounts you have to pay before your insurer pays the rest), and expenses that other insurance plans do not cover. As with other SPAPs, you can hold additional coverage, such as Medicare coverage, while you are enrolled in the Texas HIV State Pharmacy Assistance Program in order to pay for prescriptions and other medical costs.

How Has Legislation Affected SPAPs?

Legislation has affected SPAPs and related insurance programs such as Medicare. Signed into law in 2010, the Patient Protection and Affordable Care Act (ACA) requires most Americans to obtain health insurance coverage and provides them with tools to find and enroll in such plans. Some provisions of the ACA give discounts on prescription drugs and rebates to help people enrolled in Medicare Part D who might have to pay some drug expenses themselves. Thus, people covered by the Affordable Care Act might need less assistance from SPAPs if they have a plan such as Medicare that covers more of their prescription expenses. Or they might need more SPAP assistance if they have a new insurance plan that does not cover all of their prescription expenses.

For More Information

BOOKS

Kronenfeld, Jennie Jacobs. *Medicare*. Santa Barbara, CA: ABC-CLIO, 2011.

"Medicaid." In *Gale Encyclopedia of Everyday Law*, edited by Donna Batten, 845–50. Detroit: Gale, 2013.

Pampel, Fred C. "The Law and Prescription Drugs." In *Prescription Drugs*, by Fred C. Pampel, 72–103. New York: Facts on File, 2010.

PERIODICALS

Bergman, Abraham B., et al. "A Political History of the Indian Health Service." *Millbank Quarterly* 77, no. 4 (1999): 571–604. This article can also be found online at http://www.ncbi.nlm.nih.gov/pmc/articles/PMC2751138/pdf/milq_152.pdf.

Gross, D., Helena Temkin-Greener, S. Kunitz, and D. B. Mukamel. "The Growing Pains of Integrated Health Care for the Elderly: Lessons from the Expansion of PACE." *Milbank Quarterly* 82, no. 2 (2004): 257–82.

Kuschell-Haworth, Holly T. "Jumping through Hoops: Traditional Healers and the Indian Health Care Improvement Act." *DePaul Journal of Health Care Law* 4 (Summer 1999): 843–60.

"The Sequester Hits the Reservation." *New York Times*, March 20 2013. This article can also be found online at http://www.nytimes.com/2013/03/21/opinion/the-sequester-hits-the-indian-health-service.html.

Washington, Donna L., Elizabeth M. Yano, Barbara Simon, and Su Sun. "To Use or Not to Use: What Influences Why Women Veterans Choose VA Health Care." *Journal of General Internal Medicine*, March 2006: S11–18. This article can also be found online at http://www.ncbi.nlm.nih.gov/pmc/articles/PMC1513176/.

WEBSITES

Barry, Patricia. "Do You Qualify for Medicare?" *AARP*. http://www.aarp.org/health/medicare-insurance/info-04-2011/medicare-eligibility.html (accessed October 21, 2014).

"Children's Health Insurance Program (CHIP)." *Medicaid.gov*. http://www.medicaid.gov/CHIP/CHIP-Program-Information.html (accessed October 1, 2014).

"Children's Health Insurance Program Financing." *Medicaid.gov*. http://www.medicaid.gov/Medicaid-CHIP-Program-Information/By-Topics/Financing-and-Reimbursement/Childrens-Health-Insurance-Program-Financing.html (accessed October 1, 2014).

"Children's Health Insurance Program Reauthorization Act (CHIPRA)." *Medicaid.gov*. http://www.medicaid.gov/medicaid-chip-program-information/by-topics/childrens-health-insurance-program-chip/chipra.html (accessed October 3, 2014).

"CHIPRA Performance Bonuses." *InsureKidsNow.gov*. http://www.insurekidsnow.gov/professionals/eligibility/performance_bonuses.html (accessed October 4, 2014).

"Coordinating Prescription Drug Benefits." *Centers for Medicare and Medicaid Services.* http://www.cms.gov/Medicare/Coordination-of-Benefits-and-Recovery/Prescription-Drug-Assistance-Programs/Coordinating-Prescription-Drug-Benefits/Coordinating-Prescription-Drug-Benefits-Page.html (accessed October 16, 2014).

"Coordination of Benefits." *Centers for Medicare and Medicaid Services.* http://www.cms.gov/Medicare/Prescription-Drug-Coverage/PrescriptionDrugCovContra/downloads/PDMChapt14COB.pdf (accessed October 14, 2014).

"Health Insurance Information, Counseling and Assistance—HIICAP." *New York State Office for the Aging.* http://www.aging.ny.gov/HealthBenefits/ (accessed October 2, 2014).

"Health Insurance Marketplace." *HHS.gov/HeathCare.* http://www.hhs.gov/healthcare/insurance/index.html (accessed October 3, 2014).

"Indian Health Service." http://www.ihs.gov/ (accessed October 2, 2014).

"Kidney Health Care Program." *Texas Kidney Foundation.* https://txkidney.org/uploads/2/8/5/5/2855229/kidney_health_care_program.pdf (accessed October 15, 2014).

"Medicare's 49th Anniversary." *National Committee to Preserve Social Security and Medicare.* http://www.ncpssm.org/Medicare/49YearsofMedicareGoodThingstoKnow (accessed October 21, 2014).

"PACE." *Medicare.* http://www.medicare.gov/your-medicare-costs/help-paying-costs/pace/pace.html (accessed October 21, 2014).

Panangala, Sidath Viranga. "Veterans Medical Care: FY 2014 Appropriations." *Congressional Research Service.* August 14, 2013. http://assets.opencrs.com/rpts/R43179_20130814.pdf (accessed October 13, 2014).

"Programs and Services." *New York State Office for the Aging.* http://www.aging.ny.gov/NYSOFA/Services/Index.cfm?id=HIICAP,#HIICAP (accessed October 2, 2014).

"Questions and Answers." *InsureKidsNow.gov.* http://www.insurekidsnow.gov/qa/index.html#Covered Services (accessed October 3, 2014).

"Sign Up/Change Plans." *Medicare.gov.* http://www.medicare.gov/ (accessed October 21, 2014).

"State Health Insurance Assistance Program National Technical Assistance Center." *HHS Grants Forecast.* http://www.acf.hhs.gov/hhsgrantsforecast/index.cfm?switch=grant.view&gff_grants_forecastInfoID=70300 (accessed October 1, 2014).

"State Health Insurance Programs." *National Association of States United for Aging and Disabilities.* http://www.nasuad.org/initiatives/state-health-insurance-programs (accessed October 1, 2014).

"State Pharmaceutical Assistance Programs." *Medicare.gov.* http://www.medicare.gov/pharmaceutical-assistance-program/state-programs.aspx (accessed October 14, 2014).

"State Pharmaceutical Assistance Programs." *Medicare Rights Center.* http://www.medicareinteractive.org/uploadedDocuments/mi_extra/SPAP-Chart.pdf (accessed October 13, 2014).

"State Pharmaceutical Assistance Programs." *My Medicare Matters*. https://www .mymedicarematters.org/about-medicare/types-of-coverage/part-d/cost/ coping-with-the-coverage-gap/spaps/ (accessed October 14, 2014).

"State Pharmaceutical Assistance Programs." *National Conference of State Legislatures*. http://www.ncsl.org/research/health/state-pharmaceutical- assistance-programs.aspx (accessed October 13, 2014).

"Texas HIV Medication Program—Frequently Asked Questions (FAQ)." *Texas Department of State Health Services*. http://www.dshs.state.tx.us/hivstd/meds/ faq.shtm (accessed October 15, 2014).

"Texas HIV Medication Program—The Texas HIV SPAP." *Texas Department of State Health Services*. http://www.dshs.state.tx.us/hivstd/meds/spap.shtm (accessed October 15, 2014).

"VA History in Brief." *U.S. Department of Veteran Affairs*. http://www.va.gov/ opa/publications/archives/docs/history_in_brief.pdf (accessed October 15, 2014).

"Veterans Health Administration." *U.S. Department of Veterans Affairs*. http:// www.va.gov/health/ (accessed October 15, 2014).

"Welcome to SHIPtalk!" *SHIPtalk*. https://www.shiptalk.org/default.aspx?Ret urnUrl=%2f&a,p;AspxAutoDetectCookieSupport=1 (accessed October 1, 2014).

"What is Pace?" *National PACE Association*. http://www.npaonline.org/website/ article.asp?id=12&title=Who,_What_and_Where_Is_PACE? (accessed October 21, 2014).

Private Health Coverage

What Is Consumer-driven Health Care (CDHC)?

Consumer-driven health care (CDHC) is a type of health-care plan that generally consists of three components: a high-deductible insurance plan (HDIP) with low premiums that cover catastrophic medical expenses; a medical savings account that allows consumers to pay for their routine care directly; and access to information about health-care options and costs.

CDHC is intended to empower consumers by granting them more flexibility to choose how much and to whom they pay for routine health care. In other, more common health-care plans such as health maintenance organizations (HMOs) and preferred provider organizations (PPOs), enrollees tend to pay high premiums to insurance companies and give some control of their care options to providers and insurance. By allowing you to pay for health care yourself instead of going through insurance, CDHC plans let you be more active in choosing your care.

© ALEXSKOPJE/
SHUTTERSTOCK.COM.

You can also get more value from your health spending because the money you contribute to your health savings account is not subject to taxes.

CDHC is intended to reduce spending on health plans and health care in general. Under these plans, employers and employees can save money on both premiums and out-of-pocket expenses. Because consumers will be less likely to pay for extra or unneeded services, overall spending on health care could decrease.

How Did CDHC Come About?

CDHC plans in the United States began in the late 1990s and have made major advances ever since. Initially conceived as a way to decrease health-care spending and to give consumers more information and choice about their health-care expenses, the concept was boosted in 2003 by the passage of the Medicare Prescription Drug, Improvement, and Modernization Act. This legislation increased the use of various medical savings accounts and increased tax incentives for the use of high-deductible insurance plans. The development and spread of the Internet also facilitated the use of CDHC plans, with information about health choices and costs readily available to consumers online.

What Are the Key Differences between CDHC Plans and Other Health-Care Options?

CDHC differs from more traditional health insurance coverage in that it provides high-deductible insurance coverage along with personal health savings accounts in order to give you more control over health expenses. In more traditional health plans such as HMOs and PPOs, you pay out of pocket until you meet a predetermined *deductible*; after this is met, insurance providers pay a high percentage of your health-care costs. Insurance companies often limit which providers and services they cover, and you are not usually given a choice of pricing options.

Deductible: *The amount of money a patient must pay for services covered by the insurance company before the plan will pay for any medical bills.*

What Are HSAs?

Health savings accounts (HSAs) are medical expense accounts available to individuals who are also enrolled in high-deductible insurance plans.

What Happens to My HSA If I Leave My Job?

In planning contributions to your health savings account (HSA), it is important to know what will happen to the funds if you leave or lose your job. Unlike flexible spending accounts (FSAs), which are terminated with employment, HSAs and all funds in them remain yours even after your employment ends. There is no time limit on the account. As long as you have funds in the account, it will remain open and you will be able to withdraw money for eligible medical expenses. The terms of the account, however, may change with your new employment status, so it is important to read the fine print. Importantly, most accounts incur a monthly administration fee. Employers generally pay these fees for their employees. After leaving your job, these fees will likely be deducted from your account each month. Over time they can deplete your balance significantly.

Once the funds in the account are depleted, weigh the benefits of keeping the account open. If you are eligible to make additional contributions to the account, you will be able to deposit funds to cover your medical bills, allowing you to continue to pay them with pretax dollars. In order to contribute additional funds to your HSA account, however, you must enroll in another qualifying, high-deductible plan (whether through a new employer, COBRA, or a private insurance plan). If you are not able make additional contributions, you may want to close the account to avoid incurring additional monthly fees.

The Internal Revenue Service (IRS) permits pretax payroll contributions to HSAs as well as posttax contributions, which can then be deducted from your gross taxable income when you file yearly taxes. These rules give HSA holders a tax advantage. You are the sole owner of your HSA, and any funds you do not use by the year's end roll over to the next year.

Employees, employers, and other parties (or some combination of the three) can pay into HSAs. The U.S. Congress sets maximum yearly contributions to HSAs, regardless of who contributes. For 2015, for example, the maximum yearly contribution permitted for an unmarried individual was $3,350. Maximum contributions are higher for married individuals and those over 55 years of age. Regardless of who contributes to the HSA, the contributions immediately belong to the account holder.

You may spend savings from these accounts without penalty on qualified medical expenses. The list of qualified expenses is determined by Congress, overseen by the IRS, and distributed to account holders. Qualified expenses can include care covered by HDIPs that fall below

Health Reimbursement Arrangement (HRA), Health Savings Account (HSA), Flexible Spending Account (FSA), and Premium Reimbursement Arrangement (PRA) Comparison

	HRA	HSA	FSA	PRA
Who may Contribute	Employer	Employer or Employee	Employee or Employer	Employee or Employer
Cost of Employer Contributions	Only pay for utilization (typically 25–50%)	100% Paid regardless of utilization	n/a	n/a
Average Cost to Cover $2,000/year Deductible	$500–$1,000	$2,000	$2,000	$2,000
Maximum Annual Contribution	No maximum	$3,350 (single) $6,650 (family) for 2015	Determined by employer; Capped at $2,550 starting in 2015	Determined by employer; usually total compensation
Eligibility Requirements	None or Determined by employer	Must have HSA-qualified health coverage ($1,250 + single/ $2,500 + family)	None or Determined by employer	None or Determined by employer
Each Employee must open new Bank Account?	No	Yes	No	No
Tax Treatment	Tax-free	Tax-free	Tax-free	Tax-free
Medical Expenses Allowed	Health Insurance Premiums + IRC 213(d)** as determined by employer	IRC 213(d) Expenses w/ no employer limitations	IRC 213(d) Expenses; but no Personal Health Insurance	Personal Health Insurance only
Use for Non-Medical Expenses	None	None	None	None
Carryover of Unused Funds to Next Year	Determined by employer	Yes	No	No
Portable after Termination	Determined by employer	Yes	No	No
Administrator	Employer or Third Party Administrator	Employee	Employer or Third Party Administrator	Employer or Third Party Administrator
Cross-Compatibility	With HSA* or FSA	Limited-Purpose or Post-Deductible FSA or HRA	With HRA or HSA*	With HRA, HSA, or FSA
Employer Reporting	Employer Views Detailed Utilization Reports	No Tracking Possible	Employer Views Detailed Utilization Reports	Employer Views Detailed Utilization Reports

*HSAs are fully compatible only with certain HRA & FSA administration platforms that enable HSA-Compatibility.
**RC 213(d) = Those expenses paid for care as described in Section 213 (d) of the Internal Revenue Code.

SOURCE: Lindquist, Rick. "Employee Health Benefits and Insurance Blog: HRA vs HSA vs FSA vs PRA Comparison Chart." ZaneBenefits, May 10, 2012. http://www.zanebenefits.com/blog/bid/143489/HRA-vs-HSA-vs-FSA-vs-PRA-Comparison-Chart.

the deductible or require coinsurance. They can also include care not usually covered by health insurance, such as dental, vision, chiropractic care, as well as the purchase of durable goods such as hearing aids.

You do not need approval before spending money from your HSA, but you must keep records of expenses paid through them. Money from HSAs spent on unqualified or undocumented expenses is subject to income tax and, as of 2014, there is a penalty payment of 20 percent of the amount spent. You can withdraw your HSA funds in several ways, including via debit card or check or through a reimbursement process.

What Are HRAs?

Health reimbursement accounts or health reimbursement arrangements (HRAs) reimburse you for out-of-pocket medical expenses and health insurance premiums. They are funded entirely by employers. You can use HRA reimbursements tax free and in combination with any type of insurance plan. Employers receive tax deductions for their contributions to HRAs.

Employers establish the parameters for use of HRAs as well as their own minimum and maximum contributions. HRAs reimburse you for services, premiums, and copays only if they are not covered by your insurance. Employers set and must provide lists of qualified reimbursable expenses. The IRS sanctions the use of HRAs, and Congress can and has voted to alter their parameters. Because of this, you should stay aware of the current laws regarding their use.

Although they are not required to prefund HRAs, employers can pay employees for qualified expenses as they occur. As with HSAs, any money left in your HRA at the end of the year rolls over to the next. If you change jobs and leave the sponsoring employer, however, you lose this money because any HRA funds you hold return to the employer.

What Are FSAs?

Flexible spending accounts or flexible spending arrangements (FSAs) are frequently offered in conjunction with traditional health insurance plans but are also available to individuals using CDHC. Like HSAs, FSAs are accounts to which individuals contribute pretax dollars. Medical FSAs, the most common type of FSA, can be used to pay for medical and health-care expenses and other fees and services not covered by health insurance. Other types of FSAs cover employees' transportation or child-care expenses.

Employers that offer FSAs should provide you with an Explanation of Benefits (EOB) for their use. Health FSAs usually cover expenses that fall below your insurance deductible, including dental and medical fees, as well as co-payments, prescription medications, and medical devices. Many users of health FSAs can access those funds through debit cards. Employers require itemized receipts to document FSA use, although this is changing as some grocery stores and pharmacies become informed of FSA-approved expenses and are able to accept or deny expenses at checkout.

As of 2015, the IRS permitted a maximum yearly contribution to FSAs of $2,550, and beginning in 2014, you could roll over up to $500 of your account at year's end. You lose access to your FSA if you leave the sponsoring employer.

How Do Employers Benefit from CDHC Plans?

Employers who offer CDHC plans could spend fewer health-care dollars than those who offer HMOs or PPOs. One reason is that high-deductible insurance plans have lower premiums than those with low deductibles. Another reason is that employers can choose what type of health savings account to offer their employees, as well as whether and how much to contribute to them. HRAs allow employers to decide how much they contribute and also return unused contributions to the employer if employees do not use them by the end of the year.

A 2012 study conducted by the Society for Human Resource Management showed that, in a sample of employers, more than half offered CDHC plans. The same study found that employers offered HSAs twice as often as HRAs, indicating that HSAs might be more economical for employers and more attractive to employees.

What Are the Advantages of CDHC Plans for Consumers?

Under CDHC plans, you are able to choose your own providers and search for the best prices for your health care. Proponents project that by allowing you to make informed choices about health care and by giving you direct access to your health-care dollars you will get more value for your money. Supporters also believe that as more people enroll in CDHC plans health-care providers will begin to repackage their services and adjust their fees to meet consumer demand. In theory, health-care providers will compete for consumers' dollars, and that competition will drive down health-care prices.

A 2012 brief by the Robert Wood Johnson Foundation found that compared to other types of health-care plans CDHC plans have led to a 5 to 14 percent reduction in enrollees' use of health services. In general, healthy CDHC enrollees spent less money on health care, often seeking fewer outpatient visits, for example.

A 2014 study conducted by health insurance provider Cigna reported that overall those enrolled in CDHC plans spent fewer health-care dollars than similar individuals covered under traditional health insurance. The study also reported that CDHC enrollees were more likely to engage in preventive care and illness management programs, used emergency care 5 percent less, and complied more often with recommended treatment.

What Are the Disadvantages of CDHC Plans for Consumers?

Advocates of CDHC plans favor consumer knowledge and choice and therefore stress that access to accurate information about diagnostics, treatments, drugs, and other services is vital to the program's success. According to the 2012 Robert Wood Johnson Foundation brief, access to tools for consumer decision making is improving but it is still a weak spot for CDHC plans in general. The same report showed that the majority of the health-care savings in CDHC plans is found in relatively healthy enrollees and that the savings are mainly from reduced spending on pharmaceuticals and outpatient visits. There is no research to prove that CDHC improves or harms the quality of health care for its enrollees.

Some physicians' groups fault high-deductible insurance programs with favoring the well and with discouraging enrollees from seeking preventive care. Their concern is that CDHC plan enrollees who are chronically ill or families that have children with high health care needs end up paying much more than the well. Also, because CDHC plan enrollees pay personally from health savings accounts, some doctors are concerned that patients will limit their routine or preventive care.

What Should I Know about the Future of CDHC?

CDHC appears to be gaining in popularity with both employers and employees. In 2009, 8 percent of covered workers in the United States were enrolled in CDHC plans, and by 2014, almost 17 percent were enrolled. Many studies show that CDHC plan enrollees tend to be wealthier, more educated, and healthier than those enrolled in other types of health-care plans. CDHC plans do appear to reduce overall health-care spending for healthy enrollees. There is no data to prove that CDHC improves the overall quality and effectiveness of health care available to its enrollees.

There are many rules and regulations regarding the elements of CDHC. Many of these change from year to year as Congress passes various health-care laws. The 2013 passage of the Patient Protection and Affordable Care Act, for instance, permitted higher annual contributions to HSAs and higher deductibles for insurance plans that accompany them. Both employers and employees are responsible for keeping track of these types of regulations and changes.

Managed Care

What Is Managed Care?

Managed care is an approach to providing health insurance coverage that places limits on the choices consumers can make in exchange for lower monthly insurance premiums and out-of-pocket costs. Managed care centers the delivery of a patient's health care on the advice and referrals of a single primary care physician (PCP) who is the patient's first point of contact when seeking medical attention. The PCP monitors the patient's health over time and helps manage and maintain it using a pre-established network of health-care providers.

Managed care is usually provided and administered by a managed care organization (MCO) that uses a variety of techniques to streamline care for greater efficiency. This results in overall cost savings for both consumers and businesses.

What Is a Managed Care Organization?

An MCO is a corporate entity that provides health insurance coverage or health care through an established network of providers. An MCO also handles the management and administration of these health plans. The amount of flexibility people have in choosing health-care providers determines how affordable a managed care insurance plan will be. Often, an MCO contracts with specific primary care doctors, hospitals, medical laboratories, diagnostic-testing facilities, and other health-care services to provide care for its members. Sometimes an MCO owns hospitals and clinics itself and employs doctors and other providers directly.

There are many factors to take into consideration when choosing a health plan. © JOHN T TAKAI/SHUTTERSTOCK.COM.

Vaccinations for Adults

Managed care programs often cover many preventive health services. One of the most important of these is immunization for adults. According to the government health-care website Healthcare.gov, adults should get regular vaccinations just as children do, because certain shots that people receive when they are young can wear off over time. Vaccinations can help keep people healthy, as well as the others around them.

The Office of Disease Prevention and Health Promotion recommends that adults obtain a flu shot each year. Children obtain a Tdap vaccine to prevent tetanus, diphtheria, and whooping cough, but this vaccine should be followed every 10 years with another shot, called a Td shot, to reinforce protection against tetanus and diphtheria. People who are 60 years of age and older should receive a shot to prevent shingles, a disease that causes a rash and pain that can last for months. For pneumonia prevention, people at least 65 and older should obtain a shot known as PPSV.

If you did not receive all of your childhood vaccinations, you should talk to your doctor about shots you may need. Pregnant women should obtain regular vaccinations during each pregnancy, including the Tdap shot. Other vaccinations that adults may need include those for hepatitis A and B and meningococcal disease, as well as one for measles, mumps, and rubella (MMR). Since most immunizations are covered under managed care plans, those who are able to should take advantage of this benefit.

This group of health-care providers makes up the plan's network in a geographical service area. When consumers visit providers within this network, much of their preventive care is covered, or paid for, by the plan. The primary way MCOs keep costs low is by restricting the number of health-care providers available. They also reduce costs at the provider level by negotiating terms with doctors that result in lower fees than the doctors would normally charge to uninsured patients. Types of managed care plans include health maintenance organizations (HMOs), preferred provider organizations (PPOs), and point-of-service (POS) plans, among others.

How Do Managed Care Plans Work?

Managed-care health plans rely on a specific network of providers that includes hospitals, clinics, physicians, specialists, testing facilities, and pharmacies. With most plans, you must choose a PCP from a list of available doctors as a point of first contact in the health-care system. The use of a PCP is central to nearly all managed care plans.

Managed care plans also focus on patient education and preventive medicine. The primary care doctor works with you on an ongoing basis to make sure that you understand lifestyle choices that lead to improved or impaired health. To facilitate this, managed care plans cover preventive health care at no additional cost to you. Such preventive care includes regular checkups, screenings (mammograms, for example), and *immunizations*.

Managed care plans typically require preauthorization for medical procedures and hospital stays. This means that you cannot decide independently that you need a specific form of treatment. Instead, treatment options are presented by your PCP and are subject to preapproval by the MCO. When needed, your primary care doctor can make referrals to specialists for additional treatment, but usually these referrals must be made to other doctors within the plan's network. Whether through contracts with groups of doctors, clinics, or hospitals or by owning and employing them outright, managed care plans seek to provide comprehensive health care at the lowest possible cost.

immunizations:
The introduction of disease-causing compounds into the body in very small amounts in order to allow the body to form antigens against the disease.

In 2014, preferred provider options were the most popular health plan for covered workers. ILLUSTRATION BY LUMINA DATAMATICS LTD. © 2015 CENGAGE LEARNING.

How Did Managed Care Plans Come About?

Managed care plans in the United States emerged around the 1930s. Most early plans were run by small groups of local doctors. They functioned as simple membership plans in which people paid a monthly fee for access to specific doctors and medical services. Some of these plans were organized by doctors to provide needed care in sparsely populated rural areas where it was difficult for people to find and afford medical treatment. Others were created to serve large groups of employees who worked for a single company.

Over the next 30 years, similar programs arose across the country as a way to deliver health care to more people at an affordable rate. Eventually, some of these group plans merged or grew in size and scope, becoming giant corporations that employed thousands of people and serviced millions of consumers. Some of the largest and most

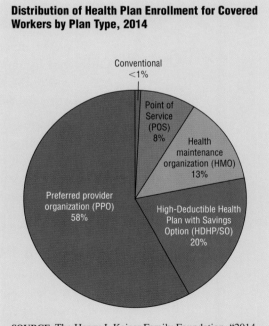

Distribution of Health Plan Enrollment for Covered Workers by Plan Type, 2014

Conventional <1%
Point of Service (POS) 8%
Health maintenance organization (HMO) 13%
Preferred provider organization (PPO) 58%
High-Deductible Health Plan with Savings Option (HDHP/SO) 20%

SOURCE: The Henry J. Kaiser Family Foundation. "2014 Employer Health Benefits Survey, September 10, 2014." Exhibit E. http://kff.org/report-section/ehbs-2014-summary-of-findings/.

well-known managed care organizations are Kaiser-Permanente, Blue Cross/Blue Shield, and Aetna.

What Is an HMO?

A health maintenance organization (HMO) is the most restrictive but also the most affordable type of managed care plan. When you participate in an HMO, you must choose a primary care doctor from a list of physicians who are part of the HMO's network of providers. Not every doctor in a certain region will participate, so your choice will be limited to those who do.

With an HMO, health-care decision making is placed in the hands of the PCP, who acts as a gateway to the other services and providers within the network. For example, when you or a covered family member gets sick, you must first see your primary care physician. Typically, the doctor will prescribe medication or order tests to diagnose the problem. If your doctor is unable to treat your condition there in the office, you will be referred to a specialist who is also in the HMO's network of doctors. However, in the case of an emergency, you are allowed to seek treatment from any doctor or hospital available.

HMOs require a minimal amount of paperwork from members. Once your insurance information is on file, all in-network providers have access to this information, so you will not have to fill out forms or make co-payments for office visits or lab tests.

HMOs seek to keep you healthy by covering 100 percent of the costs of preventive care. The goal is to discover health problems early and make sure to treat them before they get worse. By keeping you informed and closely monitoring your health over time, PCPs keep a close eye on their patients' condition and can address problems before they become more difficult and costly to treat.

What Is a POS?

A point-of-service (POS) plan (sometimes known as an "open-ended HMO") offers more flexibility than an HMO by allowing you to use some providers outside its network, but it still requires you to select a PCP from within the network. If you have this type of plan, you can choose to see a specialist either in or outside the network, but this choice must first be approved by your PCP. Depending on the plan, if PCP approval is not granted, only a portion of the cost of being treated by the specialist will be covered, and there may be a *deductible* that has to be met before this partial coverage kicks in. A POS plan encourages in-network care by making visits to those providers more affordable.

POS plans tend to have higher premiums and larger co-payment amounts than HMOs, especially with out-of-network care, but they offer a greater choice of providers. As with HMOs, preventive care is usually covered at no additional cost when provided in-network.

Deductible: *The amount of money a patient must pay for services covered by the insurance company before the plan will pay for any medical bills.*

What Is a PPO?

A preferred provider organization (PPO) is the most expensive and least restrictive of managed care plans. It is structured like an HMO, with a predetermined network of health-care providers that the plan prefers you use, but you are free to see doctors or other providers outside the plan's network without a referral. The co-payment amounts for a PPO are higher than with an HMO, and there is often a yearly deductible that must be met before the health-care benefits apply. However, preventive care is not always fully covered, especially if this care is provided by an out-of-network doctor.

PPOs do not require you to choose a primary-care physician. Instead, you can choose to visit any doctor you prefer, whether inside or outside the plan's network, but the amount of coverage is greater for doctors and other providers within the network.

Sometimes the rates of coverage are expressed in terms such as "80/20," which means that, once the yearly deductible has been met, the plan will pay 80 percent of the cost of care while the patient is responsible for the remaining 20 percent. For example, if your doctor charges $1,000 for a procedure, the plan will pay $800 and you will be responsible for the remaining $200. This $200 is called a coinsurance payment. Coinsurance amounts can vary greatly, so you must decide how much you are willing to spend on certain aspects of care when going outside the provider network.

A PPO requires you to take a more active role in your own health care, since there is not always a primary care physician to coordinate care within the network. This means that you may have a greater amount of paperwork to fill out with each doctor visit, but these records will not be linked or shared with other providers unless you takes steps to make this happen.

What Are the Key Differences between Managed Care Plans and Other Health-Care Options?

The use of a predefined network of providers is what distinguishes managed care plans from other forms of private health insurance. With traditional indemnity health insurance plans, often known as "fee-for-service" plans, there is no network, and you are free to visit any doctor or specialist as needed. While it is possible for you to see any doctor you want under a PPO plan, it is common for participants in managed care plans to receive the majority of their care from in-network providers. Rather than being coordinated and evaluated by a single primary care doctor, your care is distributed among a number of doctors and specialists who may not communicate with each other.

Indemnity plans generally do not provide incentives for preventive care, and they usually have higher yearly deductibles and require larger coinsurance payments than managed care plans. A visit to the doctor for a routine exam may be fully covered by a managed care plan, but the same exam would be subject to a deductible and coinsurance with a private indemnity plan. However, with an indemnity plan there is no preauthorization requirement, and you are free to make all of your own health-care decisions using any available physician.

What Are the Advantages of Managed Care Plans?

The greatest advantage of managed care plans is affordability. Usually, an HMO is the most affordable choice. Managed care plans have low monthly premiums and smaller (if any) co-payments, and they generally require less paperwork than other forms of insurance. They also cover preventive care, such as regular checkups and immunizations, at little or no additional cost.

Through the use of a primary care physician, managed care is centralized and coordinated within one fixed network. This allows the PCP to be the consumer's gateway to the rest of the services within the network, and it also makes it possible for the organization to provide advice and referrals based on intimate knowledge of a patient's history.

Managed care organizations usually encompass all areas of available health care, from hospitals and clinics to laboratories and pharmacies, often in a single location. This means that you may be able to see a doctor and get a blood test, and possibly a scan or an X-ray, from providers who coordinate with one another on your behalf and who may even be located in the same building.

What Are the Disadvantages of Managed Care Plans?

The greatest disadvantage of managed care plans is limited choice. To varying degrees, managed care plans place limits on the available health-care providers that are covered by the plan's insurance benefits. If, for example, you are not satisfied with the choice of physicians available and want to see a doctor outside the network, you will be responsible for some or all of the costs associated with this out-of-network care.

Limited consumer choice means that managed care plans have a great degree of control over patient care, and changes in a plan mean changes for the consumer. For instance, because each managed care plan has its own network of providers, if you or your employer change plans for any reason, you will likely not be able to keep the same primary care doctor unless the new plan has the same network as the old one.

Managed care plans also place an emphasis on keeping costs down, and this may lead to your not receiving the most advanced or up-to-the-minute care available. Not every medical procedure is covered, and because of the preapprovals required for most specialist care, patients may experience longer wait times for treatment. People who are well informed about the latest medicines and treatments may find that they cannot receive them under their managed care plan or they will have to pay a lot more out of pocket to get them.

What Does the Future Look Like for Managed Care Plans?

The popularity of managed-care plans makes it likely that they will remain one of the dominant health plan options. Employers often favor managed care plans because of the low cost to both the company and its employees. Also, managed care organizations typically provide a number of insurance options and handle the administration and implementation of the plans, which makes them like "one-stop shopping" for an employer. In short, MCOs make it easy for employers to offer a wide variety of plans at competitive prices. The preventive-care aspect of most managed care plans also helps keep a company's workforce healthy and productive with fewer illness-related absences over the long term.

Managed care has grown over time to become the dominant health-care delivery mechanism in the United States. With the passage of the Patient Protection and Affordable Care Act in 2010, many people who had previously been uninsured were given the option to sign up for health coverage, and the majority of plans made available were managed care plans. The act single-handedly funneled millions of people into managed care plans of all kinds, helping to make managed care the number one type of health plan in the United States.

Employer-Sponsored Health Plans

What Is an Employer-Sponsored Health Plan?

An employer-sponsored health plan is a health-care plan that a company offers to employees at no or relatively low cost as a benefit of their employment. The type and amount of health-care coverage that an employee receives may vary widely, as well as the financial contribution required from both employers and employees. Typical plans include coverage for some or all of the costs of hospitalization, emergency care, routine or preventive care, disability, dental or vision care, mental health, long-term care, and prescription drugs. Plans may also provide coverage for an employee's spouse or dependent children.

Employer-sponsored plans are most typically found in the United States, since unlike many other countries, it does not rely on a national health system. Employers sometimes offer robust employer-sponsored health plans in order to attract or retain employees. Employers can also get a variety of tax benefits from offering employer-sponsored health plans, and some companies may offer their employees a variety of plans to choose from. Individual plans can vary by the degree of coverage, amount of costs to the employee, and by which health-care providers or institutions the employee can use.

Government workers are more likely to have employer-sponsored health plans than those who work for private employers. The Employee Benefit Research Institute found that 85.7 percent of government employees had employer-sponsored plans in 2009, compared to 67.5 percent of employees in the private sector. Those who worked for larger businesses, were full-time workers, had high-skilled jobs, or were in managerial or professional positions were also more likely to be covered by employer-sponsored plans.

Health Insurance Plan Types

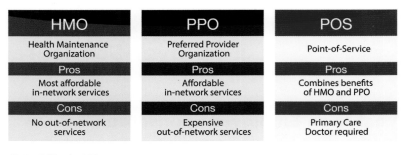

HMO	PPO	POS
Health Maintenance Organization	Preferred Provider Organization	Point-of-Service
Pros	**Pros**	**Pros**
Most affordable in-network services	Affordable in-network services	Combines benefits of HMO and PPO
Cons	**Cons**	**Cons**
No out-of-network services	Expensive out-of-network services	Primary Care Doctor required

Out-of-Pocket Expenses

Co-pays	Co-insurance	Deductibles	Out-of-Pocket Maximums

Each health plan has its pros and cons. It is wise to consider your personal and family needs when selecting coverage. © JOHN T TAKAI/SHUTTERSTOCK.COM.

What Is the History of Employer-Sponsored Health Plans?

Labor union: *A group of workers who have joined together to negotiate with employers in order to bargain for better wages, benefits, and working conditions.*

In the late nineteenth century, some industries, such as the railroad and mining industries, had company doctors who were available to workers. The first *labor union* to offer medical services to its members was the International Ladies Garment Workers Union (ILGWU) in 1914. Before World War II (1939–45), there were very few group insurance contracts, though department store Montgomery Ward had such a contract as early as 1910.

During World War II the National War Labor Board froze workers' wages. Meanwhile, the need for goods was high because of war shortages, and many would-be workers were enlisted in the armed services, which meant there were fewer workers available. Since employers could not attract workers by offering high wages, they began to offer employer-sponsored health plans. The government ruled that workers did not have to pay taxes on these plans, which increased their value and made them more appealing to potential employees. Unions also supported these plans.

The number of people with employer-sponsored plans grew exponentially after World War II. This number peaked in 2000, when 69.3 percent of the nonelderly population in the United States had employer-sponsored health plans, according to a 2012 survey by the Employee Benefit Research Institute. The survey also showed, however, that in the

Monitoring Employee Lifestyles

In order to offset rising health-care costs, some employers are looking for ways to distribute costs among employees according to their lifestyle choices. Most notably, because of the high medical costs associated with smoking, a number of companies have instituted policies that incentivize a tobacco-free lifestyle by providing small health-care subsidies to employees who abstain from tobacco or by charging higher rates to tobacco users. Such initiatives often also include employer-sponsored tobacco-cessation programs that help employees who want to quit smoking succeed. Tobacco users who enroll in cessation programs may be eligible for the same rates as colleagues who do not use tobacco.

Employers are also looking at ways to avoid the high costs associated with obesity or to distribute those costs to the employees most likely to incur them. In doing so, some have required employee physicals, setting certain biometric parameters that must be met in order to qualify for the lowest rates. Targets may be set for any number of health measures, including blood pressure, cholesterol levels, and Body Mass Index (BMI), a measure of body fat based on your height and weight. Although many employees find such screenings to be intrusive, in addition to keeping health-care costs as low as possible, they can provide employees with valuable information about their risks for preventable diseases.

early twenty-first century the percentage of the nonelderly population covered by employer-sponsored plans was decreasing. In 2011 only 58.4 percent had employer-sponsored plans. The high unemployment rate of the times was cited as a main reason for the decline in these plans.

What Are Premiums?

The amount employers contribute to health-care plans to cover the costs for their employees varies widely. With some plans, employers take full or major financial responsibility for premiums, which are periodic payments toward the overall cost of the health plan. Many plans require employees to pay premiums on a regular basis, often monthly. Some plans may necessitate that employees pay a premium as well as a percentage of costs for certain services. For example, an employee may be allowed to have an annual checkup for no fee, but he or she may have to pay 50 percent of the cost of a follow-up visit.

Depending on the type of plan, employers and employees pay different percentages for both premiums and procedures. Both the general cost of health plans and the percentage of financial responsibility paid by employees increased in the early twenty-first century. A 2014 Employer

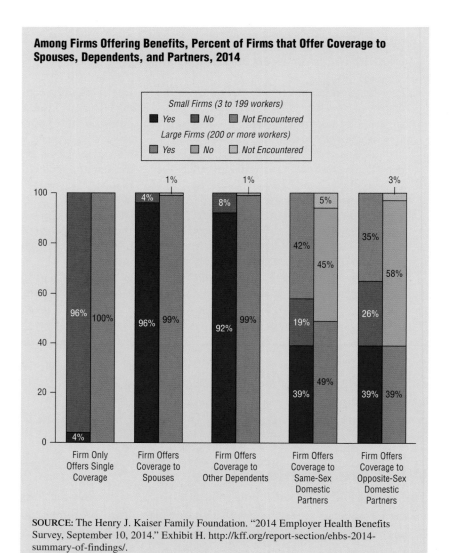

Among Firms Offering Benefits, Percent of Firms that Offer Coverage to Spouses, Dependents, and Partners, 2014

Small Firms (3 to 199 workers)
■ Yes ■ No ■ Not Encountered

Large Firms (200 or more workers)
■ Yes ■ No ■ Not Encountered

SOURCE: The Henry J. Kaiser Family Foundation. "2014 Employer Health Benefits Survey, September 10, 2014." Exhibit H. http://kff.org/report-section/ehbs-2014-summary-of-findings/.

As shown in this illustration, companies offer different health coverage depending on an employee's marital status and dependents. ILLUSTRATION BY LUMINA DATAMATICS LTD. © 2015 CENGAGE LEARNING.

Health Benefits Survey by the Kaiser Foundation found that worker contributions to employee health plans increased 81 percent from 2004 to 2014, while the costs of premiums generally rose 69 percent.

What Is a Managed Health-Care System?

In a managed health-care system, a group of health-care providers and facilities will provide care for free or at a reduced rate to those who are enrolled in specific plans. This group of providers is called the plan's network.

Preferred provider organizations (PPO) are managed health-care plans. PPOs were the most common employer-sponsored plans in 2014, with 58 percent of workers enrolled in them, according to the Kaiser Foundation. A PPO requires you to use a specified network of contracted health-care providers, clinics, and hospitals that are available within the network. If you use providers or establishments outside the network, you receive less or no coverage.

A health maintenance organization (HMO) is another form of managed health care that has been commonly used as an employer-sponsored plan. An HMO requires you to choose a primary-care physician from a specific list of providers within the network. The primary-care physician provides all of your basic health care. Generally, you can only see a specialist, such as an oncologist or a physical therapist, if your *primary-care physician* provides a referral to that specialist and he or she is also within the HMO's network.

A point-of-service (POS) plan is a managed-care plan that combines some features of HMOs and PPOs. If you are enrolled in this type of plan, you have to choose a physician from the network, who is called the point-of-service physician. This physician can make referrals outside the network of health-care providers, but you usually have to pay a high percentage of the fee for services.

Primary care physician: *The doctor who is responsible for the total care of a patient and refers patients to other doctors or specialists.*

What Are Some Other Types of Health Plans?

In the early twenty-first century more employers are offering employees high-deductible insurance plan (HDIP) coupled with health savings accounts (HSA). An HDIP generally has a low premium with a high deductible. A deductible is the amount you are required to pay before your health insurance plan starts contributing money. Authorized by the U.S. Congress in 2003, HSAs are similar to personal savings accounts, but they are tax free and are used exclusively to pay for medical expenses not covered by insurance. Both employees and employers can contribute to an HSA.

The least commonly used employer-sponsored plan as of the early twenty-first century is the indemnity health plan, sometimes called a conventional health plan. Indemnity plans allow enrollees to choose any doctor or hospital they want, as long as the particular service, such as an annual exam or a strep-throat test, is covered. Indemnity plans are generally more expensive than managed-care plans. In 2014 only 1 percent of employers offered indemnity plans.

What Are Some Advantages and Disadvantages of an Employer-Sponsored Health Plan?

Employer-sponsored plans are paid for partly or fully by employers and are tax free for employees. Since these plans offer substantial economic advantages, employers can use them to compete for highly qualified workers. Employers, employees, and labor unions use different types of employer-sponsored plans as negotiating tools when renewing work contracts.

Employers choose the plan, however, which means you may have little or no choice in the type of health plan your company offers, and it may not fit well with your needs. Your ability to choose among doctors or facilities may be limited, and a service that you, or even your physician, may see as essential may not be covered fully or at all by your plan. For example, an employer-sponsored plan may see fertility treatment as an elective and refuse to cover it. If you seek this type of treatment, you might be required to pay the entire bill or purchase an additional insurance plan.

Since employers are paying toward health-care costs, they may take what could be considered an invasive interest in your health in order to keep their costs down. In order to be covered by their plan, some employers may require preventive health-related behavior, such as exercising or not smoking, to maintain your health.

How Did the Patient Protection and Affordable Care Act (2010) Affect Employer-Sponsored Health Plans?

In 2010 Congress passed the Patient Protection and Affordable Care Act, commonly known as the Affordable Care Act or Obamacare. One important purpose of the act was to help people who don't have employer-sponsored plans by providing better access to Medicaid or tax credits. However, the Affordable Care Act also greatly impacts employer-sponsored health plans.

The Affordable Care Act requires that, as of 2014, medium- and large-sized companies have to provide a certain level of health insurance to their employees or pay financial penalties to the federal government. Employers who have at least 50 full-time workers or the equivalent have to pay at least 60 percent of health insurance for full-time workers, and the cost to employees must be less than 9.5 percent of the employee's household income. When the act became effective, most large employers already met the requirements and did not have to make any changes.

Employers who do not meet the ACA's requirements are charged annual penalties per employee. If an employer-sponsored plan does not meet other requirements of the act, employers have to pay some fees. Employers with fewer than 50 full-time employees are exempt from the requirement to offer health insurance. Employers with 25 or fewer employees with average annual wages of $50,000 or less can get tax credits if they pay at least 50 percent of their employees' premiums.

What Happens to My Employer-Sponsored Health Plan If I Change or Lose My Job?

The federal government enacted two laws in the late twentieth century to help employees maintain health insurance if they changed or lost their jobs. The Consolidated Omnibus Budget Reconciliation Act of 1985 is commonly known as COBRA. COBRA requires that health coverage be continued for employees and their families if a certain qualifying event takes place, such as the loss of a job or a reduction in hours, that leaves an individual unqualified for his or her employer-sponsored plan. Employers are legally obligated to inform their employees of their COBRA rights.

COBRA is generally more expensive than employer-sponsored plans because employees are required to pay for the portion of the plan's costs that was previously maintained by their employer. COBRA entitles you to all the same health benefits as any employee on the employer-sponsored plan. Coverage generally lasts 18 months from the day your employment ended or when your hours were changed, but it can be extended to 36 months under certain circumstances, such as if you become disabled. Coverage can also be extended if you experience a "second qualifying event," such as a divorce from an individual who is covered by COBRA.

The Health Insurance Portability and Accountability Act of 1996 (HIPAA) addressed the issue of what happens to your health plan when you move from one job to the next. Before this act, employer-covered plans often required a waiting period before you were allowed to be covered by a new plan. Also, if you had a preexisting condition, such as asthma or arthritis, the employer could make you wait for coverage or deny coverage for that condition, even if you were covered under a previous plan from a previous employer. Under HIPAA, any coverage from a previous plan counts against the new plan's waiting period. There cannot be more than a 63-day break between plans, and you cannot be denied coverage or made to wait because of a preexisting condition.

Nonmedical Health Insurance

What Is Nonmedical Health Insurance?

Disability insurance and long-term care insurance are two common types of nonmedical health coverage. Disability insurance replaces income when ill health prevents a person from working, either temporarily or permanently. Injuries, back problems, joint deterioration, heart disease, and cancer are among the most common causes of disability. Many people experience a sickness or an injury that prevents them from working for at least three months, but few have the resources to support their families during an extended period with no income. Disability insurance may be used to pay rent and other living expenses, in addition to costs related to the disability itself, such as building a wheelchair ramp or hiring someone to buy groceries and mow the lawn.

The second type of nonmedical health coverage, long-term care insurance, provides services for people who need help with daily activities, such as eating and bathing. Sometimes the insurance pays for physical therapy, hospitalization, and certain other medical expenses. It provides care at home or in a facility such as a nursing home. Most beneficiaries are elderly, but the insurance covers people of any age who require assistance due to sickness, injury, age, or impaired mental ability. This typically includes patients with *Alzheimer's disease* or Parkinson's disease.

Alzheimer's disease:
A serious condition usually found in older adults that affects the parts of the brain that control thought, memory, and language.

What Types of Disability Coverage Are Available?

Insurers do not always use the same definition of disability. Some policies cover accidents but not illness, some pay benefits to people who are partially disabled, and some presume complete disability if the person has become blind or deaf or cannot speak. Some policies pay benefits even if the recipient is able to work part time.

Disability insurance replaces your income when you are prevented from working either temporarily or permanently by ill health. © PHOTOGRAPHEE. EU/SHUTTERSTOCK.COM.

Between the start of the disability and the first payment of benefits, most policies require a waiting period, also called the elimination period. This may last anywhere from two weeks to six months, with 60 to 90 days being the usual recommendation. The shorter the waiting period, the more expensive the policy will be. The first benefit payment is typically made about 30 days after the end of the waiting period. Payment of benefits continues throughout the benefit term, which is the length of time stipulated in the policy.

Short-term disability (STD) coverage usually includes a waiting period of up to two weeks and a benefit period of up to two years. Long-term disability (LTD) coverage usually includes a waiting period of a few weeks or months and a benefit period that lasts a few years or until the recipient dies. The amount of each payment is typically about 60 percent of the base salary the person earned before becoming disabled. More costly policies often pay about 70 percent, and some feature a cost-of-living adjustment (COLA) to compensate for inflation.

What Government Programs Offer Disability Coverage?

Among the various government programs for people with disabilities, workers' compensation is operated primarily by states. These programs require employers to pay into the fund to cover their employees.

Social Security Benefits, October 2014

Type of beneficiary	Beneficiaries		Total monthly benefits (millions of dollars)	Average monthly benefit (dollars)
	Number (thousands)	Percent		
Total	**58,862**	**100.0**	**70,176**	**1,192.21**
Old-Age and Survivors Insurance	47,936	81.4	59,249	1,235.99
Retirement benefits	41,810	71.0	52,583	1,257.67
Retired workers	38,876	66.0	50,665	1,303.24
Spouses of retired workers	2,304	3.9	1,518	658.94
Children of retired workers	629	1.1	399	634.45
Survivor benefits	6,127	10.4	6,666	1,088.04
Children of deceased workers	1,877	3.2	1,530	815.05
Widowed mothers and fathers	145	0.2	134	922.39
Nondisabled widow(er)s	3,845	6.5	4,817	1,252.73
Disabled widow(er)s	258	0.4	184	712.53
Parents of deceased workers	1	(L)	1	1,101.78
Disability Insurance	10,926	18.6	10,927	1,000.12
Disabled workers	8,958	15.2	10,259	1,145.22
Spouses of disabled workers	150	0.3	46	309.00
Children of disabled workers	1,818	3.1	622	342.32

Note: (L) = less than 0.05 percent.

SOURCE: Social Security Administration. "Master Beneficiary Record, 100 percent data." http://www.ssa.gov/policy/docs/quickfacts/stat_snapshot/.

As this table shows, disability is a large part of the Social Security system after retirements. ILLUSTRATION BY LUMINA DATAMATICS LTD. © 2015 CENGAGE LEARNING.

In addition, the U.S. Department of Labor offers workers' compensation for federal employees, victims of black lung disease, and people who work in the energy or longshore and harbor industries. When a worker suffers a job-related illness or injury, workers' compensation generally pays about two-thirds of the person's previous wage. Most disabled people do not qualify for this program, however, because most disabilities are not job related.

The Social Security Administration, which manages the national retirement system, also operates the Supplemental Security Income (SSI) and Social Security Disability Insurance (SSDI) programs. SSI is for low-income people who do not own many assets (all items of value owned by a person). The recipient must be at least age 65 or have a severe visual impairment or other long-term disability that prevents the person from earning a living. This program serves children as well as adults.

The second program, SSDI, is available for people who previously held a job and then became too disabled to earn a significant income. The affliction must be expected to cause death or to last for at least one year. A spouse who is at least 62 years old and any children younger than

Medicare: *The federal health insurance program for older adults and people with disabilities.*

19 or disabled before age 22 would be covered. In 2013, the average yearly benefit from SSDI was $13,584 for an individual and $23,028 for a married person with at least one dependent child, according to America's Health Insurance Plans, a national trade association. After receiving SSDI payments for two years, recipients are automatically enrolled in *Medicare.*

What Other Disability Coverage Is Available?

Military veterans may obtain disability benefits through the federal Veterans Administration. Labor unions and other organizations often provide group coverage for their members. Individuals may purchase private disability coverage from an insurance company. This coverage typically offers more flexibility and pays larger benefits, which are not subject to income tax.

Most states require employers to provide short-term disability (STD) insurance, also known as sick leave, for their workers. This coverage usually lasts 6 to 12 months. The benefits are subject to income tax. For disabilities that continue for more than six months, many companies offer long-term disability (LTD) insurance, with the employer paying all or part of the premiums. Benefits from this insurance are often paid out for five years or more, sometimes ending when the recipient reaches age 65 or dies. The amount of the benefit is usually about 60 percent of the recipient's base salary, with monthly payments capped at about $10,000.

What Types of Long-Term Care Are Available?

Long-term care insurance is designed for people who need assistance with daily living. It covers a broad array of services not ordinarily provided by major medical insurance. These services are categorized as skilled, intermediate, or custodial care. The first two categories are intended to improve the patient's condition, while the third helps with routine tasks and provides a safe place to live if necessary.

Skilled care is often required when a person is hospitalized due to a grave injury or sickness. It includes daily medical treatment, nursing care, and therapy. The second category, intermediate care, provides similar services, but the services are not provided every day. This is sometimes a transition stage as the patient continues to recover after receiving skilled care.

The third category, custodial care, is for people who are elderly, injured, or have some other physical or mental impairment that prevents them from independently performing routine "activities of daily living." These include eating, bathing, dressing, using the toilet, and "transferring" (being able to move from a chair into a bed, for example). Custodial care may be provided every day or as little as a few hours each week, and it can be in the individual's home or in a facility, such as a nursing home. Long-term care insurance pays for services in all of these settings.

If I Am in Custodial Care, Where Will I Live?

Home care allows you to maintain a degree of independence in your own home instead of having to move into a care facility. This can be a workable option for elderly people with deteriorating abilities, as well as people of any age who have disabilities or other ongoing health problems. Home-care workers may provide medical and nursing services, perform therapy, help with daily living activities, and sometimes attend to essentials such as cooking or buying groceries. If you live at home with a caregiver, adult day care centers are also available, where you can stay in a safe environment while the caregiver is at work, for example.

When remaining at home is no longer practical, long-term care insurance pays for residency in an assisted-living facility or a nursing home. At an assisted-living facility, residents typically enjoy the privacy of their own living quarters and have access to common areas for recreation, dining, and other activities. The staff provides around-the-clock supervision, attending to each resident's personal needs and health concerns. Nursing homes operate in much the same way as assisted-living facilities, but in addition they usually provide more psychological, medical, nursing, and rehabilitation services. Private and semiprivate rooms are usually available.

Should I Purchase Long-Term Care Insurance?

If you have no insurance, the high price of long-term care can rapidly deplete your life savings. The cost varies widely from state to state. In 2014 the median price for the most expensive kind of care, which provides private quarters in a nursing home, ranged from $57,500 annually in Oklahoma to $240,900 in Alaska, according to Life Happens, a nonprofit organization founded by the insurance industry. Nationwide, the median cost of a private room in a nursing home was about $88,000 annually. For care in a person's own home, the median cost for one health aide to work 44 hours per week ranged from about $34,000 to $59,000 annually, or $15 to $26 per hour.

The federal government offers limited benefits through Medicare, a program that provides health care for elderly people and certain others. This pays for up to 100 days of skilled treatment in a nursing home after you have spent at least three days in a hospital. It also pays for short-term skilled care in your home if you have an unstable medical problem. Medicare pays nothing toward custodial care, since long-term care is not its primary purpose.

Another federal program, Medicaid, will pay for medical costs, some home care, and the cost of staying in a nursing home. It is available only to people with few assets, however. To qualify, recipients must meet federal poverty guidelines. Medicaid does not cover all long-term care facilities and might not pay for services at the site you prefer.

Long-term care insurance offers broad coverage, but the premiums can be costly—sometimes more than paying for services out-of-pocket. Therefore, insurance is not necessarily the best choice for people with assets of more than about $1.5 million, according to the Insurance Information Institute. If you have few assets and little income, Medicaid may be your best option. If your income is somewhere in the middle and you can afford the premiums, long-term care insurance offers peace of mind. It can guarantee that you will receive care when you need it, without having to depend on help from friends and family, and you will not need to sell assets to pay for that care. The coverage also allows you greater freedom to choose a nursing home or other facility.

Since a devastating injury or illness can happen to anyone at any age, it is generally recommended that you purchase long-term care insurance before age 60. To make the coverage more affordable, ask an insurance agent about partnership programs offered by states and insurance companies, in addition to federal and state tax incentives.

Supplemental Health Coverage

What Is Supplemental Health Coverage?

Supplemental health insurance, also known as voluntary insurance, helps pay out-of-pocket expenses that are not covered by major medical insurance. For example, it could provide funds for traveling to and from medical centers or for child care while a parent is confined to a hospital. Money from supplemental insurance can also pay the *deductibles*, co-payments, and co-insurance expenses related to other insurance policies.

There are many types of supplemental insurance available, with benefits varying by state and level of coverage. Some supplemental plans cover specific medical conditions only, such as cancer or the loss of a limb. Other plans help pay for hospitalization, dental or vision examinations, general wellness examinations, mammograms, and other routine care.

Since the mid-twentieth century the price of health care has soared. Many people fail to realize how high these costs can be, and they lack insurance to cover every health expense. In a 2013 report by Aflac, a private insurer, 44 percent of workers surveyed said they would need to borrow money to pay for out-of-pocket expenses if they suffered a major sickness or accident. About half of the respondents said they had less than $1,000 on hand to pay these expenses, while 25 percent had less than $500. In 2014 an individual's responsibility for deductibles, co-payments, and co-insurance was limited by law to a total of $6,350 annually, while the family limit was set at $12,700. There is no legal limit on other out-of-pocket expenses, however.

In the three years leading up to the Aflac study, half of the businesses surveyed had reduced their budgets by adopting high-deductible health plans. This meant that employees were required to pay a larger sum of money before an insurance company would begin distributing funds. It has been part of a trend toward the "consumerization" of health care, in which patients make more of their own decisions and pay a greater

Deductible: *The amount of money a patient must pay for services covered by the insurance company before the plan will pay for any medical bills.*

share of the cost. By offering a variety of coverage options and helping to pay deductibles and other expenses, supplemental insurance can play an important part in an individual's health-care strategy.

How Does Supplemental Insurance Work?

Supplemental insurance is different from major medical insurance, which costs more and pays for most hospitalization expenses and treatment by medical professionals. With major medical insurance, the amount of the payment varies, depending on the price of the care provided. After the insurer receives an invoice for those charges, the money is sent to the health-care provider.

In contrast, supplemental insurance usually pays a fixed sum of cash directly to you. The money can be spent in any way you choose. People who are sick or injured may use it for daily living expenses such as rent, utility bills, car payments, help with household tasks, and child care. It can also be applied to charges for health-care specialists and hospitals, experimental treatments, and other medical bills. Supplemental insurance helps prevent these expenses from becoming unmanageable, and it has saved some people from *bankruptcy*.

Bankruptcy: *A process by which a debtor who is deemed unable to pay off all his or her debts seeks legal protection from his or her creditors.*

Supplemental insurance claims are typically paid regardless of any other insurance you might have. To qualify for a payment, you must meet the conditions stated in your policy. For example, if you have accident insurance, you would receive a payment if you fall and break your leg but not if you have a heart attack or develop leukemia. Some plans require that you pay a deductible before receiving benefits, but many do not.

After a claim is approved, the insurer pays whatever amount the policy specifies, often within a few days. Some plans give the full amount in a single "lump sum" payment. Others provide a specific amount of money for certain categories of care. For instance, some dental plans pay a fixed dollar amount, depending on what service was performed, while others pay 100 percent of the cost for examinations and cleanings, 80 percent for filling cavities, and 50 percent for crowns and false teeth.

What Is Supplemental Cancer Insurance?

Some supplemental policies cover only cancer or other specific illness. About one in three residents of the United States is likely to be diagnosed with cancer, the nation's second most common cause of death in 2013. Treatment for cancer can be enormously expensive, and major medical insurance does not cover all of the related costs. Although supplemental insurance pays a smaller amount than major medical insurance, the premiums are affordable, and the benefits can add up to a substantial total.

For example, one insurance company offers a supplemental cancer policy at group rates to members of AAA, the auto and travel organization. It costs about $5 per month for an adult and 75 cents per month for each eligible child. If you are diagnosed with cancer, the policy pays $30 to $60 for each day you are confined in a hospital, $200 per day for extended hospital care, $30 per day for home health care, $30 a day for private nursing services, and $10 each for certain doctor visits. It also offers as much as $750 for chemotherapy, $600 for blood transfusions, $1,000 for surgeries, and $500 for ambulance transport. Each insured person may collect up to $250,000 in lifetime benefits.

AAA also sponsors a second cancer policy underwritten by a different insurance company. The price varies by age group, about $6 to $16 per month for an adult and $10 to $26 per month for a family. The insurance continues as long as you pay the premiums on time and remain a member of AAA, unless the group master policy is discontinued. If you die of anything other than cancer, suicide, or intentional self-inflicted injury, 100 percent of the premiums for this policy would be returned to your heirs.

Vision and dental insurance are two types of supplemental coverage. © BSIP SA/ALAMY.

Keep in mind that most insurance companies will only sell you a cancer policy (or similar supplement insurance for other chronic conditions and diseases) if you have not yet been diagnosed with cancer. It is important to weigh your risk of getting cancer with the cost of this supplemental coverage.

What General Health Coverage Is Available?

Some other types of supplemental insurance work essentially the same as a cancer policy, but they cover different health conditions. Critical illness insurance, sometimes called critical care and recovery insurance,

Additional Information about Medigap

Medicare Supplement Insurance (Medigap) is a supplemental coverage program available through private insurance companies for people already on Medicare. The program is designed to pay for health-care costs not covered by Medicare such as co-payments and deductibles. Before applying for a Medigap policy, here are some additional facts about the program.

- Medigap is only available for people already on Medicare Part A (hospital insurance) and Part B (medical insurance).

- You must pay a monthly premium to the company providing the Medigap policy, not to Medicare.

- A Medigap policy only covers one person and cannot be obtained for two or more people. If both you and your spouse wish to receive coverage, you must apply separately and purchase separate policies.

- You can purchase a Medigap policy from any insurance company licensed to sell one.

- The Medigap program has a guaranteed renewal, so the insurance company cannot cancel your policy even if you develop additional health problems.

- You may not participate in the Medigap program if you are currently enrolled in the Medicare Advantage Plan or if you have a Medicare Medical Savings Account Plan.

For people already on Medicare and in need of supplemental coverage, Medigap is an option for additional health-care expenses. However, it is important to discuss with a private insurance company which costs a policy will cover since the policy does not cover certain services, including long-term care, hearing aids, eyeglasses, and private-duty nursing.

pays cash if you suffer a stroke, heart attack, paralysis, kidney failure, severe burns, or another major calamity; have coronary bypass surgery; or are in a coma. Some short-term disability policies pay a percentage of your normal income each month while you are disabled. They offer a range of prices and benefits, and the length of the coverage period varies.

Hospital confinement insurance pays a benefit when you are admitted to a hospital due to sickness or injury. The most basic policies cover only hospitalization, while others include expenses for services such as transportation by ambulance, diagnostic examinations, outpatient surgery, treatment for accidents, visits to a doctor, and wellness examinations. Aflac sells a policy specifically for hospital intensive care, which includes ambulance transportation and transplantation of major human organs. Hospitalization policies typically pay a cash benefit for each day that you are confined, and often those benefits increase if the confinement lasts more than one week.

Supplemental accident insurance helps pay for treatment of injuries such as concussions and broken teeth, as well as services such as ambulance transportation and treatment in an intensive care unit. This type of coverage is frequently sold as accidental death and dismemberment (AD&D) insurance attached to a major health or life insurance policy. Sometimes called double indemnity, it often pays twice the usual amount for a death or for the loss of specific body parts, typically arms, legs, or eyes. Most AD&D policies cover losses due to accidents only. Usually they will not pay for a death caused by a drug overdose, bacterial infection or other physical illness, or mental illness. Some will also refuse to pay for accidents that happened while the person was participating in an extraordinary dangerous activity, such as car racing or skydiving.

For retirees and others on Medicare, private insurers sell Medicare Supplement Insurance to pay for out-of-pocket expenses not covered by Medicare. Also known as Medigap, this insurance can be used to pay deductibles, co-payments, and co-insurance, but not if they are part of a Medicare Advantage plan. In most cases, Medigap does not cover dental or vision care, private-duty nursing, or long-term care. Because each Medigap policy covers only one individual, spouses must buy their own policies.

Dental Industry Revenues, 2013

Other
28.7%

Restorative dental
services
22.2%

Preventive
services
15.6%

Fixed
prosthodontics
8.8%

Orthodontics
9.8%

Diagnostic
services
14.9%

SOURCE: "Dental Industry Revenues, 2013." *Market Share Reporter, 25th Edition*. Detroit: Gale, 2015, 270. First published as "Dentists in the U.S." [online] from http://guides.lib.ua.edu/loader.php?typed&id818069 [Published June 2013], from IBISWorld.

ILLUSTRATION BY LUMINA DATAMATICS LTD. © 2015 CENGAGE LEARNING.

What Is Dental and Vision Insurance?

Dental and vision policies are two separate types of insurance that typically offer a considerable discount on services and products. These policies may cover the entire cost of annual examinations, dental cleanings, dental X-rays, and eye glasses. Usually they pay part of the cost for dental fillings, root canals, and other expensive procedures. Comprehensive vision insurance costs more than basic coverage but is more likely to help pay for eye surgery and the treatment of major conditions such as macular degeneration, cataracts, and retinal detachment.

When a dental or vision plan is linked to a health maintenance organization (HMO), it will pay for services only within a certain network

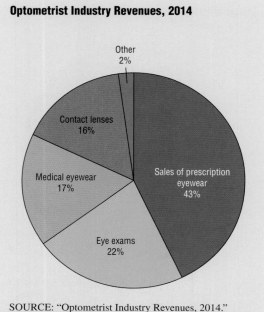

Optometrist Industry Revenues, 2014

- Other 2%
- Contact lenses 16%
- Medical eyewear 17%
- Sales of prescription eyewear 43%
- Eye exams 22%

SOURCE: "Optometrist Industry Revenues, 2014." *Market Share Reporter, 25th Edition*. Detroit:Gale, 2015, 577. First published as "Optometrists in the U.S." [online] from http://www.ibisworld.com [Published January 2014], from IBISWorld.

ILLUSTRATION BY LUMINA DATAMATICS LTD. © 2015 CENGAGE LEARNING.

of health-care providers. Other plans allow you to choose any dental or vision professional, but they offer reduced rates for those within their preferred provider network (PPO). A third option, an indemnity plan, pays a specific percentage of the bill from any service provider.

Unlike most other types of supplemental insurance, dental and vision policies do not pay you cash to spend in any way you like. Usually the money is sent to the health-care provider, but sometimes you are reimbursed for out-of-pocket expenses. For dental coverage, most policies will pay no more than $1,200 to $1,500 each year. For either dental or vision coverage, you might be required to pay an annual membership fee, co-pays, and a deductible in addition to monthly or annual premiums.

How Do I Obtain Supplemental Insurance?

Employers who provide a group health plan for their workers frequently offer supplemental insurance options, or riders, allowing the policy to be tailored to individual needs. You pay an additional premium for attaching these riders to the basic group policy. Unions, school districts, associations, and other organizations sometimes sponsor supplemental insurance plans for their members. Some group health plans accept new members and changes to existing policies only during their open enrollment period, which occurs once a year.

If you have individual private insurance, you can buy supplemental coverage as a rider attached to a major medical or life insurance policy, or you can purchase it separately. Dental and vision coverage can be attached to some major medical insurance plans purchased through the Health Insurance Marketplace (http://www.healthcare.gov), a website operated by the federal government. You may also purchase stand-alone dental plans at the Marketplace but not stand-alone vision plans. In addition, you may buy supplemental coverage at the websites of private insurance companies or through insurance agents.

COBRA

What Is COBRA?

The Consolidated Omnibus Budget Reconciliation Act (COBRA), passed by the U.S. Congress in 1985, allows employees and their families to have a temporary continuation of their group health insurance coverage. Group health insurance is an important benefit that many businesses provide for employees and their families. Historically, an employee who lost his or her job or began working fewer hours usually lost access to this coverage. If a person died or went through a legal separation or divorce, his or her children and former spouse also would most likely have been dropped from the group health plan.

Although COBRA can prevent gaps in health insurance coverage, it is not meant to be a permanent health-care solution. COBRA insurance ends after a specific length of time, usually 18 or 36 months, and the employer is not required to help pay for it. For someone living on a reduced income, the premiums can be financially challenging. Other options are available and should be considered. In the interim, COBRA can help people weather the transition from one insurance plan to the next.

Who Is Eligible for COBRA?

COBRA is available only to people who meet certain criteria. One important requirement is that you are enrolled in a group health plan at your place of employment. Sometimes contractors and agents who are enrolled in a group health plan can qualify for COBRA coverage even though they are independent workers and not employees of a company. Continuation coverage is not available to employees of the federal government, very small companies, churches, or certain other religious organizations. In order to offer COBRA coverage, a private-sector business must have had at least 20 full-time workers during the previous year or part-time workers with enough hours to add up to about the same

Cover of the COBRA benefits publication. U.S. DEPARTMENT OF LABOR, EMPLOYEE BENEFITS SECURITY ADMINISTRATION (EBSA).

total hours. Local or state governments can also provide COBRA to their employees.

If a specific event causes you to lose group health coverage, you must be enrolled in your employer's group health plan on the day before that event took place in order to be eligible for COBRA. Events that may qualify you for eligibility, known as qualifying events, include quitting your job, being laid off or fired, having your work hours cut, or becoming eligible for Medicare. If your employer declares bankruptcy, that would also be considered a qualifying event, but the loss of your job due to gross misconduct (such as embezzlement or sexual assault) would not be.

Your spouse, former spouse, or dependent children are usually entitled to continuation coverage if you die or become divorced or legally separated. Children born or adopted during the period of COBRA coverage would qualify, and a dependent child who is about to become independent might also be eligible.

What Does COBRA Cover, and How Long Does It Last?

For a specific period of time, COBRA coverage allows you to remain on your previous group health plan. You will be eligible to receive the same services, benefits, and options as other participants in the plan, with the exception of disability and life insurance benefits. COBRA includes any dental, vision, medical, or prescription drug benefits that are offered by the group health plan. If the company alters the terms of its health plan for active employees, your coverage will also change.

An employer is usually required to continue COBRA health coverage for a maximum of either 18 or 36 months. The length of time is determined by the qualifying event that caused you to lose your group health coverage. In most cases your employer has the option of ending your coverage after that interval or allowing you to remain on the group health plan for a longer period. If you or a family member is disabled

A Marketplace Alternative to COBRA Coverage

Although COBRA is a valuable option for many Americans who lose their insurance benefits, under the Affordable Care Act (ACA), it is not the only option. As of 2013 Americans who no longer have insurance coverage through an employer can purchase coverage through the state marketplaces that were created by the legislation. In many cases, these plans provide more affordable coverage than COBRA. Individuals whose incomes fall between 100 and 400 percent of the federal poverty level qualify for premium tax credits when purchasing through the marketplaces.

These tax credits can significantly lower the cost of coverage.

Before signing up for COBRA coverage, you should evaluate your insurance needs to determine whether you need the same level of coverage that was provided through your employer. You can then investigate all of the options available to you through your state's insurance marketplace and weigh the costs and benefits at different levels of coverage. Making an informed decision can potentially save you a significant sum of money each year.

and you were initially granted 18 months of COBRA coverage, you are likely to be entitled to an additional 11 months. You may also be allowed to receive extended coverage if you experience a second qualifying event.

COBRA continues only as long as you pay the premiums on time. It will cease if you become eligible for *Medicare* or if your employer's group health plan is terminated. Continuation coverage usually ends if you sign up for a different group health plan, but it may continue if the new plan offers limited coverage for a preexisting condition or excludes it entirely. If you commit wrongdoing such as fraud or another act that would be grounds for expulsion from your employer's group health plan, your COBRA coverage may be withdrawn.

Medicare: *In the United States, a national health-insurance program for citizens age 65 and older and disabled people.*

How Much Will I Have to Pay for COBRA Coverage?

Under COBRA, employers who sponsor group health plans are required to offer an extension of coverage, but they are not required to pay for it, which means that you may be responsible for the entire price of the premiums, or periodic payments, with no further help from your employer. For this reason, COBRA can be expensive. You might be charged a 2 percent administrative fee in addition to your premiums, along with any deductibles specified in the health plan. COBRA sometimes costs less

Health savings account: *A tax-exempt trust or custodial account to pay or reimburse certain medical expenses. Also called HSA.*

The coverage periods under COBRA are set by U.S. law. ILLUSTRATION BY GGS INFORMATION SERVICES. © 2015 CENGAGE LEARNING.

than private health insurance, but not always. It can also be less expensive than paying directly for medical care instead of relying on insurance.

If you or a family member is disabled and receiving extended COBRA coverage, your premiums could be as much as 50 percent higher than the usual amount. During the time you are covered under COBRA, the group health plan might also raise the price of its premiums. To lower the cost, you may have an opportunity to revise your coverage within the plan by selecting a less expensive option. Usually this can be done once a year during the group plan's open enrollment period, which is a designated period of time when people are allowed to sign up for new coverage or make changes to an existing plan.

If you have a *health savings account*, you can use any money left in the account to pay COBRA premiums. If your premiums and other medical expenses amount to more than 7.5 percent of your annual income, they are not subject to federal income tax. Some COBRA beneficiaries are entitled to a refundable federal tax credit of up to 65 percent of their premiums.

How Do I Enroll in COBRA?

The administrator of your employer's group health plan must be notified when a qualifying event takes place. Depending on the type of qualifying event, you, your family, or your employer may provide this notification. You or a family member must also inform the administrator if you are involved in a divorce or legal separation or if your child will soon cease to be a dependent. The health plan might impose a time limit for reporting these circumstances, but it must allow you at least 60 days to deliver the notification. Your employer is responsible for reporting other qualifying events within 30 days after they happen.

After receiving notification of a qualifying event, the group health plan administrator must advise you and other eligible beneficiaries of your right to apply for COBRA. This must occur within 14 days. After you receive that notice, you have at

COBRA Coverage Periods

Qualifying Event	Person(s) Eligible for COBRA	Duration of Coverage
Loss of job for any reason other than gross misconduct	Employee Spouse Dependent child(ren)	18 months
Quit voluntarily	Employee Spouse Dependent child(ren)	18 months
Working hours are reduced	Employee Spouse Dependent child(ren)	18 months
Employee is eligible for Medicare	Spouse Dependent child(ren)	36 months
Employee becomes divorced or legally separated	Spouse Dependent child(ren)	36 months
Employee dies	Spouse Dependent child(ren)	36 months
Loss of dependent-child status	Dependent child(ren)	36 months

SOURCE: U.S. Department of Labor, Employee Benefits Security Administration (EBSA). *An Employee's Guide to Health Benefits Under COBRA*, November 2012, 18. http://www.dol.gov/ebsa/pdf/cobraemployee.pdf.

least 60 days to inform the administrator if you wish to enroll in COBRA coverage. If your request is denied, the administrator has another 14 days to inform you of that decision and state a reason for the denial.

If your enrollment request is accepted, you must pay the first premium within 45 days after mailing the election form to the administrator. Your COBRA rights can be terminated if you fail to make this payment when it is due. Subsequent payments are usually required each month, but with some group plans you may have the option of making payments on another schedule, perhaps weekly or quarterly.

What Other Coverage Options Should I Consider?

If you are leaving your job on good terms, your employer might be willing to include you in the organization's group health plan and pay for the premiums as part of a retirement or severance package. You would then still have the option of electing COBRA after the severance agreement reached its conclusion. Alternatively, you might be able to stay with the company and remain on its group health plan by working at a different position, perhaps for a lower salary. You could also consider a part-time or secondary job with another company that offers employer-paid group health care.

If your group health coverage is about to end, you have special rights granted by the Health Insurance Portability and Accountability Act. These include the right to enroll in a new group health plan outside its open enrollment period. If you are married, this could provide an opportunity to enroll in your spouse's health plan if necessary. You can apply for special enrollment in another plan before or after you have selected COBRA. After COBRA or other health coverage has ended, you have 30 days to request special enrollment in another group plan.

Another option, private health insurance, is sometimes less costly than continuing your enrollment in a group health plan through COBRA. If you have private insurance, you might qualify for tax credits on the premiums or discounts on other health expenditures. These credits or discounts may vary depending on how many people are in your household and how much money you make. Government programs are also available to help family members obtain insurance. For instance, the website InsureKidsNow.gov (http://www.insurekidsnow .gov) offers insurance for children. The Health Insurance Marketplace (http://www.healthcare.gov) is a website operated by the federal government on which you can shop for private insurance plans that are available at a variety of prices. The procedure for switching from COBRA coverage to an insurance plan via the marketplace can be handled in two different ways. This depends on the time of year and whether your COBRA coverage is still in effect.

If your COBRA insurance is terminated before its coverage period has expired, you can obtain insurance through the marketplace during the annual open enrollment period, which runs from November 15 through February 15. Early termination of COBRA can happen if you fail to pay the premiums in full and on time. It can also occur if your coverage is canceled because the group health plan has been discontinued or you commit an offense such as fraud. However, if you continue your COBRA insurance until the end of its coverage period, you can enroll in a private insurance plan through the marketplace without waiting for open enrollment to begin.

For More Information

BOOKS

America's Health Insurance Plans (AHIP). *Guide to Disability Income Insurance.* Washington, DC: AHIP, 2014. This guide can also be found online at http://www.ahip.org/templates/Issues/documentResults.aspx?id=14458&cat=2147484864.

Coombs, Jan. *The Rise and Fall of HMOs: An American Health Care Revolution.* Madison: University of Wisconsin Press, 2005.

Merlis, Mark. *The Affordable Care Act and Employer-Sponsored Insurance for Working Americans.* Washington, DC: Academy Health, 2011. This report can also be found online at http://www.academyhealth.org/files/nhpc/2011/AH_2011AffordableCareReportFINAL3.pdf.

O'Toole, Marie T., ed. *Mosby's Medical Dictionary.* 9th ed. St. Louis: Elsevier/Mosby, 2013.

Yoo, Hannah, Dan LaVallee, Teresa Mulligan, and Karen Heath. *Small Group Health Insurance in 2010: A Comprehensive Survey of Premiums, Product Choices, and Benefits.* Washington, DC: America's Health Insurance Plans, Center for Policy and Research, 2011. This report can also be found online at http://www.ahip.org/templates/Issues/documentResults.aspx?id=14175&cat=2147484864.

PERIODICALS

Revell, Janice. "Don't Let Illness Derail Your Retirement." *Fortune,* July 12, 2012. This article can also be found online at http://fortune.com/2012/06/26/dont-let-illness-derail-your-retirement/.

WEBSITES

"2014 Employer Health Benefits Survey." *Henry J. Kaiser Family Foundation*. September 2014. http://kff.org/health-costs/report/2014-employer-health-benefits-survey/ (accessed October 19, 2014).

"COBRA Coverage and the Marketplace." *HealthCare.gov*. https://www.healthcare.gov/what-if-i-currently-have-cobra-coverage/ (accessed August 5, 2014).

DiGiacomo, Robert. "Is Dental Insurance Worth the Cost?" *Bankrate*. http://www.bankrate.com/finance/insurance/dental-insurance-1.aspx (accessed August 15, 2014).

"Disability Benefits." U.S. Social Security Administration. http://www.ssa.gov/disabilityssi/ (accessed August 14, 2014).

"Disability Insurance." *Insurance Information Institute*. http://www.iii.org/insurance-topics/disability-insurance (accessed August 10, 2014).

Employee Benefit Research Institute. http://www.ebri.org/ (accessed October 19, 2014).

"An Employee's Guide to Group Health Continuation Coverage under COBRA: The Consolidated Omnibus Budget Reconciliation Act." *U.S. Department of Labor*. November 2012. http://www.dol.gov/ebsa//faqs/faq_compliance_cobra.html (accessed August 6, 2014.)

"Fact Sheet: Consolidated Omnibus Budget Reconciliation Act (COBRA)." *U.S. Department of Labor*. http://www.dol.gov/ebsa/newsroom/fscobra.html (accessed August 5, 2014).

"FAQs about COBRA Continuation Health Coverage." *U.S. Department of Labor*. http://www.dol.gov/ebsa/faqs/faq-consumer-cobra.html (accessed October 20, 2014).

Fontinelle, Amy. "Vision Care Insurance: Will You See A Benefit?" *Investopedia*. http://www.investopedia.com/articles/pf/11/vision-care-insurance.asp (accessed August 15, 2014).

———. "What You Need to Know about COBRA Health Insurance." *Investopedia*. http://www.investopedia.com/articles/insurance/11/intro-cobra-health-insurance.asp (accessed August 15, 2014).

Goodell, Sarah, and Kate Bundorf. "Consumer Directed Health Plans: Do They Deliver?" *The Robert Wood Johnson Foundation*. October 2012. http://www.rwjf.org/content/dam/farm/reports/reports/2012/rwjf402405/subassets/rwjf402405_1 (accessed August 5, 2014).

"The Health Insurance Portability and Accountability Act (HIPAA): Fact Sheet." *U.S. Department of Labor*. December 2004. http://www.dol.gov/ebsa/newsroom/fshipaa.html (accessed October 20, 2014).

"Health Ownership Transformed." *8th Annual Cigna Choice Experience Study*. April 2014. http://newsroom.cigna.com/images/9022/874630_ExecutiveSummary_FINAL.pdf (accessed August 15, 2014).

Kusuma, Sharat, et al. "Issues Facing America: Consumer-Directed Health Care." *American Academy of Orthopaedic Surgeons*. April 2008. http://www.aaos.org/news/aaosnow/apr08/reimbursement1.asp (accessed August 5, 2014).

"Long-Term Care Insurance." *Insurance Information Institute*. http://www.iii .org/insurance-topics/long-term-care-insurance (accessed October 20, 2014).

"Long-Term Care Insurance." *Life Happens*. 2014. http://www.lifehappens.org/ insurance-overview/long-term-care-insurance/ (accessed October 20, 2014).

"Managed Care and Medical Benefits." *California State University, Sacramento*. http://www.csus.edu/indiv/h/heflintl/group/section-1/group-5/Website/ index.htm (accessed October 27, 2014).

Miller, Stephen. "Consumer Driven Plans Are Now Second Most Common Design." *Society for Human Resource Management*. September 20, 2012. http://www.shrm.org/hrdisciplines/benefits/articles/pages/cdhps- increasingly-popular.aspx (accessed August 5, 2014).

———. "Consumer Driven Plans Increased Health Management." *Society for Human Resource Management*. April 28, 2014. http://www.shrm.org/ hrdisciplines/benefits/articles/pages/cdhps-health-management.aspx (accessed August 5, 2014).

———. "For 2015, Higher Limits for HSA Contributions and Deductibles." *Society for Human Resource Management*. April 24, 2014. http://www.shrm .org/hrdisciplines/benefits/articles/pages/2015-hsa-limits.aspx (accessed August 5, 2014).

"Preventive Health Services for Adults." *HealthCare.gov*. https://www .healthcare.gov/preventive-care-benefits/ (accessed August 5, 2014).

"What's Medicare Supplement Insurance (Medigap)?" *Medicare.gov*. http:// www.medicare.gov/supplement-other-insurance/medigap/whats-medigap .html (accessed October 29, 2014).

"Why Supplemental Insurance Matters." *Aflac*. October 16, 2013. http://www .aflac.com/healthcare_reform/articles/why_voluntary_benefits_are_more_ relevant_now_than_ever.aspx (accessed October 29, 2014).

Personal Identity, Mental Health, and Behavior

Overview: Personal Identity, Mental Health, and Behavior

How Is Personal Identity Defined?

You have a unique personal identity that grows and changes throughout your life, and it distinguishes you as an individual. Some aspects of your identity are with you from birth and cannot be changed, such as your racial identity. Other aspects change over time and can be more fluid, such as your values, your relationships to others, or even the style of clothing you prefer. During your lifetime you might change careers, become a parent, or move to a different country.

From ancient to contemporary times, philosophers, theologians, scientists, and psychologists have debated what exactly makes up personal identity. While theories vary, your personal identity generally embraces all the roles you have in your life, as well as your behaviors and the qualities you associate with yourself. It can include your family or social roles, physical attributes, occupation or volunteer work, religious affiliation, and hobbies, as well as groups you are born to, such as an ethnic group, or groups you join, such as a political party. Your identity is also defined by your significant characteristics and abilities, such as being kind, energetic, or funny, and it can be influenced by cultural values. What may be viewed as success in one culture may not be viewed as such in a different culture.

How Is Mental Health Defined?

Mental health is often defined as including emotional, social, and psychological facets. People who are emotionally healthy generally feel happy or at peace with themselves. Those who are socially healthy have a positive outlook and see themselves as part of social groups, communities, and society at large. Those with psychological health generally have a positive sense of their own worth and purpose, feel hopeful about themselves and the world, and understand and appreciate change.

Insomnia: *Chronic
sleeplessness or sleep
disturbances.*

When you are mentally healthy, you are able to be productive and have positive nurturing relationships, from intimate relationships to more casual or business connections. You can also cope well with stresses and challenges and can be a contributing member of society. Your environment can also have an impact. For example, if you are constantly dealing with the stress of racism, it may be challenging for you to maintain good mental health.

How Is Mental Illness Defined?

Your emotional, social, and psychological well-being are adversely affected if you have a mental illness. You may experience negative moods, behaviors, or thinking; you may experience *insomnia* or uncontrolled anger. Mental illness can be connected to genetic factors or family history, or it may originate from environmental or societal factors such as traumatic experiences. Living in a war zone, experiencing abuse, or dealing with chronic poverty are examples of such negative influences. According to a 2013 brochure by the National Alliance on Mental Illness, "One in four adults—approximately 60 million Americans—experiences a mental health disorder in a given year."

Having a mental illness can impair your ability to function in daily life. It can also make you more likely to engage in risky behavior, such as smoking, overeating, or drug or alcohol abuse. Some research has shown that mental illness can heighten your risk of getting other chronic illnesses such as diabetes, heart disease, or asthma. Conversely, the stress of having a major chronic illness can lead to mental illness.

Major diagnosed mental illnesses include depression, bipolar disorder, schizophrenia, borderline personality disorder, post-traumatic stress disorder (PTSD), obsessive-compulsive disorders, and eating disorders. Depression is the most commonly diagnosed mental illness in the United States. There are different types of depression, including postpartum depression, which affects some women after the birth of a child, or seasonal affective disorder (SAD), a kind of depression that can occur in some people during the winter. According to a 2014 report by the National Center for Health Statistics, 7.6 percent of Americans age 12 and over had moderate or severe symptoms of depression from 2009 to 2012. In 2012 a World Health Organization report stated that depression was the leading cause of disability in the world, affecting over 350 million people.

How Has Mental Illness Been Perceived Historically?

In many ancient cultures, mentally ill people were believed to be possessed by the devil and in need of a religious "cure," such as an exorcism. The Greek physician Hippocrates (460 BCE–370 BCE) was one of the first to suggest that mental illness was not a religious issue but a medical one that could be treated through environmental changes or with medicines. Despite the theories of Hippocrates, people with mental illness continued to be thought of as possessed for many centuries. Negative attitudes toward and stigmatization of people with mental illness continued in the West well into the nineteenth century. At that time, most people diagnosed with mental illness were placed in institutions, often in inhuman conditions. Some lessening of stigmatization began in the mid-1800s, when government funding and oversight of institutions increased.

Changes in how mental illness was viewed and treated, as well as some lessening of stigmatization, happened in the United States in the twentieth and early twenty-first centuries, when new laws and initiatives helped improve the mental health-care system. The National Mental Health Act of 1946 created and provided funding for the National Institutes of Mental Health to research causes and management of mental illnesses. The Mental Retardation Facilities and Community Health Centers Construction Act of 1963 provided funding for community-based mental health services. In 2013, $50 million of funding was made available through the Affordable Care Act to establish or expand behavioral health services for people living with mental illness and drug and alcohol problems. The Affordable Care Act also established that mental health had to be covered by all insurance plans with no lifetime or annual dollar limits.

Despite increased understanding of and respect for people with mental illness, many have still been stigmatized or faced discrimination. The National Alliance on Mental Illness was founded in 1979 as a nonprofit to "advocate for access to services, treatment, supports and research" and "to raise awareness and build a community for hope for all of those in need." Some believed that those diagnosed with mental illnesses were treated in inhuman and abusive ways by the government, medical institutions, pharmaceutical companies, and other institutions, and a number of organizations were founded to protect their rights. MindFreedom, a nonprofit founded in 2005, united hundreds of grassroots advocacy groups to "win human rights and alternatives for people labeled with psychiatric disabilities."

How Do Self-Esteem and Self-Perception Relate to Personal Identity?

Self-esteem is a term that refers to the way you feel about yourself. This concept includes your feelings about your skills, traits, and capabilities, as well as your limitations. Self-perception refers to how you think about yourself and how you interact with your environment. Your self-perception may be that you have physical strength, but your self-esteem describes how you feel about the strength you have. When you have high self-esteem, you feel positively about yourself and how others see you. If you have low self-esteem, you may feel that you do not matter or that nothing you do is good enough.

As your personal identity changes throughout your life, your self-perception and self-esteem may change. For example, imagine that a young man has a self-perception that he is athletic. He plays on a soccer team, jogs daily, and works out. Some of his self-esteem derives from feeling positive about his physical abilities and the mental abilities needed for team sports. As he enters middle age, he develops arthritis and gains new responsibilities, both as a parent and in his career. These factors mean that he now has less time, energy, and capacity for playing soccer or jogging. His self-perception changes, and instead of seeing himself as an athlete, he now sees himself as a busy, middle-aged person with a disability. At first, his self-esteem suffers as he tries to adjust to his new limitations. Then, he decides to become a soccer coach and start a speed-walking group for people over 50. His self-perception changes again with his new roles, and his self-esteem grows as he affirms his new skills as a coach, an organizer, and a person committed to good physical health at any age.

The way you think and feel about yourself can change in relationship to your immediate environment or the world at large. You might feel great if you just got married, or you might be unhappy if you unexpectedly lost your job. People with positive self-esteem and self-identity can cope with the ups and downs of daily life. They see their strengths and limitations realistically, and they accept who they are and work on limitations that they would like to change. People without a strong sense of self-esteem and self-identity tend to be more affected by external events. If you do not get a promotion at work, for example, it doesn't matter if the position required five years of experience and you had only worked in that field for one year. The external event may still reinforce a belief that you are incompetent. Even positive feedback may not last long if you return to a negative self-perception.

How Do Self-Esteem and Self-Perception Relate to Mental Health?

Studies have found that healthy self-esteem can help prevent mental illness. Having positive self-perception and self-esteem allows you to be productive, have healthy relationships, and form good habits and behaviors. It also helps you to be confident, flexible, and resilient and to deal with and recover from life's challenges. All of these elements are important for good mental health.

Research also shows that poor self-esteem is related to many types of mental illnesses, particularly depression, anxiety, and eating disorders. Low self-esteem can lead to negative behaviors such as substance abuse or a tendency to stay in an abusive relationship because you believe that it is what you deserve. Often a negative cycle occurs in which low self-esteem makes people more vulnerable to mental illness, but mental illness and its societal stigma further lowers self-esteem. Conversely, building positive self-esteem can help address certain mental illnesses or associated behaviors such as obsessive dieting or smoking.

Your self-perception and self-esteem can also be affected by experiences with discrimination, such as sexism, and therefore they can affect your risk of mental illness. A 2014 report by the National Center for Health Statistics noted that the highest rate for depression between 2009 and 2012 was in women aged 40 to 59. In that same period, people living below the poverty level were nearly 2.5 times more likely to suffer from depression than those at or above the poverty level. People living with poverty often feel insecurity and hopelessness about their lives, have poor physical health, and live with a high risk of experiencing or witnessing violence. Environmental factors such as these may cause poor self-esteem that can lead to mental illness. Mental illness can also be a cause of poverty since it poses challenges to a person's ability to live a productive life.

How Can I Change My Behaviors and Improve My Self-Esteem and Mental Health?

Becoming more aware of your thoughts and emotions and finding healthy ways to express them can help you improve your self-esteem and mental health. This awareness can be particularly important if you are going through major life changes or if a current event triggers memories of a past trauma. Having people you trust to talk with and share what is happening in your life can help you deal with challenges. If you are working on changing a negative behavior such as smoking or trying to incorporate a positive behavior into your routine such as a daily walk, having a friend, partner, or support group can help keep you on track.

 Having a variety of healthy relationships is vital. People with whom you have intimate relationships, whether a romantic partner, a best friend, or a family member, will likely be there in good times or bad. They can give you an honest assessment of how you are doing because they care about you and believe that you are worthwhile. It is also important for you to develop other relationships, such as with work colleagues or people you meet at your place of worship or in your neighborhood. These relationships can help you feel good about your place in the world. However, it is essential for you to have a good relationship with yourself, because the messages that you communicate to yourself will affect your self-esteem.

Everyone experiences stress. To maintain mental health, it is important to recognize sources of stress and how you behave when you are under pressure. For example, an occasional drink with friends might be a good way to relieve stress temporarily, but drinking alcohol every time you feel stress can lead to problems. Generally, maintaining your physical health is essential for mental health—a connection referred to as the mind-body connection. Exercising, eating well, getting enough sleep, and balancing work and relaxation can make a critical difference in how you feel about yourself and your life. Exercise releases endorphins, which are hormones in your brain and nervous system that help you feel a sense of well-being. Other ways to deal with stress include learning new things, being out in nature, helping others, or using your creativity to develop hobbies such as cooking or singing.

What Are Symptoms of Mental Illness?

Sometimes, despite efforts to address poor self-esteem or self-identity, mental illness develops due to biological or environmental factors. Environmental factors may be so significant that it may be very difficult to combat the stress they cause. If you are without financial means and can't afford healthy food or adequate housing, for example, your ability to maintain positive self-esteem and mental health may be severely compromised. Other risk factors for mental illness can include having been abused as a young child or having parents who are addicts, experiencing severe trauma such as extreme violence, or dealing with a chronic illness, especially if it isolates you from others. Mental illness may also be provoked by substance abuse, or it may be a side effect of a medication, including certain drugs specifically prescribed for mental illness.

Some common symptoms of mental illness include isolating yourself from others, having an inability to sleep or eat, feeling hopeless, or engaging in addictive behaviors. Other signs may be an inability to concentrate, memory loss, low energy, or having angry or violent feelings toward yourself or others. Some people experience unexplained headaches, stomach aches, or general pain, and they may worry excessively or even have thoughts of suicide. Some of these signs may be temporary and not associated with mental illness. Isolating yourself to heal may be an appropriate response to a traumatic experience. Unexplained headaches may be due to a physical issue, such as hormone changes, and should be checked out by a medical professional. However, if you or someone else has a number of these signs, or if they persist, you should take serious note and make an effort to get help. Suicidal thoughts should always be taken seriously and treated immediately.

There are many professional treatments and programs that can help people cope with mental health issues. These resources include professional therapists and medical personnel who can provide a variety of

Homeopathy: *A system of natural remedies that relies on the idea that "like cures like."*

therapeutic treatments and prescribe medications. Alternative medical practices such as *homeopathy* and acupuncture can effectively reduce symptoms. In dealing with depression and anxiety, some people have benefited from the use of support groups, massage, or relaxation techniques such as meditation.

When it comes to treating mental illness or maintaining positive self-esteem, it is important to remember that what may work for one person may not be right for another. Maintaining mental health and healing from mental illness are processes, and there is no one magic or immediate answer. Each person is unique. Working on and understanding your personal identity, your self-esteem, and your mental well-being is a lifelong journey of challenges and opportunities.

For More Information

BOOKS

Crilly, Lynn, and Natasha Devon. *Fundamentals: A Guide for Parents, Teachers and Carers on Mental Health and Self-Esteem.* London: John Blake Publishing, 2015.

Gold, Joel, and Ian Gold. *Suspicious Minds: How Culture Shapes Madness.* New York: Free Press, 2014.

Hartwell-Walker, Marie. *Unlocking the Secrets of Self-Esteem: A Guide to Building Confidence and Connection One Step at a Time.* Oakland, CA: New Harbinger Publications, 2015.

PERIODICALS

Luhrmann, T. M. "Redefining Mental Health." *New York Times*, January 18, 2015. This article can also be found online at http://www.nytimes.com/2015/01/18/opinion/sunday/t-m-luhrmann-redefining-mental-illness.html?_r=0.

Mershon, Erin. "Will 'Obamacare' Fill the Gaps in Our Mental Health System?" *National Journal*, December 28, 2012. This article can also be found online at http://www.nationaljournal.com/healthcare/will-obamacare-fill-the-gaps-in-our-mental-health-system-20121228.

WEBSITES

"Community Conversations about Mental Health: Information Brief." *MentalHealth.gov.* July 2013. http://www.mentalhealth.gov/talk/community-conversation/information_brief_english_07-22-13.pdf (accessed January 23, 2015).

"Depression: Fact Sheet No. 369." *World Health Organization.* October 2012. http://www.who.int/mediacentre/factsheets/fs369/en/ (accessed January 23, 2015).

"Mental Health Basics." *Centers for Disease Control and Prevention*. October 4, 2013. http://www.cdc.gov/mentalhealth/basics.htm (accessed January 23, 2015).

"Mental Illness: What You Need to Know." *National Alliance on Mental Health*. 2013. http://www.nami.org/Content/NavigationMenu/Inform_Yourself/ About_Mental_Illness/By_Illness/MentalIllnessBrochure.pdf (accessed January 24, 2015).

Pratt, Laura A., and Debra J. Brody. "Depression in the U.S. Household Population, 2009–2012." NCHS Data Brief, No. 172. *National Center for Health Statistics, Centers for Disease Control and Prevention*. December 2014. http://www.cdc.gov/nchs/data/databriefs/db172.pdf (accessed January 23, 2015).

Self-Concept and Self-Esteem Behaviors and Habits

What Is Self-Perception?

Self-perception is what you think of yourself. It's how you think about who you are and how you interact with the environment around you. Self-perception can include how you see yourself physically, such as how strong you are, and your personality traits, such as whether or not you are kind. Self-perception can also include more abstract ideas, such as your sense of spirituality.

You can form your self-perception by observing how you typically behave in different situations, noticing what comes naturally to you, such as meeting new people, and understanding what is unique about you. Self-perception can also come from noticing how others see and relate to you. Self-perception is what you *think* about yourself rather than how you *feel* about yourself, which is your self-esteem.

Psychologist Daryl J. Bem formulated the theory of self-perception, which states that people evaluate their own behavior in a similar way that other people evaluate their behavior. For example, if you drink 10 cups of coffee a day at work, your coworkers would conclude you love coffee because you drink so much of it. In self-perception theory, if someone asked you why you like coffee, you would say that you must like it because you drink it all the time rather than saying, for example, that you love the taste of coffee.

What Is the Relationship between Self-Perception and Personal Identity?

Your personal identity is made up of your individual qualities, your social relations, and all the groups you consider yourself part of. Your personal identity can include, for example, your family roles (child, sister, parent) and work roles (construction worker, supervisor), as well as your race, gender, ethnicity, religion, and sexuality. Your personal identity distinguishes you as an individual separate from other people.

Aspects of your personal identity can change over time. Changes are particularly pronounced as you move from childhood to adulthood. However, adult personal identities change too. You can change your religion or career or go from being single to married or from childless to being a parent.

As your personal identity changes, your self-perception may also change. Your personal identity could include being a well-known doctor, a Muslim who is very active at your mosque, and a swimmer and skier. This may lead you to have a self-perception that you are very energetic, professionally successful, social, spiritual, and physically fit. If later in life you retire and take heart medication that makes you tire easily, your personal identity can change as can your self-perception. You are no longer a doctor, you may stop skiing, and you may not have as much energy to volunteer at the mosque. Your self-perception could change from seeing yourself as a high-energy person to a person with limited energy. Your identity as a Muslim can remain strong, but you can change from being an active participant at the mosque to a respected elder. You can have new roles, too, perhaps you are now an active grandparent.

How Is Self-Perception Developed?

Self-perception starts developing at a very young age and continues to change throughout your life. Psychologist Dr. Susan Harter, in her book *The Construction of Self: A Developmental Perspective*, explains that self-concept usually begins about the age of two. This is when children begin to understand that they have bodies separate and unique from others.

As children grow, especially between adolescence and young adulthood, their self-perception can develop and change radically as their bodies and brains undergo major developments. A young child could have the self-perception that he is short, but then he has a sudden growth spurt in adolescence. He goes from being the shortest in his class to one of the tallest. He starts seeing himself as very tall.

Some self-perceptions that start developing at a very young age can remain basically the same throughout our lives. Even at a young age, you might have a particular sense of compassion for others. While you may develop a stronger or more mature and refined sense of compassion as you age, your basic self-perception as a compassionate person remains.

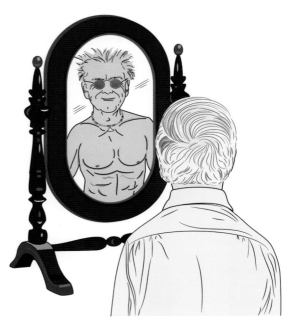

How we think about ourselves can be very different from how we really are. © GAIL DRINNAN/SHUTTERSTOCK.COM.

What Is the Difference between Realistic and Unrealistic Self-Perception?

Self-perception is not necessarily realistic. You may think of yourself as extremely short, but statistically you may be of average height. Self-perceptions about personality or more abstract notions can be more unrealistic than physical perceptions. Having charisma or being understanding, for example, can have various and sometimes complex interpretations.

It can be particularly difficult to distinguish between realistic and unrealistic self-perceptions when your self-perception is heavily based on what others think. You might believe you are a big eater because your coworkers constantly remark about how much food you bring for lunch. Realistically, you eat an average amount of food for your size and active lifestyle. Your coworkers could also be excessively dieting, so your lunch looks large because they only eat a small piece of fruit and yogurt for lunch. Others can influence you to have an unrealistic self-perception.

If your self-perception doesn't change as events in your life change, you can develop unrealistic self-perceptions. If you grew up in New York, you may see yourself culturally as a New Yorker. If, however, you moved to Paris when you were 12 and lived there all your adult life, you may develop many Parisian cultural characteristics. After decades of living in France, you might still have some cultural characteristics of a New Yorker but your self-perception as primarily a New Yorker may be skewed.

Sometimes self-perceptions are unrealistic if they are based on how you would like to see yourself in the future or on who you would like to be. You may think of yourself as an accomplished actor, even though you have only had a few nonspeaking roles in small community theater productions. You have an unrealistic self-perception, since hoping to be a professional actor in the future and wishing that you were already one do not make you an accomplished actor.

How Can I Evaluate How I Think about Myself?

When evaluating how you think about yourself, think about how you are in different situations and with different people. Are you always fairly quiet in social settings or is it just in big groups? You can have different roles in different relationships. If you are middle-aged, you might feel old around your teenage children and their friends but young when volunteering at a senior center. Of course, different environments require that you use appropriate characteristics. A good sense of humor makes sense at a party but, obviously, not at a funeral.

Another way to evaluate how you think about yourself is by listening to how other people talk about or react to you. If people often come to you with their problems, it can indicate you are a good listener. If you are unsure about your self-perceptions, you can ask other people their opinions. Remember to consider who you are asking and that what type of person they are influences their response. A person from a particular culture may consider you easy going, while someone from another culture may see you as being too informal. You can also learn about yourself by seeing how you react to opinions others have of you. Are you able to take criticism well or do you react defensively, for example?

When evaluating how you think of yourself, bear in mind what's realistic and current. Are you are still thinking of yourself the way your parents thought of you as a child, even though your life now is very different? Keep in mind your current self and environment, as well as who you might have been in the past and who you wish to be in the future.

Can Self-Perception Change over Time?

As children become adults, their self-perceptions can radically change as their bodies and minds go through enormous shifts and they become independent. While perhaps not as dramatically as in childhood, over your lifetime as an adult, your self-perception can also change.

Your self-perception can change when you experience major life events, such as getting married or divorced, changing jobs, moving to a different country, or witnessing the death of a parent. Your self-perception can also vary as you age and your body continues to change. Sometimes, your self-perception doesn't change as quickly as the changes in your life might merit. People who are newly retired, for example, might continue to perceive themselves in the ways they were in their workplace, even though they are no longer there. It can take time for one's self-perceptions to change.

Even in the absence of major life events, your self-perception can change. You might have viewed yourself as socially awkward because you didn't feel comfortable at parties. As you mature, your analysis can get more refined as you realize people often feel differently about particular social situations. You may not like parties, but you do great socially in more intimate and personal settings with family or friends. You haven't changed who you are, but your self-perception has changed from being socially awkward to someone who loves to socialize, just not in large settings.

Your self-perception can change about your physical being too. You may have always thought of yourself as overweight and unattractive. Through educating yourself about healthy eating, exercise, and body sizes, you may see that people come in different sizes and that eating well and exercising is what's important. You can change your self-perception to being someone who is healthy and beautiful.

What Can I Do to Change How I Think about Myself?

There are many strategies you can use if you want to change how you think about yourself. An important place to start is with personal awareness. What is it you want to change? What would you change it to? Are you thinking about yourself realistically? Are you taking into account what others think of you too much or not enough? Being aware of what you realistically want to change is a first step.

Be specific about what you want to change, and create a plan for how you will accomplish it. Motivate yourself by writing a list of why you want to change. Don't be judgmental when evaluating your self-perceptions, even if how you think about yourself has been harmful in the past. If believing that you were overweight led to anorexia, it is important to change your perception. Judging yourself for what you previously thought or did, however, is counterproductive.

You needn't change the entire way you think about yourself or even make lots of big changes at once. Start small. If you think of yourself as someone who is unable to be on time, notice when you do get somewhere in a timely fashion. Reinforce the positive: I made it to the bus on time today. If you begin telling yourself old negative self-perceptions, stop the negative thinking immediately. When you've accomplished a goal, reward yourself and take a new next step.

Self-Esteem: How Do You Feel about Yourself?

What Is Self-Esteem?

Self-esteem refers to the way you feel about yourself. People who possess healthy self-esteem have a positive sense of their own value, and they tend to be capable of assessing both their accomplishments and their failures in a balanced manner. People with low self-esteem, however, may believe that they are incapable of success. These individuals often see themselves very differently from the way others see them, and they often assume that others' opinions of them are negative.

How you feel on a daily basis can fluctuate based on any number of things. However, the concept of self-esteem goes beyond the range of moods you experience in a usual day. According to the University of Texas at Austin Counseling and Mental Health Center, individuals with healthy self-esteem are able to face normal ups and downs, while those with low self-esteem are intensely affected by everyday challenges.

Some people consider certain qualities to be markers of success, such as physical attractiveness, intelligence, or financial standing, but these factors do not necessarily determine your self-esteem. However, self-esteem can influence how you perceive your relative attractiveness or success. Those with healthy self-esteem tend to present themselves more positively, both in dress and demeanor, which can cause them to appear more attractive or successful. On the other hand, a person with low self-esteem may not make an effort to dress attractively or may be reluctant to engage in positive social interactions, which can cause others to see him or her as less outgoing.

Why Is Having a Healthy Level of Self-Esteem Important?

Individuals with healthy self-esteem are more able to acknowledge both their strengths and their flaws. They feel confident expressing themselves

© FOTOHUNTER/
SHUTTERSTOCK.COM.

Self-esteem

and making decisions. They also have more realistic expectations of their abilities and thus experience greater levels of personal satisfaction when they meet goals. They are often less critical of themselves and others, which results in fewer instances of depression or negative emotions such as shame. These individuals also tend to build stronger relationships and are more likely to realize when relationships are unhealthy.

People with good self-esteem tend to make better decisions regarding responsible conduct at work or school. They are less likely to engage in destructive behaviors such as alcohol and drug abuse or eating disorders. Because they are more able to admit their imperfections, people with healthy self-esteem are not easily weakened by occasional mistakes or hardships. They are more willing to appreciate their own positive attributes, and they are more able to receive positive and negative feedback without becoming discouraged.

How Can I Find Out Whether I Have a Healthy Level of Self-Esteem?

Since self-esteem is so personal and subjective, it can be difficult to measure. Researchers divide the concept into two general categories. Global self-esteem refers to the overall way you feel about yourself, while domain-specific self-esteem refers to self-evaluation based on specific criteria, such as intelligence or attractiveness. Global self-esteem is often measured with the use of quizzes and response tools, and many of these are readily available online.

American social psychologist Morris Rosenberg designed the most widely used test for measuring self-esteem, the Rosenberg Scale, in 1965. This test asks people to express their relative agreement with 10 statements that focus on personal worth, comparison with others, satisfaction,

Social Media and Self-Esteem

Social media are increasingly present in everyday life. Americans use platforms such as Facebook, Pinterest, Tumblr, and Twitter to keep up with friends, gather entertainment news, and share project ideas. Users have become accustomed to sharing photographs of themselves and their achievements online and receiving feedback on these images from members of their social circle. With the growth of such media, however, has come increasing concern that these forums may be having a negative impact on self-esteem, particularly for women, who tend to be more active on many social media sites than males.

One of the criticisms of social media is that it offers idealized images of everything from homemaking and parenting to weight loss and physical fitness. Such images may cause pressure to conform to standards that are unattainable for many, which can have a negative impact on self-esteem. This concern motivated Pinterest to ban so-called "thinspiration" pin boards, in which posters sought to inspire others by demonstrating their own weight loss or physical fitness accomplishments. These posts created controversy, since many viewers felt that they were boastful and judgmental rather than inspirational and that they induced feelings of shame for those who were unable to demonstrate similar results.

respect, and ability. Examples include "I feel that I am a person of worth, at least on an equal plane with others"; "I feel I do not have much to be proud of"; and "I wish I could have more respect for myself." Respondents can agree or disagree with each statement, and their answers are scored from 0 to 30. Scores below 15 indicate low self-esteem.

What Are Some Factors That Influence Self-Esteem?

Your self-esteem can be affected by a number of personal factors. One essential aspect of self-esteem involves the way you think about yourself and others. People who focus on their own imperfections and have difficulty controlling negative thoughts about themselves may have damaged self-esteem. Those who hold themselves to overly high standards often have unreasonable expectations for others and may focus their thinking on criticism. Physical health and negative body image can affect self-esteem, and some believe that genetic makeup may also play a role in how you feel about yourself.

Self-esteem can be impacted by your identification with various types of social groups and your feelings about how those groups are viewed by society. It can also be affected by perceptions you see reflected in media. Advertising and social media may encourage you to compare yourself to others in a way that may have a negative impact on your self-image. Your self-esteem is also likely to be influenced by your relationships with others and your experiences in the world, especially during childhood and adolescence.

Childhood experiences can have an especially powerful effect on self-esteem. Children are more likely to have healthy self-esteem if they are listened to and spoken to appropriately and given proper attention and kindness. They should also receive acknowledgment of their successes and be taught to accept their mistakes. Children who are criticized, ignored, or held to unreasonable standards of perfection may experience low self-esteem. Such experiences can stem from the behavior of parents, family members, teachers, peers, or other authority figures.

How Can Low Self-Esteem Affect My Life?

Anxiety: *An abnormal and overwhelming sense of worry and fear that is often accompanied by physical reaction.*

Varying degrees of emotional distress are common for people with low self-esteem, including depression, *anxiety*, and loneliness. People experiencing these symptoms frequently are less likely to take on personal, professional, or academic challenges, since they may believe that they are more likely to fail. When they do take on challenges, they may be more likely to procrastinate or expect too much of themselves. Those with low self-esteem tend to set unrealistically high standards for themselves that often ensure disappointment.

People with low self-esteem may believe themselves incapable of good decisions and may therefore resign themselves to making poor decisions, which can cause their perceptions of their own self-worth to decrease. They may be more likely to pursue unhealthy or abusive relationships and may struggle to connect with others. They may also cause themselves physical harm as a result of alcohol and substance abuse, violence, sexual risk, or eating disorders.

How Can I Improve My Self-Esteem?

Improving self-esteem requires a conscious adjustment of thinking patterns, and it can take time. The Mayo Clinic suggests that you start by trying to identify where and when your self-esteem might be challenged. This can make you more aware of your feelings and help you analyze why these situations are difficult for you. By paying attention to the way you feel, you can begin to question your negative thinking. You can then practice challenging those patterns by thinking positively instead of negatively. It can be beneficial to remember that, with practice, you can learn to control and retrain your mind.

If you are suffering from low self-esteem, you may also benefit from improving your physical health. Wholesome living practices such as eating well, getting enough exercise and sleep, and practicing meditation can have a positive impact on your self-esteem. Similarly, avoiding harmful practices such as drinking, using recreational drugs, or smoking can also help you to feel better about yourself. If you are struggling with negative feelings, other people in your life may be able to help you. Reaching out to friends and family can be an essential part of building healthy self-esteem.

"I'll be the first 5'4" center in the NBA."

Self-confidence is one part of a healthy self-esteem.
© CARTOONRESOURCE/
SHUTTERSTOCK.COM.

What Professional Help Is Available to Help Me Build My Self-Esteem?

There are a number of resources that can help you improve your self-esteem. Many books and articles related to psychology, counseling, and wellness are available in public libraries and online. These materials can help you understand the source of your self-esteem issues and can provide tips for improving your confidence.

Many community colleges and adult learning centers offer courses aimed at managing stress and anxiety, and similar courses are also available through educational institutions online. Building stress-management skills can give you a sense of empowerment as well as faith in your ability to manage life's challenges, which are key factors in self-esteem. Creative study in such fields as visual art, writing, or music can also be therapeutic and can improve your sense of well-being. Since many people with low self-esteem also struggle with negative body image, environments that foster physical wellness can help you to view

Yoga: *A form of exercise and a system of health that incorporates a series of exercises utilizing regulated breathing, concentration, physical postures, and flexibility.*

your body in a more positive way. *Yoga* and meditation classes promote physical fitness as well as stress reduction, mental discipline, and general health.

Seeking the advice of a counseling professional can be extremely helpful in building healthy self-esteem. Licensed therapists and counselors are trained to help you examine and alter harmful thinking and actions. Most communities offer both group and individual counseling opportunities, and fees vary among institutions. Insurance policies often cover some or all of the costs of mental health counseling. Counselors can help you develop reflective and behavioral skills that will continue to be valuable even after you have completed your counseling sessions.

Factors That Influence Personal Identity

What Is Personal Identity?

Your personal identity is the way you understand and define yourself and what makes you unique compared to other human beings. Your personal identity is separate from your social identity, which refers largely to your socioeconomic class and ethnicity. Demographic factors such as your ethnic heritage or sexual orientation also form part of your identity, as do personal relationships, life experiences, attitudes, and values, among other factors. Your personal identity is your own idea of who you are, or the total of what characterizes your individuality. It also naturally includes what you like about yourself and is the primary source of your self-esteem.

Your identity develops over time as the circumstances of your life change. Also, since identity is multifaceted, you might describe yourself differently in different situations or to different people. In one setting, you might emphasize your professional status and credentials, while in another you might talk about your fashion sense and favorite genres of music. Social scientists and psychologists debate whether personal identity is a fixed, essential property within each of us or whether it is socially constructed, continually evolving through our relationships and how we act. Either way, we tend to experience identity as a continuous, complex sense of who we are.

German-born American psychologist Erik Erikson had an influential theory of identity. Unlike Austrian neurologist Sigmund Freud, who believed that identity is formed primarily in childhood, Erikson took a developmental view, arguing that people build their identities in stages that span their entire lives. Adolescence may be the most challenging of all the life stages, since young people seek to carve out an independent place in the world while also negotiating a new role in the family. In many cultures, rites of passage give adolescents a formal way to mark the change from juvenile to adult identity and social roles. As people grow

© GUSTAVO FRAZAO/
SHUTTERSTOCK.COM.

older, they develop greater self-knowledge. The jobs you have held, your hobbies and interests, the people you associate with, and the roles you fulfill in your family and community all reflect and help reinforce your sense of self.

How Can Genetics Influence Personal Identity?

Genetics forms an important part of your identity. It may not determine who you are, in terms of your moral character and important choices in life, but your genes determine a great deal of *what* you are. Gender is one significant component of your identity that is clearly genetically determined. Your body type is another. Certain physical and intellectual traits are inherited, as is the likelihood that you will be vulnerable to certain illnesses and diseases. People often compare babies' physical appearance and behavior to those of their parents. They may notice that a child has inherited his or her mother's eyes, for example, or his or her father's temper. In a way, genetics arranges the order of many of the building blocks of identity.

The Human Genome Project, a major scientific advance of recent years, succeeded in its goal of mapping the entire sequence of genes in human DNA. The researchers discovered that more than 99 percent of our genetic structure is the same for everyone. The things we have in common vastly outnumber the genetic differences between individuals. However, the small differences in our genetic makeup create important variations. Genetic advances have provided evidence for those who claim that identity is fixed from birth rather than influenced by social factors. However, studies of human genetic content have largely disproven the idea that human characteristics are in any way determined or influenced by race. Research shows greater genetic variation within each racial group than between one group and another.

How Can Health Influence Personal Identity?

Researchers have found that aspects of identity and personality, such as your emotional temperament, cognitive habits, and self-esteem, can have a major impact on your long-term health. The reverse can also be

Erik Erikson and Developmental Psychology

Born in 1902 in Frankfurt-am-Main, Germany, Erik H. Erikson (1902–94) is one of the best-known psychoanalysts of the twentieth century for his theories on psychosocial development, including the evolution of an individual's personal identity. He is credited with coining the term *identity crisis*.

As a boy Erikson was interested art, and in 1927, after graduating from high school, he moved to Vienna to teach art at a school focusing on psychoanalysis run by Anna Freud (1895–1982), the daughter of Austrian neurologist Sigmund Freud (1856–1939). There Erikson became fascinated with the study of the human mind and enrolled in the Vienna

Psychoanalytic Institute. After completing his training, Erikson immigrated to the United States, and in 1936 he joined Yale University's Institute of Human Relations.

Erikson contributed to the area of psychoanalysis that studies developmental progression in humans. He theorized that, at each stage of life, human beings undergo a psychological struggle that contributes to specific aspects of the personality. Since Erikson first developed these ideas, his theories have been challenged by the scientific community. Still, the concept of confusion of roles, or an identity crisis, continues to be one of his best-known ideas.

true. At any stage of life, your health can affect the way you think about yourself. For example, if an injury or illness during your childhood left you with a limp, this physical impairment could become a source of frustration as you grow older. By contrast, good health and fitness can help you form a positive self-concept or contribute to your body's ability to fight off sickness or handle stress.

Disabilities, whether or not they are genetically inherited, can have an impact on the character of those who have them. Some disabled people find it challenging to cultivate a sense of identity that is separate from their disability. Society tends to view disability as a personal tragedy, but in many cases those who deal with a disability eventually find that they are able to establish a new approach to life and a new understanding of themselves on their own terms.

Physical and mental health are equally important when it comes to influencing identity. The onset of mental health conditions such as traumatic brain injury, *Alzheimer's disease*, or dementia can make you feel as if you have undergone a fundamental change that affects your identity. If an injury or illness impairs physical or cognitive functioning, the loss of specific abilities can diminish your sense of competence and threaten

Alzheimer's disease:
A serious condition usually found in older adults that affects the parts of the brain that control thought, memory, and language.

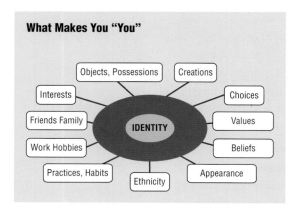

There are many factors that make you who you are.
ILLUSTRATION BY LUMINA DATAMATICS LTD. © 2015 CENGAGE LEARNING.

your sense of identity. Memory loss can have an equally profound effect since adults, especially older ones, rely on their memories as a basis of identity and self-esteem. However, it is important to remember that no single factor captures the entirety of who you are.

How Can Life Challenges Influence Personal Identity?

Your identity is a work in progress, and the events in your daily life contribute to making you who you are. Each day you construct your life story, and your experiences shape your character. Many people believe that your strength of character emerges through the way you respond to the challenges life puts in your path. A major event, such as a severe injury, surviving physical or sexual abuse, getting a divorce, or living through a war, can become a permanent and defining aspect of identity. However, such trauma can also help you discover unexpected courage or resilience.

Finding the right career and earning a living are among the most important challenges of adult life, and they can represent a central part of your life story. Periods of unemployment or unsatisfying work can have detrimental effects on your self-esteem and self-worth. If you spend most of your waking hours in activities that are poorly suited to your skills and natural talents, you may feel as if your life lacks a meaningful purpose. However, facing such challenges can help you find the drive to overcome obstacles and make positive changes. Setting goals and striving to reach them are fundamental steps toward taking charge of your life and identity.

How Can Family Relationships Influence Personal Identity?

Parents and other principal caregivers are a powerful influence on the people we become. No matter where you grew up, your family was most likely your main environment when you were a child. Children develop a concept of self as early as the second or third year of life, a crucial developmental stage. During these early years, parents or caregivers give children feedback that helps them establish their sense of what it means to be alive, to be a person, and to be unique. Other close family relationships, such as with siblings or grandparents, also help children come to understand their place in the world. Love and patient encouragement from parents contributes to the healthy development of self-esteem in the young. However, undue or excessive criticism or punishment, researchers have found, can cause harm to a child's self-image. Parents are also typically the most important influence on a child's values and moral beliefs.

People often learn to see themselves the way they are viewed within their family. The ways in which your parents described you while you were growing up can all too easily become part of your core beliefs and identity. For example, if they told you that you were smart, lazy, beautiful, or had a difficult temper, you might continue to believe this about yourself as you grow older. Later in life, often during the teenage years, people may resent or rebel against these characterizations. However, more often they carry into adulthood the ways they have learned to think of themselves since childhood.

How Can Peer Relationships Influence Personal Identity?

Peer relationships reinforce identity and provide positive feedback. Friends are people who see you in a positive light and who notice and appreciate your good qualities. A good friend can reassure you in moments of self-doubt and even remind you of the strengths you have if you have forgotten them. Through shared activities or conversation, your closest friends can bring out the best in you and make you feel like your true self.

Relationships with friends and peer groups are especially important during adolescence, a time when many young people experiment with their identity. Friends and classmates can sometimes be a more powerful influence in a teenager's life than parents. Children in the adolescent years are seeking to assert their independence and uniqueness, while at the same time they want to belong to their peer group. In middle school and high school, young people learn all about how social networks function. They categorize one another and form cliques, or groups, with other people their age. These years may be difficult, but they are enormously important in the development of self-awareness and personal identity.

You exhibit your identity through your roles in your family, your community, and the social groups and structures in which you participate. You also show your identity while you are at your job, shopping in stores, or even passing by strangers on the street. In everything you regularly do that puts you in contact with other people, you have opportunities to demonstrate the nature of your identity. This is why some theorists believe that identity is socially constructed. In a sense, you invent yourself, or reinvent yourself, every day through your social interactions.

Behaviors and Habits

What Are Behaviors and Habits?

Behaviors and habits help define who you are. Whether you are shy or outgoing, energized or lazy, your behaviors and habits are what people observe and ultimately use to describe you. Recognizing and breaking certain habits—whether they are unhealthy, destructive, or just annoying—can help you improve your overall well-being and strengthen your personal and professional relationships.

Behaviors are actions that are choices. Habits, on the other hand, are behaviors that have become automatic through repetition. For example, when a baseball player comes to the plate to bat, he plans his batting stance, checks the bases, remembers the pitcher's history, knows the inning and the score, and reads the hand signals from the coach. Over time and repeated practice, these simple behaviors become ingrained to the point that the batter doesn't have to think much before he swings. His repeated behaviors have become habits.

It is difficult to determine where behaviors end and habits begin. Many behaviors that end up becoming habits are started when we're young, with little understanding of what impact they will have later in life. Other habits, however, are developed in adulthood. If you understand how habits are formed, it may be easier to break those that have a negative impact on your life. It also helps to understand the role your brain has in causing you to react out of habit when exposed to certain cues or triggers.

How Do Behaviors Become Habits?

Habits begin as routine behaviors that you do regularly without thinking much about them. An example may be your weekday morning routine. Your alarm goes off, and you reach over to the bedside table toward your alarm. You hit the snooze button to allow yourself to doze for 10 more

Some habits, such as smoking cigarettes and excessive drinking, can be unhealthy and even life threatening.
© DAN KOSMAYER/
SHUTTERSTOCK.COM.

minutes. The alarm rings again, and you reach over to turn it off. You throw back the covers and swing your legs out of bed. You head to the kitchen, fumble for the coffee, add water, and start the brew. While that is perking, you head outside to grab the newspaper. At this point, you might actually be fully awake. You have basically performed all of these tasks without putting any thought into them.

Habits allow you to complete regular and familiar tasks quickly and effectively. In fact, if you look at each hour of your day, you will probably find dozens of examples of habits you have developed, many of which have been with you since early childhood. These little habits rule your day, in the sense that they allow you to use your creativity and brain power on more productive or challenging activities that make each day unique.

What Is Happening in My Brain as I Perform Habitual Behaviors?

The basic components of a habit include cues, behaviors, rewards, and cravings. If you take the morning routine example again, a cue that triggers your behavior is the alarm clock going off twice. The rewards are drinking a hot cup of coffee, reading the newspaper, and getting to work on time.

Over time, you begin to enjoy and then crave the coffee, reading the paper, and the perks that go with being on time to work. If your alarm doesn't go off, you may miss your coffee and have to explain why you are running late—both of which can feel unsettling. Craving is the component that makes habits so hard to break.

What Are Some Examples of Good and Bad Habits?

Habits—both good and bad—have an impact on your life. Good habits can contribute to a more positive outlook on your day and to less stressful situations and relationships. Some positive habits, such as exercising

Pepsodent Ad Campaign

If you thought that people always brushed their teeth, you would be wrong. During World War I (1914–18), the U.S. military observed how unhealthy a number of young men were because of their decaying teeth. Few brushed daily, and just telling people they need to clean their teeth for better health was not enough to change their habits.

It took advertising giant Claude Hopkins and his promotional campaign for Pepsodent toothpaste to get people to the new normal of daily brushing. Hopkins took a scientific approach to advertising and sales, using what he understood about human nature and studying dental textbooks to learn about plaque, a film on the teeth. For the

Pepsodent campaign, Hopkins used the "cue" of the cloudy, yellow film that forms on your teeth when you don't brush your teeth. The "reward" for brushing with Pepsodent came in the form of a minty, clean, and tingly feeling, plus a prettier smile. He used the catchy jingle, "You'll wonder where the yellow went, when you brush your teeth with Pepsodent" to reinforce his message.

After engaging several times in the behavior of brushing their teeth and enjoying the reward of a clean feeling and nice smile, people began to "crave" that feeling and, ultimately, Pepsodent. Hopkins's campaign was so successful that, by the end of World War II (1939–45), the military downgraded their concerns about dental health.

and practicing good hygiene, can even extend your life. Getting enough sleep each night, eating healthy, and being punctual are other good habits that can set the right tone each day.

Getting out of sync with your morning routine and craving a cup of coffee are rather inconsequential examples of habits that you may or may not want to control or change. However, some habits, such as using illegal drugs, smoking cigarettes, and excessive drinking, can be unhealthy and even life threatening. Unfortunately, these are also some of the more difficult habits to quit because of the extremely strong cues, rewards, and cravings these substances elicit. Most people wanting to stop these habits ultimately need to seek professional help. A good place to start is to talk to your physician honestly about your concerns and your desire to end unhealthy habits.

Some people have bad habits relating to eating, including overeating or indulging in foods that are high in fat or high in sugar. For example, a small cup of black coffee has a minimal number of calories, under five. But by adding sugar and cream, the calorie count jumps by 100 or more calories. Worse, if you develop the habit of treating yourself to a specialty coffee drink such as a peppermint white chocolate mocha, your one cup of coffee now has over 500 calories. Drinking 500 calories is the equivalent of drinking four cans of soda.

Overeating has a number of triggers, many of which can be linked to behaviors developed during childhood. Some people eat meals or dishes they remember from their childhood as "comfort food"—reminding them of a happier or simpler time. Foods high in sugar provide an immediate reward to the taste buds and the brain. Like stopping the use of addictive drugs or alcohol, curbing bad eating habits may require help from a professional. Again, speak to your physician if you are unable to change your eating habits on your own. Be prepared to be honest about how much, and what, you are eating.

How Does My Behavior Affect Others?

Behaviors that affect how you treat other people are important to recognize. In some cases you may not even be aware of your negative behaviors. For example, what you consider a direct conversation with family and friends may come off as snappish to others. Offering unsolicited advice or observations about others' lives may come off as rude or judgmental. Asking friends, colleagues, and family members for honest feedback about your behavior is the first step to learning about areas that may need improvement.

If you are the family member who always seems to be in the middle of controversy, determine your role in the problem and see if a certain pattern of behavior emerges. Perhaps you have a tendency to gossip about others, or maybe you give others the cold shoulder when something is bothering you instead of discussing the issue. Over time, these types of behaviors can become habits that can potentially destroy relationships.

How Can Behaviors and Habits Shape How Others Perceive Me?

It is human nature for us to judge and be judged by others based on the good and bad habits we display. And, considering repetition is how behaviors become habits, your habits are likely seen repeatedly by those around you. Those closest to you know that there is more to you than your good or bad habits, but it's easy for coworkers or casual acquaintances to define you based on behaviors they witness regularly. Making a poor first impression can have a negative impact on your professional as well as your personal life. You may be passed up for opportunities at work or struggle to build a professional network all because of the way you are perceived by others.

Fair or not, it is important to understand the impact certain behaviors have on how others perceive you. For example, your manager at work may strongly disapprove of cigarette smoking. While he or she cannot forbid you to smoke, continuing to smoke during work hours could affect your relationship with your boss and even your potential for promotion. On the flip side, a positive habit such as walking during your lunch break every day may cause you to be seen as a positive, take-charge member of the staff.

Take stock of your habits. Do they represent who you are or who you want to be? Understanding this will help you get closer to the person you want to be and how you want others to perceive you.

What Are Some Things I Can Do to Break Bad Habits?

Not all bad habits require medical attention. For example, if you want to get out of the habit of biting your fingernails or cracking your knuckles, you can begin your efforts at home. The first step in fighting any bad habit is to understand it. Pay careful attention to what triggers the undesirable behavior. Spend a few days keeping a log. Make a note every time you catch yourself acting out your bad habit. After a few days, review the data and look for a pattern. This will help you figure out what is triggering the behavior if you don't already know.

Once you have identified the trigger, work to address it. If possible, change your routine to avoid the trigger. If this is not possible, look for a more benign behavior to substitute in its place. For example, if you discover you tend to bite your nails during certain times of the day or in certain situations, chew gum or suck on a hard candy to keep your mouth occupied. If you find that you overeat when you become bored in the afternoon, change up your schedule. Go for a walk instead of snacking.

If you feel negative reinforcement is more likely to work for you, many experts recommend putting a rubber band on your wrist and snapping it each time you catch yourself engaging in the bad habit. This will help your brain associate the habit with pain rather than pleasure.

What Are Some Effective Treatments for Bad Habits?

Despite our best efforts, many bad habits require the intervention of a trained health-care provider. If you discuss your concerns with your primary care provider, he or she will be able to decide whether to offer you treatment or refer you to another physician or therapist who specialized in treating your specific habits.

The therapy recommended for you will depend on the habit you are trying to break and your own personal circumstances. Available therapies range from medication to hypnosis or even inpatient therapy. Your physician or therapist will help you find a treatment program that is right for you.

For More Information

BOOKS

Bem, Daryl J. "Self-Perception Theory." In *Advances in Experimental Social Psychology: Volume 6*, edited by Leonard Berkowitz. New York: Academic Press, 1972.

Contrada, Richard J., and Richard D. Ashmore, eds. *Self, Social Identity, and Physical Health: Interdisciplinary Explorations*. New York: Oxford University Press, 1999.

Duhigg, Charles. *The Power of Habit: Why We Do What We Do in Life and Business*. New York: Random House, 2012.

Erikson, Erik H. *Childhood and Society*. New York: W. W. Norton, 1950.

Harter, Susan. *The Construction of Self: A Developmental Perspective*. 2nd ed. New York: Guilford Press, 2012.

McShane, Steven L., and Mary Ann Von Glinow. "Self-Concept: How We Perceive Ourselves." In *Organizational Behavior: Emerging Knowledge, Global Reality*. 6th ed. New York: McGraw-Hill, 2013.

Oyserman, Daphna, Kristan Elmore, and George Smith. "Self, Self-Concept, and Identity." In *Handbook of Self and Identity*, edited by Mark R. Leary and June Price Tangney. 2nd ed. New York: Guilford Press, 2012.

Perry, John, ed. *Personal Identity*. 2nd ed. Berkeley: University of California Press, 2008.

Taylor, Charles. *The Sources of the Self: The Making of the Modern Identity*. Cambridge, MA: Harvard University Press, 1989.

PERIODICALS

Gleason, Philip. "Identifying Identity: A Semantic History." *Journal of American History* 6 (1983): 910–31.

Klitzman, Robert. "'Am I My Genes?': Questions of Identity Among Individuals Confronting Genetic Disease." *Genetics in Medicine* 11 (2009): 880–89.

Kokkoris, Michail D., and Ulrich Kuhnen. "'Express the Teal You': Cultural Differences in the Perception of Self-Expression as Authenticity." *Journal of Cross-Cultural Psychology* 45, no. 8 (2014): 1221+.

Moskowitz, Nancy Heller. "Queen-Sized: Body Image and Self-Perception." *Advocate*, November 2010: 18+.

Murugami, Margaret Wangui. "Disability and Identity." *Disability Studies Quarterly* 29, no. 4 (2009).

WEBSITES

Chaganti, Subba Rao. "The Ad That Created a Habit!" *BuildingPharmaBrands*. http://buildingpharmabrands.com/tag/pepsodent/(accessed October 21, 2014).

Ciotti, Gregory. "5 Scientific Ways to Build Habits That Stick." *99U*. http://99u.com/articles/17123/5-scientific-ways-to-build-habits-that-stick (accessed October 22, 2014).

De Guzman, Maria R. T. "Friendships, Peer Influence, and Peer Pressure during the Teen Years." *Institute of Agriculture and Natural Resources, University of Nebraska-Lincoln*. http://www.ianrpubs.unl.edu/epublic/pages/publicationD.jsp?publicationId=837 (accessed December 14, 2014).

Dubigg, Charles. "The Power of Habit: How the History of Toothpaste Explains Why You Can't Lose Weight." *Slate*. http://www.slate.com/articles/arts/culturebox/2012/02/an_excerpt_from_charles_duhigg_s_the_power_of_habit_.1.html (accessed October 21, 2014).

Grohol, John M. "Changing Our Routines and Habits." *Psychcentral.com*. http://psychcentral.com/lib/changing-our-routines-and-habits/000903 (accessed October 22, 2014).

McLeod, S. A. "Self Concept." *Simply Psychology*. http://www.simplypsychology.org/self-concept.html (accessed November 6, 2014).

"Psych Basics: Self-Esteem." *Psychology Today*. http://www.psychologytoday.com/basics/self-esteem (accessed October 30, 2014).

Robins, Richard W., Kali H. Trzesniewski, and M. Brent Donnellan. "A Brief Primer on Self-Esteem." *Prevention Researcher*. http://www.tpronline.org/download-free-article.cfm?id=599 (accessed October 29, 2014).

"Rosenberg's Self-Esteem Scale." *W. W. Norton & Company*. http://www.wwnorton.com/college/psych/psychsci/media/rosenberg.htm (accessed October 31, 2014).

"Self-Esteem." *University of Texas at Austin Counseling and Mental Health Center*. http://cmhc.utexas.edu/selfesteem.html (accessed October 30, 2014).

"Self-Esteem: Take Steps to Feel Better about Yourself." *Mayo Clinic*. http://www.mayoclinic.org/healthy-living/adult-health/in-depth/self-esteem/art-20045374 (accessed October 31, 2014).

"Self-Esteem Check: Too Low or Just Right?" *Mayo Clinic*. http://www.mayoclinic.org/healthy-living/adult-health/in-depth/self-esteem/art-20047976 (accessed October 31, 2014).

Mental Health and Mental Illness

How Does My Mental Heath Affect My Physical Health and Relationships?

Mental health is generally understood to be a state of personal well-being that allows an individual to function successfully in daily life. Mentally healthy people are able to cope with stress and are typically productive and engaged, both professionally and socially. A growing body of research has also demonstrated that mental health and physical health are closely connected.

Mental illness, which may take a variety of forms, can have a number of adverse effects on your physical health. Untreated mental illness may also strain your relationships with parents, siblings, significant others, and friends. With treatment, many people experience not only relief from mental health symptoms but also improvements in physical health and the quality of personal relationships.

What Is Mental Illness?

Many people experience mental health issues at some point in their lives, particularly following the death of a loved one or a major life transition

How Do Chronic Physical Conditions Affect Mental Health?

While researchers have found that mental illness can precede poor physical health, the reverse has also been shown to be true. Individuals with health problems, particularly chronic diseases, are more likely to develop depression or anxiety than those not suffering from a chronic condition.

With some conditions, research has suggested that biological disease processes are a factor in the development of mental illness. For instance, depression often seems to develop with neurological disorders such as Parkinson's disease or multiple sclerosis. However, other factors may also be at play, especially when disease progression has profound effects on a patient's speech, mobility, and cognitive function.

Finally, health-care costs associated with treating chronic conditions can be burdensome, which can further exacerbate a mental health condition. If a physical illness is severe enough to prevent patients from working, medical costs may be an extreme hardship and an additional trigger for depression and anxiety.

such as divorce or the loss of a job. When such issues linger for long periods of time and lead to a breakdown in a person's ability to cope with stress and to function in everyday life and relationships, a clinically defined mental illness may be suspected. Mental illness is diagnosed by a *primary care physician* or by a qualified mental health professional such as a psychologist or psychiatrist.

Primary care physician:
A doctor who manages the health care of a patient with HMO insurance, referring the patient to specialists and authorizing procedures.

While the exact causes of mental illness have not been pinned down, experts generally agree that a mixture of biological, environmental, and social factors influences their development. Mental illness affects people of all ages and races and from all socioeconomic backgrounds. Most people diagnosed with a serious mental illness can be treated effectively, either with medication, therapy, or some combination of the two. A growing number of people have also found relief using alternative approaches such as yoga, medication, and acupuncture either instead of or in conjunction with more traditional forms of treatment.

Can Mental Illness Cause or Worsen Physical Conditions?

Research has shown that a mental health condition can have a significant impact on physical health and that it may often precede physical illness. People living with mental illness often experience physical symptoms such as lethargy, which can result from the illness itself or can be a side effect of medication being used to treat the malady. In addition, mental illness can affect various body processes, such as the sleep cycle. This, in turn, depresses the *immune system* and makes the body more vulnerable to infection.

When you suffer from mental illness, it may be more difficult to take care of yourself. For example, you may have a hard time making healthy food choices and getting regular exercise, which can lead to weight gain. Carrying extra weight impacts physical health by, say, raising blood pressure. It can also lower self-esteem and worsen mental health symptoms in some cases. Mental illness may also make you more likely to self-medicate with alcohol or drugs. This obviously can have adverse effects on your health, especially over a long period of time.

Immune system: *The body's system of natural defenses that helps the body resist harmful substances or microorganisms— bacteria, viruses, parasites, and fungi.*

Which Diseases Are Associated with Poor Mental Health?

Research has linked mental illness to an increased risk of developing a number of diseases or physical problems, including diabetes, heart disease, stroke, cancer, musculoskeletal problems such as back pain, and irritable bowel issues. Research also suggests that people with severe mental disorders tend to die on average 10 to 25 years earlier than the general population.

According to some studies, the risk of developing diabetes is significantly higher for people with mental illness. Depression and schizophrenia in particular are risk factors for the development of type 2 diabetes. These disorders are both thought to have an effect on the body's resistance to insulin. People suffering from mental illness are also more prone to other risk factors for diabetes, including high cholesterol levels and obesity. Conversely, high blood sugar levels associated with diabetes have been implicated in the development of depression in people with the disease. In the case of diabetes and depression, it may be hard to say with certainty which condition comes first. Regardless, both maladies need to be treated to achieve better overall health.

Additionally, mental illnesses can be a risk factor for both heart conditions and stroke. Those experiencing problems with anxiety in particular may experience high blood pressure and elevated levels of stress hormones, which increase the heart rate. Antipsychotic medication used to treat schizophrenia and sometimes bipolar disorder has been associated with the development of an abnormal heart rhythm. These types

When a person has trouble coping with stress and functioning in everyday life and relationships, it is time to get help. © CHAMELEONSEYE/ SHUTTERSTOCK.COM.

of physical changes in cardiovascular functioning increase the risk of heart attacks and various cardiac diseases. Furthermore, mental illness, especially among the poor, has been linked to poor nutrition, inadequate amounts of physical activity, and a lack of attention to preventive health care.

Research conducted at Johns Hopkins University has suggested that people with serious mental illnesses such as schizophrenia and bipolar disorder are more likely to develop cancer. While the findings did not conclusively establish why this may be the case, researchers theorized that there may be higher rates of smoking in this population, contributing to an increased risk of lung cancer, among other factors.

Finally, mental illness, especially anxiety, has been connected to musculoskeletal and gastrointestinal problems. While likely not the cause of these types of problems, anxiety can exacerbate them. Individuals suffering from anxiety or major depression may have greater-than-average difficulties coping with ongoing physical pain. Chronic stomach or back pain, in turn, may worsen psychological symptoms, particularly for people whose pain limits mobility.

How Does Mental Illness Affect Relationships in General?

Mentally healthy people tend to have good relationships, probably in part because they have solid social skills and the energy to invest in bonding with others. In turn, those social relationships can be an important support during times of stress. Conversely, a lack of social support is a known risk factor for developing mental illnesses such as depression and anxiety. Mental illness, then, can make it more difficult to form and maintain relationships.

How Does Mental Illness Affect Family Relationships?

The effects of mental illness on family relationships vary greatly, depending on factors such as the closeness and strength of the bond prior to the episode of illness, among other things. Members of the affected individual's immediate family may quickly jump into a caretaking role, particularly if this dynamic was part of the relationship beforehand, such as parent to child. In other cases, family members may be in denial, especially if they do not know much about mental illness. Some family members may have a hard time understanding the debilitating nature of mental illness and interpret associated behaviors as "lazy" or "underachieving." Such characterizations can damage the relationship on both sides. It is particularly important for parents of adolescents to be aware of the symptoms of mental illness so that the proper treatment, rather than discipline, is administered.

Children whose parents suffer from mental illness may not receive adequate care. Some low-functioning parents may not be able to care for children at all and may lose parental rights. In less severe cases, mentally ill parents may provide necessities such as food and shelter but may not possess the internal resources to be models of healthy behavior and to give their children the necessary emotional support.

Siblings may feel helpless, frustrated, and even angry with, say, a brother experiencing mental illness because he may seem like a stranger, no longer interested in once-shared activities. In addition, parental energy and attention may be so focused on the ill child that little time is left to address the needs of the other kids.

Other family relationships can also be affected by mental illness. Someone suffering from depression may stop participating in activities involving the extended family. Worse, close family members may not feel comfortable sharing a diagnosis, which can lead to misunderstandings or assumptions about the absent individual. On the other hand, grandparents, aunts, uncles, and other extended family members can be sources of both practical and emotional support, both to the affected individual and to those who are dealing with the situation on a daily basis.

How Does Mental Illness Affect Marriage or Other Romantic Partnerships?

Most long-term partnerships face challenges over time and have both good and bad periods. When both partners are mentally healthy, dealing with life's difficulties is challenging enough. Still, good communication skills and habits, such as making time for each other, can strengthen the relationship and make it a source of support in the face of external stressors.

In contrast, marriages in which one or both partners have a mental illness are more likely to end in divorce. Many people with mental health concerns have difficulty communicating feelings and achieving intimacy and may also be unable to fulfill household obligations in an equitable way. The chances of divorce are especially high for couples coping with major depression or addictions. Certain personality disorders, such as antisocial personality disorder and borderline personality disorder, are also associated with high divorce rates. Divorce itself often worsens mental illness, bringing with it a significant amount of change, financial stress, and the loss of companionship.

Couples counseling is sometimes helpful in teaching good communication and listening skills. In addition, couples who have strong networks of social support outside the relationship may be able to draw on these to help cope with difficulties in the marriage. If a marriage is able to survive the burden of mental illness, the union may actually be strengthened by the experience.

How Does Mental Illness Affect Friendships?

Friendships can change in several ways because of mental illness. Sometimes friends will step up to provide support and practical help to the person who is ill. Other times, however, friends might not know what to do, prompting them to distance themselves in order to avoid feeling uncomfortable.

It is also possible that the person who is mentally ill will do the distancing in order to avoid being a burden or having to share the distress. Unfortunately, a loss of important relationships may worsen symptoms of mental illness. Social isolation is known to contribute significantly to the development and worsening of depression in particular.

How Does Mental Illness Affect Professional Relationships?

Relationships in the workplace can also be affected by mental illness. People in the throes of an episode of depression may not be as productive as usual and may experience difficulty making decisions. Absenteeism and a lack of productivity in particular create difficulties. Coworkers may be forced to pick up slack without understanding what is causing the ill person's behavior. Such situations breed resentment, causing a breakdown in professional relationships. In addition, poor performance places the employee's job in jeopardy, which results in further stress and a potential worsening of the mental illness.

Employees who are able to share their struggles with a sympathetic supervisor or coworkers are often more likely to preserve workplace relationships. Coworkers are more inclined to be understanding when an employee is actively taking steps to receive treatment and making a good-faith effort to perform job duties during the recovery process. Many companies have helplines or programs designed to assist employees struggling with mental health issues or addictions.

Common Mental and Psychological Illnesses and Disorders

What Are Mental and Psychological Illnesses and Disorders?

Mental or psychological illnesses and disorders comprise a wide range of conditions that affect a person's emotions and actions. Everyone at times experiences stress, emotional suffering, and mood changes. The symptoms of stress can be similar to those of mental illness, but there are important differences. Symptoms of mental illness are more intense, last at least two weeks, and impair a person's ability to function for an extended period of time. Examples of mental illness include depression, anxiety, and mood disorders; schizophrenia; and addictive behaviors. Mental and psychological disorders can also include neurodevelopmental disorders, such as autism.

The signs and symptoms of mental illness may include confused thinking or reduced ability to concentrate; extreme mood changes; withdrawal from friends and activities; significant tiredness, low energy, or problems sleeping; detachment from reality, which may involve delusions or hallucinations; trouble understanding and relating to situations and to people; alcohol or drug abuse; excessive anger, hostility, or violence; and suicidal thinking. These conditions can cause problems in daily life at work and school. They can also cause problems in relationships with friends and family. Mental health, like physical health, exists on a continuum that can include stages of illness, recovery, and wellness. There are many strategies that have proven successful in helping people achieve mental health recovery and wellness.

Medical and psychological professionals have a variety of theories about what causes mental and psychological disorders. Most health practitioners believe the causes to be biological, psychological, or environmental factors or a combination of those factors. Examples of biological causes are toxic exposure and genetic susceptibility. Psychological causes include psychological trauma resulting from emotional, physical, or sexual abuse. Environmental factors include the conditions of a person's past or current living situation.

If you seek treatment for a psychological disorder, a mental health professional might inquire about your biological family history, your physical health, your mother's or your own exposure to toxic chemicals, your exposure to stress or abuse, and your use of mood-altering drugs. In order to diagnose mental disorders, mental health practitioners in the United States use a manual called the *Diagnostic and Statistical Manual of Mental Disorders*, fifth edition (DSM-5), published by the American Psychiatric Association. The DSM provides a standardized classification of hundreds of disorders and their symptoms. Health insurance companies require a diagnosis based on the DSM in order to reimburse for a patient's treatment.

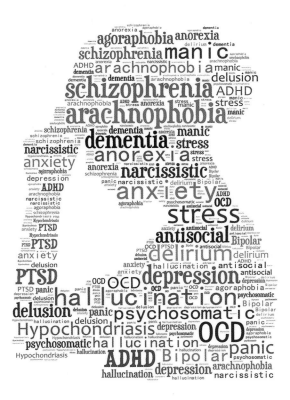

© AMIR RIDHWAN/
SHUTTERSTOCK.COM.

What Are Anxiety Disorders?

Anxiety disorders include post-traumatic stress disorder (PTSD), obsessive-compulsive disorder (OCD), and other phobias and panic disorders. If the kind of anxiety you feel before a test or a job interview doesn't go away and just gets worse over time, you may have an anxiety disorder. Other symptoms may include chest pains, frequent nightmares, and feelings of terror when there is no danger.

PTSD is caused participating in or witnessing a traumatic event such as war; a serious accident; physical, sexual, or emotional abuse; or a natural disaster such as a tornado or flood. Anyone, including children, can experience PTSD. The symptoms of PTSD may begin soon after the traumatic experience, or they may not develop until months or years later. The symptoms include feeling like you are living through the trauma again; frequent nightmares; angry outbursts; and feeling lonely, sad, and guilty.

A person with OCD experiences frequent, upsetting thoughts, called obsessions, which he or she tries to control by repeating particular behaviors, called compulsions. These thoughts and behaviors interfere with a person's daily life. For instance, someone with OCD might not be able to stop thinking that everything around her is dirty and may engage in repeated hand washing because it gives her temporary relief from the thoughts.

What Are Mood Disorders?

Bipolar disorder and depression are considered to be types of mood disorders. Bipolar disorder is characterized by very extreme mood swings that range from uncontrollably active and happy to extremely hopeless and unable to be active. Bipolar disorder is sometimes called manic-depressive illness. The up feeling is the "manic," and the down feeling is depression.

Depression may be experienced as a part of bipolar disorder, or it may be a condition by itself. It ranges widely from mild and temporary feelings of sadness to a more serious, persistent form known as major depression or clinical depression, in which individuals lose all interest in activities and relationships they used to enjoy and have profound feelings of sadness and worthlessness. Other symptoms of clinical depression may include a loss of energy, frequent thoughts of death or suicide, and unexplained physical pain.

What Are Schizophrenia Spectrum and Psychotic Disorders?

Schizophrenia spectrum disorders is the twenty-first-century term that groups together a range of various psychotic disorders. Psychotic disorders are conditions in which people interpret and react to reality in ways significantly different from other people around them. Psychotic disorders are characterized by clusters of symptoms that might include delusions, hallucinations, confused thinking, or abnormal behavior. A delusion is a belief that something is happening that is not in reality happening. For instance, if you are experiencing a delusion, you may believe that inanimate objects are speaking to you, that other people are controlling your thoughts, or that you can control other people's thoughts. A hallucination involves seeing or hearing something that is not really present. Confused thinking and speech describes a condition in which answers to questions seem unrelated and effective communication is impaired.

Psychotic disorders may also be characterized by a cluster of symptoms referred to as "negative symptoms," meaning a decisive lack of emotional expression, a reduced ability to take care of oneself, and a loss of interest in everyday activities. Schizophrenia often appears for the first time between the ages of 18 and 24 and rarely begins after age 45.

What Should I Do If I Suspect I Am Suffering from a Mental/Psychological Illness or Disorder?

If you think you may be suffering from a mental illness, it is a good idea to keep track of any symptoms you, or those close to you, have noticed. You may, for instance, be experiencing changes in your normal patterns of sleeping or eating or your ability to carry out daily activities at home, school, or work. Make a list and note how long you have experienced the symptoms. You can also keep track of different things you do in response to your symptoms. For example, if you exercise more, get more sleep, or change your diet, are there any changes in how you feel? When you have an appointment with a mental health professional, your answers to these questions will provide him or her with useful information.

Before you make an appointment, consider what type of mental health provider you need. The different types of providers include psychiatrists, psychologists, psychiatric mental health nurses, physician assistants, licensed clinical social workers (LCSWs), and licensed professional counselors (LPCs). Mental health professionals should be able to diagnose your condition, offer treatment options, and provide treatment. Not all mental health professionals can provide all kinds of treatment. For instance, some are not licensed to prescribe medication.

Mental health professionals often specialize in different types of mental health issues. You may want to seek out someone who has experience helping people with the types of symptoms you are experiencing. Asking your trusted friends, family, primary care physician, or clergy for referrals or recommendations is a good way to gather names of mental health providers. If possible, look into your private, Medicare, or Medicaid insurance plan's mental health benefits to see what types of mental health services are covered and what your benefit limits are. Your health insurance coverage may specify particular providers or types of providers and may only cover some diagnoses.

When choosing a counselor, therapist, or doctor, ask plenty of questions. You should ask questions about the provider's training and specializations, office hours, what insurance they accept, and the length of therapy sessions. You can also ask providers about their approaches to mental illness and treatment. What are their beliefs about the causes of mental illness and about the use of medication and therapy? In order to get the most out of your treatment for mental health issues, it is important to find the right person to work with. Many therapists offer free initial consultations so that you can get to know them a little, ask questions, assess your comfort level, and decide if this person is a good match for you. It is a good idea to interview a few different practitioners before you begin treatment.

What Should I Do If I Think Someone I Know Is Struggling with Mental Health Issues?

When someone you know seems to be developing a mental health problem or is experiencing a mental health crisis, there are ways you can help. The things you can do include assessing the risk of self-harm or harming others, listening respectfully and nonjudgmentally, offering reassurance and information, and encouraging the person to seek appropriate professional help as well as to do things that will help him or her feel better.

The first thing to do is assess the person's risk of harming himself or herself or others. It is important to look for signs of suicidal thoughts and behaviors, self-injury, or other harm. If someone you know is feeling hopeless; withdrawing from friends and family; and talking or writing about death, dying, or suicide, you should try to determine if there is imminent danger. If you need immediate help, you can seek emergency medical assistance by calling the National Suicide Prevention Lifeline: 1-800-273-TALK (8255).

If you determine that the person is not in immediate danger, the next thing you should do is listen to him or her and have a conversation in which the person feels respected and accepted. Mental illnesses are real and treatable, and they are not the person's fault. In your conversation with someone you think is struggling with mental health issues, you should try to offer emotional support and practical information.

You can encourage the person you know to help himself or herself by engaging in strategies that are known to contribute to wellness and recovery. These include relaxation and meditation; getting physical exercise; and talking with friends, family, or others about how he or she is feeling. Another way to help is to encourage the person to participate in a peer support group and to become socially engaged in other ways.

What Kind of Treatment Options Should I Expect If I Am Diagnosed with a Mental or Psychological Illness or Disorder?

If you are diagnosed with a mental or psychological illness or disorder, your treatment options will be influenced by a number of factors, including the beliefs and training of the mental health practitioner that you choose, what treatments are available in your location, what treatments your health insurance covers, and your own ability or willingness to participate in your mental health care. The options offered to you by a mental health practitioner will also depend on your diagnosis and the kind of treatments that have worked for you in the past.

The two broad categories of treatment options offered by mental health practitioners are medications and therapy. There are many different kinds of medications and approaches to therapy. Your treatment options may include therapy alone or therapy with medication. Some of the most common psychiatric medications are antidepressants, anti-anxiety medications, mood stabilizers, and antipsychotics. Mental health experts are careful to point out that medication does not cure mental illness but rather manages symptoms. A medication's dosage, side effects, and efficacy are unique to each person and should always be closely monitored both by you and by the professional who prescribed it.

Therapy is a kind of treatment that entails talking about your condition and gaining insight and knowledge about your moods, feelings, thoughts, and behavior. There are many different approaches to therapy, including psychoanalytic therapy, cognitive-behavioral therapy (CBT), and interpersonal therapy (IPT). Psychoanalytic therapy (also called psychoanalysis) focuses on changing behaviors by exploring unconscious motivations. Cognitive-behavioral therapy blends therapies that focus on how thoughts affect behaviors. In this approach, the therapist helps you change behaviors by learning to identify unhelpful thinking patterns. Interpersonal therapy helps you identify troubling emotions, what triggers those emotions, and how you communicate your feelings to others.

Complementary and alternative approaches to treatment are also widely used. These include taking supplements of omega-3 fatty acids, vitamin B12, and other vitamins, particularly those that are depleted by stress. Aerobic exercise has also been shown to enhance the action of endorphins and stimulate the neurotransmitter norepinephrine, both of which can improve and stabilize your mood.

What Does the Future Look Like for the Treatment and Cure of Mental and Psychological Illnesses and Disorders?

The goal of mental health treatment is recovery, a process of restoring or developing a positive and meaningful sense of identity and rebuilding one's life. Recent medical research shows the plasticity of the brain and its ability to heal. The mental health field is increasingly focusing on recovery and wellness and the use of peers in the delivery of services. These factors paint a hopeful picture for the future of mental health. Most people with mental health issues can and do get better. An important principle of treatment is that recipients of service need to be informed partners in their mental health care. The Affordable Care Act of 2013 requires insurance companies to cover costs of mental health care to the same extent as physical health care. This requirement is one step toward eliminating the stigma of mental and psychological illness and emotional crisis.

Mental Health Therapies and Treatment Options

Why Do People Seek Treatment for Mental Health Issues?

Most people have concerns about their mental health from time to time, especially in the wake of a stressful life event such as the death of a loved one or a divorce. Sometimes these concerns become significant enough to be considered mental illness. Statistics have suggested that up to 20 percent of the U.S. adult population has a diagnosable mental illness. Mental illnesses vary in type and severity, but many cause a significant enough disruption in the lives of sufferers to prompt them to seek treatment. Major depression, for example, can negatively impact moods, along with the ability to work, sleep, and enjoy recreational activities.

Not everyone with a mental illness seeks treatment. Some people are unaware of the signs of mental illness or do not realize the condition is treatable. Others feel ashamed to seek help, even though the stigma attached to mental illness has lessened in recent decades. Still others are unable to afford treatment, which can be prolonged and expensive, especially if it is not covered under the patient's insurance policy.

Where Can I Seek Treatment for Mental Illness?

Even if you do have health insurance, your options for treatment may be limited by your type of coverage. Many patients must start by visiting a primary care physician, most of whom can diagnose cases of mental illness and prescribe medications to treat them. Your primary care doctor may also provide a referral to a counselor or other type of therapist for treatment.

If your insurance allows it, you may bypass your primary care physician and go directly to a psychologist, psychiatrist (a medical doctor with specialized training in the treatment of mental illness), or other mental

Sigmund Freud (1856–1939), seen here on a 50 Shilling 1986 Banknote from Austria, is considered the father of psychoanalysis. © GEORGIOS KOLLIDAS/SHUTTERSTOCK.COM.

Psychoanalysis:
A theory of psychotherapy, based on the work of Sigmund Freud, involving dream analysis, free association, and different facets of the self (id, ego, superego).

health professional. You should be aware, however, that only psychiatrists are licensed to prescribe medication.

Can Mental Illness Be Treated with Medication?

Many types of mental illness are treated with medication, either alone or in conjunction with other therapies. Depending on the illness, as well as factors such as the patient's age, lifestyle, and family history, medication may be proposed as either a short- or long-term treatment. While the effectiveness of medication alone in treating mental illness is a subject of debate, research suggests that many drugs do help to manage symptoms and can greatly improve a patient's ability to function in daily life.

Medications have drawbacks, however, some of which are severe. Some drugs, especially those used to treat anxiety, can be addictive. Further, many medications have unpleasant side effects or cause significant withdrawal symptoms when patients stop taking them. Before committing to a course of medication, weigh the pros and cons with your doctor.

What Types of Talk Therapies Are Available to Treat Mental Illness?

Talk therapy, sometimes referred to as psychotherapy, is a family of treatments that includes counseling, cognitive behavioral therapy, or CBT (directed toward altering destructive behaviors), dialectical behavior therapy, or DBT (a form of cognitive behavioral therapy also designed to change harmful thinking), and *psychoanalysis*, among others. Talk therapy may occur as individual sessions between you and a mental health professional or could include couples, families, or groups of people being counseled together.

Austrian neurologist Sigmund Freud is generally considered to have pioneered the use of talk therapy, which he began with his patients in the late nineteenth century. Freud suggested that an unconscious part

What Can I Do If I Suspect a Family Member or Friend Is Struggling with Mental Illness?

If you suspect a loved one is suffering from mental illness, a good first step is to educate yourself about mental health issues. If your loved one is undiagnosed, you might try sharing this information in a supportive way. Many people suffering from a mental illness are not aware that their symptoms are abnormal. It can be hard to speak up, but doing so is vital in order to get appropriate medical care.

When discussing mental illness, you should be prepared to listen without judging. Do not attempt to make your own diagnosis or push your friend or loved one to seek treatment before he or she is ready to do so. Some people will remain in denial for a period of time, especially in communities in which mental illness is looked upon as a sign of weakness. It can be hard to deal with someone who is exhibiting dysfunctional behavior while denying having a problem;

however, you are more likely to get a positive response if you avoid being pushy and impatient.

While most mental illnesses respond well to treatment, you should not expect your loved one to recover instantly or to be unchanged by the experience. Disorders that have been undiagnosed for a long time may not respond to treatment immediately. Medication often takes several weeks to take effect and even longer for a patient to notice significant improvement. Talk therapy and lifestyle changes also may require months or years to be truly effective. Therefore, patience and a commitment to provide support over a long period, during which time setbacks may occur, is key. Check in with your loved one to make sure that treatment is helping. If it is not, you might encourage the person to talk to his or her health-care providers about additional options.

of the human mind is what drives maladaptive behavior—behavior that prevents you from adjusting to certain situations or environments. The purpose of psychoanalysis, as it came to be known, was to examine the patient's life for signs of early trauma, which Freud believed was repressed or stored in the unconscious. While psychoanalysis was widely practiced well into the twentieth century, it has fallen out of favor, and many of Freud's theories have been largely discredited. In addition, psychoanalysis is typically open ended, involving years of sessions that many insurance companies do not cover.

Psychotherapy is a more general term used to describe almost any type of talk therapy administered by a mental health professional. Sometimes simply called "therapy" or "counseling," it can be provided by psychologists, psychiatrists, social workers, and other licensed professionals. Therapy may be prescribed to treat mental illnesses such as depression and is usually completed in a matter of months, depending on how frequently a patient attends. Some therapists employ a combination of techniques and approaches, while others are more specialized.

What Exactly Is CBT?

CBT has become the preferred form of treatment for addressing a number of mental illnesses, especially depression. In CBT a therapist helps the patient examine beliefs and thoughts that lead to maladaptive patterns of behavior. The goal is to modify these thought patterns deliberately, often through exercises. Modifying beliefs and thoughts, according to the principles of CBT, should then help the patient make better life choices.

Anxiety: *An abnormal and overwhelming sense of worry and fear that is often accompanied by physical reaction.*

For example, if you are depressed, you begin to believe you are incompetent in various areas of your life. This belief can manifest in an inability to complete, or even start, tasks. A CBT therapist will help you examine such beliefs and then challenge them through behavioral experiments. Unlike psychoanalysis, which is open ended, CBT is goal focused and short term. Patients develop skills that enable them to monitor and confront negative thinking on their own. In addition to depression, CBT has been used to treat *anxiety* disorders; post-traumatic stress disorder, or PTSD (a condition that occurs after a person goes through a particularly difficult episode, such as the death of a loved one); phobias (paralyzing fears of certain objects or situations); and even schizophrenia (a severe mental disorder in which a person loses touch with reality).

What Exactly Is DBT?

DBT is a specific type of CBT that was originally developed for patients diagnosed with borderline personality disorder, or BPD (a malady characterized by extreme emotional volatility), but it is now also used to treat a number of other mental disorders, including severe depression. DBT therapists focus on validating a patient's uncomfortable thoughts, feelings, and maladaptive behaviors.

Once some amount of acceptance is achieved, the therapist teaches the patient to change problematic behavior and the thoughts and feelings associated with it. DBT typically incorporates some version of mindfulness practice, with therapists calmly and nonjudgmentally teaching clients to be conscious of the thoughts and feelings they experience.

Can Peer Support Groups Be Used to Treat Mental Illness?

While they do not constitute treatment in the traditional sense of the word, numerous organizations administer peer support groups. Many people have found this approach to be helpful when struggling with mental illness. Some groups are facilitated by a mental health professional, while others are peer driven. Many organizations also offer online support groups, which can be important to individuals suffering from anxiety or other disorders that make real-life interaction uncomfortable.

Alcoholics Anonymous (AA), a 12-step program that is designed to help people recover from alcoholism, is among the best-known support organizations. AA and the numerous other 12-step programs that are modeled after it focus on modifying problematic behaviors by providing people with peer support as they work through the series of steps. Many such groups have meetings across the United States. These meetings can be easily found online (http://www.aa.org) or by calling a local chapter.

When Is Electroconvulsive Therapy Used to Treat Mental Illness?

Electroconvulsive therapy (ECT), often known in popular culture as shock treatment, is a procedure in which a brief seizure is triggered by passing electrical currents through the brain in a controlled way. ECT is generally not used as a first line of treatment for mental illness but has been shown to alter brain chemistry in a manner that provides significant relief of symptoms for some patients.

Introduced in the 1930s, ECT still has a bit of a stigma. In the first decades of its use, ECT was administered in high doses that sometimes caused injuries and memory loss. In the early twenty-first century ECT is given under general anesthesia in the smallest doses deemed therapeutically beneficial. The treatment usually occurs in a hospital or clinic on an outpatient basis, most often two to three times a week until symptoms have improved. Studies have suggested that ECT is effective in treating depression, anxiety, schizophrenia, and various personality disorders. However, the procedure does have a number of potential side effects and may need to be undertaken again if the mental illness returns.

What Types of Alternative Treatments Are Available for Mental Illness?

 A growing number of people suffering from mental illness have turned to alternative therapies that are employed alongside, or even instead of, more traditional treatments. Alternative therapies include relaxation practices such as meditation and yoga, acupuncture, and plant-based dietary supplements such as St. John's wort and kava.

Yoga is known to increase physical fitness, lung capacity, strength, and flexibility in those who do it regularly. Some studies have suggested that it also has benefits for treating mental illness, especially depression and anxiety disorders. The exact nature of the benefit is unclear. In part, some experts have suggested, the social aspect of yoga classes may be beneficial. In addition, yoga sessions often incorporate meditation. Practitioners learn breathing and other techniques to stay in the moment and maintain focus. Like other practices that emphasize mindfulness, yoga may teach techniques that can then be applied to the management of thoughts and emotions in daily life.

Acupuncture, which is the practice of inserting needles into specific points on the body to correct energy imbalances, has shown promise in treating anxiety disorders in particular. In 2011 *CNS Neuroscience and Therapeutics* published an essay suggesting that people who were given acupuncture to treat anxiety received a benefit comparable to CBT.

Several plant-based dietary supplements used to treat mental illness are available over the counter. Some patients suffering from depression take St. John's wort, which is made from a flower of the same name. Research has indicated that the supplement is as effective as antidepressants in treating mild to moderate depression but relatively ineffective against major depression. Kava, extracted from a plant of the same name, has been found to be a relatively effective short-term treatment for anxiety, though it has also been linked to reports of liver damage. Dietary supplements are not regulated by the Federal Drug Administration (FDA) in the same way prescription drugs are regulated. Always consult your doctor before you start taking dietary supplements, especially if you are already using other medications.

Where Do I Go to Receive Treatment?

In most cases, mental illness is treated on an outpatient basis. If your doctor prescribes medication, you may need to return for one or more follow-up appointments to make sure the medication is working properly and that you are not suffering any serious side effects. Most people see therapists out of a medical office or sometimes even a private residence. The frequency of visits varies depending on the course of the treatment, as well as the number of sessions allowed by your insurance provider, if you have one.

Treatments for more severe mental illness may occur on an inpatient basis in a hospital or clinic. Inpatient treatment is most often undertaken when patients are in significant danger of harming themselves or others. Inpatient services are also available for individuals with serious substance abuse problems. Such detox facilities treat withdrawal symptoms, if applicable, and then use some form of psychotherapy that is often administered in both individual and group sessions to help teach coping skills. The cost of inpatient mental health services is extremely high and is not always covered by insurance plans. For this reason, outpatient treatment is much more common.

Managing Stress

What Is Stress?

Stress is a physical and psychological reaction to positive or negative change. People can experience different degrees of stress depending on the amount of change in their lives. Stress can come from a one-time event, such as going out on a first date, or can be chronic or last for a long time, such as an adult dealing with a chronically ill child. Sometimes people under extreme stress can become traumatized, which can happen for those who live in a war zone, for example.

Stressful events can provoke what is known as the flight-or-fight response, an automatic primitive reaction by your body. When animals are threatened, perhaps by a predator, their bodies prepare to either fight or run away. Our bodies automatically prepare a similar response when perceiving danger. Our hearts beat faster, our breathing becomes more rapid, more blood flows to our brains and muscles, we sweat more, and hormones such as adrenaline and cortisol course through our bodies.

The flight-or-fight response can be an important tool or it can become harmful. When you remove your hand quickly from a hot stove so you don't get burned, your body is having a flight-or-fight response. However, if you react with a flight-or-fight response every time you see a stove, your body and mind can become overloaded. You may start to have adverse physical and psychological symptoms. Stress can become a serious issue if it starts to interfere with your ability to cope with daily life.

What Are the Different Types of Stress?

The American Psychological Association defines three main types of stress: acute stress, episodic acute stress, and chronic stress. Acute stress usually comes from a specific event or situation, but it can also be an event you imagine, such as fear of your plane crashing. It is the most

Possible consequences of stress

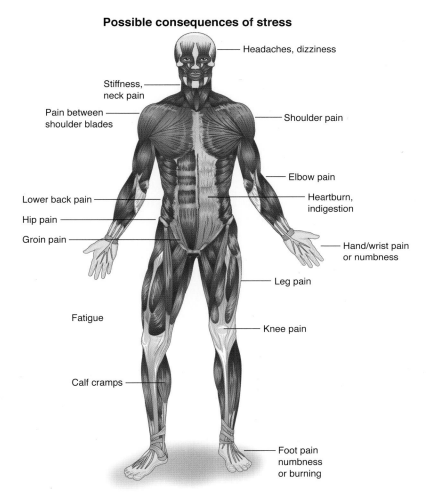

Headaches, dizziness

Stiffness, neck pain

Pain between shoulder blades

Shoulder pain

Elbow pain

Lower back pain

Heartburn, indigestion

Hip pain

Groin pain

Hand/wrist pain or numbness

Leg pain

Fatigue

Knee pain

Calf cramps

Foot pain numbness or burning

Stress reduction techniques:

- Identify your stressors
- Don't fret over small details
- Try and find positive solutions to stressful situations
- Turn to friends and family for help and support
- View stress as a challenge to be overcome, rather than as a roadblock

Activities that help manage stress:

- T'ai chi
- Massage therapy
- Yoga
- Meditation
- Guided imagery
- Breathing exercises
- Cognitive behavioral therapy

ILLUSTRATION BY ELECTRONIC ILLUSTRATORS GROUP. REPRODUCED BY PERMISSION OF GALE, A PART OF CENGAGE LEARNING.

common kind of stress and is usually short term. In small amounts, acute stress can be exciting, such as the stress you can feel when auditioning for a play, or it can be disconcerting, such as how you feel after a minor car accident.

Episodic acute stress is when you frequently experience acute stress. Episodic acute stress can happen if you are often disorganized, frequently make unrealistic demands on yourself, live from crisis to crisis, or worry all the time. People with "Type A" personalities often have episodic acute stress. They are usually very competitive, aggressive, impatient, or overworked. Episodic acute stress can come and go; it happens in "episodes."

Chronic stress is long term and constant. Chronic stress is when you are continuously exposed to unrelenting stressful situations, such as living in poverty or in politically unstable countries, are in a dysfunctional or abusive relationship, or dealing with chronic illness. Chronic stress wears people down physically and mentally, and it can be the cause of serious health issues and can even be life threatening.

What Are the Symptoms of Stress?

When our brains perceive stress, they alert the sympathetic nervous system, which is the part of the nervous system that prepares our body for action. Your body may react by your heart beating faster, and you breathe more rapidly than normal, sweat more, tense your muscles, and feel a rush of energy from the hormone adrenaline being released. If you have too much stress, you may experience headaches, stomach or other digestive problems, back pain, anxiety, insomnia or other sleep problems, and you can even develop high blood pressure. Chronic stress can lead to serious physical and mental health problems, including heart disease, depression, and substance abuse.

While there are general stress symptoms that most people experience, individuals react differently to stress, even if they experience the same stressful situation. One person may start sweating profusely and feeling nauseated on a scary amusement park ride, while another may love the thrill of the adrenaline rush they get and have no other negative symptoms.

Why Is It Important to Manage Stress?

Stress is a common occurrence in the modern world. Whether trying to manage and balance the demands of a family, a job, and your health or keeping up with the fast-paced connected world of smart phones and computers, many people deal frequently with stress. A 2007 American Psychological Association poll, "Stress in America," found that

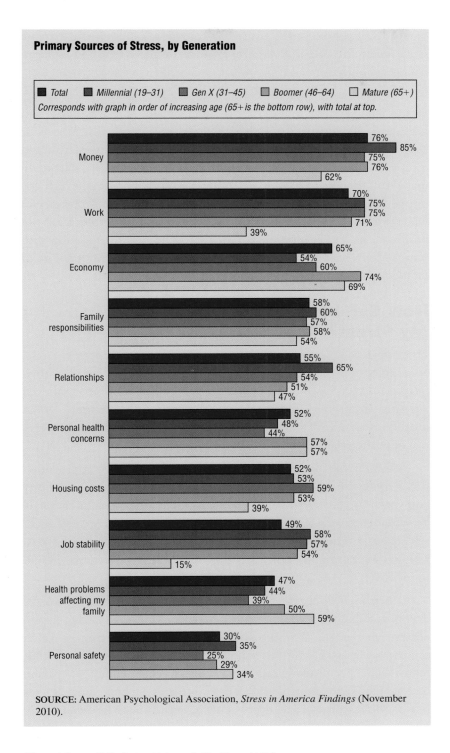

Primary Sources of Stress, by Generation

■ Total ■ Millennial (19–31) ■ Gen X (31–45) ■ Boomer (46–64) ☐ Mature (65+)
Corresponds with graph in order of increasing age (65+ is the bottom row), with total at top.

Money
- 76%
- 85%
- 75%
- 76%
- 62%

Work
- 70%
- 75%
- 75%
- 71%
- 39%

Economy
- 65%
- 54%
- 60%
- 74%
- 69%

Family responsibilities
- 58%
- 60%
- 57%
- 58%
- 54%

Relationships
- 55%
- 65%
- 54%
- 51%
- 47%

Personal health concerns
- 52%
- 48%
- 44%
- 57%
- 57%

Housing costs
- 52%
- 53%
- 59%
- 53%
- 39%

Job stability
- 49%
- 58%
- 57%
- 54%
- 15%

Health problems affecting my family
- 47%
- 44%
- 39%
- 50%
- 59%

Personal safety
- 30%
- 35%
- 25%
- 29%
- 34%

SOURCE: American Psychological Association, *Stress in America Findings* (November 2010).

one-third of people in the United States report experiencing extreme stress levels and one in five reported high levels of stress 15 or more days per month.

Some amount of stress is part of ordinary life. However, it is important to manage stress so it doesn't become a major part of your life and begin to adversely affect you physically and psychologically. After your body goes into fight-or-flight mode when experiencing stress, it should return to a calm state. If you frequently experience stress, your body may think it needs to be in fight-or-flight mode all the time, which can put you at risk for mild to serious health problems. It is wise to try to manage stress before you start experiencing even mild problems. Mild problems, such as headaches, can themselves be stressful and grow into more serious, hard-to-manage health concerns or disrupt your ability to manage relationships, jobs, or daily life.

How Can I Identify the Sources of My Stress?

To manage your stress, you need to identify the sources of your stress. Sometimes they are easy to identify. A divorce or losing a job is an obvious source of stress. It may be hard to remember, however, that even a positive event, like becoming a grandparent, can create stress. When identifying sources of stress, pay attention to major events that are negative or positive.

Stress doesn't always come from events or situations. Stress sometimes comes from inside you, from your thoughts or fears or the way you speak to yourself. The risk of an accident from a plane trip may be extremely small, but if you are afraid of flying, you may cause yourself stress by repeatedly telling yourself all the things that could possibly go wrong. Sources of stress that are less concrete can be harder to identify.

When identifying stress, examine your way of thinking, internal dialog, and habits for dealing with different situations. You should also observe whether you are using excuses not to identify the things that are causing you stress. Do you tell yourself this is "just life" instead of attending to what specifically is causing you stress, which could be a person or your job? Do you blame others for your stress, telling yourself your boss is the reason you feel overwhelmed, even though you constantly procrastinate when you have deadlines? Looking realistically at what is causing you stress will help you to manage it effectively.

How Can I Avoid Stress?

Sometimes you can control a situation and avoid a stressor completely. Is there a person or place that causes you particular stress? If you feel stress because a coworker complains in the break room every day, you can take a break in a different place or at a different time to avoid the person and the stress completely.

> **Stressful Life Events**
>
> Death of spouse, family member, or close friend
> Divorce
> Marital separation
> Jail term/sentencing of close family member or friend
> Personal injury or illness
> Marriage
> Loss of job due to termination
> Retirement
> Pregnancy
> Change in financial state

Some stress can't be avoided, but you can prepare for the situation and adapt to it. If you feel stress because your boss says you need to meet with her, you may have to go to the meeting no matter how you feel about it. However, you can ask her exactly what she wants to talk about to feel more in control. You can prepare notes so you don't forget important points you want to make. Making sure you eat healthy food and get a good night's sleep before a stressful situation will help you feel less stress.

Having too much to do and being overwhelmed can also make you feel stress. Setting priorities about what's most important to accomplish, setting limits on what you will or won't do, and organizing your plans can help avoid stress. You can avoid the stress of being overwhelmed if you balance your tasks with rest and relaxation and time with family and friends.

How Can I Manage the Effects of Stress When I Begin to Feel It?

Everyone has some stress. When stress is internal, you can try to think in a different way about what is causing the stress. If you keep telling yourself there is too much to get done, you can try to give yourself more positive messages instead. Tell yourself that you will get done what is necessary. You can put the issue in a broader context: Is getting a particular task done really as important as you think? Will it be important in a year from now? Having a sense of humor can also be helpful in managing stress.

Talking to a friend or a counselor to get a different perspective on a situation can help you figure out how to best eliminate some of your stress. Keeping a stress journal to track the times you feel stress and how you react in stressful situations can help you see patterns and triggers for stress, which can help you come up with a specific plan for stress management. Writing in a journal can help you manage your stress and provide the opportunity to process your feelings and thoughts.

Yoga: *A form of exercise and a system of health that incorporates a series of exercises utilizing regulated breathing, concentration, physical postures, and flexibility.*

There are a lot of healthy habits that can help you deal with stress. Relaxation techniques, *yoga*, massage, meditation, breathing exercises, or taking a walk are just some strategies to help you calm down before you enter a stressful situation; doing any of these regularly will help you manage your overall stress. Eating healthy, getting enough sleep, and regular exercise all are crucial to managing your stress.

There are also many unhealthy ways to deal with stress. They may seem good at first, and some even temporarily reduce stress, but in the long run they are harmful. Smoking, drinking too much, overeating or not eating enough, withdrawing from people, and spacing out in front of a computer or television are some common ways people use to try to manage stress. In the long run, none is effective, and all are harmful.

How Can Medical Professionals Help Me Manage Stress?

Biofeedback: *The technique of teaching people to control involuntary bodily processes (such as heartbeats or brain waves).*

Medical professionals can help you manage stress and deal with its symptoms. If your stress is beginning to feel out of control and affecting your sleep, eating habits, relationships, or moods, a psychotherapist may be of assistance. The therapist can help you understand your experiences and find new ways to deal with your stress and its adverse symptoms. Psychiatrists are therapists who are also medical doctors. They can prescribe medication that may be useful. Other types of therapies, such as dance therapy, massage therapy, or *biofeedback*, can help you relax and cope with stress, as well as help with issues such as insomnia. If you are suffering from chronic stress and trauma, it is important to seek medical help.

Your family doctor or a clinic can help you manage issues related to stress such as high blood pressure, back pain, and heart disease. They may recommend medications or lifestyle changes, such as diet and exercise programs, or they might send you to a medical specialist. Alternative health-care providers also can help with many of the symptoms of stress. Chiropractors and acupuncturists can help with pain management, for example, and naturopaths (health-care professionals who treat disease using natural methods) can help with a variety of symptoms, from headaches to digestive problems to anxiety.

For More Information

BOOKS

Donnelly, Joseph W., and Norm Eburne. *Mental Health: Dimensions of Self-Esteem and Emotional Well-Being.* Boston: Allyn and Bacon, 2001.

Ford, Julian D., and Jon Wortmann. *Hijacked by Your Brain: How to Free Yourself When Stress Takes Over.* Naperville, IL: Sourcebooks, 2013.

Hicks, James Whitney. *50 Signs of Mental Illness: A Guide to Understanding Mental Health.* New Haven, CT: Yale University Press, 2006.

Sederer, Lloyd I., and Glenn Close. *The Family Guide to Mental Health Care.* New York: W. W. Norton & Company, 2013.

Whitaker, Robert. *Anatomy of an Epidemic: Magic Bullets, Psychiatric Drugs, and the Astonishing Rise of Mental Illness in America.* New York: Broadway Books, 2011.

PERIODICALS

Ahn, Woo-kyoung, Caroline C. Proctor, and Elizabeth H. Flanagan. "Mental Health Clinicians' Beliefs about the Biological, Psychological, and Environmental Bases of Mental Disorders." *Cognitive Science* 33, no. 2 (2009): 147–82. This article can also be found online at http://www.ncbi.nlm.nih.gov/pmc/articles/PMC2857376/.

Myers, Neely Lorenzo. "Update: Schizophrenia across Cultures." *Current Psychiatry Reports* 13, no. 4 (2011): 305–11. This article can also be found online at https://www.academia.edu/650212/Update_Schizophrenia_across_Cultures.

WEBSITES

"Cancer and Injuries More Likely in People with Serious Mental Illness." *Johns Hopkins Medicine.* http://www.hopkinsmedicine.org/news/media/releases/cancer_and_injuries_more_likely_in_people_with_serious_mental_illness (accessed January 28, 2015).

"Evidence Map of Acupuncture for Mental Health." *National Center for Biotechnology Information.* http://www.ncbi.nlm.nih.gov/books/NBK185076/ (accessed January 6, 2015).

"Fact Sheet on Stress." *National Institute of Mental Health.* http://www.nimh.nih.gov/health/publications/stress/index.shtml (accessed October 15, 2014).

Kolappa, Kavitha, David C. Henderson, and Sandeep Kishore. "No Physical Health without Mental Health: Lessons Unlearned?" *World Health Organization.* http://www.who.int/bulletin/volumes/91/1/12-115063/en/ (accessed January 28, 2015).

"Mental Health First Aid." *Substance Abuse and Mental Health Services Administration's National Registry of Evidence-Based Programs and Practices.* http://nrepp.samhsa.gov/ViewIntervention.aspx?id=321 (accessed October 15, 2014).

"Mental Health Information." *National Institute of Mental Health.* http://www.nimh.nih.gov/health/topics/index.shtml (accessed October 15, 2014).

"Relationship with Physical Health and Healthy Lifestyles." *The UK's Faculty of Public Health.* http://www.fph.org.uk/relationship_with_physical_health_and_healthy_lifestyles (accessed January 28, 2015).

"Stress: The Different Kinds of Stress." *American Psychological Association.* http://www.apa.org/helpcenter/stress-kinds.aspx (accessed October 17, 2014).

Resources for More Information

The following is an alphabetical compilation of books, periodicals, and websites relevant to the topics found in this volume of the *Life and Career Skills Series*. Although the list is comprehensive, it is by no means exhaustive and is intended to serve as a starting point for gathering further information. Gale, Cengage Learning, is not responsible for the accuracy of the addresses or the content of the materials or websites.

Books

American Medical Association. *American Medical Association Guide to Talking to Your Doctor*. New York: John Wiley and Sons, 2001.

Askin, Elisabeth, and Nathan Moore. *The Health Care Handbook: A Clear and Concise Guide to the United States Health Care System*. 2nd ed. St. Louis, MO: Washington University Press, 2014.

Brill, Steven. *America's Bitter Pill: Money, Politics, Backroom Deals, and the Fight to Fix Our Broken Healthcare System*. New York: Random House, 2015.

Brownlee, Shannon. *Overtreated: Why Too Much Medicine Is Making Us Sicker and Poorer*. New York: Bloomsbury USA, 2008.

Crilly, Lynn, and Natasha Devon. *Fundamentals: A Guide for Parents, Teachers and Careers on Mental Health and Self-Esteem*. London: John Blake Publishing, 2015.

Ernst, Edzard, and Simon Singh. *Trick or Treatment: The Undeniable Facts about Alternative Medicine*. New York: W. W. Norton, 2008.

Fuhrman, Joel. *Eat for Health*. Flemington, NJ: Gift of Health Press, 2012.

Gold, Joel, and Ian Gold. *Suspicious Minds: How Culture Shapes Madness*. New York: Free Press, 2014.

Hartwell-Walker, Marie. *Unlocking the Secrets of Self-Esteem: A Guide to Building Confidence and Connection One Step at a Time*. Oakland, CA: New Harbinger Publications, 2015.

Hoffman, Beatrix Rebecca. *Health Care for Some: Rights and Rationing in the United States since 1930*. Chicago: University of Chicago Press, 2013.

Kirschmann, John. *Nutrition Almanac*. New York: McGraw-Hill, 2007.

Knight, Joseph A. *A Crisis Call for New Preventive Medicine: Emerging Effects of Lifestyle on Morbidity and Mortality*. River Edge, NJ: World Scientific, 2004.

Lipman, Frank, and Danielle Claro. *The New Health Rules: Simple Changes to Achieve Whole-Body Wellness*. New York: Artisan, 2015.

Mayo Clinic. *Mayo Clinic Book of Alternative Medicine.* New York: Time Inc. Home Entertainment, 2010.

McKeown, Thomas. *The Role of Medicine: Dream, Mirage, or Nemesis?* Princeton, NJ: Princeton University Press, 1979.

Niles, Nancy J. *Basics of the U.S. Health Care System.* Burlington, MA: Jones & Bartlett Learning, 2010.

Rath, Tom. *Eat Move Sleep: How Small Choices Lead to Big Changes.* Arlington, VA: Missionday, 2013.

Rosenberg, Robert. *Sleep Soundly Every Night, Feel Fantastic Every Day: A Doctor's Guide to Solving Your Sleep Problems.* New York: demosHealth, 2014.

Sultz, Harry A. *Health Care, USA: Understanding Its Organization and Delivery.* Burlington, MA: Jones & Bartlett Learning, 2014.

Weil, Andrew. *Natural Health, Natural Medicine: The Complete Guide to Wellness and Self-Care for Optimum Health.* Boston: Houghton Mifflin, 2004.

Willett, Walter C., with P. J. Skerrett. *Eat, Drink, and Be Healthy: The Harvard Medical School Guide to Healthy Eating.* New York: Free Press, 2005.

Periodicals

Aschwanden, Christie. "Need a Mental Health Professional? Here's How to Find One." *Washington Post*, August 19, 2014, E4.

Farley, Thomas A. "The Public Health Crisis Hiding in Our Food." *New York Times*, April 21, 2014, A21. This article can also be found online at http://www.nytimes.com/2014/04/21/opinion/the-public-health-crisis-hiding-in-our-food.html.

Gillespie, Lisa. "Parity for Mental Health Care Is Still Lagging, Study Says." *Washington Post*, January 6, 2014, E5.

Graetz, Ilana, Cameron M. Kaplan, Erin K. Kaplan, James E. Bailey, and Teresa M. Waters. "The U.S. Health Insurance Marketplace: Are Premiums Truly Affordable?" *Annals of Internal Medicine* 161, no. 8 (2014): 599–604.

Landro, Laura. "Doctors Dole Out Prescription for Exercise: Activity Regimens Become the New Vital Signs." *Wall Street Journal*, December 8, 2014.

Luhrmann, T. M. "Redefining Mental Health." *New York Times, Sunday Review*, January 17, 2015. This article can also be found online at http://www.nytimes.com/2015/01/18/opinion/sunday/t-m-luhrmann-redefining-mental-illness.html?_r=0.

Newcomer, Laura. "Looking for Alternative Treatments? Look Here." *Washington Post*, April 29, 2014, E4.

Ornish, Dean. "Eating for Health, Not Weight." *New York Times*, September 23, 2012, SR4. This article can also be found online at http://www.nytimes.com/2012/09/23/opinion/sunday/the-optimal-diet.html?_r=0.

Rabin, Roni Caryn. "You Can Find Dr. Right, with Some Effort." *New York Times*, September 29, 2008. This article can also be found online at http://www.nytimes.com/2008/09/30/health/30find.html?_r=0.

Taubes, Gary. "Why Nutrition Is So Confusing." *New York Times*, February 9, 2014, SR5. This article can also be found online at http://www.nytimes.com/2014/02/09/opinion/sunday/why-nutrition-is-so-confusing.html.

Websites

"About the Law." *U.S. Department of Health and Human Services.* http://www.hhs.gov/healthcare/rights/ (accessed February 12, 2015).

ChooseMyPlate.gov. http://www.choosemyplate.gov/ (accessed March 25, 2015).

"Costs in the Coverage Gap." *Medicare.gov.* http://www.medicare.gov/part-d/costs/coverage-gap/part-d-coverage-gap.html. (accessed January 17, 2015).

"CPS Health Insurance Definitions." *United States Census Bureau.* 2012. https://www.census.gov/hhes/www/hlthins/methodology/definitions/cps.html (accessed January 17, 2015).

"Depression." *World Health Organization.* October 2012. http://www.who.int/mediacentre/factsheets/fs369/en/ (accessed January 23, 2015).

"Fitness and Nutrition." *New York Times.* http://www.nytimes.com/pages/health/nutrition/ (accessed October 30, 2014).

"Focus on Health Reform: A Guide to the Supreme Court's Decision on the ACA's Medicaid Expansion." *Henry J. Kaiser Foundation.* 2012. http://kaiserfamilyfoundation.files.wordpress.com/2013/01/8347.pdf (accessed January 17, 2015).

"Food Pyramids and Plates: What Should You Really Eat?" *Harvard School of Public Health.* http://www.hsph.harvard.edu/nutritionsource/pyramid-full-story/ (accessed March 25, 2015).

"Health Insurance." *USA.gov.* http://www.usa.gov/Citizen/Topics/Health/HealthInsurance.shtml (accessed February 12, 2015).

"Health Plans and Benefits." *United States Department of Labor.* http://www.dol.gov/dol/topic/health-plans/ (accessed January 17, 2015).

"Mental Health Basics." *Centers for Disease Control and Prevention.* July 2011. http://www.cdc.gov/mentalhealth/basics.htm (accessed January 23, 2015).

"Preventive Health Care Helps Everyone." *World Research Foundation.* http://www.wrf.org/preventive-healthcare/preventive-healthcare.php (accessed March 25, 2015).

Rice, Thomas, Pauline Rosenau, Lynn Y. Unruh, and Andrew J. Barnes. "United States of America Health System Review." *World Health Organization.* 2013. http://www.euro.who.int/__data/assets/pdf_file/0019/215155/HiT-United-States-of-America.pdf (accessed January 17, 2015).

"Sleep." *New York Times.* http://topics.nytimes.com/top/news/health/diseasesconditionsandhealthtopics/sleep/index.html (accessed March 25, 2015).

"Wellness." *Washington Post.* http://www.washingtonpost.com/lifestyle/wellness/ (accessed March 25, 2015).

List of Key Organizations

The following is an annotated alphabetical compilation of organizations and advocacy groups relevant to the topics found in this volume of the *Life and Career Skills Series*. Although the list is comprehensive, it is by no means exhaustive and is intended to serve as a starting point for assembling further information. Gale, Cengage Learning, is not responsible for the accuracy of the addresses or the contents of the websites, nor does it endorse any of the organizations listed.

Academy of Nutrition and Dietetics

A professional organization that advocates for the dietetics profession, offers accreditation and certifications, and educates professionals and the public on nutrition-related topics.

> 120 South Riverside Plaza, Suite 2000
> Chicago, IL 60606
> Phone: (800) 877-1600
> Website: http://www.eatrightpro.org/

Alcoholics Anonymous

An organization that supports recovering alcoholics using the Twelve-Step program.

> P.O. Box 459, Grand Central Station
> New York, NY 10163
> Phone: (212) 870-3400
> Website: http://www.aa.org/

America's Health Insurance Plans

An organization that lobbies for the insurance industry.

> 601 Pennsylvania Avenue NW
> South Building, Suite 500
> Washington, DC 20004
> Phone: (202) 778-3200

> Fax: (202) 331-7487
> Email: ahip@ahip.org
> Website: http://www.ahip.org/

American Academy of Allergy, Asthma, and Immunology

A professional organization of allergists, immunologists, and other medical professionals that is dedicated to improving the treatment of allergic and immunologic diseases. Users can search website by symptoms and terms.

> 555 East Wells Street, Suite 1100
> Milwaukee, WI 53202
> Phone: (414) 272-6071
> Email: info@aaaai.org
> Website: http://www.aaaai.org/home.aspx

American Academy of Ayurvedic Medicine

An organization that supports the widespread recognition and acceptance of Ayurvedic medicine in the United States and India.

> 100 Jersey Avenue, Building B, Suite 300
> New Brunswick, NJ 08901
> Email: info@ayurvedicacademy.com
> Website: http://www.ayurvedicacademy.com/

American Academy of Family Physicians

A professional organization of family physicians that is dedicated to improving family health care.

P.O. Box 11210
Shawnee Mission, KS 66207
Phone: (800) 274-2237
Fax: (913) 906-6075
Email: contactcenter@aafp.org
Website: http://www.aafp.org/home.html

American Academy of Orthopedic Surgeons

A professional organization that provides continuing musculoskeletal education to orthopedic surgeons.

9400 West Higgins Road
Rosemont, IL 60018
Phone: (847) 823-7186
Fax: (847) 823-8125
Email: custserv@aaos.org
Website: http://www.aaos.org/home.asp

American Association of Naturopathic Physicians

A professional organization that supports the practice of naturopathic medicine in order to promote people's wellness.

818 18th Street NW, Suite 250
Washington, DC 20006
Phone: (866) 538-2267
Fax: (202) 237-8152
Email: member.services@naturopathic.org

American Board of Preventive Medicine

An organization that promotes the advancement of preventive medicine and provides certificates to physicians who have preventive medicine experience.

111 West Jackson Boulevard, Suite 1340
Chicago, IL 60604
Phone: (312) 939-2276

Fax: (312) 939-2218
Website: https://www.theabpm.org/

American Celiac Disease Alliance

A membership organization that lobbies for people who have celiac disease.

2504 Duxbury Place
Alexandria, VA 22308
Phone: (703) 622-3331
Email: info@americanceliac.org
Website: http://americanceliac.org/

American Chiropractic Association

A professional organization that supports the practice of chiropractic medicine.

1701 Clarendon Boulevard, Suite 200
Arlington, VA 22209
Phone: (703) 276-8800
Fax: (703) 243-2593
Email: memberinfo@acatoday.org
Website: http://www.acatoday.org/

American Cleaning Institute

An organization that lobbies for the cleaning industry. Its website provides much useful information on how to clean people and things.

1331 L Street NW, Suite 650
Washington, DC 20005
Phone: (202) 347-2900
Fax: (202) 347-4110
Email: info@cleaninginstitute.org
Website: http://www.cleaninginstitute.org/

American College of Sports Medicine

A membership organization that focuses on the research and advancement of sports medicine and exercise.

401 West Michigan Street
Indianapolis, IN 46202
Phone: (317) 637-9200
Email: publicinfo@acsm.org
Website: http://www.acsm.org/

American Herbalist Guild

A professional organization that is dedicated to supporting the practice of herbalism.

125 South Lexington Avenue, Suite 101
Asheville, NC 28801
Phone: (617) 520-4372
Email: office@americanherbalistsguild.com

American Massage Therapy Association

A professional organization that supports the practice of massage therapy through education, professional support, and scientific research.

500 Davis Street, Suite 900
Evanston, IL 60201
Phone: (877) 905-0577
Email: info@amtamassage.org
Website: http://www.amtamassage.org/

American Medical Association

A professional organization that supports physicians in the practice of medicine through advocacy, education, and medical publications.

AMA Plaza
330 North Wabash Avenue
Chicago, IL 60611
Phone: (800) 621-8335
Website: http://www.ama-assn.org/ama/home
.page

American Mental Health Counselors Association

A professional organization that advocates for the profession of mental health counseling.

801 North Fairfax Street, Suite 304
Alexandria, VA 22314
Phone: (800) 326-2642
Fax: (703) 548-4775

American Osteopathic Association

A professional organization that supports the research and practice of osteopathic medicine.

142 East Ontario Street
Chicago, IL 60611

Phone: (800) 621-1773
Fax: (312) 202-8200
Email: info@osteopathic.org
Website: http://www.osteopathic.org/

American Physical Therapy Association

A professional organization that supports the practice of physical therapy through advocacy and education.

1111 North Fairfax Street
Alexandria, VA 22314
Phone: (800) 999-2782
Fax: (703) 706-8536
Website: http://www.apta.org/

American Psychiatric Association

A professional organization that supports the practice of psychiatry through advocacy, continuing education, and research.

1000 Wilson Boulevard, Suite 1825
Arlington, VA 22209
Phone: (888) 357-7924
Email: apa@psych.org
Website: http://www.psychiatry.org/

American Red Cross

A nonprofit organization that provides disaster relief in the United States and abroad, assists military families, receives blood donations, and performs other tasks that further the public good.

2025 E Street NW
Washington, DC 20006
Phone: (800) 733-2767
Website: http://www.redcross.org/

Bureau of Indian Affairs

A federal government organization that is a part of the U.S. Department of Interior and oversees the government's relationship with American Indian and Alaska Native tribes, providing education and economic support, among other services.

1849 C Street NW
Washington, DC 20240
Phone: (202) 208-3710
Fax: (202) 501-1516
Website: http://www.bia.gov/

Center for Nutrition Advocacy

An organization that lobbies for the rights of nutrition care providers and provides information to that community.

Website: http://nutritionadvocacy.org/

Centers for Disease Control and Prevention

A federal government organization that is a part of the Department of Health and Human Services and works to ensure the health security of citizens through education and information.

1600 Clifton Road
Atlanta, GA 30329
Phone: (800) 232-4636
Website: http://www.cdc.gov/

Centers for Medicare and Medicaid Services

A federal government organization that administers Medicaid, Medicare, and associated programs (see below).

7500 Security Boulevard
Baltimore, MD 21244
Website: http://www.cms.gov/

Children's Health Insurance Program

A federal government program that provides health insurance for eligible children.

Website: http://medicaid.gov/CHIP/CHIP-Program-Information.html

Medicaid

A federal government program that provides health insurance for people who have a low income.

Website: http://medicaid.gov/

Medicare

A federal government program that provides health insurance for the elderly and some others with disabilities.

Website: http://www.medicare.gov/

Program for All-Inclusive Care for the Elderly

A federal government program that helps elderly or disabled people receive health care in their community instead of in a facility.

Website: http://www.medicare.gov/your-medicare-costs/help-paying-costs/pace/pace.html

State Health Insurance Assistance Program

A federally funded, state-run program that offers counseling to people who are interested in Medicare.

Website: https://www.shiptalk.org/

State Pharmaceutical Assistance Programs

State-funded programs that offers prescription assistance to eligible individuals.

Website: http://www.medicare.gov/pharmaceutical-assistance-program/state-programs.aspx

Cleveland Clinic

A nonprofit medical organization that offers health care, conducts medical research, and provides health-care education.

9500 Euclid Avenue
Cleveland, OH 44195
Phone: (216) 444-2200
Website: https://my.clevelandclinic.org/

Employee Benefit Research Institute

An organization that lobbies for comprehensive employee benefits.

100 13th Street NW, Suite 878

Washington, DC 20005
Phone: (202) 659-0670
Fax: (202) 775-6312
Email: info@ebri.org
Website: http://www.ebri.org/

Employee Benefits Security Administration

A federal government organization that is a part of the Department of Labor and monitors, regulates, and enforces the distribution of employee benefits.

Frances Perkins Building
200 Constitution Avenue NW
Washington, DC 20210
Phone: (866) 444-3272
Website: http://www.dol.gov/ebsa/

Energy Star

A federal government organization that is a part of U.S. Environmental Protection Agency and assists citizens and businesses to improve their energy efficiency.

1200 Pennsylvania Avenue NW
Washington, DC 20460
Phone: (888) 782-7937
Website: http://www.energystar.gov/

Federal Trade Commission

A federal government organization that protects consumers' rights through a variety of means, including the promotion of competition in the marketplace.

600 Pennsylvania Avenue NW
Washington, DC 20580
Phone: (202) 326-2222
Website: http://www.ftc.gov/

Feldenkrais Guild of North America

A professional organization that supports the practice of Feldenkrais in North America through professional support and education.

401 Edgewater Place, Suite 600

Wakefield, MA 01880
Phone: (781) 876-8935
Fax: (781) 645-1322
Website: http://www.feldenkrais.com/

Healing Touch Program

An organization that provides information on Healing Touch for the public and support for Healing Touch professionals.

15439 Pebble Gate
San Antonio, TX 78232
Phone: (210) 497-5529
Fax: (210) 497-8532
Email: info@HealingTouchProgram.com
Website: www.HealingTouchProgram.com

Indian Health Service

A federal government organization that is a part of the U.S. Department of Health and Human Services and provides health care to American Indians and Alaska Natives.

The Reyes Building
801 Thompson Avenue, Suite 400
Rockville, MD 20852
Website: http://www.ihs.gov/

Institute for Safe Medication Practices

A nonprofit organization that supports the safe use of medications and medication-error prevention.

200 Lakeside Drive, Suite 200
Horsham, PA 19044
Phone: (215) 947-7797
Fax: (215) 914-1492
Website: http://www.ismp.org/

Insurance Information Institute

An organization that provides information to the public about insurance.

110 William Street
New York, NY 10038
Phone: (212) 346-5500
Website: http://www.iii.org/

International Center for Reiki Training

An organization that provides trainings for Reiki professionals or students and information to the public about Reiki.

21421 Hilltop Street, Unit 28
Southfield, MI 48033
Phone: (800) 332-8112
Fax: (248) 948-9534
Email: center@reiki.org
Website: www.reiki.org

International Scientific Forum on Home Hygiene

A nonprofit organization that focuses on promoting good hygiene to improve health in the home.

Old Dairy Cottage
Woodhouse Lane
Montacute, Somerset TA15 6XL
United Kingdom
Website: http://www.ifh-homehygiene.org/

International Society for Orthomolecular Medicine

A professional organization that advocates for the practice of orthomolecular medicine and unites orthomolecular professionals.

16 Florence Avenue
Toronto, ON
Canada M2N 1E9
Phone: (416) 733-2117
Fax: (416) 733-2352
Email: centre@orthomed.org
Website: http://www.orthomed.org/

Kaiser Family Foundation (The Henry J. Kaiser Family Foundation)

A nonprofit and bipartisan organization that researches health-care issues in the United States.

2400 Sand Hill Road
Menlo Park, CA 94025
Phone: (650) 854 9400

Fax: (650) 854 480
Website: http://kff.org/

Life Happens

A nonprofit organization sponsored by insurance companies that educates the public about life insurance and other insurance plans.

1655 North Fort Myer Drive, Suite 610
Arlington, VA 22209
Phone: (888) 543-3777
Fax: (202) 464-5011
Email: info@lifehappens.org
Website: http://www.lifehappens.org/

Mayo Clinic

A nonprofit organization that provides health-care services, conducts medical research, and educates the public on health issues.

200 First Street SW
Rochester, MN 55905
Phone: (507) 284-2511
Fax: 507-538-7802
Website: http://www.mayoclinic.org/

Medicare Rights Center

A nonprofit organization that helps people navigate the Medicare system and advocates for Medicare users.

520 Eighth Avenue
North Wing, Third Floor
New York, NY 10018
Phone: (212) 869-3850
Fax: (212) 869-3532
Email: info@medicarerights.org
Website: http://www.medicarerights.org/

Mental Health America

A nonprofit organization that supports the mental health of Americans through prevention and treatment.

2000 North Beauregard Street, Sixth Floor
Alexandria, VA 22311

Phone: (800) 969-6642
Fax: (703) 684-5968
Website: http://www.mentalhealthamerica.net/

MindFreedom

A nonprofit organization that supports the
rights of people with psychiatric disabilities to
resist coercive psychiatric treatment.

P.O. Box 11284
Eugene, OR 97440
Phone: (877) 623-7743
Fax: (480) 287-8833
Email: office@mindfreedom.org
Website: www.mindfreedom.org

My Medicare Matters

An educational organization that is sponsored by
the National Council on Aging and Aon Retiree
Health Exchange™ that provides assistance to
people who have questions about Medicare.

251 18th Street South, Suite 500
Arlington, VA 22202
Phone: (571) 527-3900
Website: http://www.ncoa.org/

National Agricultural Library

A federal library that is a part of the U.S.
Department of Agriculture and houses
literature about agriculture and related topics.

10301 Baltimore Avenue
Beltsville, MD 20705
Phone: (301) 504-5755
Email: NALSpecialCollections@ars.usda.gov
Website: http://www.nal.usda.gov/

National Alliance on Mental Illness

A nonprofit organization that supports people
who have mental illness through advocacy and
education.

3803 North Fairfax Drive, Suite 100
Arlington, VA 22203
Phone: (703) 524-7600

Fax: (703) 524-9094
Website: http://www.nami.org/

National Association of Nutrition Professionals

A professional organization that advocates for
nutrition professionals, educates members, and
certifies nutrition programs and professionals.

P.O. Box 1884
Rancho Cordova, CA 95741
Phone: (800) 342-8037
Fax: (510) 580-9429
Website: http://www.nanp.org/

National Ayurvedic Medical Association

A professional organization that represents
Ayurvedic medicine in the United States.

8605 Santa Monica Boulevard, #46789
Los Angeles, CA 90069
Phone: (800) 669-8914
Fax: (612) 605-1989
Email: info@ayurvedaNAMA.org
Website: http://www.ayurvedanama.org/

National Center for Biotechnology Information

A federal government organization within the
U.S. National Library of Medicine that offers
biomedical and genomic information.

U.S. National Library of Medicine
Building 38A
Bethesda, MD 20894
Phone: (888) 346-3656
Website: http://www.ncbi.nlm.nih.gov/

National Center for Complementary and Integrative Health

A federal government organization that is a
part of the National Institutes of Health and
supports scientific research on the efficacy of
alternative health care.

9000 Rockville Pike
Bethesda, MD 20892
Phone: (888) 644-6226

Email: ninfo@nccih.nih.gov
Website: https://nccih.nih.gov/

National Center for Health Statistics

A federal government organization that is
a part of the Centers for Disease Control
and Prevention and makes available data
on health issues.

3311 Toledo Road, Room 5419
Hyattsville, MD 20782
Phone: (800) 232-4636
Website: http://www.cdc.gov/nchs/

National Certification Commission of Acupuncture and Oriental Medicine

An organization that provides certification
for practitioners of acupuncture and Eastern
medicine.

76 South Laura Street, Suite 1290
Jacksonville, FL 32202
Phone: (904) 598-1005
Fax: (904) 598-5001
Website: http://www.nccaom.org/

National Coalition for Mental Health Recovery

A membership organization that advocates for
people who have or are recovering from mental
illness.

611 Pennsylvania Avenue SE, #133
Washington, DC 20003
Phone: (877) 246-9058
Website: http://www.ncmhr.org/index.htm

National Heart, Blood, and Lung Institute

A federal government organization that is part of
the National Institutes of Health and supports
research on heart, blood, and lung diseases.

P.O. Box 30105
Bethesda, MD 20824
Phone: (301) 592-8573
Email: nhlbiinfo@nhlbi.nih.gov
Website: http://www.nhlbi.nih.gov/

National Hospice and Palliative Care Organization

A professional organization that supports
the advancement of end-of-life care through
professional support, advocacy, regulatory and
quality monitoring, and education.

731 King Street, Suite 100
Alexandria, VA 22314
Phone: (703) 837-1500
Fax: (703) 837-1233
Email: nhpco_info@nhpco.org
Website: http://www.nhpco.org/

National Human Genome Research Institute

A federal government organization that is a part
of the National Institutes of Health and supports
scientific research on the human genome.

9000 Rockville Pike, Building 31, Room
4B09
31 Center Drive, MSC 2152
Bethesda, MD 20892
Phone: (301) 402-0911
Fax: (301) 402-2218
Website: http://www.genome.gov/

National Institute of Allergy and Infectious Diseases

A federal government organization that is part
of the U.S. Department of Health and Human
Services and supports research on allergic,
immunologic, and infectious diseases.

5601 Fishers Lane, MSC 9806
Bethesda, MD 20892
Phone: (866) 284-4107
Fax: (301) 402-3573
Email: ocpostoffice@niaid.nih.gov
Website: http://www.niaid.nih.gov/

National Institute of Neurological Disorders and Stroke

A federal government organization that is
part of the National Institutes of Health and

promotes research on the brain in order to treat neurological problems.

> P.O. Box 5801
> Bethesda, MD 20824
> Phone: (800) 352-9424
> Website: http://www.ninds.nih.gov/index.htm

National Institutes of Health

A federal government organization that is a part of the U.S. Department of Health and Human Services and supports research on human health.

> 9000 Rockville Pike
> Bethesda, MD 20892
> Phone: (301) 496-4000
> Email: NIHinfo@od.nih.gov
> Website: http://www.nih.gov/

National Registry of Evidence-Based Programs and Practices

A federal government organization that is a part of the Substance Abuse and Mental Health Services Administration and offers a comprehensive list of intervention programs.

> 1 Choke Cherry Road
> Rockville, MD 20857
> Phone: (866) 436-7377
> Email: nrepp@samhsa.hhs.gov
> Website: http://www.nrepp.samhsa.gov/

National Sleep Foundation

A nonprofit organization that works for improved sleep health through advocacy, research, and education.

> 1010 North Glebe Road, Suite 310
> Arlington, VA 22201
> Phone: (703) 243-1697
> Email: nsf@sleepfoundation.org
> Website: http://sleepfoundation.org/

National Suicide Prevention Lifeline

A federal government organization that is a part of the Substance Abuse and Mental Health Services Administration and offers telephone counseling for people who are considering suicide.

> Phone: (800) 273-8255
> Website: http://www.suicidepreventionlifeline.org/

Occupational Safety and Health Administration

A federal government organization that is a part of the U.S. Department of Labor and ensures that workers are safe on the job through regulation and outreach.

> 200 Constitution Avenue NW
> Washington, DC 20210
> Phone: (800) 321-6742
> Website: www.osha.gov

Office of Dietary Supplements

A federal government organization that is part of the National Institutes of Health and supports the scientific research of dietary supplements and provides information on them to the public.

> 6100 Executive Boulevard
> Room 3B01, MSC 7517
> Bethesda, MD 20892
> Phone: (301) 435-2920
> Fax: (301) 480-1845
> Email: ods@nih.gov
> Website: http://ods.od.nih.gov/

Palo Alto Medical Foundation

A nonprofit medical organization that offers health care to people living in California's Bay Area.

> Phone: (888) 398-5677
> Website: http://www.pamf.org/

People's Organization of Community Acupuncture

A cooperative organization of acupuncture practitioners, patients, and others who support affordable acupuncture.

> 3526 NE 57th Avenue

Portland, OR 97213
Phone: (503) 781-9740
Website: https://www.pocacoop.com/

President's Council on Fitness, Sports, and Nutrition

A federal government organization that promotes healthy lifestyle choices such as eating well and being physically active.

1101 Wootton Parkway, Suite 560
Rockville, MD 20852
Phone: (240) 276-9567
Fax: (240) 276-9860
Email: fitness@hhs.gov
Website: http://www.fitness.gov

Robert Wood Johnson Foundation

A nonprofit organization that works for the public health of Americans.

P.O. Box 2316
Princeton, NJ 08543
Phone: (877) 843-7953
Website: http://www.rwjf.org/en.html

Social Security Administration

A federal government agency that oversees the distribution of retirement, disability, and survivors' benefits.

Office of Public Inquiries
1100 West High Rise
6401 Security Boulevard
Baltimore, MD 21235
Phone: (800) 772-1213
Website: http://www.ssa.gov/

Society for Human Resource Management

A professional organization that represents human resources professionals and provides information regarding the human resources field.

1800 Duke Street
Alexandria, VA 22314
Phone: (800) 283-7476
Fax: (703) 535-6490
Website: http://www.shrm.org/

Special Diabetes Program for Indians

A federal government organization that is part of the Indian Health Service and provides support to American Indians and Alaska Natives with diabetes-related health issues.

801 Thompson Avenue, Suite 300
Rockville, MD 20852
Phone: (844) 447-3387
Fax: (301) 594-6213
Email: diabetesprogram@ihs.gov

Substance Abuse and Mental Health Services Administration

A federal government organization that is a part of the U.S. Department of Health and Human Services and supports the treatment of substance abuse and mental illness.

1 Choke Cherry Road
Rockville, MD 20857
Phone: (877) 726-4727
Website: http://www.samhsa.gov/

Therapeutic Touch® International Association

A professional organization that supports Therapeutic Touch® professionals and students through education and professional support as well as provides information to the public.

P.O. Box 130
Delmar, NY 12054
Phone: (518) 325-1185
Fax: (509) 693-3537
Email: info@therapeutic-touch.org
Website: http://therapeutic-touch.org/

TRICARE
A federal government organization that
provides health care for the military
community.

> *7700 Arlington Boulevard, Suite 5101*
> *Falls Church, VA 22042*
> *Website: http://www.tricare.mil/*

World Health Organization
An organization that is a part of the
United Nations and focuses on shaping
global health care.

> *Avenue Appia 20*
> *Geneva 27, 1211*
> *Switzerland*
> *Phone: + 41 22 791 21 11*
> *Fax: + 41 22 791 31 11*
> *Website: http://www.who.int/en/*

World Research Foundation
A nonprofit organization that distributes
information on both allopathic and
complementary and alternative medicine.

> *P.O. Box 20828*
> *Sedona, AZ 86341*
> *Phone: (928) 284-3300*
> *Email: info@wrf.org*
> *Website: http://www.wrf.org/*

U.S. Department of Agriculture
A federal government organization that oversees
and execute policy on farming, agriculture,
and food safety. It also works to end hunger
and obesity with its Food and Nutrition
Service, which implements programs such as
Supplemental Nutrition Assistance Program
(SNAP) and the Women, Infants, and Children
(WIC) program.

> *1400 Independence Avenue SW*
> *Washington, DC 20250*
> *Phone: (202) 720-2791*
> *Website: http://www.usda.gov/wps/portal*
> */usda/usdahome*

**U.S. Department of Health and Human
Services**
AA federal government agency that provides
human and social services through offices
including the Centers for Disease Control,
Centers for Medicare and Medicaid Services,
and the Health Resources and Services
Administration.

> *200 Independence Avenue SW*
> *Washington, DC 20201*
> *Phone: (877) 696-6775*
> *Website: http://www.hhs.gov/*

U.S. Department of Veterans Affairs
A federal government agency that oversees
patient care and benefits for veterans and their
dependents.

> *810 Vermont Avenue NW*
> *Washington, DC 20420*
> *Phone: (877) 222-8387*
> *Website: http://www.va.gov/*

U.S. Drug Enforcement Agency
A federal organization that is a part of
the U.S. Department of Justice and enforces
drug laws.

> *Phone: (202) 307-1000*
> *Website: http://www.dea.gov/*

U.S. Food and Drug Administration
A federal government organization that
is a part of the U.S. Centers for Health
and Human Services and ensures the safety

of food, drugs, medical devices, radiation-emitting products, vaccines, veterinary medicine and foods, cosmetics, and tobacco products.

> *10903 New Hampshire Avenue*
> *Silver Spring, MD 20993*
> *Phone: (888) 463-6332*
> *Website: www.fda.gov*

Veterans Health Administration
A federal government organization that is part of the U.S. Department of Veterans Affairs and that provides health care for military veterans.

> *810 Vermont Avenue NW*
> *Washington, DC 20420*
> *Phone: (877) 222-8387*
> *Website: http://www.va.gov/health/*

Index

This index is sorted word-by-word. Italic page locators indicate images. A *t* following a page number indicates the citation is to information in a table or other illustration.